THE MODERN LANGUAGE ASSOCIATION OF AMERICA

MONOGRAPH SERIES

XVIII

CONGREVE'S PLAYS
ON THE EIGHTEENTH-CENTURY STAGE

CONGREVE'S PLAYS

ON THE

EIGHTEENTH-CENTURY STAGE

BY

EMMETT L. AVERY

Professor of English
State College of Washington

NEW YORK
THE MODERN LANGUAGE ASSOCIATION
OF AMERICA
1951

In BCL

PRINTED IN THE UNITED STATES OF AMERICA BY THE
VAIL-BALLOU PRESS, INC., BINGHAMTON, N. Y.

To
Paul P. Kies

PREFACE

This study of the stage history of Congreve's plays has grown out of materials which I have collected in compiling a calendar of theatrical performances in London from the reopening of the theaters in 1660 to the end of the eighteenth century. The newspapers and playbills for that period offer a wealth of theatrical data for appraising the vogue of individual plays as well as types of drama, and in writing this monograph I have tried to present the fortunes of Congreve's plays, with some attention to their relation to other late-seventeenth-century comedies in the following century, against the background of the principal events in the London theatrical world of the eighteenth century. Although it has been difficult at times to keep background and foreground in proper perspective, I feared that presenting simply a record of the performances and criticism of Congreve's plays alone would not only be less comprehensive but would suggest that they were performed in a theatrical vacuum.

Through the years in which I have been collecting material concerning Congreve's plays and stage history in general, I have become very much indebted to many scholars and libraries. The major portions of the details were collected in the British Museum, whose officials were unfailingly helpful in assisting me with the newspapers and playbills in the Burney Collection and the manuscript calendars and theatrical account books. Mr. George Nash, of the Enthoven Collection in the Victoria and Albert Museum, kindly permitted me to examine playbills and other stage documents in his charge. In this country I have examined the extensive collection of late-eighteenth-century playbills in the Henry E. Huntington Library, the Winston Calendar and other manuscripts in the Folger Shakespeare Library, the eighteenth-century newspapers in the Library of Congress, and the resources of the University of Chicago Library. I was fortunately able to check again the many details of performances and casts while on a John Simon Guggenheim Fellowship in London during 1949–50, a year's study in which I was also assisted by the Committee on Research of the State College of Washington.

To Professor George Sherburn, who first introduced me to eighteenth-century drama and who read an early version of this study, I am greatly indebted for encouragement and enlightenment during many years. I have also profited greatly from the suggestions of those who read the manuscript for the Modern Language Association; of these, the only scholars whom I can thank individually are Professor Henry Ten Eyck Perry of the University of Buffalo, Professor John C. Hodges of the University of Tennessee, and Professor William R. Parker, Secretary of the Association. Among my colleagues, Professor Murray W. Bundy assisted me with the organization of the study, and Professor Paul P. Kies has not only read and criticized the manuscript but listened patiently a great many times while I stated my perplexities and asked his advice. Professor A. H. Scouten of the University of Pennsylvania has been of invaluable assistance in checking performances and casts and in aiding me with other problems. Dr. Giles E. Dawson of the Folger Shakespeare Library generously permitted me to use some quotations from the unpublished diaries of Richard Cross which the Folger Library possesses. For assistance less easily particularized I am indebted to Professor Allardyce Nicoll, Miss Sybil Rosenfeld, Professor Louis Landa, Professor G. E. Bentley, and Professor Roland Botting. And I could not have completed the study without the assistance of my wife, who patiently searched for performances and criticism of Congreve's plays in the London newspapers. To these individuals is due whatever virtue this study may have.

E. L. A.

CONTENTS

CONGREVE'S PLAYS
ON THE EIGHTEENTH-CENTURY STAGE

CHAPTER I

THE STAGE REPUTATION OF CONGREVE'S PLAYS

More than two hundred and fifty years ago William Congreve offered his first play, *The Old Batchelor* (1693), to a London audience. Seven years later, with the production of *The Way of the World,* he virtually retired as a dramatist. In that brief period he produced one tragedy and four of the finest comedies of manners. All of these plays, with fluctuations, remained on the stage for nearly a hundred years, and some have had successful revivals in the present century. The popularity of a dramatist's work upon the stages of several generations is, of course, one mark of his stature as a playwright, certainly a visible standard which, unlike the private enjoyment of his dramas, can be measured. In addition, public offerings of his plays, especially in a repertory system, invite frequent reviews and critical appraisals of his merit. Hence, an account of the fortunes of Congreve's plays in the eighteenth century should clarify the degree to which they were appreciated by the changing tastes of three or four generations. And because he was then regarded as representative of the most brilliant comic drama of the late seventeenth century, the reception of his plays should illuminate the status of Restoration comedy as a whole, especially the work of such comparable authors as Wycherley, Etherege, and Vanbrugh.

Nearly all of Congreve's plays were well received at their premières, particularly by the wits, critics, and courtiers, although, as everyone knows, their tone displeased the moralists who, led by Jeremy Collier's attack upon the stage in 1698, kept them under censure for many years. In spite of this opposition, Congreve's dramas early established themselves as valuable theatrical properties. With slight fluctuations they appeared more and more frequently on the boards until their share in the theatrical offerings was a very impressive one. Statistically the clearest indication of their vogue lies not in the total number of performances season by season but in the share which the five plays had in the repertories. At the beginning of the century his dramas accounted for roughly 2.5 per cent of the London performances. (For a detailed statement of their share in the repertory, see a table in Chapter VIII.) They rose steadily in popularity even after Drury Lane, which had given Congreve more attention than any other playhouse, lost its monopoly in 1714. Their vogue was enhanced by the opening of a third major theater

1

(Goodman's Fields) in 1729, and from that year to the passage of the Licensing Act in 1737 performances of Congreve's plays comprised 5.5 per cent of the repertory. At their peak a few years later their share had risen to more than 6 per cent, a remarkably good showing for a playwright with only five plays. At that time they were competing with Shakespeare's dramas, which were rapidly growing in esteem, with the whole of late seventeenth-century drama, and with the new plays of each season, some of which, like *The Beggar's Opera,* were extraordinarily well received. A decline in Congreve's popularity, becoming apparent in the 1750's, grew at an accelerated pace in the closing years of David Garrick's career. In 1776 the managers revised and revived all five plays, but on the whole the experiment was not very successful. For a few years they were acted more frequently; then, resuming their decline, they were by 1800 even less frequently given than they had been in the closing years of Garrick's management.

What was the critical and popular opinion of the dramas during their rise and decline? In the early years of the century, when they were achieving their larger share in the repertories, only two themes were represented with any vitality. One was a forthright opposition by the moralists who pointed to Congreve as an example of the gross immorality which, they insisted, characterized the stage as a whole. The other was an adulatory comment which, although it gave the plays a high critical place, was likely to be very general and unanalytical in tone. Of the two, the moralistic critics were by far the more vocal, and they maintained an offensive during the early decades of the century. They initiated prosecutions of actors for uttering profane and licentious expressions or for swearing upon the stage. Among the professional moralists, Arthur Bedford, one of the most zealous and powerful, illustrates both the legal zeal and didactic criticism. In *The Evil and Danger of Stage-Plays* (1706) he cited example after example of immoral behavior and language in scores of plays. He noted with approval the indictment in the Easter Term of 1701 of the players in Lincoln's Inn Fields for using *"scandalous Expressions"* when acting *Love for Love* and *The Provoked Wife* and rejoiced that they were found guilty. Later, attacking Congreve as associate manager with Vanbrugh of the Queen's Theater during 1705–06, Bedford emphasized that the two producers had stipulated in the letters patent that they would act nothing "to the prejudice of *Religion and Good Manners,*" yet they continued to present objectionable plays, including, of course, some of their own.[1] For many years

---

[1] Pages 4, 116, 204. He also referred (pp. 12–13) to the acting of the same comedies in Bristol by Power, who intended to offer only "sober and modest" plays. Power's choice of these comedies convinced Bedford that the stage could not be easily re-

the moralists pamphleteered against the stage [2] and cited hundreds of plays as evidence of its evil. Agitation was renewed in 1726 by William Law, a devout and distinguished man, whose *Absolute Unlawfulness of the Stage-Entertainment Fully Demonstrated* was an influential and frequently reprinted work. Occasionally in the 1720's and 1730's there was support from a periodical like the *Universal Spectator,* which tended to make moral criteria the principal standards for judging a play. It is doubtful, however, whether at that time the moralists had any considerable effect upon the vogue of Congreve's plays in the theaters.

While the Jeremy Colliers were denouncing Congreve, commentators with less biased views accorded him a very high place among comic dramatists, although some of the praise was stated in generalities which were perfunctorily echoed many times in histories of the stage or in lists of dramatic authors and their works. Occasionally, however, there was lively and genuine discussion of his merits, such as appeared in *A Comparison between the Two Stages* (1702), in which the author is highly appreciative of Congreve in spite of his inclination to be severe with actors, plays, and authors. In an exchange of opinions concerning Congreve, Ramble, Sullen, and Critick spoke first of *Love for Love,* which Ramble characterized as "an extraordinary good Comedy, the like has scarce been heard of." Sullen added that *"Congreve* has a great Character for Comedy, and in my poor Judgment has perform'd well in Tragedy." Several times the three speakers tentatively ventured upon a full discussion of Congreve's merits but always turned aside from the task. Once Critick ventured an objection to *The Mourning Bride,* but Sullen silenced the projected argument by remarking that he could not "tell whether it be civil to pry into the Merits of so establish'd an Author: Mr. *C.* is a Gentleman of Wit and good Sense, and above my Strength." After a long analysis of Dryden, the commentators returned again to Congreve, and Critick asserted that, although Congreve's reputation then arose from *The Old Batchelor, Love for Love,* and *The Mourning Bride,* in his opinion *The Double Dealer* was the dramatist's finest play. Toward the end of their talk, they recalled that they had originally intended a full examination of Congreve's dramas, whereupon Critick remarked that his own "Forces [were] so weaken'd already,

---

formed and that plays must be banished. In *A Serious Remonstrance in Behalf of the Christian Religion, against the Horrid Blasphemies and Impieties which are still used in the English-Playhouses* (1719), Bedford returned to the attack, citing *The Old Batchelor* (p. 144) and *Love for Love* (p. 145) as in part responsible for the many licentious plays produced after 1700.

[2] An extensive list appears in F. T. Wood's "The Attack on the Stage in the Eighteenth Century," *Notes and Queries,* CLXIII (1937), 218–222.

[he had] not strength enough left to incounter such a gigantick Author." [3]

During the next two decades several influential critics gave Congreve very high praise. Although Steele and Addison did not systematically examine Congreve's works, their genuine admiration for his comedies in the *Tatler* and *Spectator* brought their authoritative judgment before the many readers of those journals. In *Tatler* No. 9 *The Old Batchelor* was complimented as "a Comedy of deserved Reputation," in which the fine gentlemen are "drawn with much Spirit and Wit, and the Drama introduced by the Dialogue of the first Scene with uncommon, yet natural Conversation." In No. 193 Congreve was praised for his brilliant "Distinction of Characters" in the same play, for "this Writer knows Men; which makes all his Plays reasonable Entertainments, while the Scenes of most others are like the Tunes between the Acts. They are perhaps agreeable Sounds, but they have no Ideas affixed to them." In No. 1 a discussion of Betterton's return to act Valentine for his benefit mentioned *Love for Love* as a "celebrated Comedy," and in No. 120 Dogget was praised for his choice of "so excellent a Play" as *Love for Love* for his benefit. In *Spectator* No. 189 it was particularized as "one of the finest Comedies that ever appeared upon the *English* Stage" and in No. 358 as one "which no Body would omit seeing that had, or had not ever seen it before." (Late in the century, the *World,* in its dramatic reviews, mentioned Addison's praise of this play as proof that even the best minds could be blinded to the immoral qualities of Congreve's plays.) This praise, influential during the lives of the two journals, was kept before the public by the many editions of the periodicals and by frequent quotation of these remarks in theatrical histories and magazines.

In 1717 John Dennis, who preferred Wycherley among contemporary writers of comedy, referred to Congreve as the "living Ornament of the Comick Scene" who possessed "Wit and Humour, and Art and Vivacity." He praised *The Way of the World,* popularly supposed to have been a failure at its première, as equal to Congreve's other comedies.[4] In 1719 Giles Jacob, compiling his *Poetical Register* (London, 1723), more systematically appraised Congreve in remarks which, like those in the *Tatler* and *Spectator,* were frequently repeated in other theatrical compendia. As to Congreve's talent, "He is the only Dramatick Poet now living, excellent for both Comedy and Tragedy; the Plays he has written in both ways, being very much applauded: And what

[3] S. B. Wells ed. (Princeton, 1942), pp. 10, 33, 34, 37, 104.
[4] "Remarks upon Pope's Homer," *The Works of John Dennis,* ed. E. N. Hooker (Baltimore, 1942–43), II, 121–122.

Mr. *Dennis* has lately observ'd of Mr. *Congreve,* is esteem'd, by most Persons, very just; That he left the Stage early, and Comedy has quitted it with him" (I, 45–46). For each play Jacob offered factual data and judgment. He saw "a genteel and sprightly Wit in the Dialogue of [*The Old Batchelor*]; and the humorous Characters are agreeable to Nature, which can be said of few other Dramatick Performances." He acknowledged that *The Double Dealer* did not succeed so well as Congreve's first play, yet he "never saw any particular Criticism on its Defects; which gives [him] leave to think its ill Reception proceeded more from a capricious Humour of the Town, than any considerable Errors in the Composure of the Play." In his praise of *Love for Love* he stated that there "is abundance of Wit in it, and a great deal of fine and diverting Humour; the Characters are justly distinguish'd, and the Manners well mark'd. Some of the nicer Criticks find fault with the unravelling of the Plot, and the Conduct of *Angelica* in it: But in spite of Envy, this Play must be allow'd to be one of the best of our modern Comedies" (I, 42–45). Next to *Love for Love* he placed *The Way of the World,* and as testimony to the excellence of *The Mourning Bride* he reprinted Sir Richard Blackmore's praise of it.

Before the death of Congreve in 1729 there had been little save moralistic denunciation or brief praise of his works.[5] The emphasis, however, was shifting. In the 1730's appeared two attacks by writers who were not professional reformers. During a very successful revival of *The Double Dealer* in Drury Lane, Aaron Hill, playwright and critic, published in the *Prompter* (Nov. 11, 1735) an extended discussion of the comedy. Although Hill praised the wit, structure of the plot, and conception of the "light" characters, he condemned the comedy as a whole. His essential point was that plays in which there are fundamentally evil characters, such as Maskwell, a *"cold, deliberate, thinking* Villain," cannot be genuinely humorous. For anyone who laughs, as does Maskwell, at the "very Notion of Virtue," should be corrected by the law, apparently by execution at Tyburn. Such characters should not appear on the stage, and because *The Double Dealer* abounds in such villains, Hill could not justify it morally. The other attack came two years later in the *Daily Gazetteer* (July 16, 1737), a criticism inspired by political controversy. The *Craftsman* and *Gazetteer* had disagreed concerning the necessity for the Licensing Act, which

---

[5] Shortly after Congreve's death there appeared the *Memoirs of the Life, Writings, and Amours of William Congreve, Esq.* (1730), in many respects the customary tribute to a deceased writer. Essentially a compilation, it offered a history of the first production of each play and of the quarrel with Collier; it presented quotations, nearly all laudatory, concerning Congreve's works; but it added little to the core of Congreve criticism.

had brought the theaters under governmental supervision. When the *Craftsman* asserted that the London stage was less libertine than the ancient Greek theater and hence did not need regulation, the *Gazetteer* cited *The Way of the World* as proof to the contrary. The indictment of the comedy was not very specific, but the *Gazetteer* asserted that all the characters in it were "immoral, indecent, and shocking in Sobriety of Thinking" and that, other opinions to the contrary, its wit could not excuse its lewdness.

Although neither article apparently affected the frequency with which the two plays were acted, the attacks were symptomatic of a renewed antagonism to the stage.[6] During 1748, for example, there was a vigorous indictment of *The Orphan,* a popular tragedy which had by then been acted approximately two hundred times. Writing in the popular *Gentleman's Magazine* for November and December 1748, the critic pointed out that it was very "difficult to find any *moral precept* that [*The Orphan*] tends to recommend or illustrate" and further argued: "That a tendency to promote the cause of Virtue is essential to Epic and Dramatic poetry, will hardly be contested; and accordingly we find the great poets not content with barely holding up *the mirror to Nature,* and exercising the virtuous affections of mankind (which yet, it must be confess'd, are valuable ends of these species of writing) but that they have constantly endeavoured to inculcate some *prudential maxim,* or *moral precept.*" Turning to the Restoration age, he declared that comedy written under the influence of the days of Charles II had as its principal character "*a fine gentleman* that could dress, dance, use his sword, and, with equal facility and address, *smoak a justice, roast a parson* or *cuckold an alderman,*" and that most of the poets and dramatists of that age were "shameless profligates" or "pestilent vermin." He concluded that "to constitute a great Poet, the primary and essential qualification is TO BE A GOOD MAN."

In the same year Edmund Burke applied similar principles in a more intensive analysis of Restoration comedy. Writing in the second issue of his periodical, *The Reformer* (Feb. 4, 1748), he set forth the qualities which mark good comedy: Humor, "without Smut or Buf-

---

6 This train of thought can be traced in the *Universal Spectator* in the 1730's. On April 10, 1731, it condemned Restoration drama and *The Beggar's Opera* for their opposition to morality. On March 11, 1732, it emphasized the need for moral instruction in plays, a point repeated on Dec. 9, 1732. *Love for Love* (Nov. 4, 1732) was disapproved because of its immorality. The production of *The London Merchant* in 1731 provided, however, a rallying point for all who desired plays with clear and unmistakable moral themes; the *Universal Spectator* (Jan. 22, 1732) stated that it was fully persuaded that frequent acting of this new play "must be of considerable Service to the *Youth* of this great City," because its effect, especially upon young persons, could only be beneficial.

foonry"; Wit; Judgment (to integrate the elements of the plot); "*Pro-priety* of Characters"; and "lastly, the whole . . . to be wrote for the Sake of one great *Moral*." He examined the works of Farquhar, Cibber, Vanbrugh, and Congreve. Farquhar, he stated, never aims at a moral; Cibber moralizes, "but it comes so awkwardly from him, that a Person is at a loss to judge which is most fulsom, his Morals or his Bawdry"; and Vanbrugh, in spite of his "deserv'd Reputation," has a "deficiency in Morals, and Plot" as great as that of any other. The "celebrated Mr. *Congreve*" was more minutely examined. He has, Burke stated, "a lively wit, solid Judgment, and rich Invention," yet he has "added such Obscenity, as none can, without the greatest Danger to Virtue, listen to; the very texture and groundwork of some of his Plays is Lewdness, which poisons the surer, as it is set off with the Advantage of Wit." Could Congreve be excused because he drew "his Pictures after the times"? Burke thought not, for "whoever examines his Plays will find, that he not only copied the ill Morals of the Age, but approved them," as demonstrated by those characters which Congreve "plainly proposes for Imitation." In Burke's opinion, Congreve meant Angelica (*Love for Love,* "the chastest of all his Plays") to be a "perfect Character, and such perhaps as he would have wished his own Mistress to have been." Yet Angelica has such "Rankness of . . . Ideas, and Expressions, in the Scene between her and old *Foresight,* (as well as in other parts of the Play) [as] are scarce consistent with any *Male,* much less *Female* Modesty." In effect, the drama must be moral, must offer a moral, and must be condemned if it fails in either respect.

In many respects Burke's views set the tone for a conception which prevailed during the later years of the century. Emphasis upon the necessity for demonstrable morality in drama was becoming a common-place, with frequent reiteration strengthening it in the public mind. To clarify this view, it will be useful to examine more closely the position of the opponents of late seventeenth-century drama. (Because *The Mourning Bride* raises other types of problems, it is discussed separately later in this chapter.) The basis was that comedy must serve didactic and instructional purposes. For example, in the *General Evening Post* (Jan. 4–7, 1772) "Longinus" stated: "The great end of the stage is to make instruction wear the garb of pleasure, and to charm our audiences into a passionate fondness for virtue. The plays best calculated to answer these essential purposes are the best plays, let the critics say what they will." When Congreve was judged by this standard, in theory an old and honorable one, his plays were disapproved because of their failure to promote virtue. A discussion of *The Double Dealer* in the *Public Advertiser* (Dec. 1, 1787) concluded: "but without a *moral* tendency, what advantage can possibly be derived from visiting the theater?"

Although many writers believed that instruction and entertainment not only should, but could, be happily blended, the extremists placed delight in second place or denied it approbation if it was achieved at the expense of virtue, a view strikingly stated by a writer in the *London Magazine* (July 1769): "It is much better to be dull than to be profligate" (p. 339). He had been brought to this conviction by hearing "admirers of the drama" complain that his age had lost the wit of Wycherley, Vanbrugh, and Congreve and that "we are no longer entertained with animated dialogue, or lively sallies of imagination, but, on the contrary, are persecuted with the dull declamations of laboured sentiment, unnatural manners, and worn out morality." He thought this state not "an unhappiness" but "the greatest piece of good fortune." More often, instead of applauding dullness as a virtue, the age used a less disheartening word: "utility," a term which usually implied that a play was "useful" in instructing man toward virtue. The *Public Ledger* (Sept. 25, 1765) realized that contemporary dramatists could not equal Wycherley, Etherege, and Congreve in wit, "but in real utility, I shall not a moment hesitate to give the poets of the present hour a considerable superiority." Restoration writers "were possessed of parts rather brilliant than useful; and they aimed infinitely more at saying fine things, than just ones; hence, decency and good sense were continually sacrificed to an ill-timed emanation of vivacity; and so an audience could be set in a roar with some sprightly sally of genius, no matter what became of their morals or their understanding." On a utilitarian basis it was only natural that Congreve should be criticized for his presumed licentiousness, an objection often expressed in generalities. The *Public Ledger* (Nov. 14, 1771),[7] for example, assailed *Love for Love*, because "through the whole, we discover a vein of licentiousness," with the result "that it is the wish of Humanity, and of Virtue, that this Play was consigned to oblivion, with all its merit, on account of this particular."

Few critics were content, however, merely to call the plays immoral. A more important problem was to determine their effect upon the

---

[7] As reprinted in the *Theatrical Review* (1771), I, 194. Some writers were much more specific. In a pamphlet reminiscent of those of the days of Jeremy Collier, the author of *The Stage the High Road to Hell* (1767) listed, with examples, the licentious failings of Restoration comic writers. He was severe with Congreve. In *The Old Batchelor,* for example, Congreve "vilely traduced" the clergy in Spintext, an old bone of contention in the quarrel between clergy and dramatist. The pamphleteer pointed to many other indecencies: disobedience to parents, women disguised as men, and, especially, adultery (pp. 16–17).

audience. Spectators, it was believed, were highly impressionable individuals who would be molded not only by provocative detail but by the tone of the play. Many writers were disturbed, therefore, to discover that nearly all of Congreve's characters were vicious. What must be the effect, they asked, of having villainous and immoral persons perpetrating their crimes before young and old and receiving insufficient punishment for guilt. As though in answer to such a question, the *Theatrical Monitor* (Nov. 14, 1767) stated: "Nay, there is hardly any play exhibited but the fool in fashion is brought on the carpet, or some other character to delude the morals of mankind. *Sharper* in the *Old Batchelor,* has made many a pickpocket; *Careless* in the *Double Dealer* has made many a worthless young fellow, if not worse; Valentine in *Love for Love* has made many a spendthrift; *Maskwell* has made many a villain." There was, in fact, a body of opinion which held that vicious characters could not be properly introduced upon the stage, yet unhappily for Congreve's reputation, according to the *Gazetteer and London Daily Advertiser* (Oct. 27, 1764), "there is hardly one of either sex, in his *Batchelor,* or his *Way of the World,* that is not a knave or a strumpet. Nobody can doubt that there are such characters in nature (perhaps they are common) but it does not follow that *every* character in nature can, with propriety, be brought on the stage."

More crucial still was the question whether, if admitted to the stage, such characters were "to glory in their wickedness and remain unpunished." Upon this matter the defenders and detractors of Congreve differed. Although the defense stressed the professed moral aims of comic dramatists, the moralists thought such professions to be perfunctory and insincere; at any rate, the villains were not genuinely punished. Furthermore, many characters possessed such engaging personalities and pleasing traits that the audiences were blinded to their inherent evil, a point which an essayist in the *Court Magazine* (Feb. 1762) stressed: "Greatly admired as Congreve's comedies may be . . . they are . . . utterly improper to be represented on any stage; . . . his fine gentlemen are generally debauchees and rascals; and the more amiable he may have dressed them up, the more dangerous they are to be exhibited, because the human mind has a natural propensity to error, and it is not always we have the resolution to avoid following an example, however contradictory to our own reason, which custom has for many years taught us to admire." To correct this danger, the *Gazetteer* (Oct. 4, 1765) urged the theatrical managers to ban every play "whose moral is too obscure to strike the inattentive; all those, whose vicious characters are so brilliant, that either by the witticism of the author, or the excellency and humour of the performer, eclipse the virtuous character, and draw off the attention from it." As *A Dissertation on Comedy* (1750) put it, "the Million" can not discern so well as the "judicious and thinking Part of Mankind" (p. 13); hence, the *Gazetteer* (Oct. 27, 1764) lamented that Congreve's plays "so qualify vice, and indeed set villainous characters in so pleasing a light, that it is to be feared there are not wanting those who may be weak enough to think them meet objects of imitation."

Another criticism of the "vicious" characters argued that they were not genuinely comic. Because they were morally obnoxious, they inhibited laughter in the spectator sensitive to ethical values, a point argued in the *General Evening Post* (June 30–July 2, 1772): "I may therefore safely conclude, that no character atrociously wicked can be properly set down as a cause of theatrical ridicule. Ridicule, in fact, ceases where criminality begins; and a laugh never grows from an object of detestation. . . . We may chuckle heartily enough at things we despise; but where we hate, a serious emotion is excited, and abhorrence immediately checks every impulse of risibility." [8] In the *General Evening Post* (May 23–26, 1772) another writer stated his preference for the laughter derived from situation (the practice of his own day) to that derived from wit (as in Congreve): "In the altered state of our comedy we sensibly make [wit] but a secondary object, and instead of labouring to raise a laugh by occasional strokes of wit, or new delineations of character, we throw the persons of our drama into such situations as must unavoidably excite a roar during the continuance of a whole scene, and advance no less the views of the entertainment, than the purposes of regularity. The veriest clod in the twelve-penny gallery can judge of *situation* as perfectly as the most elaborate scholar in the boxes, though he cannot judge equally of *humour*."

The essence of this moralistic criticism lay, then, in an insistence that comedy must have a didactic and instructional effect whose force would be genuinely felt by even the least perceptive auditor. A comic view which presented life realistically or as the dramatist saw it was likely to be unsatisfactory, especially if the characters or actions were not conventionally moral. However true to their age Congreve's comedies may or may not be, their licentiousness and their brilliance would trap the unwary spectator into overlooking viciousness and into admiring what he should reject. Hence, there was relatively little ap-

---

[8] Thirty years before, *The Prompter* (Nov. 11, 1735) had made much the same criticism of Maskwell in *The Double Dealer*. And in 1776 James Beattie published an essay in which he discussed fully the relationship between laughter and morality. He agreed that "to have a just sense of the enormity of a crime, and at the same time to laugh at it, seems impossible, or at least unnatural." *Essays* (Edinburgh, 1776), pp. 661–662.

preciation of Congreve's comedies as works of art, for there was great concern lest a theatergoer witnessing a well-bred, attractive rascal upon the stage would think of him, not as an author's artistic creation, but as a person whom he would emulate unless it was made perfectly clear that it was wrong to do so. To the reformer of this period, Congreve's plays bred moral confusion instead of clarity and their brilliance was more dangerous than admirable. These views, it should be noticed, are considerably those of writers for the periodicals, yet the very frequent reiteration of them in several decades impressed them more closely upon the minds of the general public than the less didactic but also less widely disseminated stand of critics of more objective stature.

There were, of course, other types of objections to Congreve. A principal one, voiced most clearly by Henry Home, Lord Kames, and frequently echoed, was made to the "barren scenes" or to the fact that the comedies were "conversation pieces." [9] To Kames, a play consisted of a "chain of connected facts, of which each scene makes a link," and each scene "ought to produce some incident relative to the catastrophe, or ultimate event, by advancing or retarding it." Even though a scene was brilliant, it could not be justified if the chain of events was complete without it. Kames illustrated his contention by listing portions of Congreve's plays which he considered barren: in *The Old Batchelor,* all the scenes in Act II except i and ii; in *The Double Dealer,* III, x and xi; in *Love for Love,* I, x–xiv. *The Way of the World* was not "entirely guiltless of such scenes." Kames did not admit that these scenes could be justified because they "help to display characters"; if necessary, a playwright could imitate Dryden and describe them in the list of characters. Ideally, of course, "a writer of genius has no occasion for such artifice; he can display the characters of his personages much more to the life in sentiment and action." [10]

Others asserted that Congreve sacrificed essential qualities, such as plot and unities as well as morality, to an excess of wit. The *Dramatic*

[9] The principal statement of this judgment, so far as Congreve was concerned, appeared in Ch. 23 of *The Elements of Criticism*. First published in 1761, the book went through many editions, to which Kames made additions and corrections. I have used the 8th ed. (London, 1805). For Congreve, see II, 324–325.

[10] Several writers for the periodicals took over Kames' objections in full. A review of *Love for Love* in the *Public Ledger* (Nov. 14, 1771) reproduced all of the argument, and a notice of *The Way of the World* (April 4, 1772) repeated the principal points. Sometimes the objection simply stated that the structure of Congreve's dramas was weak, and in *Lloyd's Evening Post* (March 9–11, 1767) it was argued that the "Comedies of Congreve have as little to boast of accuracy in their construction, as the Plays of Shakespeare," yet Shakespeare, even in "most open violation of the lesser critical unities," pursued one point more steadily, showed one character more uniformly, and developed more consistently "one grand purpose of the fable" than Congreve ever did.

Censor (1770), though praising the language, mentioned as a fault "of a very heavy nature" that Congreve's "flashes of wit are too frequent, often too much for the person who utters them, his dialogue rather profuse" (II, 467). Every character, no matter what his station, spoke brilliantly. *A Dissertation on Comedy* (1750) argued that wit "in the Mouth of a *Wittol* . . . degenerates into Absurdity and Nonsense." [11] Samuel Johnson criticized *The Old Batchelor* because the "dialogue is one constant reciprocation of conceits, or clash of wit, in which nothing flows necessarily from the occasion, or is dictated by nature." [12] In spite of an admiration for the wit of Congreve, "undoubtedly the most witty author that ever existed," Horace Walpole felt that, although Congreve marked each character with wit proper to him alone, "each play is unnatural . . . because four assemblages of different persons could never have so much wit as Congreve has bestowed on them." As a result, we "want breath or attention to follow their repartees; and are so charmed with what every body says, that we have not leisure to be interested in what any body does." [13] Johnson, writing from memory, was certain that excess of wit made Congreve's characters "commonly fictitious and artificial, with very little of nature, and not much of life." He thought Heartwell and "the Ladies" in *The Old Batchelor* artificial, and Ben in *Love for Love* "very pleasant" but not "very natural." [14] Convictions such as these appeared also in the periodicals. The *Morning Post* (Nov. 22, 1776) stated that Congreve drew "a great deal more from life than from nature, a distinction of the utmost importance, tho' little attended," and to the *St. James' Chronicle* (March 5–7, 1776) the characters in *The Double Dealer* were "most Caricatures."

Interestingly enough, nearly every quality of Congreve's comedies which was condemned by some critics was praised by others. Although there were relatively few attempts to speak well of Congreve's morality, there were some. Horace Walpole's approach, like that of Charles Lamb, was rather negative. To him the comedies had the air of an unreal society and "our passions cannot be engaged" by them. In fact, we "even do not believe that a company who seem to meet only to show their wit, can have any other object in view. Their very vices seem affected, only to furnish subject for gaiety: thus the intrigue of Careless and Lady Pliant does not strike us more than a story that we know

[11] Page 55. To these complaints Horace Walpole made a succinct rejoinder: "We may blame the universality of wit in all his personages, but nobody can say which ought to have less"—"Thoughts on Comedy," *Works* (London, 1798), II, 316.
[12] *Lives of the English Poets*, "World's Classics" (Oxford, 1920), II, 25.
[13] *Works*, II, 316–317.
[14] *Lives of the English Poets*, II, 31, 26.

is invented to set off the talents of the relator." [15] *A General View of the Stage* (1759) saw in Congreve, Cibber, and Vanbrugh an intent "to lash the commonest vices" and to laugh "out of their faults and follies" the "loosest sorts of livers. . . . Thus we see blended in Comedy pleasure and utility" (pp. 56–57). Thomas Davies found in *Love for Love* and *The Way of the World* moral intentions, though somewhat obscured by licentiousness.[16] In the *Morning Chronicle* (Nov. 4, 1776) a writer argued, apropos of Samuel Johnson's statement that in the age of Charles II "Intrigue was plot, obscenity was wit," [17] that "Congreve certainly is no less to blame on this score than the bad taste of the age he lived in. Writers, especially writers for the stage, must accommodate their dramatic manners to the prevailing dramatic taste." Congreve and his contemporaries "gave the 'living manners as they rose.' " [18]

Praise of Congreve usually centered, however, in less controversial subjects than the moral effects of his works. There was, naturally, commendation of his dramatic skill by the best critics and the journalists. Although the *Gazetteer* (Jan. 2, 1777) condemned his licentiousness, it had "ever considered and admired our Congreve as the first of all dramatic writers in comedy." According to the *London Chronicle* (Oct. 12–14, 1758) "Congreve was richer in wit, I mean in wit of the true sterling kind, than any man whatsoever." Samuel Johnson gave his authoritative praise of Congreve's language: "He formed a peculiar idea of comick excellence, which he supposed to consist in gay remarks and unexpected answers; but that which he endeavoured, he seldom failed of performing; . . . his personages are a kind of intellectual gladiators; every sentence is to ward or strike; the contest of smartness is never intermitted; his wit is a meteor playing to and fro with alternate coruscations." [19]

There were also many writers who considered Congreve's characters expertly individualized. To Arthur Murphy, writing in the *Gray's Inn Journal* (July 6, 1754), Congreve had much the same talent for characterization as Shakespeare and Jonson. Murphy stated that he had heard it objected that many of Congreve's characters were "obvious in human life," but he thought that a "strong proof of his superior genius." Heart-

---

[15] *Works*, II, 317.
[16] *Dramatic Miscellanies* (Dublin, 1784), III, 210.
[17] Prologue at the opening of Drury Lane in the autumn of 1747.
[18] Edmund Burke, in *The Reformer* (Feb. 4, 1748), objected to this type of excuse: "I know 'tis said in his Excuse, that he drew his Pictures after the times; but whoever examines his Plays will find, that he not only copied the ill Morals of the Age, but approved them."
[19] *Lives of the English Poets*, II, 31.

well was an example: "he must pass through such an imagination as *Congreve's* to support several scenes in the drama with exquisite pleasantry. The character was not new; yet his management of it has all the graces of novelty, and the situations in which we see him are exquisitely ridiculous." This type of character may prove tiresome in the hands of a weak writer, "but in this excellent poet's hands nothing suffers." Sir Paul Plyant similarly has "perhaps as much comic force as in any one piece on the stage." [20] In the same journal (July 20, 1754) a comparison between Shadwell and Congreve argued that Shadwell ridiculed absurdities or odd characters insufficiently universal, but not so with Congreve's Heartwell, Foresight, and Lady Wishfort. "We all can vouch for the existence of such characters; and, when we see them properly acted, we acknowledge the truth of imitation." James Boaden was in essential agreement with this stand: "Notwithstanding the eternal wit of Congreve's comedies . . . it is not true that they have no real character." *Love for Love* "abounds in characters admirably discriminated and preserved." [21] Let the *Dramatic Censor* (II, 467) sum it up: "No man who ever wrote for the stage has shewn more capital, more correct, or more pleasing delineations of life; his characters are beautifully contrasted."

To many writers Congreve's comedies represented the best in entertainment, but only for sophisticated audiences. *The Gazetteer* (Nov. 30, 1776) declared Congreve "not fit food for every man's palate," yet "never were plays that could afford a more rational entertainment." In the *Morning Post and Daily Advertiser* (Dec. 28, 1776) "The Ghost of Gay," lamenting the "fallen condition" of the contemporary theater, set Congreve in contrast to the sentimentalists. He argued that the best French and English dramatists believed it necessary "only to *expose,* in order to *reform,* the folly of the world." Therefore, they "drew men as they found them, to *shew* what they *ought* to be," whereas a sentimental dramatist "drew men as they should be, and not as they *are.*" Because "immaculate characters are rarely to be met with," Congreve and Jonson, "our first-rate authors," people their dramas with *"knaves, fops,* and *fools;* no deck'd virtue or brilliancy of sentiment, but men conforming their characters, by manners and language, deducing from the tenor some truly comic effect." Congreve was praised as far superior to contemporary comic writers who "are too pious to expose, and too fashionable to admit, that fops, fools, or rascals exist." Expressing its rating of Congreve in a way popular among periodicals of the mid-century, the *Literary and Antigallican Magazine* (III, 6) published (Jan.

---

[20] Quoted from *The Works of Arthur Murphy, Esq.* (London, 1786), VI, 344–345.
[21] *Mrs. Jordan* (New York, n.d.), I, 101.

1758) a table of the major dramatists on a scale of one to twenty (perfection):

Poet	Genius	Judgment	Learning	Versification
Shakespeare	19	14	14	19
Otway	17	10	10	17
Lee	16	10	10	15
Dryden	18	16	17	18
Congreve	15	16	14	14
Vanbrugh	14	15	14	10
Rowe	14	16	15	16
Farquhar	15	16	10	10

With vigorous disapproval of Congreve's alleged licentiousness on the one hand and warm praise of his brilliance and wit on the other, the critics and especially the theatrical managers ultimately needed to weigh these conflicting judgments. So far as the stage was concerned, the opposition to Congreve won, in the sense that the practical men of the theater bowed to the weight of objections. As Garrick expressed it in the preface (1766) to his alteration of Wycherley's *The Country Wife* into *The Country Girl*, "There seems indeed an absolute Necessity for reforming many Plays of our most eminent Writers: For no kind of Wit ought to be received as an Excuse for Immorality, nay it becomes still more dangerous in proportion as it is more witty.—Without such a Reformation, our *English* Comedies must be reduced to a very small Number . . . or . . . continue shameless in spite of publick Disapprobation." As a result of this conviction, which was expressed in many ways by many dramatic reviewers and correspondents for the periodicals, Congreve's plays, after declining rapidly in popularity during the 1760's, were revised and restored to the stage in 1776. Although reviewers disagreed concerning the merit of the revisions, the plays had a brief renewal of popularity.

In the early decades of the nineteenth century Restoration comedy, with considerable emphasis upon Congreve, was examined by Hazlitt, Lamb, Hunt, and Macaulay. Although their analysis falls outside the eighteenth century proper, their judgments have a continuity with the thinking of the preceding century and have had a considerable influence upon later opinion of Restoration comedy. Of the four authors, Hazlitt first published his views, in 1819, in his lectures on the English Comic Writers. In Lecture IV he discussed Wycherley, Congreve, Vanbrugh, and Farquhar, the four whom Leigh Hunt edited twenty years later. Unlike Lamb and Macaulay, Hazlitt did not genuinely examine the morality or immorality of the plays, although, somewhat like Lamb, he seemed inclined to think of the world of the comedies

as one set apart from the early 1800's. "In turning over the pages of
the best comedies," he stated, "we are almost transported to another
world, and escape from this dull age to one that was all life, and whim,
and mirth, and humour." The domain of the plays was a "happy
thoughtless age, when kings and nobles led purely ornamental lives;
when the utmost stretch of a morning's study went no farther than the
choice of a sword-knot, or the adjustment of a side-curl; when the soul
spoke out in all the pleasing eloquence of dress; and beaux and belles,
enamoured of themselves in one another's follies, fluttered like gilded
butterflies, in giddy mazes, through the walks of St. James's Park." Of the
four authors, Congreve was to Hazlitt the "most distinct" and "most
easily defined," the one who excelled in "wit and elegance," with a
style "inimitable, nay perfect. It is the highest model of comic dialogue." [22]

With an intense enjoyment of the plays of Congreve and his contemporaries, Lamb approached them as a spectator in a theater, enjoy-
ing the portrayal of certain characters—Ben in *Love for Love*, for example—by actors whom he admired, and discussing them through an
appreciative account of "The Old Actors." In a second article [23] he
turned his attention to the morality and realism of what he called the
"Artificial Comedy of the Last Century." He discovered that he had
differing reactions to it and to modern drama, or sentimental drama,
or the drama of common life, as it was variously called. What made the
difference? In the first place, Lamb was not inclined to see in a stage
character an approximation of a real-life individual, particularly when
the author made no attempt to offer such a parallel. Although the drama
of Lamb's day constantly confronted him with parallels of that kind,
the "artificial comedy," in Lamb's opinion, suspended the inclination
to identify stage personalities with real ones, a suspension which enabled Lamb to avoid the eighteenth-century concern with the moral im-
plications of the comedy.[24] Lamb frankly acknowledged that in his day
"Congreve and Farquhar show their heads once in seven years only, to
be exploded and put down instantly." Why had this happened? Not

[22] *Lectures on the English Poets and the English Comic Writers,* ed. W. C.
Hazlitt (London, 1906), pp. 91–92. Of the comedies, only *Love for Love* still held the
stage when Hazlitt wrote; it he praised as being "full of character, incident, and
stage-effect," and surpassing in wit all others by Congreve except *The Way of the
World. Love for Love,* in his opinion, still acted well.

[23] The three essays were "On Some of the Old Actors," "On the Artificial Comedy
of the Last Century," and "On the Acting of Munden." They appeared in the *London
Magazine* for Feb., April, and Oct. 1822. The text I have used is *The Works of Charles
Lamb,* ed. William MacDonald (London, 1903), I, 263–294.

[24] See also W. E. Houghton, Jr., "Lamb's Criticism of Restoration Comedy," *ELH,*
x (March 1943), 61–72.

"altogether" because of a "few wild speeches" or "an occasional licence of dialogue." The causes, more fundamental, turned back to the complaints of the eighteenth century. The "business" of their dramatic characters "will not stand the moral test. We screw every thing up to that. Idle gallantry in a fiction, a dream, the passing pageant of an evening, startles us in the same way as the alarming indications of profligacy in a son or ward in real life should startle a parent or guardian." [25] Lamb convinced himself, however, that, because these were essentially comedies of wit and did not directly present an emotional view of man, they did not intrude themselves into the moral world of here and now. He eventually claimed that the plays could not be judged immoral because the world in which the characters lived and acted was not Christendom. Their society was one in which morality did not exist and consequently was not an issue.

In 1840 Leigh Hunt edited the works of Wycherley, Congreve, Vanbrugh, and Farquhar. In an introduction he discussed not only the authors and their plays individually, but also the drama of that age. Hunt approved of Lamb's attempt to vindicate these authors from charges of immorality, but he disagreed with Lamb's defense, which Hunt referred to as "the entire fancifulness of the states of society described by Congreve and others." He did not, however, undertake a defence of them on new grounds. Of the four, Congreve was to him the "wittiest, most scholarly, most highly bred, the most elaborate in his plots and language, and most pungent but least natural in his characters," and had the "least heart." [26]

In January 1841, in the *Edinburgh Review*, Macaulay, reviewing Hunt's edition, had the last and perhaps most devastating word in a reappraisal of Wycherley and Congreve. Noting that there were objections to a republication of their works, Macaulay argued, however, that no work or class of works which "has exercised a great influence on the human mind" should wholly disappear and that, if these plays were to be regarded as unprintable, a great many ancient authors must, on the same basis, be excluded from the eyes of modern man. But he much feared the immoral in them. As to their morality, he disagreed

---

25 *Works*, I, 281.

26 *The Dramatic Works of Wycherley, Congreve, Vanbrugh, and Farquhar* (London: Edward Moxon, 1840), p. lxxviii. In considering the plays individually, Hunt displayed some of the attitudes prevalent in the preceding century. Although he thought *The Double Dealer* superior to *The Old Batchelor*, he emphasized its hardness of sentiment. Act II, Scene v, was "exquisite for the grossness of the overtures made under pretence of a delicacy in alarm," and it has a very "black . . . villain." Sir Paul was guilty of remarks "no decent person would hear with patience between father and child" (p. xxxvii). *Love for Love*, the "most amusing," also had the "least unpleasant" characters, with no "revolting scoundrel" (p. xxxviii).

with Hunt, "who seems to hold that there is little or no ground for the charge of immorality." The indecency was not the most disagreeable fault but rather the fact that, although the dramas were brilliantly entertaining, they were "earthly, sensual, devilish" and imbued with a singularly inhuman spirit. The characters were all distinguished by "foreheads of bronze, hearts like the nether millstone, and tongues set on fire of hell." What, Macaulay asked, of the excuse that justified these comedies by the coarseness of expression in still earlier English dramatists? He could not so defend them. Whereas to the Elizabethan, infidelity was either a serious crime or the laughter was turned against the gallant, the Restoration dramatist evidently did his "best to make the person who commits the injury graceful, sensible, and spirited, and the person who suffers it a fool, or a tyrant, or both." Macaulay then raised an objection which the preceding century had voiced: the late seventeenth-century point of view was deplorable, because morality was "deeply interested in this, that what is immoral shall not be presented to the imagination of the young and susceptible in constant connection with what is attractive." [27]

And what of Lamb's defense of this way of writing? Macaulay did not doubt that it was possible to create "a conventional world in which things forbidden by the Decalogue and the Statute Book shall be lawful" without making such an exhibition harmful. But this was not what was done in Restoration comedy. In it, a "hundred little touches are employed to make the fictitious world appear like the actual world." Macaulay could not believe that morality was not present in this comic world or that the reader or spectator made the suspension of judgment which Lamb expected. "Sound morality" was, in Restoration comedy, "insulted, derided, associated with everything mean and harmful"; "unsound morality" was set off to "every advantage, and inculcated by all methods, direct and indirect." [28] It was unfortunate that Macaulay, writing in so influential a journal as the *Edinburgh Review,* perpetuated with such force so many of the narrowest conceptions which the late eighteenth century had fostered. Although Macaulay did not advocate banning these works from the library or stage (they had nearly disap-

[27] *The Complete Works of Thomas Babington Macaulay* (New York: Houghton Mifflin, 1910), VIII, 48, 51, 53, 52.

[28] VIII, 54, 56–57. In appraising Congreve's talent, Macaulay found some of the plays admirable. Although he felt that the plot of *The Old Batchelor* lacked both interest and probability, the "dialogue is resplendent with wit and eloquence" (VIII, 81). In *The Double Dealer* the powers demonstrated in the first play had matured and improved. *Love for Love* was thought "superior both in wit and in scenic effect" (VIII, 83) and *The Way of the World* "the most deeply meditated and the most brilliantly written of all his works" (VIII, 94).

peared from the stage by then), his pronouncements, as the last in this
series of reappraisals of late seventeenth-century dramatists, confirmed
rather than softened the moralistic denunciation which, dating from
the attack by Jeremy Collier, had for nearly one hundred and fifty
years harmed the reputation of Congreve and his fellow writers.

The Mourning Bride

The Mourning Bride, the only tragedy among Congreve's plays,
stands in a somewhat exceptional position. Although it was occasionally discussed in an eighteenth-century commentary upon all of Congreve's works, much more frequently it was singled out for individual
attention and received more special analysis than any one of the comedies. The principal early statement concerning it was a highly laudatory account in Sir Richard Blackmore's Preface to King Arthur (1697)
in which Blackmore stated that the play had received, quite justly,
"Universal Applause" as being "the most perfect Tragedy that has been
wrote in this Age." He selected for praise the "Fable" as "a very Artful
and Masterly Contrivance"; the characters as "well chosen, and well
delineated," especially Zara; the "Passions" as "well touch'd, and skill-
fully wrought up"; the diction as "Proper, Clear, Beautiful, Noble, and
diversify'd agreeably to the variety of the Subject"; the moral as quite
proper, vice being punished and "Opprest Innocence at last Rewarded";
and "Nature . . . very happily Imitated." He could not find in it any
"immodest Images or Expressions" or any "wild, unnatural Rants." It
was "Chast, Just, and Decent." [29] The moralizing Collier did not, of
course, find the tragedy chaste or free of "immodest Images," and in
A Comparison between the Two Stages (1702) Critick remarked that "I
can by no means consent to the great Reputation his Mourning Bride
has, because I can point to several Blots in't unmention'd by Collyer"
(pp. 33–34). On the other hand, a discussion of English tragedy in the
Spectator (April 16, 1711) listed it as one of the "very noble Tragedies"
among the small group which "have ended happily." Giles Jacob, in
his Poetical Register (1719), stated that he could not better describe
the "Excellence of this Tragedy" than had Blackmore, whose comment
he quoted.

Not until later in the century, however, did critics give the tragedy
much more attention. As was true of the comedies, there was a mixture of praise and disparagement of The Mourning Bride, but the un-

[29] E. B. Potter, "The Paradox of Congreve's Mourning Bride," PMLA, LVIII (1943),
977–1001, has discussed Blackmore's motives in writing this tribute.

favorable views stressed the structure of the play and the nature of the characters more than the moral or immoral tone. Lord Kames, in his *Elements of Criticism,* focussed attention upon its structure, for it, he pointed out, did not wholly observe the unities. In the last act there was a "capital error with respect to unity of place," with the first three scenes set in a room of state, the fourth in a prison. The "chain" of the actors was broken, "as the persons introduced in the prison are different from those who made their appearance in the room of state." To Kames this interruption suggested two acts rather than one, and he wondered whether a tragedy might be written in an unconventional six acts (II, 341).[30] A more fundamental objection was that the tragedy was unnatural, in both language and characters, a view briefly stated in *Lloyd's Evening Post* (March 4–6, 1767): "This Play met with more applause than any of his other pieces, though it is, in general, bombast and unnatural."

In 1770 the *Dramatic Censor* devoted fifteen pages to an analysis of the play (chiefly summary of the plot) which stressed its "unnatural qualities." The author stated that the play at the end "draws a very moral inference" in showing that, "though virtue may labour under occasional chastisement, yet perseverance in rectitude cannot fail of reward." In spite of this virtue and of able performances before "many brilliant audiences," *The Mourning Bride* "is one of the worst living tragedies: it is apparently laboured, the sentiments in general strained, the versification in many places monotonous, and the plot equivocal" (II, 413). As to the characters, the King was considered a "weak, blustering, tyrannical object; a credulous lover, and a harsh father. His passions, especially in the fourth act, are laughable; . . . he is altogether the most ungracious load that ever lay heavy on the shoulders of a performer." Osmyn also could not be considered a genuine hero, being rather an "affectionate, constant husband," whose "situations and embarrassments raise sensations of pity," yet because he is "totally out of the fourth act, and so immaterially concerned in the first and fifth, he becomes a very imperfect hero for representation." Almeria was thought "amiable in her principles, and pitiable in her circumstances; . . . yet her royal highness is undoubtedly too much upon the whine." Less satisfactory was Zara, "beyond dispute, the most indelicate Queen that can well be imagined; she is vicious and mean, gross in sentiment, and vulgar in expression." On the whole, "scarce any degree of merit can

---

[30] Kames' views were given wide currency by reviewers. In similar language the substance of his criticism was reproduced in a long review of the play in the *Public Ledger* (Sept. 28, 1771), as reprinted in the *Theatrical Review,* I, 22–23, and also in the *General Evening Post* (Oct. 1–3, 1771).

save expiring Zara and her dismal attendants from being laughed at"
(II, 413–416).[31]

There were, however, several critics who offered a more balanced
view of the virtues and defects of the tragedy. Dr. Johnson, in his *Life
of Congreve*, thought that there was "more bustle than sentiment" in
it. It had a plot "busy and intricate" and the "events take hold on the
attention; but, except a very few passages, we are rather amused with
noise, and perplexed with stratagem, than entertained with any true
delineation of natural characters." Nevertheless, it continued "to be
acted and applauded." [32] When Thomas Davies wrote his *Dramatic Miscellanies,* he gave it a higher standing than had the author of the
Dramatic Censor. Davies believed the fable "not ill chosen" and the
characters not "weakly drawn." The King, though a mixture of "pomp-
ous phraseology with an outrageous vehemence of temper," was "still
. . . a character." Almeria, Zara, and Osmyn all aroused admiration,
pity, or terror. The "intricate" plot demanded close attention and there
was a satisfactory moral. Yet the play was not wholly pleasing: "If the
composition . . . with respect to sentiment, passion, and diction, were
equal to the well-studied oeconomy of the fable, it might challenge a
rank with our most frequented tragedies." In spite of its deficiencies,
he concluded that *The Mourning Bride* possessed some scenes "which
never fail to attract the attention and engage the heart of the spectator" and the "happy conclusion will for ever cause joy and exultation
in the audience, who will continually dismiss the players with the loud-
est approbation" (III, 204–209).

During the late years of the century, the most damning indictment
of the tragedy accused it of being a pantomime. Charles Churchill early
applied that term to it, in referring to Hannah Pritchard's acting:
"When Congreve's favour'd pantomime to grace, / She comes a captive queen of Moorish race." But it was the *World* which gave it wide
currency. On May 21, 1787, its reviewer stated his objections to the
play: "And yet it is, in spite of all that astonishing acting can do for
it, signifying nothing. Sound without cause, and fury without effect.
If Zara's passions outstrip the wind, they neither interest the mind, nor
impress the heart. The play is very worthless. That it is a pantomime,

[31] Some of the attacks were unreasonably severe. In the *St. James' Chronicle*
(March 12–15, 1768), a writer, discussing the art of tragedy, asserted that modern
writers of tragic drama were weak because "their Attention has been too much fixed
upon Plot and Intrigue, which is the proper Business of Comedy, to amuse the
Audience . . . but this is beneath the Dignity of Tragedy." To illustrate his point,
he cited an incident in *The Mourning Bride:* "The King putting on the Dress of
Osman to surprise his Daughter, which is the Occasion of his being murdered by
Gonsales, in the Habit of a Slave, is an Incident fitter for a Romance than a Tragedy."
[32] *Lives of the Poets,* II, 27.

is not its greatest fault. Inasmuch as it offends manners no less than taste; and hurts with ribaldry more than nonsense." On January 7, 1789, it blackened the reputation of the tragedy by heading a review: "CONGREVE'S PANTOMIME."

In the last decade of the century a series of articles in the *Thespian Magazine* argued the merits and defects of the tragedy. "Censor Dramaticus," who initiated the discussion, undertook an objective analysis. He acknowledged that few plays had "caused more disputation" than Congreve's tragedy, with friends extolling it beyond reason and enemies execrating it "beyond all probability." In examining it "according to the rules of the Drama," the writer thought its fable "perfectly dramatic" with a single action "conducing to a single object, the happiness of Osmyn and Almeria." With respect to the unities, "this is one of the most perfect pieces in our language," with only a slight deviation in the fifth act. He judged the character of Osmyn to be "eminently beautiful," with all the "conspicuous virtues" represented in "their utmost perfection." To keep Osmyn from being a perfect and hence unnatural hero, Congreve made Osmyn's principal distresses "brought on him by his own means" but without preventing "our pity for his sufferings, and satisfaction at their completion." The critic agreed that the "sentiments and diction" have been open to just criticism, but these defects "form but a small part of the whole, and lose all comparison when opposed to the number of beauties" (I, 163–166).

In a later issue (I, 209–212) a reply by "Criticus" appeared. He wished to rectify "a few errors into which the author has fallen either from a glowing partiality to that production, or from a want of thoroughly considering it." He examined one by one the points made by "Censor Dramaticus" and argued that the "characters are *caricatures*—the incidents *monstrous*—the situations *pantomimic*—the sentiments *uncongenial*—the language *bombast*." As to the tragedy's being commended for "being one entire action," he wondered whether there was any tragedy, except perhaps the "tragic comedies of Dryden," which did not have "one proposed end in view." He also did not believe that the incidents developed naturally from the history of Osmyn and Almeria or that the observance of the unities was more than a minor virtue, for they could be observed in an otherwise wretched tragedy. He was caustic concerning the diction and, quoting a short passage, argued that it resembled many other portions of the play in that in sound "it has the appearance of involving something sublime and interesting; but a very narrow examination has not permitted me yet to discover any meaning at all in it."

The dispute then deteriorated into a quarrel over details and went from rejoinder to counter-rejoinder; nothing new was added to the argument. A further defense of the tragedy was offered by James Boaden in his *Memoirs of Mrs. Siddons* (pp. 221–227). Because he admired the actress very much in her performance in this tragedy, he tried to refute the charge that it was a pantomime. He pointed out that in the 1780's a "very mischievous tone of criticism" became "prevalent in the daily press" and a "despicable sort of commentary" called the tragedy a pantomime, a charge which "implies that the play, however aided by speech, retains too much of this character—that it is a show, and little but a show." In reply, Boaden argued first that if critics meant that the play was "more complex in its action than perhaps the French stage admits," then the same charge could be made "equally to the whole series of English authors, and to Shakespeare very particularly indeed." In further denial of the charge, he stated that in respect to the "other nerves of the drama—description, sentiment, and passion," he found Congreve not wanting. Boaden quoted many "beauties" of the play, one naturally being the opening line. Asserting that "Congreve, as a poet, has a seat the proudest that a poet can occupy," he called for "an attentive reconsideration of this neglected tragedy," not upon the stage, "for now we could not act it—but in the closet." In conclusion, not only was *The Mourning Bride* "replete with description, sentiment, and passion," but the abundance of these qualities, which some, because of their plenitude, found painful, "must not be supposed to diminish the lustre of his figures or sentiments; they are admirable however numerous."

Quite recently E. B. Potter has discussed a paradox which exists in the contrast between the stage vogue of *The Mourning Bride* and its apparent lack of critical acclaim.[33] There is a contradiction, certainly, between the continued performance of the tragedy and the rather severe attacks upon it, but the paradox is certainly not unique and may not be so great as Potter implies. It is a question whether critical opinion, in the best sense of the term, was a decisive factor in the vogue of plays on the eighteenth-century stage. One might similarly speak of the paradox of *The Way of the World,* which, far less warmly received at its première than was *The Mourning Bride,* was more frequently acted in the eighteenth century. Or of *The Double Dealer,* which held the stage well during and following the revival in 1735 when Aaron Hill in the *Prompter,* one of the few periodicals devoting a great deal of its space to the stage, denounced it roundly. There is the fact, too, that *The Mourning Bride* at its first appearance had a reception which was little, if at all, superior to that offered *The Old Batchelor* and *Love for Love*

[33] *PMLA,* LVIII, 977–1001.

in the 1690's, yet all three managed to remain on the stage for a considerable time in spite of a good deal of adverse criticism. The vogue of all the plays was a fluctuating one, not an evenly sustained popularity, and *The Mourning Bride* does not represent a unique problem. The problem reappears from time to time in the following chapters, which narrate the stage history of the plays, and is discussed more fully at the end of Chapter viii.

Chapter II

THE EARLY YEARS, 1693–1714

Toward the end of 1690 William Congreve, a young man anxious to try his fortune in a new environment, settled himself in London. By the close of the next year he had entered upon the study of law by becoming a resident of the Middle Temple. There, in the Inns of Court where Etherege, Wycherley, Shadwell, and many others had enjoyed leisurely lives as law students, Congreve directed his attention to writing. In a short time he published a novel, *Incognita: or Love and Duty Reconcil'd* (1692); but he was also already at work on a comedy. For some time—how long is not clear—he mulled over the manuscript of his first play.[1] It was in many ways a fortunate time for Congreve to turn to the theater. The older comic writers—Wycherley and Etherege—had left off playwriting, and although their plays remained on the stage no one had very successfully followed their vein of comedy. In the early 1690's, in fact, no one of the promising authors soon to appear had yet made his debut as a dramatist: young Colley Cibber had not yet ventured to turn from actor to actor-dramatist; John Vanbrugh did not offer his first play until late in 1696; and George Farquhar was not to appear until 1699. Congreve was to have three plays on the boards before any of these three writers produced his first play.

The Old Batchelor, Congreve's first venture, was in the hands of the actors by the end of 1692, but its première was delayed for several months, perhaps because of the deaths of several principal actors belonging to the Theater Royal. Early in 1693, about three years after his arrival in the capital, it was acted and Congreve entered upon his short but brilliant career. Between 1693 and 1700, when *The Way of the World* appeared, he saw three of his plays receive unusual acclaim at their premières and the other two gain the praise of the critics, if not the theatergoing public as a whole. Not alone because of his dramatic successes were these important and exciting years in the London theaters. It was, in fact, a time of great change in both the playhouses and society. The older school of actors—among them the illustrious Thomas Betterton—were nearing the end of their supremacy; the young performers—among them the colorful Colley Cibber and Thomas Dog-

[1] John C. Hodges, *William Congreve, the Man* (New York, 1941), pp. 33–39, and "The Composition of Congreve's First Play," *PMLA,* LVIII (Dec. 1943), 971–976.

get—were rising to dominance, and with them rose Congreve. When *The Old Batchelor* was produced, London had a single company of players, the "United Company" formed in 1682; yet before the end of Congreve's career this monopoly was broken. His last three plays were produced after the secession of the actors in 1695, a revolution which he assisted by offering *Love for Love,* his third play, to the dissenting actors as the opening attraction for their new playhouse. From that day, except for a very few years in the early eighteenth century, London had competing playhouses and the advantages of rivalry. In addition, a new theatergoing public was forming and tastes were changing. The repertory system permitted currents of sentimentalism to appear in the main stream of the drama at the same time that the comedy of manners sustained itself not only in repeated performances of the plays of Etherege and Wycherley but also in new productions by Congreve, Vanbrugh, and Farquhar. And in the midst of Congreve's success, the playwrights and theaters were ruthlessly attacked by Jeremy Collier, who, in his *Short View of the Immorality and Profaneness of the English Stage* (1698), stirred the dramatists to angry reply and precipitated a turmoil which did not subside for many years. Although Congreve may have been sufficiently disappointed in the reception of his fifth play in 1700 to abandon playwriting, he surely could never have looked back upon those seven years as dull and unprofitable ones.

When *The Old Batchelor* (1693) was offered to a London audience, the city had not for a long time seen so extraordinarily successful a first play by such a young man, and youth and talent were warmly received by spectators who saw it achieve in March 1693 the great success of fourteen successive performances.[2] Like many another play, it owed much of its initial success to the actors, for Congreve had the good fortune to cast it, as well as his others, with many of the best players of his day. In the role of Heartwell appeared the pre-eminent Thomas Betterton. Among the actresses, Anne Bracegirdle was a charming and vivacious woman whose fame as an actress had hitherto been of slow growth. After playing Araminta, however, she very rapidly gained the recognition long due her, and thereafter Congreve created his heroines with her in mind. According to Cibber, Congreve wrote Fondlewife for Dogget, whom he had known in Ireland and whose association with the dramatist was mutually profitable; Tony Aston remarked that in this part and later in Ben (*Love for Love*) Dogget "vegetated fast." Sir

---

[2] Hodges, *Congreve,* p. 41, argues for March. To the middle of the next century a play with an initial run of nine performances, which would permit the author three benefit nights, could be considered a moderate success, and those which ran twelve consecutive nights or more were the exceptional ones.

Joseph was acted by Bowen, another friend of the dramatist. To Joe Haines, a popular comedian, was assigned Bluff, a part which in Aston's opinion "none ever touch'd but *Joe Haines*." [3] Elizabeth Barry, possibly the most accomplished actress of the time, played Laetitia and spoke the epilogue, and Mrs. Mountfort, whose actor-husband had recently been killed in a duel, acted Belinda. The lesser parts were also in capable hands: Jack Verbruggen (Sharper), Joseph Williams (Vainlove), Cave Underhill (Setter), Mrs. Bowman (Sylvia), and Mrs. Leigh (Lucy). Nearly all of these players had parts in Congreve's later comedies.

Although *The Old Batchelor* began brilliantly, we have little knowledge of its stage history in the closing years of the seventeenth century, for exact data concerning the daily offerings of the London theaters before 1702 are scarce. Of one performance, in 1695, there is mention in Cibber's *Apology* (I, 205–209), where he relates how he first came to act Fondlewife. The company in Drury Lane, to nettle the opposition in Lincoln's Inn Fields, determined to offer George Powell as Heartwell, Powell to mimic Betterton in the role. In casting the play, the manager overlooked Fondlewife until a late moment; once aware of his oversight, Powell permitted young Cibber, who had expressed a desire for the part, to attempt it. Diligently observing Dogget's portrayal of Fondlewife, Cibber undertook a close imitation in voice and manner. The occasion was a triumph for the fledgling actor, who was pleased that Dogget was in the audience. In fact, the entire venture was successful: "the Curiosity to see *Betterton* mimick'd," Cibber remarked (I, 207), "drew us a pretty good Audience, and *Powel* (as far as Applause is a Proof of it) was allow'd to have burlesqu'd him very well." [4] Not until the early eighteenth century is there record of another London performance.[5]

After the success of *The Old Batchelor*, it was only natural that Congreve should hasten another comedy to the stage. It was *The Double Dealer*, acted in Drury Lane probably by December of 1693,[6] less than a year after his first play. Although it did not meet with so favorable a reception, John Downes, the prompter, included it among the "good Plays" of the season and mentioned the "Unparrell'd" performance of

[3] *A Brief Supplement to Colley Cibber, Esq.* (n.d.), rptd. in R. W. Lowe's ed. of Cibber's *Apology* (1889), II, 309, 316.

[4] Benjamin Victor, an admirer of Cibber, gave an extended account of the episode in *The History of the Theaters of London and Dublin* (London, 1761), II, 36–43.

[5] It probably was given frequently, but the principal record is of an intended performance for Nov. 3, 1700, "On Friday last there was a full House at the Playhouse in Drury Lane, the play of the Old Batchelor being to be acted; but Capt. Griffin, who was chief actor therein, being taken ill, they were dismissed all having their money returned." *English Post* (Nov. 8–11, 1700).

[6] Hodges, *Congreve*, p. 46.

Dogget (Sir Paul Plyant) and Mrs. Barry (Lady Touchwood). John Dryden stated that the comedy met with censure from the "greater part of the Town," but in his own opinion the adverse criticism came not from the "best Judges." In spite of the cool reception, it had been acted eight times when Dryden wrote,[7] a fair though possibly disappointing number. An extended account of its reception appeared in a letter written in London on March 22, 1694, in which a correspondent discussed several new plays:

The first that was acted was Mr. Congreve's, called The Double Dealer. It has fared with that play, as it generally does with beauties officiously cried up; the mighty expectation which was raised of it made it sink, even beneath its own merit. The character of The Double Dealer is artfully writt, but the action being but single, and confined within the rules of true comedy, it could not please the generality of our audience, who relish nothing but variety, and think any thing dull and heavy which does not border upon farce.—The criticks were severe upon this play, which gave the author occasion to lash 'em in his Epistle Dedicatory, in so defying or hectoring a style, that it was counted rude even by his best friends; so that 'tis generally thought he has done his business, and lost himself: a thing he owes to Mr. Dryden's treacherous friendship, who being jealous of the applause he had gott by his Old Batchelour, deluded him into a foolish imitation of his own way of writing angry prefaces.[8]

Many years later, in 1719, Colley Cibber referred to *The Double Dealer* as an example of a playwright's difficult relations with his public, a subject on which Cibber could easily have been an authority: "If he [a dramatist] succeeds in a first Play, let him look well to the next, for then he is enter'd the Herd, as a Common Enemy, and is to know that they, who gave him Fame, can take it away; he is then to be allow'd no more Merit or Mercy, than the rest of his Brethren: Of which nothing can be a stronger Instance, than the Torrent of Applause that was deservedly thrown in upon the *Old Batchelor,* and the boisterous Cavils that the next Year unreasonably over-run the same Author's Play of the *Double-Dealer.*"[9]

The cast was an excellent one. Betterton (Maskwell), Williams (Mellefont), Verbruggen (Careless), and Powell (Brisk) had had parts in *The Old Batchelor.* Kynaston and Bowman acted Lord Touchwood and Lord Froth for their first Congrevean roles. All the actresses had appeared in the earlier comedy. Mrs. Barry (Lady Touchwood) and Mrs. Bracegirdle (Cynthia) were accompanied by Mrs. Mountfort, the "Mistress of more variety of Humour than I ever knew in any one

[7] *Roscius Anglicanus,* ed. Montague Summers (London, n.d.), p. 42; *The Letters of John Dryden,* ed. C. W. Ward (Durham, N.C., 1942), p. 63.

[8] In Edmond Malone, "An Historical Account of the Stage," in *The Plays and Poems of William Shakespeare* (London, 1821), III, 162–163.

[9] Introduction to *Ximena* (London, 1719), pp. xix–xx.

Woman Actress," [10] as Lady Froth and Mrs. Leigh as Lady Plyant. Not long after the première Congreve's reply to the critics appeared in the first printed version of the comedy. The quarto included also a laudatory poem by Dryden, and no doubt many others among the "best Judges" consoled him for his failure to equal the success of his first comedy. A month later, on January 13, 1694, *The Double Dealer* was given by command of Queen Mary. On that evening Cibber took a part on short notice—as he was to do the following year with Fondlewife—and made a success of it. Having been asked by Congreve personally to attempt Lord Touchwood, Cibber was as pleased as any young actor could be when "Mr. *Congreve* made me the Compliment of saying, That I had not only answer'd, but had exceeded his Expectations, and that he would shew me he was sincere by his saying more of me to the Masters.—He was as good as his Word." [11] Five years later (March 4, 1699) the comedy was again given, as we know from a letter from Dryden to Mrs. Steward: "This Day was playd a reviv'd Comedy of Mr Congreve's calld the Double Dealer, which was never very takeing:—in the play bill was printed,—Written by Mr Congreve; with Severall Expressions omitted: What kind of Expressions those were you may easily ghess; if you have seen the Monday's Gazette, wherein is the King's Order, for the reformation of the Stage: but the printing an Authours name, in a Play bill, is a new manner of proceeding, at least in England." [12] With no other performance known before 1703, the principal comment upon it appeared in *A Comparison between the Two Stages* (1702) when Critick praised it by saying that, although Congreve's reputation rose from *The Old Batchelor, Love for Love,* and *The Mourning Bride,* he thought *The Double Dealer* "the best he ever writ." When Ramble reminded him that Critick's judgment was "against the Opinion of all the Town," Critick replied, "I can't help that . . . but without being byass'd or prejudic'd, I do take the *Double Dealer* to be among the most correct and regular Comedies: Mr. *C.* intended it so, and it cost him unusual Labour to do't; but as he says, he has been at a needless Expence, and the Town is to be treated at a cheaper rate" (pp. 37–38).

It was a year and a half after *The Double Dealer* before Congreve's third piece reached the theaters. The delay was not altogether his doing, because *Love for Love* was apparently ready late in 1694; an impending theatrical revolution, however, kept it from the stage until the early spring of 1695. For several years there had been incipient revolt

10 Cibber, *Apology,* I, 165.
11 *Apology,* I, 186.
12 *Letters,* pp. 112–113.

among the actors against the patentees of the United Company formed in 1682. Previous to that year there had been two theaters, and a dissatisfied, restless, or mistreated actor could seek an engagement with the opposition; after 1682, however, the performers felt themselves at the mercy of the holders of the patent. Finally the principal actors, particularly Betterton, Mrs. Barry, and Mrs. Bracegirdle, all of whom had acted in Congreve's first two plays, sought the aid of Lord Dorset and Sir Robert Howard and eventually secured a license for a new company, in which, according to Downes, Congreve owned a share. Congreve contributed greatly to the success of the theater by withholding *Love for Love* so that it might open the new playhouse. At its initial performance, on April 30, 1695, there was a distinguished audience, with King William present to lend royal approval. With a run of thirteen consecutive performances,[13] the comedy was highly successful. Cibber states that it "ran on with such extraordinary Success that they had seldom occasion to act any other Play 'till the End of the Season," [14] and *A Comparison between the Two Stages* (1702) remarked that the "New-house opened with an extraordinary good Comedy, the like has scarce been heard of" (p. 10).

The cast was a distinguished one, so excellent, in fact, that Downes implied that it was responsible for much of the success. Once more the cast was headed by Betterton, who acted Valentine. The characterization which apparently created the greatest stir, however, was "little, lively, spract" Dogget's handling of Ben. According to tradition, Dogget in preparation for the part "took Lodgings in *Wapping,* and *gather'd thence a Nosegay* for the whole Town." [15] Downes thought him exceptionally good, and Cibber believed that Dogget so valued the reputation he made as Ben that he came to prefer comedy to tragedy, in due time overvaluing "Comedy for its being nearer to Nature than Tragedy" (I, 229). Concerning Cave Underhill as Sir Sampson there was disagreement. Cibber praised him highly because "he shew'd all that true perverse Spirit that is commonly seen in much Wit and Ill-nature. This Character is one of those few so well written, with so much Wit and Humour, that an Actor must be the grossest Dunce that does not appear with an unusual Life in it: But it will still shew as great a Proportion of Skill to come near *Underhil* in the acting it, which (not to undervalue those who soon came after him) I have not yet seen" (I, 155). Aston stated, however, that Underhill "did great In-

[13] *Roscius Anglicanus,* pp. 43–44.

[14] *Apology,* I, 197. If Cibber's statement is taken literally, *Love for Love* may have had the most successful première among Congreve's plays. It is notable that three commentaries characterize its reception as extraordinary.

[15] *An Essay on Acting* (London, 1744), p. 10.

justice to Sir *Sampson Legend* . . . unless it had been true, that the Knight had been bred a Hog-driver" (II, 308). Aston thought better of Sandford (Foresight), who, though "not usually deem'd an Actor of the first Rank," did very well in this type of character, for "his Figure, which was diminutive and mean, (being Round-shoulder'd, Meagre-fac'd, Spindle-shank'd, Splay-footed, with a sour Countenance, and long lean Arms) render'd him a proper Person to discharge . . . *Foresight*" (II, 306). Mrs. Bracegirdle was certainly well suited to Angelica, which Congreve created for her, as was Mrs. Barry for Mrs. Frail. In the cast also were Mrs. Ayliff (Prue), Mrs. Bowman (Mrs. Foresight), and Mrs. Leigh (Nurse).

After such a remarkable first season, *Love for Love* was certainly revived frequently, but it is as difficult to trace its stage history before 1702 as it is to follow that of Congreve's other plays. There are records of two additional performances before 1700: one by royal command at Whitehall (Feb. 6, 1697),[16] the other at the Inner Temple (Nov. 1, 1697).[17] The next known performance occurred at Lincoln's Inn Fields toward the end of June 1700, when it was offered at a benefit to raise funds "to'ards the Redemption of the English now in Slavery at Machanisso in Barbary." [18] Shortly thereafter, in the Easter Term of 1701, legal action was taken against the players for acting *Love for Love* and other plays in Lincoln's Inn Fields.[19] Although not all of these indictments for licentiousness brought convictions, the attacks may have made the managers wary of offering some Restoration comedies as frequently as they might wish. At any rate it was not until 1704 that *Love for Love* was again certainly played.

After three comedies Congreve turned to a tragic theme, his new play appearing almost two years after *Love for Love*. Apparently he spent a good deal of time in the creation of *The Mourning Bride,* which shared with Vanbrugh's *The Provoked Wife* the honors for the season of 1696–97. It was first given in February 1697 at Lincoln's Inn Fields, where it was acted on thirteen consecutive days. According to a con-

---

[16] "On Monday the King visited the Princess of Denmark and invited her to Whitehall on Saturday next, it being her Royal Highnesses Birth Day, and his Majesty has been pleased to give the Right Honourable the Lord Chamberlaine Orders to have the Play called Love for Love, written by Mr Congreve, acted there the better to Celebrate the Day." *Post Boy* (Feb. 2–4, 1697), quoted by Sybil Rosenfeld, *MLR*, XXX (1935), 449.

[17] Allardyce Nicoll, *A History of Restoration Drama* (Cambridge, 1928), p. 385; see also Rosenfeld, p. 449.

[18] *London Post*, June 28–July 1, 1700.

[19] Bedford, *The Evil and Danger of Stage-Plays*, p. 4. For a discussion of these attacks, see J. W. Krutch, *Comedy and Conscience after the Restoration* (New York, 1924), pp. 166–191.

temporary, the theater was "full to the last." [20] Although some contemporaries emphasized that it was the best received of Congreve's plays,
it did not surpass *The Old Batchelor* or *Love for Love* in the length of
its initial run. Once again there was a distinguished cast. Betterton,
aging but still master of the stage, spoke the prologue and played Osmyn.
Mrs. Bracegirdle had in Almeria another part written expressly for
her, but according to Aston, "Mrs. *Barry* outshin'd Mrs. *Bracegirdle* in
the Character of ZARA . . . altho' Mr. *Congreve* design'd Almeria for
that Favour.—And yet, this fine Creature was not handsome, her Mouth
op'ning most on the Right Side, which she strove to draw t'other Way,
and, at Times, composing her Face, as if sitting to have her Picture
drawn" (II, 302). Jack Verbruggen, a promising actor, played the King;
Sandford, who specialized in villains because of his "bodily Defects," [21]
was cast as Gonsalez, but Aston thought him weak in that role.[22] The
lesser parts were in the hands of Scudamore (Garcia), Bowman (Heli),
and Mrs. Bowman (Leonora). In spite of its initial success there are few
recorded performances during the next ten years. It was acted at
Lincoln's Inn Fields on February 27, 1700,[23] but waited several years
for a genuine revival.

The intervals between Congreve premières grew steadily longer. It
was three years after *The Mourning Bride* before he brought his fifth
play onto the stage, but he had not been idle. He had been embroiled
in argument and counter-argument with Jeremy Collier, who apparently
hoped either to reform drastically or destroy the stage and who singled
out Congreve as a principal target for his moral indignation. In the
midst of this controversy Congreve retained his active interest in the
affairs of Lincoln's Inn Fields, where conditions were not wholly satisfactory. Competition between the two playhouses had become severe,
and Betterton's company was no longer so strong as it had been. Perhaps a new play by Congreve would bring it new vitality. At length,
probably in the first week of March 1700, *The Way of the World* was
presented. Undoubtedly it was a disappointment to the principals of
the theater and to some of the spectators. John Dryden, writing to Mrs.
Steward on March 12, stated that it "had but moderate success," [24] and
Lady Marow on the same day that it "doth not answer expectation." [25]

[20] John Coke to Thomas Coke, Cowper MSS., Historical MSS Commission, 12th
Report, Appendix, Part II (London, 1888), p. 368.

[21] Cibber, *Apology*, I, 131.

[22] *Brief Supplement*, II, 306. The *Tatler*, No. 134, referred to his excellent performance in tormented characters and his skill in moving an audience.

[23] R. W. Lowe, *Thomas Betterton* (London, 1891), p. 14.

[24] *Letters*, p. 134.

[25] Dartmouth MSS., Vol. III. Historical MSS Commission, 15th Report, Appendix,
Part I (London, 1896), p. 145.

Each implied that it warranted a better reception, Dryden declaring that it "deserves much better" and Lady Marow that, in spite of deficiencies in plot, it had "many witty things to ridicule the Chocolate House, and the fantastical part of the world." To Downes the comedy "curiously *Acted . . .* had not the Success the Company Expected," apparently because it was "too Keen a Satyr" (p. 45). Discussing the attitude of the town, John Dennis in 1717 stated that Congreve had written "at last a Play, which besides that it was equal to most of the former in those pleasant Humours which the Laughers so much require, had some certain Scenes in it, which were writ with so much Grace and Delicacy, that they alone were worth an entire Comedy." Yet the "Play was hiss'd by Barbarous Fools in the Acting; and an impertinent Trifle was brought on after it, which was acted with vast Applause." After Congreve quit the stage, "those nice great Persons, whose squeamish Palates rejected Quails and Partridges, have pin'd ever since in such a Dearth, that they greedily feed upon Bull-Beef." [26]

Like Congreve's previous comedies, this one had a good cast. Mrs. Bracegirdle dominated it as Millamant. Downes reported that "Madam *Bracegirdle* performing her Part so exactly and just, gain'd the Applause of Court and City" (p. 45), and Cibber, naming Millamant as one of two parts "in which she acquitted herself with uncommon Applause," praised her in a sentence which was many times repeated in later theatrical biographies: "As when she acted *Millamant,* all the Faults, Follies, and Affectations of that agreeable Tyrant were venially melted down into so many Charms and Attractions of a conscious Beauty" (1, 173). Mrs. Marwood was acted by Mrs. Barry; Lady Wishfort by Mrs. Leigh, who was "extremely entertaining, and painted in a lively manner the blind Side of Nature." They were accompanied by Mrs. Bowman (Mrs. Fainall), Mrs. Willis (Foible), and Mrs. Prince (Mincing). Nearing retirement but still titular head of the players, Betterton acted Fainall. Jack Verbruggen was Mirabell. Underhill, who played "Characters that may be called Still-life, I mean the Stiff, the Heavy, and the Stupid," [27] was not miscast as Sir Wilful. Bowen (Witwoud), Bowman (Petulant), and Bright (Waitwell) rounded out the cast. How long a run the comedy had is not known, but it marked Congreve's retirement as an active playwright, although he later had a hand in some lesser pieces. It might almost be said that the comedy temporarily retired with him, for it was infrequently acted in the next fifteen years, only *The Double Dealer* being equally neglected. *The Way of the World*

[26] "Remarks upon Mr. Pope's Translation of Homer," *Works,* ed. Hooker, II, 121-122.
[27] *Apology,* I, 163, 154.

was given on December 17, 1705, and on May 17, 1715, according to the extant records. It waited until 1718 for a genuine revival.

After 1700 Congreve's five plays became a part of the large collection of dramas which constituted the theatrical repertory, a body of plays written in Shakespeare's age and succeeding decades. For many years a typical season consisted of those old plays in considerable demand (*Hamlet*, for example), those warranting occasional revival (*The Country Wife*), and whatever new plays, moderately or greatly successful, contemporary dramatists produced. The season usually opened with a change of bill nightly, the more reliable plays being then offered—quite often *Love for Love* or *The Old Batchelor* was one of the first eight or ten offerings—and in the spring a round of benefits usually brought the familiar and popular plays forward again, especially those which offered parts in which the actors receiving the benefit could draw the largest crowds. Into this mixture of the familiar and the novel, the established and the experimental, Congreve's plays eventually fitted themselves. During the early years of the century, however, they were slow in finding a large share in the seasonal offerings, for repercussions of the Collier controversy possibly restricted the offerings and the theaters were not wholly prosperous. For example, William Morley wrote on August 2, 1701, "and I believe there is no poppet shew in a country town but takes more money than both the play houses. Yet you wonder that immorality and profaneness should reign as much as it does." [28] A year later (March 11, 1702) Sir John Perceval wrote that no one "will suffer by the King's death but the poor players, who are ready to starve; neither are they to act till the coronation. . . . I accidentally met yesterday the boxkeeper, who swore to me he had not drunk all day, for that now they are all out of pay, none will trust them so much as for a pot of ale." [29] *Love for Love* and *The Old Batchelor* were the only Congreve plays certainly acted in the two years following the première of *The Way of the World,* and during 1702–03 *The Old Batchelor* alone appeared. [30] When it was given on November 19, 1702, the advertisements omitted the cast in order to emphasize the entertainments, especially singing by Richard Leveridge, a popular entertainer, who did the

[28] Cowper MSS, Historical MSS Commission, 12th Report, Appendix, Part II (London, 1888), II, 434.

[29] Egmont MSS, Historical MSS Commission (London, 1909), II, 208. Sir John added, "One cannot pass by the Play-house now it is dark but you are sure to be stripped."

[30] The performances hereafter listed in this chapter are taken from the *Daily Courant* and the *Spectator,* the principal papers in which the theaters then advertised. These performances have been checked against those in the Latreille Calendar (British Museum) and Winston Calendar (Folger Shakespeare Library).

"mad Song in *Don Quixote,* beginning, Let the dreadful Engines, &c." [31]

In 1703-04 Congreve's plays appeared more frequently but still formed only a small portion of the repertory. *The Old Batchelor* was given twice, *The Double Dealer* once, and *Love for Love* twice. Even so, they were not nearly so popular as *The Squire of Alsatia,* which, unacted for twelve years, was played 13 times, or *The Emperor of the Moon* (7 performances), or such new pieces as *Abra Mule* (probably 15 times) and *Liberty Asserted* (11). Among Congreve's plays *The Old Batchelor* was the first to appear, at Drury Lane on October 13, 1703, and again on November 18, with Captain Griffin as Heartwell. On November 29 *The Double Dealer* was advertised for Lincoln's Inn Fields as "Never Acted there but Twice," but nothing concerning the cast is known. On April 26, 1704, *Love for Love* was acted there, with Dogget in his original role of Ben. It was repeated on June 1 as a benefit for Mrs. Bowman, who presumably acted her original part of Mrs. Foresight. There was a new prologue, and Bowman sang "The Misses Lamentation for want of their Vizard Masks in the Play-house." There was a slight increase in Congreve performances in 1704-05, with *The Old Batchelor* acted 3 times early in the season, *Love for Love* 3 times near the end. On October 26 Richard Estcourt, newly arrived from Dublin, undertook Bluff; Downes stated that he could be depended on "in Comedy always to Laetificate his Audience, especially Quality." On January 15 Dogget, "very Aspectabund, wearing a Farce in his Face," [32] had his original role of Fondlewife. In the spring (April 9, 1705) the company lately in Lincoln's Inn Fields moved into a new playhouse, the Queen's Theater in the Haymarket, in which Congreve was financially interested.[33] Strangely, *The Old Batchelor* was not acted there at all during the early months of its operation, and *Love for Love* not until June. When it was acted on June 25, 1705, it was advertised as "Acted all by Women." During this period a play given only by the actresses was a rare phenomenon, but no comment survives which explains why this performance and two others on June 27 and 29 were given in this fashion. Neither is there any evidence as to who played the parts.

[31] *Love for Love* was given at Oxford on July 5, 1703, by the Theater Royal players, with a Prologue to the University spoken by Betterton. See R. C. Rhodes, *TLS,* Feb. 21, 1929, p. 140.

[32] *Roscius Anglicanus,* pp. 51-52.

[33] Arthur Bedford once thought that this theater was "to be built only to *reform* the *Stage,*" but he was soon disillusioned, for *Love for Love,* not to mention other plays of which he disapproved, was among its offerings (*The Evil and Danger of Stage-Plays,* p. 20).

During the next two years there was no major change in the status of Congreve's plays. In 1705–06 emphasis was so strongly upon musical rather than dramatic pieces that plays seemed at a disadvantage. Drury Lane again offered Italian operas—principally *Arsinoe* and *Camilla*—and the Queen's produced English operatic pieces: *The British Enchanters, The Wonders in the Sun,* and *The Island Princess.* Drury Lane found time for a very successful new comedy, *The Recruiting Officer,* and had a fair success in Rowe's *Ulysses;* the Queen's successfully produced Vanbrugh's *The Confederacy.* Somewhat overshadowed were 2 performances of *The Old Batchelor* at Drury Lane, with 2 performances of portions of the comedy; at the Queen's, 2 of *Love for Love.* For its only recorded performance between 1700 and 1715 *The Way of the World* appeared at the Queen's on December 17, 1705. Although the cast was not advertised, very probably Betterton, Bowen, Verbruggen, Bowman, Mrs. Bracegirdle, Mrs. Barry, Mrs. Bowman, and Mrs. Willis, all members of the original production and now of the Queen's, acted their original parts. There is no evidence, other than the failure of the comedy to appear again for ten years, as to its reception. In 1706–07 it was *The Mourning Bride* which reappeared for a single performance, its only known presentation since 1700 and the only Congreve play acted in London that season. Given on May 28, 1707, it was a benefit for Cave Underhill, with Mrs. Bracegirdle probably acting Almeria for the last time. It is strange, particularly since Congreve was associated with one theater, that all of his comedies should be absent from the stage in that season, but London was so enthusiastic about *The Recruiting Officer* as to call for 21 performances of it and Farquhar completed his domination of the season by bringing on *The Beaux Stratagem* for 12 performances. These two comedies, accounting for a seventh of the season's offerings, left less time than usual for old plays.

The next three years were more eventful both for the theaters generally and for Congreve's plays. During the early months of 1707–08 the two companies competed vigorously, with occasional Italian operas at Drury Lane. In mid-season, however, the companies united, the first union in more than a decade. On January 10, 1708, the actors took possession of Drury Lane; the singers, of the Queen's. As a result, the full strength of the town was available for casting plays. *Love for Love,* with 5 performances, had its best season in some time and was one of the six or seven most popular old plays. Two members of the original cast of 1695 still played in it: Bowen as Jeremy, a role he kept until 1717, and Mrs. Barry as Mrs. Frail. As the older actors retired, younger ones stepped into their parts and held them for many years. The "unrivalled

fine Gentleman of the Stage for more than twenty Years," [34] Robert
Wilks, who had gained fame in Farquhar's comedies, assumed the role
of Valentine. He was to keep it until 1731. Downes thought him "Proper
and Comely in Person, of Graceful Port, Mein and Air; void of Affectation; his Elevations and Cadencies just, Congruent to Elocution: Especially in Gentile Comedy. . . . The Emission of his Words free, easy
and natural; Attracting attentive silence in his Audience, (I mean the
Judicious) except where there are Unnatural Rants." [35] Of still greater
value to comedy generally and Congreve's plays in particular was Mrs.
Oldfield, who owed a good deal to Farquhar's assistance and who now
succeeded Mrs. Bracegirdle as Angelica. Cibber thought that "Mrs.
Oldfield and Mr. *Wilks,* by their frequently playing against one another
in our best Comedies, very happily supported that Humour and Vivacity which is so peculiar to our *English* Stage" (1, 314). Whenever Mrs.
Oldfield took on a part in another Congreve comedy, the play gained
steadily in popularity. Once she began to play Angelica, *Love for Love*
was to be seen much more frequently. In 1709-10 she undertook Laetitia
and *The Old Batchelor* rose steadily in popularity. When *The Way of
the World* was revived in 1717-18, her Millamant established a new
standard for comic excellence.

In addition, there was Benjamin Johnson, who, with interruptions,
acted Foresight until 1742. According to Victor, the judgment of "all
the Criticks" was that Johnson possessed "the Sterling *Vis Comica,*"
and the *Comedian* (October 1732) stated: "I believe if I say of *Johnson*
that a truer Comedian never trod the Stage, I shall have the Assent of
all who have seen him on it." Barton Booth, a man of many talents,
played Valentine occasionally and Scandal fairly regularly. Henry
("Jubilee Dicky") Norris, who derived much of his "Merit from the
Oddity of his little, formal Figure, and his singular, squeaking Tone of
Voice," [36] acted Trapland until 1730. Richard Estcourt, once an ap-
prenticed apothecary in Dublin, played Sir Sampson; Colley Cibber
succeeded Dogget as Ben; and George Pack, formerly a singer, appeared
as Tattle. Among the actresses were Jane Rogers (Mrs. Foresight), Mrs.
Bicknell (Prue), who excelled as Margery Pinchwife in Wycherley's
The Country Wife, and Mrs. Willis (Nurse). One of the five performances was a benefit for Cibber, who did not act on that occasion, and
Dogget played Ben then and on an occasional evening. With this cast
remaining relatively unchanged for several years, *Love for Love* entered
upon several decades of growing popularity.

[34] Victor, *History of the Theaters,* II, 53.
[35] *Roscius Anglicanus,* p. 51.
[36] *History of the Theaters,* II, 63-64.

In the same season *The Old Batchelor,* after a year's absence, reappeared in Drury Lane on March 15, 1708. Betterton (Heartwell), Dogget (Fondlewife), and Mrs. Barry (Laetitia) continued their original roles. Wilks, "the finished and polite libertine," [37] was Bellmour, with Estcourt continuing as Bluff. From 1708 to 1721 Booth usually acted Vainlove, and until 1732 John Mills played Sharper. William Bullock and Henry Fairbank attempted Sir Joseph and Setter for a brief period. Mary Bicknell was Sylvia; Araminta, Belinda, and Lucy were acted by Mrs. Bradshaw, Mrs. Rogers, and Mrs. Saunders, the latter one of the best of chambermaids. With this competent cast, *The Old Batchelor* vied with *Love for Love* for first rank among Congreve's comedies.

The Mourning Bride made only one appearance during the season, at Drury Lane on March 25, 1708. Mrs. Barry, "solemn and august," [38] retained her original role of Zara. Booth—"of Mellifluent Pronuntiation, having proper Gesticulations, which are Graceful Attendants of true Elocution; of his time a most Compleat Tragedian" [39]—played Osmyn, as he did for some years thereafter. George Powell, who had joined Drury Lane in November, was the King. The cast was completed by Theophilus Keen as Gonsalez, Mrs. Bradshaw as Almeria, and Mrs. Porter as Leonora. In spite of this good cast, the tragedy was once cited by a Drury Lane player to a stroller at Nottingham as one of the good plays which "will hardly fetch us a tolerable audience, unless we stuff the bills with long entertainments of dances, songs, scaramouched entries, and what not." [40] A glance at the theatrical advertisements for these years will show how greatly the companies relied upon miscellaneous entertainments to fortify the bills and attract a crowd.

Although the season of 1708–09 did not differ markedly from the preceding one, Richard Steele on October 7, 1708, dismally concluded that the "taste for Plays is expired. We are all for Operas, performed by eunuchs every way impotent to please." [41] Operas, it is true, were very popular, but plays were by no means ignored.[42] Drury Lane, retaining its monopoly of legitimate drama, offered *The Old Batchelor* twice and *Love for Love* three times. Cibber resumed Fondlewife, in which, according to his great admirer, Tom Davies, he "was much, and justly, admired and applauded." Ben Johnson undertook Bluff, for forty years one of his best parts; according to Davies, it was "as complete a piece of

37 Davies, *Dramatic Miscellanies,* III, 219.

38 Aston, *Brief Supplement,* II, 303.

39 Downes, *Roscius Anglicanus,* p. 52.

40 Percy Fitzgerald, *A New History of the English Stage* (London, 1882), I, 240.

41 *The Correspondence of Richard Steele,* ed. Rae Blanchard (Oxford, 1941), p. 25.

42 In 1707–08 and 1708–09 there were several moderately successful plays, of which two—Cibber's *Lady's Last Stake* and Mrs. Centlivre's *The Busy Body*—became popular additions to the permanent repertory.

acting as I ever saw; his person was against him; for he was old and thin when I first saw him, which is now above fifty two years since, and I remember I thought him ill chosen for a bully; but his exquisite performance soon cured me, and the whole audience, of any diffidence of his abilities." [43] On April 28, 1709, when Mrs. Cross played Belinda, the *Tatler* (No. 9) spoke of it as a "Comedy of deserved Reputation. In the Character which gives Name to the Play, there is excellently represented the Reluctance of a battered Debauchee to come into the Trammels of Order and Decency: He neither languishes nor burns, but frets for Love." The third performance of *Love for Love* (April 7, 1709) was a gala benefit for Thomas Betterton, who returned to play Valentine, his original part, for that night only. Honoring him were three others from the original cast: Dogget (Ben); Mrs. Barry (Mrs. Frail), who spoke the epilogue, which was separately printed in the same year; and Mrs. Bracegirdle (Angelica), who made her farewell appearance. Not only had the four players been intimately associated for many years, but all except Dogget had been in the original casts of all of Congreve's plays, and Dogget's success in *The Old Batchelor* had been of great importance to his career. The *Tatler* for April 12, 1709, gave a long account of the occasion. [44]

At the conclusion of this season the union of the companies, which had begun on January 10, 1708, was terminated by the Lord Chamberlain's silencing of Drury Lane on June 4, 1709. When the new season began, London again had two playhouses. Wilks, Cibber, and Dogget, seceding from Drury Lane, joined with Owen Swiney to establish a company at the Queen's. Contrary to their expectations, a group of actors continued to offer plays at Drury Lane, which had the only marked success of the season—Shadwell's *Fair Quaker of Deal,* given 13 times there and 3 times in Penkethman's summer theater in Greenwich. The Queen's alone offered *The Old Batchelor,* whose cast included most of the usual actors, Betterton and Dogget again playing Heartwell and Fondlewife. Opening a summer of benefits for themselves, the managers on July 6 again offered it with Mrs. Oldfield as Laetitia. It is uncertain whether this was her first appearance in that part, but thereafter it was one of her principal roles. The occasion was a benefit for Dogget, who induced the *Tatler* (No. 193) to give him a puff. [45]

---

[43] *Dramatic Miscellanies,* III, 219.

[44] The Tatler's remarks were reprinted in *The History of the English Stage* (London, 1741), p. 119. Thomas Whincop, *A Compleat List of all the English Dramatic Poets* (London, 1747), stated that Betterton, past seventy and lame with the gout, "seemed but to burlesque the Part of youthful *Valentine*" (p. 175).

[45] Zacharias Conrad von Uffenbach, a zealous traveler and diarist, saw this performance. The early entries in his journal give detailed comments upon plays he saw, but by this performance he was less inclined to write at length. He said only that

The progress of Congreve's plays appeared most clearly, however, in the increased vogue of *Love for Love*. With 9 performances in 1709–10, it was equalled only by *Hamlet* and *The Emperor of the Moon* and exceeded only by *The Busy Body*, with 10 performances. Five of the 9 presentations were at the Queen's, in whose cast were nearly all the principals of the Drury Lane casts of the previous year: Estcourt, Wilks, Johnson, Bowen, and Dogget, for whose benefit on January 16, 1710, *Tatler* No. 120 lent its hearty support. Husband acted Scandal, a part he had played before; Cibber played Tattle in place of George Pack, who remained at Drury Lane. Mrs. Oldfield (Angelica) dominated the cast, and Mrs. Porter, "to whom Nature had been niggard in Voice and Face" yet "mov'd Astonishment," [46] acted Mrs. Frail, as she had done at least once before. For the 4 Drury Lane performances, a few members of the old cast were present: Booth (Valentine), Pack (Tattle), and Norris (Foresight). Replacing the seceding actors were some newcomers to London: John Leigh (Sir Sampson), John Bickerstaff (Ben), Theophilus Keen (Scandal), and Josias Miller (Jeremy), nearly all of whom were to have successful careers. On December 3 Hester Santlow (later Mrs. Barton Booth) made her debut as an actress in Prue, and on June 6 the comedy was offered again for her benefit.

The division of the companies extended briefly into 1710–11, but because competition had been a financial strain upon both houses, they reunited in the autumn under an agreement that Drury Lane would have exclusive right to plays, the Queen's to operas. Although similar compacts had been arranged before and sometimes quickly suspended, this one endured for four years. During its monopoly of plays Drury Lane prospered [47] and *The Old Batchelor* and *Love for Love* continued to rise in popularity. In 1710–11, with no really successful new play, *Love for Love*, with 6 performances, was given more frequently than any other old play. *The Old Batchelor* was offered twice. For it the principal addition was Theophilus Keen, "an excellent Scholar, and a very good Actor" who had been trained under Joseph Ashbury in Dublin; [48] he succeeded Betterton, who died on April 28, 1710, at the age of seventy-five. In the following season both comedies were acted almost as frequently, but they were eclipsed by some new and revived plays. *The Distrest Mother* and *The Wife's Relief* both had successful pre-

---

The Old Batchelor was a "most diverting Comedy." *London in 1710*, ed. W. H. Quarrell and Margaret von Uffenbach (London, 1934), p. 123.

[46] W. R. Chetwood, *A General History of the Stage* (London, 1749), p. 29.

[47] R. H. Barker has estimated that in 1712–13 the managers of Drury Lane made £4,000; in 1713–14, £3,600; in the first three months of 1714–15, £1,700. See *Mr. Cibber of Drury Lane* (New York, 1939), p. 99.

[48] Chetwood, *General History*, p. 177.

mières, with 8 and 11 performances respectively; *The Tempest,* with
new scenes and machines, was revived for 12 performances; and *Philas-
ter* was brought on 7 times. *Love for Love,* with 5 performances, was less
in the limelight.[49] After Estcourt left the stage in 1711—he died in 1712
—Leigh acted Sir Sampson; and when Mrs. Oldfield was occasionally
absent, Mrs. Bradshaw played Angelica. *The Mourning Bride* reappeared for 2 performances.

In 1712–13, performances of the older plays were again restricted by
new plays, with 20 performances of *Cato* and 8 of *The Heroick Daughter. Love for Love* appeared 5 times; *The Old Batchelor,* 3; *The Mourning Bride,* once. On May 25, 1713, at a benefit for Henry Norris, Miss
Younger assumed Prue, a part she was to hold for many years. In the
last season of Drury Lane's monopoly there was no appreciable change
in the status of Congreve's plays. *The Old Batchelor* and *Love for Love*
had 3 performances apiece; *The Mourning Bride,* its customary one.
None of Congreve's plays was as popular as *Cato,* in its second season,
or *She Would and She Would Not,* newly revived; and *The Mourning
Bride* had a new rival in Nicholas Rowe's *Jane Shore,* which came on
for 19 performances.

In the first fourteen years of the century, the principal fact concerning the popularity of Congreve's plays was that two—*Love for Love*
and *The Old Batchelor*—established themselves securely in the repertory. Beginning in 1707–08 *The Old Batchelor* was acted in London
during every season through 1750–51; from the same season *Love for
Love* held the stage regularly through 1766–67. Hardly less important
was the fact that during this period both comedies acquired the excellent casts which were to remain relatively unchanged until the 1730's.
The Mourning Bride, however, did not become a stock play for several
years, and the other two comedies were so infrequently performed as
hardly to be noticeable to the average playgoer.

The relative standing of Congreve's comedies may be seen by a comparison with the frequency of performance of other comedies. Between
1700 and 1714 *The Old Batchelor* was acted 26 times; *Love for Love,*
43. The latter compared well with *The Committee* and *The Spanish
Fryar,* with around 40 performances each. *The Amorous Widow, The
Emperor of the Moon,* and *The Lancashire Witches,* with approximately 30 performances, barely exceeded *The Old Batchelor,* which
was about equally popular with *Rule a Wife and Have a Wife, The
Constant Couple, The Man of Mode,* and *She Would if She Could.*

---

[49] It was also acted by the Duke of Norfolk's Servants at Norwich during this
season. See Sybil Rosenfeld, *Strolling Players and Drama in the Provinces, 1660–
1765* (Cambridge, 1939), p. 50.

All of these were surpassed by *The Recruiting Officer*, with some 66 performances since 1706; and other new plays had a better frequency of performance: *The Careless Husband*, with better than 40 performances since 1704; *Love Makes a Man*, at least 42 since 1700; and *The Tender Husband*, about 30 since 1705.

Chapter III

DRURY LANE AND LINCOLN'S INN FIELDS
COMPETE, 1714–1729

On December 18, 1714, Drury Lane's monopoly ended once and for all. Ever since the opening of the playhouses in 1660 there had been revolutions and counter-revolutions, unions of the companies and revolts of the players. In 1714 a London theatergoer might well have assumed that the opening of Lincoln's Inn Fields was simply another venture at competition, perhaps as short-lived as the opening of the Queen's in 1705. No doubt, sooner or later the companies would again discover that in union lay prosperity. Yet never again did London have only one legitimate theater. Thereafter, at least two companies, occasionally three, sometimes even four, competed, until the Licensing Act of 1737 restored the two-theater system which, at least in theory, endured into the nineteenth century.

It was John Rich who opened the new house in 1714, a playhouse which his father, Christopher Rich, had constructed in place of the old one in Portugal Street. Although John Rich often had an inferior set of actors, his enterprise and ingenuity for a long time—he directed his theater until his death in 1761—had a great influence upon the dramatic world. Certainly his new venture "not only terrified the managers at *Drury-Lane*, but was in fact, for a great Time, a Draw-back to their Profits." [1] Under the impact of competition the theaters varied their offerings and experimented with novelty, although Rich was usually more ingenious in experimentation than the actor-managers at Drury Lane. They developed ballad opera; they turned to musical masques, pantomimes, and a great variety of song and dance when the town seemed surfeited with the routine repetition of plays; and they dug out of their libraries neglected plays with which to enlarge their repertories. The roles of the two theaters were not, of course, the same. At first Drury Lane had the advantages accruing to an established house, with excellent actors at its command, yet it had to adjust itself to the loss of some of its younger performers and to declining income. Unable to match Drury Lane's finer acting, Lincoln's Inn Fields more often turned to novelty and spectacle. Rich was greatly interested in scenic and pantomimic effect—his enemies charged that he preferred spectacle to drama—and he excelled in theatricality of that type.

[1] *Apology for the Life of Mr. T. C., Comedian* (London, 1740), p. 68.

Both theaters also showed a considerable interest in older plays. For Drury Lane the neglected or infrequently acted dramas were a means of broadening its repertory and displaying the skill and variety of its actors. For Lincoln's Inn Fields the inactive plays were the source of a working repertory which would not involve a duplication of Drury Lane's offerings. As a result, within five years after the opening of the new theater there were several very successful revivals of old plays, some long neglected, others only a short while dormant. Congreve's less familiar comedies shared in this revival. *The Double Dealer* and *The Way of the World,* soon newly staged, became standard parts of the repertory; in time *The Mourning Bride* secured for itself a firmer place among the tragedies. The resurgence of the old also brought renewed appreciation of plays as varied as *The Country Wife, The Emperor of the Moon, The Fair Penitent, Greenwich Park, Henry VIII, The Island Princess, The Prophetess, The Provoked Wife,* and *Tamerlane.*

From the very first Rich left little doubt that he also intended to capitalize upon novelty. Because his theater had a larger stage than that in Drury Lane, he offered singing and dancing specialties for entr'acte entertainment and for afterpieces, and eventually spectacles of pantomimic action. On the opening night, when he offered *The Recruiting Officer,* a very popular comedy which could draw a good audience upon its merits alone, he advertised also a miscellany of song and dance. There was a large audience, as indicated by receipts of £143,[2] very nearly the highest for the season. Rich's seventh play was *The Old Batchelor,* acted on January 4, 1715, and from that evening through 1745–46 the comedy appeared in at least two theaters during every season except 1719–20 and 1720–21. For its first performance the comedy brought receipts of £50 19s 6d, just about average for the week in which it appeared; for its second, on February 4, £38 18s 6d, distinctly below the average for the current week.

A week after the first offering of *The Old Batchelor, Love for Love* was acted at Rich's theater, where it appeared twice later in the season. According to the receipts, it did not bring particularly large crowds. For the first night, January 12, the sum of £39 14s was below the nightly average of £50 for the first three weeks of January. Repeated

---

[2] The receipts for Lincoln's Inn Fields and its successor, Covent Garden, have been preserved for many seasons in the Latreille Calendar (B.M.) and Winston Calendar (Folger) and in some other manuscript compilations. It should be noted that these collections do not always give the same receipts for the same day. Some of the data have been published by F. T. Wood, "The Account Books of Lincoln's Inn Fields Theater, 1724–1727," *Notes and Queries,* CLXIV (1933), 220–224, 256–260, 272–274, 294–298. Unfortunately the receipts for Drury Lane in the early years have not survived.

on February 2 it brought £46 13s; on May 10, at a benefit for Mrs. Hunt, who for novelty attempted Ben, £65 7s 6d, rather small for a benefit. Quite possibly it, as well as *The Old Batchelor,* lacked the skilled players which would give Congreve's comedies their distinction. Rich faced the same problem four months later when he produced *The Way of the World,* which did rather poorly at the box office. Acted on May 17 as a benefit for Mrs. Spiller, it was augmented by dances and a prologue by Spiller riding on an ass, a novelty which Will Penkethman had popularized, yet the receipts were only £58 4s 6d. There seems little doubt, however, that Rich tried to offer a good program of plays. He produced three of Congreve's, one of which had rarely been given before; but the fact that the three achieved only 8 performances as contrasted with 14 for *The Island Princess* alone, may well have influenced Rich's thinking concerning the role of play versus spectacle in achieving theatrical prosperity.

Rich had, of course, to organize a company of actors and he was for some time handicapped by the fact that Drury Lane could usually offer a better cast for a play. His company, however, was not recruited from amateurs. He engaged some of the younger members from Drury Lane, some experienced strollers, and several performers from Ireland.[3] In the casts of *The Old Batchelor* and *Love for Love* there were, in fact, some players who had previously appeared in them. Theophilus Keen, to whom Rich gave a share in the management, acted Heartwell, and the elder Bullock played Sir Joseph and Sir Sampson, parts which they had recently performed in Drury Lane. From the same theater came Mrs. Kent (Laetitia), Bullock (Fondlewife and Trapland), Spiller (Jeremy), Pack (Tattle), Francis Leigh (Valentine), and Mrs. Knight (Mrs. Frail). From Ireland came John Leigh (Bellmour) and John Hall (Bluff), the latter a corpulent man with a thickness of speech which gave a peculiar quality to his voice. Benjamin Husband (Vainlove) had played in both Dublin and Drury Lane; Miss Schoolding (Sylvia and Prue) was relatively inexperienced.

During the first season of rivalry *Love for Love,* with 7 performances in Drury Lane and Lincoln's Inn Fields, and *The Old Batchelor,* with 8 appearances, ranked rather high. Only one of the new dramas, *Lady Jane Grey,* surpassed them. Among the older pieces *The Island Princess,*

---

[3] According to one journal, the exodus from Dublin was of considerable proportions: "About 12 Gentlemen-Actors, who were reckoned the best Comedians at Dublin, are arrived here from thence, and have settled themselves at the New Play-House in Lincolns-Inn-Fields" (*Weekly Journal,* May 5, 1715). Thomas Davies, *Memoirs of the Life of David Garrick, Esq.* (London, 1780), I, 91, states that Rich had many difficulties: "he was very young and inexperienced, and the governing players, Bullock, Keen, and others, considered him as one very unfit to give laws to them, and manage the business of a theater."

a dramatic opera with 22 performances, dominated the season; and *The Emperor of the Moon* (12), *The Tempest* (11), and *The Recruiting Officer* (10) did better than either of Congreve's plays. For four years both theaters offered both comedies [4] with few changes in the cast, Drury Lane presenting *The Old Batchelor* 14 times to Lincoln's Inn Fields' 10, and *Love for Love* 16 to 11. In spite of the weakness of his casts, Rich was not deterred from offering plays competitively and turned to other Restoration comedies as well. In 1715–16, for example, he restored Wycherley's *The Plain Dealer,* unacted for ten years, and gave it 7 times. Yet the receipts show that attendance, especially when the bills listed plays only, was often distressingly small. On November 7, 1715, for example, *The Old Batchelor* brought in only £12 10s, too small to meet expenses; even a benefit (June 5, 1716), came to only £63 17s 6d.[5] Sometimes *Love for Love* fared almost as badly.

Indeed, there was at least one time when rumor hinted that Rich might close his theater. Writing on June 11, 1717, at the close of the third season at Lincoln's Inn Fields, Richard Steele stated that there might again be only one playhouse, with Rich, "who is almost broke," [6] given a salary, presumably by Drury Lane, so long as only one theater was open. However serious Rich's plight may have been, Lincoln's Inn Fields did not close. Instead, the management fell into the hands of Christopher Bullock and Theophilus Keen, and after Keen's death to Pack, a situation which lasted for several years. During 1717–18 the new managers were able to engage Mrs. Thurmond, the best actress yet obtained there, to play Laetitia and other principal parts. Lincoln's Inn Fields was also fortunate in that plans for importing a troupe of French comedians to act in the King's Theater did not mature; by the following season, 1718–19, when the foreign actors arrived in London, the theater was more secure financially. The new company was not able, however, to continue offering Congreve's plays with distinction. In 1718–19 it gave *The Old Batchelor* only once, and in the next two seasons not at all. *Love for Love* was dropped after 1719–20, probably because of casting difficulties. The magnitude of the problem may be seen in the fact that in 1719–20 over half the parts in *Love for Love* at Lincoln's Inn Fields were assigned to players new to their roles and that the actresses particularly were of indifferent ability. The

---

[4] *The Mourning Bride* was acted only once from 1714–15 through 1717–18—at Drury Lane on Dec. 12, 1716—but nothing is known of the cast. *The Way of the World,* after a single performance in 1714–15, went unacted until 1717–18.

[5] Congreve's plays were not, of course, the only ones occasionally to have low receipts. On Jan. 12, 1716, *The Confederacy* secured only £7 4s. At the other extreme, *The Prophetess* during its first run brought in about £100 nightly.

[6] *Correspondence of Steele,* ed. Blanchard, p. 353.

company was losing valued members. Theophilus Keen, one of the managers, died. Benjamin Husband returned to Ireland, and Mrs. Thurmond, after one season at Lincoln's Inn Fields, joined the company in Drury Lane.

In the meantime, Congreve's plays, with occasional changes in the casts, continued to do well in Drury Lane. During 1716–17 John Bickerstaff attempted Ben. William Bowen, "fiery to a Fault, and passionate to his Prejudice," [7] performed Sir Joseph and Jeremy. When the temperamental Bowen, creator of three of Congreve's comic parts, was killed in a theatrical quarrel, Josias Miller replaced him.[8] With *The Old Batchelor* as the attraction, the customary benefit for the family of a deceased player was tendered Mrs. Bowen and her children in Drury Lane on May 3, 1718. On March 25, 1717, another famous comedian retired from Congreve's plays when Dogget, "so famous for playing the Fool," [9] for the last time acted Ben, a part he had held for twenty years. He was succeeded by Miller. When Mrs. Oldfield was absent, Mrs. Thurmond played Angelica and Laetitia, roles to which she succeeded after Mrs. Oldfield's death. And on August 9, 1718, *Love for Love* was acted at Richmond, apparently for the first time there.

By 1718 the casual playgoer might well have forgotten that Congreve had written any dramas other than *The Old Batchelor* and *Love for Love*. *The Double Dealer* had been staged only once and *The Way of the World* but twice since 1700 (so far as we know now); even *The Mourning Bride* could not have been greatly familiar. Within two years, however, all three experienced successful revivals. First to appear was *The Way of the World*, which Drury Lane, on January 8, 1718, introduced upon its stage for the first time and which it offered 8 times, a very good showing for a restored play in a season of successful revivals. It shared honors with *Cymbeline* (8 performances), *The Committee* (7), and *The Fair Example* (7). For some years thereafter, *The Way of the World* held a respectable, though never dominant, position in Drury Lane. It had a good cast, with the excellence of Wilks and Mrs. Oldfield setting the standard. Davies spoke of the "accomplished Mirabel of Wilks," and as Millamant, Mrs. Oldfield's "fine figure, attractive manner, harmonious voice, and elegance in dress, in which she excelled all her predecessors and successors except Mrs.

---

[7] Chetwood, *General History of the Stage*, p. 101.

[8] Fitzgerald, *New History of the Stage*, I, 306, refers to a print designed and executed by William Hogarth as a ticket for Joe Miller's benefit, a performance of *The Old Batchelor* on April 25, 1717.

[9] *Weekly Journal, or Saturday's Post*, Sept. 9, 1721. Cibber (*Apology*, II, 159) stated that in this part and Fondlewife "no Author and Actor could be more obliged to their mutual masterly Performances."

Abington, left her without a rival." [10] Cibber's characterization of Witwoud was judged by Davies to be more "finished" than that later achieved by Thomas Chapman. They were ably supported by Barton Booth (Fainall), John Bowman (Petulant), William Penkethman (Sir Wilful), and John Leigh (Waitwell). Among the actresses the principal figures were Mrs. Porter (Mrs. Marwood) and the comely Mrs. Horton (Mrs. Fainall), who was beginning her rise to stardom. Although this cast went essentially unchanged for three seasons, the number of performances decreased. In that respect the comedy merely followed the usual pattern of revived plays: a good first season followed by less frequent appearances. In 1718–19 it was given 3 times, the performance on March 3, 1719, being for Mrs. Oldfield's benefit; in 1719–20, but once; in 1720–21, twice; and in 1721–22, once, with Mrs. Oldfield again testifying to her high regard for Millamant as a role by choosing the comedy for her benefit. For the rest of the decade the comedy never fell below 3 performances a season or exceeded 5.

Not long after *The Way of the World* was revived early in 1718, *The Double Dealer* was restored to the stage. Perhaps Drury Lane's offering of Congreve's last play suggested to Lincoln's Inn Fields that *The Double Dealer* might bring it prestige and perhaps profit, but it waited until 1718–19 to bring on the play. Appearing first on October 18, 1718, it was acted 4 times that season. It ranked considerably below the successes of the season: *Sir Walter Raleigh,* a new play with 12 performances; *The Committee* and *The Chitchat* (new), with 11 each; and *All for Love,* with 10. Although *The Double Dealer* did not prove a particularly popular attraction, Lincoln's Inn Fields continued to offer it without competition until 1735–36. It had a satisfactory cast. The theater's best actors, James Quin and Lacy Ryan (Heartwell and Vainlove in *The Old Batchelor*), played Maskwell and Careless. George Pack and Christopher Bullock—Tattle and Trapland in *Love for Love*— acted Sir Paul and Brisk. Supporting them were Leigh (Mellefont), Corey (Lord Touchwood), and Spiller (Lord Froth), all superior to many of the players with whom Rich opened his theater. Lady Froth was played by Mrs. Christopher Bullock, the natural daughter of Wilks; according to Chetwood, she "pleas'd in several dramatic characters, assisted by a graceful Form and Figure." [11] Mrs. Knight, who already played Zara (*The Mourning Bride*), Mrs. Frail (*Love for Love*) and Laetitia (*The Old Batchelor*), added Lady Plyant to her distinguished roles.

In all probability, *The Double Dealer* disappointed the managers

[10] *Dramatic Miscellanies,* III, 221–222.
[11] *General History of the Stage,* p. 112.

of Lincoln's Inn Fields, who would have been grateful for profitable plays. They may have looked enviously at Drury Lane's greater success with *The Way of the World* and with *All for Love,* successfully revived for the first time since 1708–09. The 4 performances of *The Double Dealer* came early in the season; the last, a benefit on December 4 for the widow of Theophilus Keen, occurred before the winter was half over. Lincoln's Inn Fields continued, however, to offer it, and in the next ten seasons it never had more than 5 performances nor less than 2. In 1720–21, when Benjamin Griffin, who "greatly distinguished himself" [12] as Sir Paul, joined the cast, the receipts fluctuated considerably. On November 2, 1720, the comedy drew £50 8s 6d, better than the November average. On November 25, however, a small audience paid only £10 19s 6d. A benefit for the treasurer on May 2, 1721, brought a good sum, £130 15s. In 1721–22, with 3 performances, the comedy was strengthened by Thomas Walker as Mellefont and Anthony Boheme as Lord Touchwood. Boheme was thought a "very extraordinary Actor" by Victor, who considered that he had a "singular Vein of Humour" but never received genuine recognition because he acted at Lincoln's Inn Fields before it was "brought into Vogue by Pantomimes." [13] Mrs. Egleton (the former Mrs. Giffard) continued as Lady Plyant, and her husband, "Baron" Egleton, excelled only by Cibber in playing fops, later undertook Brisk. Given twice in 1722–23, the comedy was further strengthened by the addition of John Hippisley, a genuine comedian, who acted Sir Paul at a benefit for the Egletons on April 4, 1723. By that time the comedy was well established in Lincoln's Inn Fields.

A few months after *The Double Dealer* was revived in 1718 at Lincoln's Inn Fields, *The Mourning Bride* reappeared at Drury Lane, from which it had been absent since the late months of 1716. Performed first on January 9, 1719, it was probably given four times later that month and twice more in the spring. Although the tragedy did not do quite so well as *The Way of the World,* it brought to four the number of Congreve's plays being presented at Drury Lane and it remained there continuously through 1732–33. Barton Booth retained his role of Osmyn, and Thomas Elrington, recently arrived from Ireland, played the King. Mrs. Thurmond, who was often understudy to Mrs. Oldfield, played Almeria, which became one of her best roles. Zara was played by Mrs. Porter, who, according to Victor, had the disadvantages of a *"plain Person* and a *bad Voice,"* the latter strained by an attempt to increase its power; "yet, being blest with a good Understanding, and a good Ear, she made herself a compleat Mistress of her Art. She acquired

---

[12] Victor, *History of the Theaters,* ii, 79.
[13] *Ibid.,* ii, 76–77.

an elevated Dignity in her Mein, and threw out a spirited Propriety in all Characters of Rage; but when Grief and Tenderness possessed her, she subsided into the most affecting Softness." [14]

By 1719, then, for the first time in the century, all of Congreve's plays were acted during the same season. Once established, they held their place well; not until 1734–35, nearly a generation later, did one of them fail to appear somewhere in London.[15] During those twenty years, when several hundred dramas formed the repertory, a play by Congreve was, on the average, among each twenty performances. His comedies probably made a better showing than *The Mourning Bride,* but it was a time when comedy seemed more in vogue than tragedy. Except for *Cato* and *Jane Shore* there were no tragedies to match the popular comedies by Farquhar, Cibber, Vanbrugh, and Congreve. Etherege's *The Man of Mode* also was fairly popular; and, like Congreve's less successful comedies, Wycherley's *The Country Wife* and *The Plain Dealer* had been revived after the opening of Lincoln's Inn Fields. After all five of Congreve's plays had appeared, they remained for several years without great change in their casts and in general grew in frequency of performance. *The Old Batchelor* was the most frequently acted until 1729–30, chiefly because it was the only one offered by both houses. *The Double Dealer* remained the exclusive property of Lincoln's Inn Fields, with Drury Lane presenting the other three without competition. The managers apparently accepted this division as mutually advantageous and made no visible effort to encroach upon each other's repertory. No doubt it assured more stable casts for each play, but the town did not, with the exception of *The Old Batchelor,* enjoy seeing rival actors play the same roles.

Superficially, the fortunes of Congreve's plays might suggest that the third decade of the century was a placid one theatrically, but it was not so. Although his plays did not suffer from violent fluctuations, the appetite for older dramas was affected by the many theatrical innovations. Some of the novelties, particularly ballad opera and pantomime, became enormously popular. In addition, companies of French and Italian players came to London and offered drama and entertainment in their native tongues. John Rich, in fact, welcomed the first large troupe by letting them act in Lincoln's Inn Fields two or three nights weekly

14 *Ibid.,* ii, 57–58.

15 In 1734–35 it was *The Double Dealer* which failed to appear. In the autumn of 1720 Congreve's plays were sufficiently among the favorites that Bullock, in his Great Booth in the Queen's-Arms Tavern Yard in Southwark, offered *Love for Love* on Oct. 3, with "all the Parts . . . perform'd to the best Advantage, by Gentlemen from both Houses," and Hall at his Booth in Bird-Cage Alley gave *The Old Batchelor* on Nov. 28.

from November 7, 1718, for the rest of the season. Soon the foreigners were his competitors. On December 29, 1720, the New Theater in the Haymarket, a small house, was opened by French players who occupied it until May. Thereafter, until the Licensing Act (1737), foreigners, in groups or individually, more and more frequently appeared in London, sometimes in the patent theaters, sometimes elsewhere. These innovations did not, of course, stop the normal process of reviving old plays and producing new ones. Although entertainments between the acts or after the play formed a large share of the evening's program, there still had to be plays—and many of them—to permit a nightly change of fare except during a successful run. The play, however, was not always the thing. Sometimes spectacle mattered more. To use a contemporary comparison, just as some worshippers attended church for the music, others for the sermon, so many Londoners went with their minds to see the play, others with their eyes and ears to be enthralled by spectacle and sound. When a particularly entrancing pantomime was running, it probably did not matter greatly to many spectators just what play was offered; the entertainment would bring a full house. Possibly plays alone, by their frequent and routine repetition, became occasionally tiresome. As the prologue to Theophilus Cibber's *The Lover* (1730) put it:

> Here Congreve oft your gay Attention warms,
> Yet, oft repeated, loses half his Charms.
> Still the same Round of Mirth fatigues your View;
> Old Pleasures tire, unless reliev'd by New:
> Reliev'd by New, again their Forms invite;
> And like other friends, grow welcome to your Sight:
> Welcome from Absence!

In this cyclic intermingling of old and new, the managers, seeking to satisfy as many people as possible, chose the plays as well as the pantomimes with an eye to their reception. In 1719–20, for example, they produced several new pieces which attained six or more performances: Theobald's *Richard II*, Malloy's *Half Pay Officers*, Griffin's *Whig and Tory*, and Hughes' *The Siege of Damascus*, most of them produced in Lincoln's Inn Fields. Several old plays—*The Committee, Hamlet, Macbeth, Oroonoko*, and *The Spanish Fryar*—fared equally well. Congreve's plays attained a total of 16 performances, a good though not remarkable showing; they compared well with Etherege's comedies (*The Man of Mode*, 3, and *She Wou'd if She Cou'd*, 1), with Wycherley's (*The Country Wife*, 4), and even with Farquhar's (*The Recruiting Officer*, 6; *The Beaux Stratagem*, 5; *The Constant Couple*, 4; and *The Twin Rivals*, 3). In 1721–22 Congreve's share in the repertory was increased by Lincoln's Inn Fields' restoring, after a two-year interval, *The Old Batchelor*. It had 4 performances there in January, but the receipts, though usually higher than in earlier years, declined from £43 10s 6d to £17 3s 6d, and Rich did not offer it again until April, when it was chosen for two benefits. Rich had been strengthening his company until the *Weekly Journal, or Saturday's Post* (March 16, 1723) thought "they are arrived even to Excellence in Tragedy." *The Old Batchelor* was improved by James Quin, Rich's best actor, as Heartwell, Lacy Ryan as Vainlove, and Thomas Walker, "a pleasant actor" in libertine parts,[16] as Bellmour. The versatile Tony Aston made his first appearance under Rich's direction as Fondlewife, a part in which he modelled himself upon Dogget, as Cibber had earlier done. None of Rich's actresses, however, could equal Mrs. Oldfield, and he was forced to choose a dancer, Mrs. Rogeir, for Araminta.

In the midst of reviving the comedy, Rich plunged more heavily into pantomimic spectacle, foreshadowing the silent dramas which later became his stock-in-trade. The box-office receipts in the early part of the season suggest how badly he needed novelty to increase attendance. The first three performances in September 1721 averaged only £25; in October the average was below £20, a poor promise for the long season ahead. In November, however, the addition of pantomimes helped greatly. For example, on November 2 *Abra Mule* unassisted brought £11 9s; on the following evening *Henry IV, Part 1*, £19 10s 6d; but on November 4 *Tamerlane* with *The Magician, or Harlequin a Director* brought £62 19s 6d. Throughout that month nearly every bill which included a pantomime brought higher income than one without, and in January three of the four performances of *The Old Batchelor* included *The Magician*, the single performance without pantomime bringing the lowest receipts the comedy had during the season. In the next season, 1722–23, the legitimate theaters felt the pinch of competitive novelty. Signora Cuzzoni, an Italian opera singer, was the rage; she made her debut at the King's Theater before His Majesty and a large audience, and she earned, so rumor reported, £2,000 for the season.[17] In addition, there was a troupe of foreign comedians at the New Haymarket, which also harbored a company of fledgling English actors who gave 11 performances there. Yet both legitimate theaters had some genuine successes. Drury Lane was the more fortunate with 26 performances of Steele's *The Conscious Lovers*, surpassing Lincoln's Inn Fields' *Mariamne* (16) and revivals of *Oedipus* and *The Cutter of Coleman Street*. Congreve's plays achieved a more even balance than

16 Davies, *Memoirs of the Life of Garrick*, I, 25.
17 *London Journal*, Jan. 12, 1723.

before. Although *The Old Batchelor* declined in Loncoln's Inn Fields
from 6 performances to 2, nearly all the other plays made gains. Quin
(Heartwell), Walker (Bellmour), and Ryan (Vainlove) were joined by
John Hippisley, who made his first appearance under Rich's management as Fondlewife, a part he retained until 1747. Drury Lane offered
it 3 times, with Heartwell by John Harper, whom *The Comedian* (October 1732) placed among the "good Comedians." Davies, however, was
not convinced of his fitness for the role: "The Old Batchelor of Drury-
lane was Harper, a good low comedian, but whose understanding was
not of that size to give force to the sarcastic poignancy of expression,
the whimsical struggles of amorous passion, or the violent rage on discovered folly, in Heartwell." [18] After the death, on March 24, 1723, of
Mrs. Bicknell, who had played Belinda since 1718, the part fell to Mrs.
Horton, a delightful coquette who also played Mrs. Foresight and Mrs.
Fainall. According to the *Grub Street Journal* (October 11, 1733), she
never failed "to please in either tragedy or comedy." Performances of
The Double Dealer declined slightly, but *The Way of the World* did
well and *The Mourning Bride* had its best season in four years. Congreve's plays achieved 19 performances for the season.[19]

By the autumn of 1723 Rich's preoccupation with pantomime was
intensifying theatrical rivalry. The managers of Drury Lane, watching
the multitude flock to Lincoln's Inn Fields to see Rich (as Lun) play
Harlequin, discovered that they could exist on a plain diet of plays.
Cibber acknowledged that he and his associates could not withstand
the cry for pantomime: "If I am ask'd (after my condemning these
Fooleries myself) how I came to assent or continue my Share of Expence
to them? I have no better Excuse for my Error than confessing it. I
did it against my Conscience! and had not Virtue enough to starve by
opposing a Multitude that would have been too hard for me." [20] By
the end of the season two of the most successful among eighteenth-
century pantomimes had taken the town. Drury Lane had the first hit
on November 26, 1723, with *Harlequin Doctor Faustus*, which ran as
an afterpiece during most of November and December. On January 7,
1724, Rich countered with *The Necromancer, or Harlequin Doctor
Faustus*, which was played as an afterpiece for 38 successive nights until a new play temporarily removed it from the bills.[21] Competition was

[18] *Dramatic Miscellanies*, III, 218.

[19] *Love for Love* was acted at Smock Alley, Dublin, on Dec. 12, 1723, and *The
Mourning Bride* there on April 1, 1723.

[20] *Apology*, II, 181–182.

[21] Even a small company of English actors in the Little Haymarket joined the
trend by reviving in January Mountfort's *Life and Death of Dr. Faustus*. Lincoln's
Inn Fields also had two other successful pantomimes, *Jupiter and Europa* and *The
Magician*, in which Rich usually played Harlequin.

no longer between one theater and another or one play and its rival but also between play and pantomime on the same bill. As *Pasquin* (Feb. 4, 1724) pointed out: "Custom indeed so far prevails, that the Play (in Point of Order only) precedes the Dance; but 'tis visible that the Audience languishes through the whole Representation, and discovers the utmost Impatience till *Harlequin* enters, to relieve them from the Fatigue of Sense, Reason, and Method, by his most incomprehensible Dexterities." The effect upon the box office was considerable. In Lincoln's Inn Fields, for example, *The Double Dealer* was acted 5 times; on three evenings *The Necromancer* completed the program. The comedy and pantomime brought £146 6s 6d, £125 8s, and £154 12s, sums which contrast sharply with £12 3s for *The Double Dealer* without a pantomime on October 24, 1722; the same contrasts appear for other plays. As the *Universal Journal* (March 25, 1724) remarked: "Harlequin takes double Prices of those, whom *Otway* and *Congreve* cannot persuade to lay out the single Price."

For the next five seasons competition continued intensely, not wholly between the two playhouses, but also among plays, Italian opera, pantomime, and French comedies. Wilks, Booth, and Cibber, writing jointly to Steele on December 12, 1724, complained, perhaps with exaggeration, "Our audiences decrease daily" because "low Entertainments . . . draw the Numbers, while we act only to the Few who are blest with common Sense." The operas, of poorer quality now, drew better, and with more French comedians arriving, "there are three Playhouses exhibiting nonsense of different kinds against us." [22] Yet the "Few who are blest with common Sense" continued to support Congreve's plays, whose frequency of performance showed no sign of declining. *The Old Batchelor* ranged from 4 to 8 performances each season; *Love for Love* from 4 to 5. Performances of all five plays fluctuated between 16 and 24.[23] Even the long runs of *The Provoked Husband* in Drury Lane and *The Beggar's Opera* in Lincoln's Inn Fields during the first two months of 1728 brought no appreciable diminution in the number of performances of Congreve's plays during that season. Neither was his death, on January 19, 1729, marked by any special attention to his

[22] *Correspondence of Steele,* pp. 184–185.

[23] Some of his plays were becoming more frequently performed in other cities. *Love for Love* was acted at Smock Alley, Dublin, on Dec. 3, 1724, as a benefit for Griffith (La Tourette Stockwell, *Dublin Theaters and Customs 1637–1820* [Kingsport, Tenn., 1938], p. 60); at Edinburgh sometime in Nov. 1727 by Tony Aston and company (J. C. Dibdin, *The Annals of the Edinburgh Stage* [Edinburgh, 1888], p. 37); at Bristol, for the opening of Hippisley's theater on June 23, 1729 (*London Weekly Journal,* June 28). *The Mourning Bride* was acted at York on Aug. 15, 1727, and at Dover in March 1728 (Rosenfeld, *Strolling Players,* pp. 112, 219).

works or memory, although both *The Old Batchelor* and *The Double Dealer* were given a few days later.

There were, of course, variations in the cast, some of significance for the future of the plays. The changes in *The Old Batchelor*, however, were relatively unimportant. In Lincoln's Inn Fields the comedy gained a good deal from the presence of Mrs. Younger, who once acted in Drury Lane, as Belinda. She and Mrs. Egleton (Lucy) were judged by *The Comedian* (October 1732) as the only actresses in Rich's company who "deserve any applause." In 1727–28 Rich engaged William Milward, a promising player who had served an apprenticeship at the Little Haymarket; he acted Sharper in a special benefit on May 11, 1728, for Tom Crawford, "lately burnt out from the Bear and Hanow Tavern." The other three comedies also continued with few changes. The cast for *The Mourning Bride* is less certainly known, for it was often presented with pantomimes and the cast omitted. On April 20, 1725, however, at a benefit for John Thurmond, who acted Gonsalez, Charles Williams (Garcia), John Bowman (Heli), William Mills (Selim), and John Watson (Alonzo) supported Booth, Elrington, John Mills, Mrs. Thurmond, and Mrs. Porter in the principal roles. The decline from 3 performances in 1726–27 to 1 in 1727–28 may have been occasioned by Booth's absence because of failing health. In 1728–29 he was succeeded by Elrington, who, proving unequal to the part, was replaced a year later by John Mills, in Victor's opinion "the only Tragic Hero in that Company, who could venture to appear in the Characters of the late Mr. *Booth*." [24] On the whole, the casts remained relatively unchanged until early in the 1730's when the deaths of Booth, Wilks, and Mrs. Oldfield deprived Drury Lane of three brilliant performers. By that time the regime of Cibber, Wilks, and Booth, the triumvirate, was at an end. The transition to a new phase was marked by the opening in 1729 of Goodman's Fields Theater, an event which affected the two patent theaters in much the same way that the opening of Lincoln's Inn Fields in 1714 had changed Drury Lane's outlook.

During the fifteen years following 1714 Congreve's plays continued to improve their position in the repertories. Before that year only *The Old Batchelor* and *Love for Love* had any noteworthy share in the theatrical offerings; in the four seasons preceding 1714 his plays accounted for approximately 4 per cent of the total performances of English plays. In the first six seasons after the opening of Lincoln's Inn Fields, they comprised 4.6 per cent of the total. In the next nine seasons their share had increased to approximately 5.1 per cent. From

24 *History of the Theaters*, I, 28.

1714–15 through 1728–29 *The Old Batchelor* was Congreve's most frequently performed play, with 89 performances—56 in Drury Lane, 32
in Lincoln's Inn Fields, 1 elsewhere. *Love for Love* was second, with 83
performances, only 15 of them in Rich's theater. Third was *The Way
of the World,* with 42 performances; then 35 performances of *The
Mourning Bride* and 34 of *The Double Dealer.* Drury Lane offered
more than two-thirds of the performances.

Another index of the standing of Congreve's plays is their comparative popularity during the period from 1714–15 to 1728–29. At that
time *The Mourning Bride,* with 35 performances, stood far below the
most frequently played tragedy, *Hamlet,* with approximately 100 performances, and Congreve's tragedy was much less popular than *Macbeth, Tamerlane, Oroonoko, King Lear, Cato, Othello, The Orphan,*
and *The Unhappy Favorite,* to list them in descending order. Roughly
approximating *The Mourning Bride* in frequency of performance were
Venice Preserved, The Distrest Mother, All for Love, and *Jane Shore.*
Among the comedies none could equal the exceeding popularity of
The Beggar's Opera, although it was on the stage only two of the fifteen
seasons. But *The Old Batchelor* and *Love for Love* were both in the
first rank of those comedies having between 80 and 100 performances,
the others being *The Beaux Stratagem, The Recruiting Officer, The
Committee,* and *The Spanish Fryar.* There were at least fourteen other
comedies more popular than *The Way of the World,* which was in a
class with *Sir Courtly Nice, The Man of Mode, The Provoked Husband*
(on the stage only two seasons), *The Double Gallant, The Conscious
Lovers, The Tender Husband,* and *The Fair Quaker of Deal.* Next
came *The Double Dealer,* which slightly exceeded *The Rehearsal, Volpone, The Plain Dealer,* and *She Would and She Would Not.* Yet few
authors, on the whole, could claim much greater dominance of the
comic offerings than could Congreve.

Chapter IV

THE OPENING OF GOODMAN'S FIELDS TO THE LICENSING ACT, 1729–1737

It had once been Colley Cibber's contention that London could not support with dignity and profit more than one theater. It might, he said, "be worth the publick Observation (if any thing I have said of it can be so) that *One* Stage may, as I have prov'd it has done, very laudably support it self by such Spectacles only as are fit to delight a sensible People; but the equal Prosperity of *Two* Stages has always been of a very short Duration." If the first decade of the century fostered this belief, the opening of Lincoln's Inn Fields in 1714 confirmed it in him: "two Sets of Actors tolerated in the same Place have constantly ended in the Corruption of the Theatre." As a result, the company "lower in Reputation" invariably turned to "some new-fangled Foppery to draw the Multitude after them." [1] No doubt the frequency with which singing, dancing, pantomime, and interludes dominated the bills after 1714 convinced him of the truth of his observation. His reactions in 1729, when a third theater became a certainty, can be easily imagined.

The new theater did not open until the new season was partly under way. It began with the offering of three of Congreve's plays during September: *Love for Love* on the 13th at Drury Lane; *The Old Batchelor* at Lincoln's Inn Fields on the 24th, with receipts of £58 8s 6d, about average; and *The Mourning Bride* at Drury Lane on the 27th with William Mills as Manuel and John Mills as Osmyn. Until October 22 the houses played on alternate evenings, with *The Old Batchelor* at Drury Lane on October 9 and *The Double Dealer* at Lincoln's Inn Fields on the 25th, the receipts of £30 7s being rather low for a play and pantomime (*Apollo and Daphne*). Then on October 31 the new playhouse in Goodman's Fields opened in a portion of London rather far removed from the section in which the two patent theaters were situated. In spite of opposition from the other playhouses, moralists, businessmen, and the City, it was a successful venture. Not until 1737 did London return to the two-theater system, and then only under the compulsion of Parliament. Even so, the theater in Goodman's Fields managed for a few years thereafter to circumvent the Licensing Act.

Under the management of Thomas Odell, an Irish actor who later

[1] *Apology*, II, 139, 179.

became the first Deputy Licenser of plays, the theater in Goodman's Fields, constructed from an old workshop, offered for its first play *The Recruiting Officer,* the same comedy with which Lincoln's Inn Fields had opened fifteen years earlier. The parallel did not end there. Just as Rich had produced *The Old Batchelor* and *Love for Love* during his first month, so Odell offered them, *Love for Love* as his fourth play on November 5 and the other comedy on November 17. Although these were the only plays by Congreve presented there during the season,[2] both were given frequently. Like Rich fifteen years earlier, Odell had to create a new comedy. Like Rich, he engaged performers from Dublin and from his competitors. He organized his casts around the Giffard family, who were his best actors; Henry Giffard, in fact, became the proprietor of the theater two years later. Henry Giffard played Bellmour and Valentine; his wife was Belinda; William Giffard acted Heartwell and Scandal. At first Odell had no other really capable actors, but he presently engaged William Penkethman, recently with Rich's company, who first played Fondlewife, then Bluff; in *Love for Love* he acted Sir Sampson. From Drury Lane Odell secured Burney, who acted Fondlewife after Penkethman relinquished it. Perhaps the best player won from the opposition was William Bullock, who made his first appearance in Goodman's Fields on November 17 as Sir Joseph and who later acted Tattle (*Love for Love*). Because the company was seriously deficient in capable actresses, Mrs. Giffard undertook a great many roles, both comic and tragic. Next to her in merit was Mrs. Mountfort, who played Sylvia and Prue. Odell's difficulties were amply illustrated in his casting of Araminta, which three actresses attempted during the first season.

There is no clear indication as to how much the prosperity of the older houses was affected by the opening of Goodman's Fields. No doubt it drew patrons from the other houses, and the attacks upon it by the moralists and businessmen suggest that it was sufficiently frequented to seem a moral menace. The receipts at Lincoln's Inn Fields also suggest a slackening of attendance there. They fell to £13 0s 6d on the opening night of Goodman's Fields and did not rise appreciably until Rich revived *The Rape of Proserpine,* one of his most profitable pantomimes. The competitive struggle was intensified by a new play, *Love and Revenge,* at the Little Haymarket during November for six performances. Although the circle of London theatergoers was enlarging, each new theater did not, of course, bring a commensurate number of new spectators. Congreve's plays, however, continued to hold their

2 Not until 1731 did Goodman's Fields venture *The Mourning Bride* and not until 1742 *The Way of the World.* It never played *The Double Dealer.*

own. In November Goodman's Fields gave *Love for Love* twice and *The Old Batchelor* once; the Prince of Wales attended a performance of *The Way of the World* at Drury Lane on November 8, apparently his first witnessing of a Congreve play that winter. In December *Love for Love* and *The Old Batchelor* were acted twice each, and *The Mourning Bride* was repeated at Drury Lane, with a revival of the eccentric Samuel Johnson's *Hurlothrumbo* enlivening the closing weeks of 1729.

During January and February Congreve's plays more than held their own with 7 performances (only *The Double Dealer* went unacted), a good showing in view of the many new plays which dominated those months. In January there was *The Humours of Oxford,* moderately successful; in early February there were *Timoleon* (Drury Lane), *The Temple Beau* (Goodman's Fields), and *The Fatal Love* (Haymarket); still later that month Samuel Johnson astounded London with another of his novelties, *The Chesire Comics.* But with *Sophonisba* at Drury Lane, *The Fatal Villainy* at Goodman's Fields, and on March 30 Henry Fielding's very successful *Author's Farce* at the Haymarket, not one of Congreve's plays was acted during March. In April, however, five performers chose the four comedies for their benefits: *The Way of the World,* April 6, at Drury Lane for Mrs. Booth; *Love for Love,* April 10, at Goodman's Fields for William Bullock and, April 18, at Drury Lane for Norris; *The Old Batchelor,* April 13, at Lincoln's Inn Fields for John Hippisley, with excellent receipts, £170 2s; and *The Double Dealer,* April 25, Lincoln's Inn Fields for Newhouse, with receipts of £104. In the late spring three of the plays were given,[3] but none was offered by the summer repertories except *Love for Love* at Richmond on August 6, 1730, as a benefit for William Milward. By this time *Love for Love* was beginning to supplant *The Old Batchelor* as Congreve's most frequently performed play. In 1729–30 it was acted 12 times to 8 for *The Old Batchelor,* 5 for *The Mourning Bride,* and 3 each for the other two plays. Although Goodman's Fields offered two of the comedies in 1729–30, the addition of a third major theater did not immediately produce any great change in the vogue of the plays. The three houses gave them 31 times, a gain of 10 over the preceding season; of these performances Goodman's Fields contributed 11, just slightly more than its proportional third of the total.

After the excitement of a first season at Goodman's Fields, the year 1730–31 was more subdued. Not only were there many dramatic failures; there were few successful revivals. The stage also lost Mrs. Oldfield, whose death on October 23 deprived London of a brilliant Laetitia,

---

[3] *Love for Love* was acted at Canterbury on May 13, 1730, by Dymer's company (Rosenfeld, *Strolling Players,* p. 220).

Angelica, and Millamant. Anthony Boheme and Charles Williams, capable though not first-rate actors, died later in the season. Coincident with these losses was much shaking of heads over declining theatrical taste. Writers of the 1730's cited many proofs for their contention that the age was inferior to the preceding century or to Shakespeare's times: the excessive fondness for pantomime, foreign comedians, Italian singers, or ballad opera, especially the many poor imitations of *The Beggar's Opera*. According to *The Templer* [4] there was evident a "strange fondness the world has for a new humour, which they are never tired of till it surfeits." It pointed to the *"Beggar's Opera,* and the inundation of ballad opera's that succeeded it. Tragedies and comedies sink in esteem, and all the playhouses subsist by *Ballads* and *Harlequins*. This custom of jading a humour is the high-road to absurdity and folly." After a long citation of current defects in taste, the *Universal Spectator* (April 10, 1731) summarized them by stating that "we are now sunk so intollerably low in respect of *Taste,* that Things at present draw an Audience of People of Fashion into our *Theatres,* which in the Days of our Fathers and Grandfathers, would have excited the Hisses of Servant-Maids and 'Prentices, at every Puppet-Show." As evidence, he offered the observation that spectators miss the point of the satire in *The Rehearsal* and *The Beggar's Opera* and he concluded that in "the present Condition of Theatrical Entertainments, the true End of the Stage is almost wholly lost; we go not thither to see Folly exposed, but to see it acted."

Possibly these complaints were merely a fashionable carping at the frailties of the moment, although there was evidence that the increase in the number of types of afterpieces had attracted many spectators who possessed little relish for true drama. The new theaters needed spectators, who must be enticed in one way or another. In 1730–31 the premières came rapidly, as though new plays might win spectators; but the failures were many: at Drury Lane *Medea* and *The Highland Fair;* at Lincoln's Inn Fields *The Coffee-House Politician, Periander, Philotas,* and *Merope;* at Goodman's Fields *The Fall of the Earl of Essex* and *The Cynic*. The genuine hits were few and came late. At the Haymarket Fielding's *Tragedy of Tragedies* and *The Letter Writers* made a flourishing spring there, and by summer *The London Merchant* gave Drury Lane a moralizing climax to a somewhat dismal year.

Yet the reception of Congreve's plays suggests that the age was not so callous to good comedy as some writers thought. During 1730–31 they were performed 27 times, only a slight decrease from the previous year. *The Old Batchelor* had 8 performances distributed among three theaters. In Drury Lane the managers chose to replace Mrs. Oldfield

---

[4] Feb. 9, 1731, as summarized in the *Gentleman's Magazine,* I (1731), 58.

with Mrs. Thurmond, who had played Laetitia before; she was joined by Mrs. Houghton as Belinda and Theophilus Cibber as Sir Joseph. In Goodman's Fields, casting Araminta remained difficult, and a Miss Smith, of whom nothing is known, attempted it. *Love for Love,* with 6 performances at Goodman's Fields, was one of its more successful plays. Undertaking Angelica was Mrs. Giffard, whom Chetwood in 1749 characterized as "an amiable Person . . . a well-esteemed Actress, both in Tragedy and Comedy." [5] On December 14 Mr. and Mrs. Morgan, from Lincoln's Inn Fields, joined Odell's company as Ben and Prue. On April 5, 1731, Charles Macklin, a promising free-lance, acted Tattle for his debut, replacing William Bullock, who was "in confinement" at the time of his benefit. At Drury Lane the performance of *Love for Love* on April 22, 1731, marked Wilks' last appearance as Valentine, a role which he had performed nearly a hundred times since 1707–08. *The Mourning Bride* and *The Double Dealer* [6] continued with few changes in their casts, but *The Way of the World* presented a problem in picking a successor to Mrs. Oldfield. According to *The History of the English Stage* (1741) Booth had often declared that no one was so capable of succeeding Mrs. Oldfield as Mrs. Horton. "Mr. *Wilks* was *of the same Opinion,* and proved it, by chusing her to play with him in several Comedies, where she appeared in Mrs. *Oldfield's* Characters. The Part of *Millamant* . . . was one of the foremost, and my intimacy with Mr. *Wilks* . . . gave me an Opportunity to be assured, that she acquitted herself in this Character to the Satisfaction of that *celebrated Actor,* as well as to the Delight of the Audience." [7] Replacing Mrs. Horton as Mrs. Fainall was not difficult, because Mrs. Heron had previously played that part well. It was she whom Cibber chose to succeed Mrs. Oldfield in his favorite characters of Lady Betty Modish and Lady Townly, but Wilks' preference for Mrs. Horton apparently prevented Mrs. Heron from securing Millamant as well. According to Victor, Cibber took great care with Mrs. Heron, "which was of singular Happiness to her; because, with that Advantage, she made but a decent Actress. She was naturally well formed, with an easy, elegant Air and Mein; and though her Voice was bad, she had a sensible Pronunciation." [8] Mrs. Horton chose *The Way of the World* for her benefit in 1730–31.

[5] *General History of the Stage,* p. 166.

[6] *The Double Dealer* appears to have been given for the first time in Dublin on May 12, 1731 (Stockwell, *Dublin Theaters and Customs,* p. 325).

[7] Page 164. Victor expressed the same opinion in curiously similar language: "*Millamant* . . . was the first Part; and my Intimacy with him [Wilks] at that Time, gave me an Opportunity to be assured that she acquitted herself in that Character to his Satisfaction. In *that* . . . she was generally allowed to be the only Copy that could remind us of that excellent Original" (*History of the Theaters,* II, 56).

[8] *History of the Theaters,* I, 39.

Although the next season (1731–32) was not an unusual one, it witnessed one theatrical event of undoubted importance: the withdrawal of Thomas Odell as manager of Goodman's Fields and his replacement by Henry Giffard. For the next ten years Giffard was a man of increasing significance, not only because of his fairly astute management of a small theater placed at a geographical disadvantage in London but also because of his possible share in the passage of the Licensing Act and his genuine share in introducing Garrick to the stage in 1741. In the meantime, he developed Goodman's Fields to near-equality with the other theaters. In January, for example, he achieved an enviable revival of *The Committee,* with Josias Miller, once of Drury Lane, playing Teague for his first appearance in London in two years; the comedy was offered about 20 times there. In the next month Drury Lane had a slight success with *Injured Innocence* and a much greater one in Fielding's *Modern Husband,* although its season was marred by a first-rate literary-political sensation in the riots which prevented Boadens' *The Modish Couple* from continuing after the third night. Just as sensational in another way was Samuel Johnson's acting Lord Wildfire in another of his own strange plays, *The Blazing Comet.*

Against this background, Congreve's plays kept their accustomed frequency, but the distribution changed. At Lincoln's Inn Fields *The Double Dealer* had its usual 3 performances, with disappointing receipts. On November 6, with *Apollo and Daphne,* it brought £52 14s; on January 19, only £18 2s 6d; and on April 28, a benefit, £54 7s 6d. Possibly these low receipts account for Rich's offering it only once in each of the next two seasons. *The Way of the World* also had a routine season, with 3 performances. *The Old Batchelor,* however, regained first place with 10 performances, divided pretty well among three playhouses. The most important changes occurred in Goodman's Fields, to which Henry Giffard brought new talent. Josias Miller, winning the town with Teague (*The Committee*), also played Sir Joseph. Giffard also acquired, from Dublin, William Havard, whose "agreeable address" [9] sustained him in Sharper, a role he kept for several years. From Ireland also came young Norris, son of "Jubilee Dicky" Norris, to act Fondle-wife. [10] From Drury Lane came Mrs. Roberts (Belinda), with Mrs. Giffard returning to Laetitia and Mr. and Mrs. Morgan acting Bluff and Lucy. Giffard offered the comedy 3 times, with 3 performances in Drury Lane and 4 in Lincoln's Inn Fields. Giffard had a greater success with

9 Davies, *Memoirs of the Life of Garrick,* II, 195.

10 Chetwood (*General History of the Stage,* p. 199) sarcastically stated that "neither he, nor his Brother (who has likewise troubled several Country Stages in *England*), resembled the Father in any Thing but Stature."

Love for Love, perhaps because Drury Lane for the first time in many years failed to offer it; the death of Wilks was probably the decisive cause. Giffard seized the opportunity to present it 7 times, although he had many casting problems. An actor named Smith, otherwise almost unknown, played Sir Sampson; Bullock resumed Tattle; Rosco joined the company as Trapland; and Collett exchanged Jeremy for Foresight. In mid-season Giffard further shifted his cast, when the Morgans left and Miller undertook Ben. Giffard's ambitious enterprise led him also to stage *The Mourning Bride* for the first time with success: 4 performances followed by 11 the next year. Given first on December 9, it introduced Dennis Delane as the King. Coming from Dublin, he had found in Goodman's Fields, as Chetwood observed, "a better Opportunity of shining without any Rival Ray." [11] Of Henry Giffard as Osmyn *The Comedian* (Oct. 1732) spoke rather sharply: "Would [he] endeavour to rid himself of a Sort of Snip-Snap . . . he would be a more agreeable Actor." Peter Bardin, a Dubliner of French extraction, acted Garcia; William Havard, "having a comely and genteel Person, a clear and distinct Voice, and commonly knowing very well the true Meaning of what he has to say," [12] acted Heli; and young Henry Woodward, rising from Harlequin roles, played Selim. Of Mrs. Giffard (Almeria) *The Comedian* somewhat unenthusiastically stated: "Nor is Mrs. *Giffard* without her Merit." And Mrs. Roberts added Zara to her Congrevean roles. All in all, Goodman's Fields did very well by Congreve by contributing 14 of the 28 performances for the season.

In 1732–33, however, the theaters recovered some of their liveliness, and from then on to the Licensing Act London's stage activities were more highly pitched. Congreve's plays shared in the increased tempo by rising to a total of 47, a figure neither before nor after that season exceeded. Part of the vitality came during these years from lively dramatic gossip in the periodicals. The *Grub Street Journal,* founded in 1730, expressed its opinions pungently, and *The Prompter,* edited from 1734 to 1736 by Aaron Hill, whose interest in the drama never flagged, devoted many issues to theatrical matters. In addition, the daily papers injected themselves into the quarrels between patentees and players, between enemies of the stage and its defenders, between admirers of an actor and those of his rivals; all in all, there was hardly a month without a spirited controversy. There were now six or seven places of entertainment, with the Little Haymarket growing steadily more important, and by 1737 there were two energetic attempts—one of them successful—to bring the stage under close governmental super-

[11] *General History of the Stage,* p. 131.
[12] Whincop, *Compleat List,* p. 245.

vision. At no time since the height of the Collier controversy had the theaters been so much a center of discussion.

In addition to its greatly increased attention to Congreve, the season of 1732–33 was marked by Henry Giffard's move to a new Goodman's Fields playhouse, by John Rich's opening his new theater in Covent Garden, by a very successful revival of *The Beggar's Opera,* and by several new successes, particularly *Achilles* and *The Miser.* There was also a pre-season series of entertainments in the Little Haymarket, where Signora Violante, famous in Dublin for her vaudeville and her Lilli-putian actors, produced *The Beggar's Opera* "after the Irish Manner," with Peg Woffington, later to act in Congreve's plays, as Macheath. On October 2 Giffard opened his new playhouse in Goodman's Fields with *Henry IV, Part I.* The building was splendidly decorated, with a statue of His Majesty in a large oval over the pit, the King attended by Peace, Liberty, and Justice and flanked by Shakespeare, Dryden, Congreve, and Betterton. Shakespeare and Betterton shared the first night with Betterton's revision of *Henry IV,* and Congreve's plays were even more successful there than they had been in the previous season. The fourth play there was *The Old Batchelor,* given 6 times in Good-man's Fields and 7 elsewhere in London, its best season to date in the century. To Giffard's cast came Mrs. Hamilton (Sylvia) from Dublin; Robert Wetherilt, from Drury Lane, to make his first appearance there as Sir Joseph, and, most important of all, Mrs. Thurmond (Laetitia) from Drury Lane. Goodman's Fields gave still greater attention to *The Mourning Bride,* which was acted on five successive nights beginning on October 18 and which attained 11 performances there. It was Mrs. Thurmond as Almeria who was primarily responsible for its success. She made her debut there in the role with considerable applause; in the same month the *Comedian,* in conscious understatement, spoke of her as being "preferable to the other women there." On the same night Charles Hulett, whom the *Comedian* described as having "Talents for Tragedy which want Improvement," first played the King, a role he kept until his death.

Although *Love for Love* was slower than usual in reaching the stage, it also fared better than in the preceding season; its success occurred in Drury Lane, where it was acted 10 times, more than any one company in the century had acted it. Its rise was due considerably to Colley Cib-ber's playing Ben on October 28 and several other nights. As the *Uni-versal Spectator* (Nov. 4, 1732) stated, it was Cibber's venture which at-tracted people to the play, one "generally allow'd to be wrote with the True Spirit of Comedy, yet in my Opinion there are some Expressions in it too loose for a Female Audience, and yet never was the House fuller of Women." They were brought by "the Curiosity of seeing the INIMITA-BLE Mr. *Cibber* appear in a Character so different from what he ever perform'd before." The writer admonished women to remember that "some of very good Sense have observed those Comedies attract the greater Female Audiences, which are wrote in the same Vein." Theophilus Cibber acted Tattle, his father's previous role, and Bridgwater succeeded Wilks as Valentine. With Mrs. Thurmond at Goodman's Fields, Mrs. Booth played Angelica. In the spring Miss Raftor, "without an equal in her walks," [13] succeeded Mrs. Cibber as Prue. Drury Lane easily surpassed the other houses in offering *Love for Love*,[14] but it is hard to understand why Goodman's Fields let its offerings of the comedy decline to three performances, especially since Mrs. Thurmond might well have been as great a success in Angelica as she was in Almeria.

After *Love for Love* and *The Mourning Bride* had won the attention of the town, *The Way of the World* became the focus of attention when John Rich selected it to open his new theater in Covent Garden on December 7. He had not staged it since 1715, and for the first time in years there was genuine rivalry, for Drury Lane stole a march on Rich by presenting *The Way of the World* on December 6, the night before the gala opening of Covent Garden, and again on December 7. On the latter night London had its choice of Bridgwater, William Mills, and Mrs. Horton in the leads at the old house, or Ryan, Quin, and Mrs. Younger at the new. Rich expended every effort to make the opening a memorable occasion. As Davies pointed out, "the scenes were new, and excellently well painted; all the decorations were suited to the grandeur and magnificence of the building." [15] A fashionable audience was expected, with the pit and boxes put together at five shillings and admission to the stage raised to half a guinea. Calculated to hold an audience of about £200, the theater took in a disappointing £115. Performed there twice later, *The Way of the World* had moderate receipts, £61 7s 6d and £67 12s 6d.

Rich's best actor, James Quin, played Fainall, a part in which Davies thought him a "judicious speaker of Fainall's sentiments, but heavy in action and deportment." Ryan's Mirabell seemed to Davies inferior to Wilks' conception, but Thomas Chapman's portrayal of Witwoud,

[13] *Grub Street Journal*, Oct. 11, 1733.

[14] On Feb. 5, 1733, it was the opening play at the new theater in Ransford Street, Dublin (Stockwell, *Dublin Theaters and Customs*, p. 69).

[15] *Dramatic Miscellanies*, III, 221. Writing on Nov. 6, 1733, Aaron Hill urged an author to bring out a new play at Covent Garden rather than at Drury Lane because "*Covent-Garden* house is larger, by one part in three;—it is more commodious for going into, and coming out of; the town's opinion of some of their actors, is very favourable; whereas there runs a strong current of prejudice against *Drury-Lane*." *The Works of the late Aaron Hill, Esq.* (London, 1753), I, 233–234.

"though not so finished as that of Colley Cibber, was of his own draw-ing, and very comic." John Hippisley as Sir Wilful, a part he continued until his death in 1748, compared favorably with his rival, Harper of Drury Lane: "Hippisley . . . was not an auricular imitator of another's manner; he was solely directed by the force of his own genius. Though he did not, in Sir Wilful, present to the spectator such a laughable figure of a superannuated lubber as Harper . . . yet he pleased by dint of comic spirit and natural humor." Mrs. Younger—very good in *The Country Wife* and as Belinda in *The Old Batchelor*—played Millamant and was, in Davies' estimation, "sprightly," though not Mrs. Oldfield's equal. Mrs. Egleton (Lady Wishfort) "was a comic actress much ad-mired by the best judges." [16] Although Rich had newly cast *The Way of the World* and given it the publicity attendant upon the opening of his new theater, it had only 4 performances and in the following season Rich put it into the bills only twice.

By late December the major revivals of Congreve's plays had occurred, with 28 performances of four of them in three months, as many as in the entire preceding season. Then other revivals and new plays crowded them off. The late weeks of December were marked by rival offerings of *The Beggar's Opera* in Drury Lane and Covent Garden. In February Covent Garden had a great success in *Achilles,* the receipts averaging £150 for the first nine performances. At this point *The Double Dealer* on February 8 at Covent Garden had its only performance, with receipts of £40 17s 6d, a decided contrast to those for *Achilles.* In March, with five theaters frequently open, not one of Congreve's plays was acted, *The Miser* and *Achilles* quite eclipsing them. In spite of such fluctua-tions, it was an exceptional season for Congreve. *The Old Batchelor* and *Love for Love,* with 13 performances each, and *The Mourning Bride,* with 12, had more performances in one season than they had had in any since their premières. *The Way of the World* equalled its best previous year. Only once later did either *The Old Batchelor* or *The Mourning Bride* exceed this season's mark; *Love for Love* never did. Although *The Double Dealer* and *The Way of the World* were yet to have their best years, never again were there so many as 47 perform-ances of the dramatist's plays in a single season.

It could hardly be expected that Congreve's plays should do so well in the next season, 1733–34, and they did not. But they did very well, with 35 performances, a considerably larger number than they had averaged in recent years. Their performance, however, was overshad-owed by several theatrical events, such as the spectacles which were prompted by the prospective marriage of the Prince of Orange to the

[16] *Dramatic Miscellanies,* III, 221–223.

Princess Royal. As soon as the Prince reached England in November, the theaters strove hard to surpass each other in honoring the approaching nuptials. Their efforts proved disappointing, however, for no sooner had the playhouses with prodigious fanfare staged their entertainments than the Prince became seriously ill and the marriage had to be postponed. Of greater importance theatrically was a crisis in the affairs of Drury Lane. In the previous spring John Highmore had bought a major share of the patent from Colley Cibber, now retiring, a sale which irked Theophilus Cibber. According to the satiric *Apology for the Life of Mr. T. C., Comedian,* young Cibber immediately reacted: "I was desperately alarm'd, and look'd on it as a Piece of Injustice done to myself: For I thought his Share, or at least the major Part of his Share, would have devolved upon me as an Inheritance; therefore I looked on myself as a *disinherited Son,* and that *Highmore* had bought, clandestinely, my *Birth-Right,* or rather by sinister Means *deprived* me of it. This may serve for a Reason why I so heartily enter'd into the Measures I afterwards prosecuted." [17] The first action was a secession of the ranking players from Drury Lane to the Haymarket, a revolt which Theophilus organized and led. For Highmore the desertion was disastrous. Not only had his theater lost most of its best actors, but he had to forego staging many of the best plays because he lacked the talent with which to cast them. For example, Highmore broke the Drury Lane tradition of presenting most of Congreve's plays each year. During the secession, from September 1733 to March 12, 1734, not a single play by Congreve was offered there.

The revolt resulted in a thorough airing of the whole relationship of players and patentees. Many individuals were genuinely concerned over the plight of comedians placed at the mercy of a new patentee whose qualification for directing a dramatic company was merely his ability to purchase it. On the other hand, there were denunciations of the players, especially of Theophilus Cibber; and Rich and Highmore in November sought legal action to have the players at the Haymarket (and, for good measure, those at Goodman's Fields as well) declared vagabonds so that the patent houses might rule without competition.[18] This action failed, as did a separate one to have Harper, who was selected as a test case, declared a vagrant. Eventually Theophilus Cibber

---

[17] Page 86. This view of Cibber's motives probably did not do him justice. In 1756, in *Two Dissertations on the Theaters,* he reviewed the situation: "'Twas in the Month of *September,* in the memorable Year 1733—myself, and a large Body of Comedians, found a happy Asylum in this little Theater, protected by a generous Town, against the despotic Power of some petulant, capricious, unskilful, indolent, and oppressive Patentees" (p. 19).

[18] An extended account of the moves in these theatrical ventures appears in Victor, *History of the Theaters,* I, 11–15, 19–28.

was victorious. In the late winter Highmore sold his share to Charles Fleetwood, who came to terms with young Cibber. The actors returned to Drury Lane on March 12, 1734, with Cibber and Charles Macklin sharing in the management,[19] and Congreve's plays returned there too.

With the Little Haymarket occupied by the seceders, the season began with four active playhouses. Goodman's Fields opened first and gave as its third play *The Mourning Bride*. Perhaps, as the natural reaction after a very good season, the tragedy was less frequently given there. In spite of Mrs. Thurmond's continuing as Almeria with a good supporting cast, it was acted only 5 times there as compared with 11 the year before. Yet it may have been Giffard's success with it that prompted Rich to stage the tragedy for the first time. Like so many of his Congreve ventures, however, this one was not an unqualified success: *The Mourning Bride* was offered in Covent Garden only twice in 1733–34 and infrequently thereafter. Its first performance, on April 22, 1734, quite late in the season, was a benefit for Mrs. Buchanan (Almeria). Ryan and Quin, both excellent actors, played Osmyn and Gonsalez. Thomas Walker, better suited to comedy, acted the King, though Davies remembered that in "several parts of tragedy Walker's look, deportment and action, gave a distinguished glare to tyrannic rage, and uncommon force to the vehemence of anger." [20] Thomas Chapman (Garcia) and Lacy (Perez) handled those parts capably, and Tony Aston, who "play'd in all the Theaters in *London,* but never continued long in any," [21] was Alonzo. Mrs. Hallam (Zara) was probably Mrs. Buchanan's equal in ability. The poor showing of *The Mourning Bride* may have been simply a part of the general decline in tragedy which the 1730's felt was evident. Writing in 1733, Aaron Hill thought that acting power, especially in tragedy, had deteriorated. When Booth, Wilks, Mrs. Oldfield, and Mrs. Porter acted, "there was a *Pathos* in their delivery, a sensation in their air, an expression in their gesture, and a spirit in their conception and execution, that compelled the dullest apprehension to receive the meaning of the dialogue." Now, however, "all this power is lost; and we may sleep in the most alarming passages; because the actors are, unnaturally *pert,* unmovingly *cold,* or elaborately tiresome, from a dull, dry, drawling monotony of declamatory stiffness." [22] Whether Hill was right or not, *The Mourning Bride* did not again gain favor until the era of Garrick.

After the early opening of Goodman's Fields, the other three houses

19 Victor (I, 31) was of the opinion that Macklin was far more capable as an aid to Fleetwood than was Theophilus Cibber.

20 *Memoirs of the Life of Garrick,* I, 24.

21 Chetwood, *General History of the Stage,* p. 88.

22 *Works of the Late Aaron Hill,* I, 232–233.

followed slowly. Covent Garden was second, with *Othello* on September 15. Drury Lane, weakened by desertion, presented *Aesop* on September 24 and had the support of the Prince of Wales in attendance. Two days later the insurgents opened the Little Haymarket with *Love for Love* to an "elegant crouded Audience." [23] Given on three successive evenings, it reappeared four times later in the season; on February 2, 1734, the comedians gave it at the revels in the Inner Temple. Although the Haymarket cast differed from that in Drury Lane before the Revolt, the principals were the same. The *Grub Street Journal* (Oct. 11, 1733) emphasized the superiority of the Haymarket and added that as Foresight "Mr. JOHNSON is certainly without a superior." *The Way of the World* was the third Congreve play to appear,[24] being offered first at Covent Garden, where it was performed only twice. On one evening it was almost overshadowed by Mlle Sallé, a famous French dancer who was filling one of her numerous London engagements. In the Haymarket the seceders offered it three times, and on their return to Drury Lane twice more, on March 26 as a benefit for Harper, whose "absurd humour, aukward bashfulness, and good-natured obstinacy of Sir Wilful [were] as diverting as any groupe of spectators could wish." On April 30 it was acted for the benefit of Mrs. Sherburn and Mrs. Pritchard, who acted Mrs. Fainall for the first time. Mrs. Pritchard had been an "addition of strength" to the seceders: "Her genteel person . . . her attractive countenance . . . her expressive, yet simple manner; her unembarrassed deportment and proper action, charmed all the spectators." [25] Upon the return to Drury Lane, Adam Hallam continued as Valentine, replacing Wilks, and Theophilus Cibber succeeded his father as Witwoud.

Although Congreve's plays came on early in the season and made a very good showing, the autumn months were theatrically dominated by entertainments honoring the approaching royal wedding. To enliven the season, Covent Garden brought from Paris two celebrated dancers, Mlle Sallé and M. Malter. Goodman's Fields, on November 12, a week after the arrival of the Prince of Orange, staged a new pastoral, *The Happy Nuptials,* in which was embodied an old favorite, *The Amorous Sportsman.* On the same evening Covent Garden presented an appropriate dance, *The Nassau.* Drury Lane announced a new "Grand Dramatick Masque" called *Aurora's Nuptials,* which it fortunately decided to delay until after the wedding. On November 24 the Haymarket gave

[23] Victor, *History of the Theaters,* I, 13.
[24] *The Way of the World* was acted at Edinburgh on Jan. 28, 1734, as a benefit for Wescomb (Dibdin, *Annals of the Edinburgh Stage,* p. 44).
[25] Davies, *Memoirs of the Life of Garrick,* I, 35; II, 176.

Love for Love followed by an "Impromptu Royal Masque on the Joyous Occasion of the Royal Nuptials." And late in November Goodman's Fields was preparing another piece to be called *The Royal Wedding, or the Loves of Germanicus and Britannia,* to be acted on a stage lengthened by thirty feet, with new scenes, new dresses, and "the most grand and magnificent" of decorations. All of these were halted by the long illness of the Prince of Orange, but his recovery and the wedding revived them, with Congreve's plays continuing to appear during the excitement: 3 performances in February and 5 in March.[26] All in all, Congreve's plays seem not to have suffered from the confusion attendant upon the entertainments.

The next three seasons—1734–35 to 1736–37—were important ones theatrically if only because they culminated in the Licensing Act. The movement toward censorship, neither new nor sudden, took legal form in 1734–35 in a parliamentary bill proposing regulation which for the moment was laid aside. In 1735–36 and 1736–37, when Henry Fielding, with headquarters at the Little Haymarket, produced a series of highly successful and politically inflammable plays, political satire proved a decisive factor in persuading Parliament to place the stage and all new plays under strict regulation. The Act also restored the patent theaters to their monopoly, a condition which prevailed until 1843. The effects of the censorship of plays have endured to this day. At the beginning of the three-season period, in 1734–35, London returned to the three-theater system, with Drury Lane recovering some of its former superiority over its competitors. True, there were French comedians at the Haymarket, but there was no division within a company which had produced the secession of the previous year, and the playhouses had to compete with Farinelli, a new "operatical" sensation. Except for Henry Fielding's plays, there were no great dramatic successes during these years to offset the attractions elsewhere. And Congreve's plays fluctuated considerably: 29 performances in 1734–35, 41 in 1735–36, and 26 in 1736–37 .

During these three seasons *The Old Batchelor* was equally popular with *Love for Love,* but nothing of great moment occurred to it. During 1734–35 it was given as a command benefit for John Harvey, painter and architect of Rich's new theater; but it was infrequently given there, perhaps because of Quin's departure for Drury Lane. Theatrical gossip had it that when Fleetwood of Drury Lane offered Quin £500 in-

26 On Jan. 16, 1734, Tony Aston, an astute observer of public taste and a caterer to the curious, presented one of his medleys at Boussler's Tavern in Bloomsbury. Like many other such exhibitions which he held in taverns, inns, and occasionally in theaters, this one had selections from popular plays. He included scenes involving Laetitia and Fondlewife from *The Old Batchelor* and Prue from *Love for Love.*

stead of the £300 he was receiving from Rich, Quin offered to remain at Covent Garden for less than £500, but Rich said that no actor was worth more than £300 yearly. He was succeeded as Heartwell by Bridgwater. In Drury Lane Quin, of course, played Heartwell, which Harper relinquished to him. The *Dramatic Censor* (1770) expressed the opinion that "we shall never see the OLD BATCHELOR . . . half so capably supported" as by Quin (II, 484). Drury Lane contributed nearly half of its performances during these three seasons, with Giffard giving it nearly as much attention. In fact, during the eight years the new theater had contributed more than a third of the performances of *The Old Batchelor* and slightly exceeded Drury Lane in its attention to the comedy.

During the seasons 1734–35 to 1736–37 *Love for Love* had 23 performances, a better showing than *The Old Batchelor* made, and during the eight seasons since the opening of Goodman's Fields it was given 78 times. Of these performances the new company was responsible for 35, the largest number by one company, with Drury Lane only slightly below that total.[27] This excellent showing was made by Giffard and his actors in spite of continuing difficulties with the cast. In 1735–36 Henry Woodward was the fifth person in five years to act Tattle there and Norris was the sixth Ben in as many seasons. In 1736–37, when Giffard gave it only once, there was another Ben—Oates; a new Tattle—the unpredictable Charlotte Charke. Once Drury Lane had recovered from the desertion in 1733, it was to give *Love for Love* without interruption through 1755–56, for it continued to have a versatile and able body of actors.

During the three seasons preceding the Licensing Act *The Way of the World* fared better than it had before, a growth achieved in spite of Drury Lane's declining attention to it. In fact, the season of 1734–35 was its only good one in Drury Lane, which gave the comedy 3 times. In the next five years, however, it was usually given there but once each season. In Covent Garden, on the other hand, it continued to do quite well: 1734–35, 4 performances; 1735–36, 6; and 1736–37, 4. An improved cast was partially responsible for the better showing. Thomas Walker, on October 7, 1734, succeeded Quin as Fainall. In Davies' opinion Walker was the superior player, because he "understood and expressed the assumed spirit and real insolence of this artful character much better." [28] Of great importance to the comedy was Mrs. Horton as Mil-

[27] It was given at Richmond on Aug. 16, 1735, with the Prince of Wales present (*Daily Advertiser*, Aug. 18), and toward the end of 1735 at Ipswich by Dymer's Company (Rosenfeld, *Strolling Players*, p. 98).

[28] *Dramatic Miscellanies*, III, 221.

lamant, a part in which she had excelled in Drury Lane and which she was to keep until 1748. A contemporary reported that the "Language, Dress, Motion, and Manners of a *Millamant* seem naturally her own; and I may say of her, what the great *Apologist* said of Mrs. *Bracegirdle* in that Part; that 'when she acts *Millamant*, all the Faults, Foibles, and Affectations of that agreeable Tyrant were venially melted down into so many Charms and Attractions of a conscious Beauty.'—But besides these Follies of the Fair Sex, she can rise into the decent Dignity of a fine Lady, and charm with the innocent Reserve of an *Indiana*, as by the fluttering *Je ne scai quoy* of a *Millamant*." [29] Adam Hallam, on March 25, 1735, replaced Ryan as Mirabell when Ryan, attacked by thieves, was so seriously wounded that at first it was thought he would not recover. After a rapid convalescence, he acted Mirabell again in May.[30]

During the three seasons *The Mourning Bride* had a varied history. After reviving it in 1733–34, Rich discontinued it in the following season, probably because Quin's departure deprived him of his principal actor. Goodman's Fields was similarly affected by Mrs. Thurmond's return to Drury Lane, for Giffard reduced it from 5 performances in 1733–34 to 1 in 1734–35. With Mrs. Thurmond returning to act Almeria, Drury Lane restored the tragedy for 4 performances. Mills (King) was then in such great demand for tragic roles that "he might be literally and truly called the *theatrical Porter*." [31] Appearing in Drury Lane for the first time in sixteen years, Quin played Gonsalez, and William Milward undertook Osmyn, a part he retained until his death in 1742. Of these two, *An Apology for the Life of Mr. T. C., Comedian* (1740) stated: Quin had the character of a "just Speaker," primarily in "the solemn declamatory Way," for either he cannot or will not "work himself into the Emotions of a violent Passion," and cannot then "give Love or Pity, Grief or Remorse their proper Tone and Variation of Features." Milward, with a "Happiness of Voice," which "is sweet, with an uncommon Strength," apparently excelled Quin be-

29 *An Apology for the Life of Mr. T. C., Comedian*, pp. 141–142.

30 On Oct. 1, 1736, *The Way of the World* was followed by a pantomime in which a serious accident occurred. Gray, present that night, wrote of it to Horace Walpole: "Covent-Garden has given me a Sort of Surfeit of Mr Rich & his Cleverness, for I was at the Way of the World, when the Machine broke t'other Night; the House was in Amaze for above a Minute, & I dare say a great many in the Galleries thought it very dextrously perform'd, & that they scream'd as naturally, as heart could wish; till they found it was no jest by their calling for Surgeons. . . . I stayed to see the poor creatures brought out of the House." *The Correspondence of Thomas Gray*, ed. Paget Toynbee and Leonard Whibley (Oxford, 1935), I, 51.

31 Victor, *History of the Theaters*, I, 29. Victor stated that Mills sometimes played on 170 of the 180 acting nights in a season.

cause "there is a Softness in it which adapts it to touch the Passions of Grief, Love, Pity, or Despair" (pp. 138–139).

In 1735–36, when Goodman's Fields omitted the tragedy after giving it 11 times in 1732–33, 5 in 1733–34, and once in 1734–35, it was given twice in Drury Lane and revived in Covent Garden for 2 performances. The receipts suggest that under Rich's management the attendance was very good—£173 18s 6d on December 17, the highest receipts that month, and £184 14s on January 28, nearly the highest for January —but on each evening it was accompanied by a pantomime. Yet in the following season Covent Garden offered it only once, as a benefit for Anne Hallam (Zara), with Adam Hallam playing Garcia. Another new-comer to the cast was Dennis Delane (Osmyn), who had risen rapidly at Goodman's Fields and was rivalling Quin. He was "esteemed a just Player," though possibly in imitation of Quin he had a "Sameness of Tone and Expression"; he also had a "loud Violence of Voice" which was useful "when Anger, Indignation, or such enrag'd Passions are to be express'd." This violence of tone gave him greater power than Quin's "sweet Cadence" possessed, though perhaps he "pleases many" because the "Million . . . are apt to be transported when the Drum of the Ear is soundly rattled." [32] These players supported Mrs. Horton (Almeria), who "has that Grace in her Presence, that clear Melody in her Voice, with Strength enough to express the Violence of some Passions, and Softness to subside into the Harmony of others, that no Actress now performing on either Stage can, in this Light, be compared to her." [33]

During these last three years before the passage of the Licensing Act the success among Congreve's plays was *The Double Dealer,* revived in 1735–36 at Drury Lane, where it apparently had not been given since its première. As a result, for the first time in its known history, Drury Lane during 1735–36 produced all five of Congreve's plays in the same season. Beginning on October 11, 1735, the comedy was acted 13 times in Drury Lane that season. The revival was noteworthy also in that it produced the first major criticism of the play in many years, an essay printed in Aaron Hill's *The Prompter* (Nov. 11, 1735). Al-though Hill believed that the revival of the comedy was, to put it mildly, a serious mistake, he nevertheless had some praise of it: it "abounds in *Wit*" and it has a plot which, "tho' very *intricate,*" is "not in the least *confused.*" It *"thickens* naturally from the Circumstances in which the Characters [are] placed. . . . Each *Light Character* has likewise a pleas-ing vein of Humour running through it, strongly *distinguished,* yet

---

[32] *An Apology for the Life of Mr. T. C., Comedian,* p. 139. On Jan. 3, 1736, Gray, again writing to Walpole, reported that "the Town . . . don't much admire Delane" (*Correspondence,* I, 36).

[33] *An Apology for the Life of Mr. T. C., Comedian,* p. 142.

theatrically PLAYING into each other." The praise was, however, only
a prelude to a thorough condemnation of the comedy. Hill assailed it
as being *"fundamentally bad."* He objected to the characters, especially
Maskwell, who as a *"cold, deliberate, thinking* Villain" does not belong
in comedy. Anyone, Hill argued, who plans his villainy and laughs at
"the very Notion of Virtue" is only to "be corrected by TYBURN." He
thought the other characters equally evil. After asking what could
justify reviving the comedy, Hill succinctly replied: "Nothing *critically*
or *morally."* He further advised the manager of Drury Lane not to
present such plays merely because spectators sometimes lend their approval to *"loose* and *immoral* Scenes," but his attack had no discernible
effect upon the frequency with which the comedy was staged.

Although the play was new to Drury Lane, the cast was not inexperienced in it. Maskwell was acted by Quin, who had for several years
performed that role in Lincoln's Inn Fields. Benjamin Griffin had also
played Sir Paul Plyant under Rich's management in 1720, where he had
impressed Victor by his making "it a finished Character; his silly important Look always excited Laughter whenever he appeared." In the
scene in which he held Careless' letter and discovered himself a cuckold,
it "was not in Nature to resist bursting into Laughter at the Sight of
him; his ridiculous, distressful Look, followed by a lamentable Recital
of his Misfortunes, in that admirable Soliloque, was as high a Subject
as any Incident I remember in Comedy." [34] Milward was also familiar
with the play, for he had played Maskwell in Lincoln's Inn Fields and
Lord Touchwood in Covent Garden. He now was Mellefont, where "the
Easiness of His Dialogue in the genteel Characters seems very amiable;
and though in his Action and Speech he does not imitate that quick
snip-snap Catch of the late Mr. *Wilks,* to express Spirit and Vigour; yet
his Voice and Gesture show such a Vivacity as are the just Effects of
Nature." [35] Miss Holliday had played Cynthia previously; and William
Mills (Careless), Theophilus Cibber (Brisk), and Mrs. Butler (Lady
Touchwood) had had wide experience in other plays by Congreve. Of
Catherine Clive as Lady Froth, Davies wrote: "Clive was in Lady Froth,
as in the rest of her comic characters, superior to all actresses." [36]

With this successful revival, the season of 1735–36 was, statistically,
the second best for Congreve's plays. As the other dramas did not appreciably decline in frequency of performance, the run of *The Double
Dealer* increased the season's total to 41. In 1736–37 there was, however,

[34] *History of the Theaters,* II, 79.

[35] *An Apology for the Life of Mr. T. C., Comedian,* pp. 139–140.

[36] *Dramatic Miscellanies,* III, 192–193. Writing on Jan. 21, 1741, Shenstone thought
her one of the very few good actresses in London. *The Letters of William Shenstone,*
ed. Marjorie Williams (Oxford, 1939), p. 16.

a decline to 26 performances, a decline in which all the plays participated. The year was marked also by the deaths of three players who
had recently appeared in Congreve's plays: John Mills, Mrs. Buchanan,
and Mrs. Porter. A performance of *The Mourning Bride,* with royalty
in attendance, was given on February 24, 1737, in honor of Mrs. Porter.

What was the position of Congreve's plays in the repertory to 1737?
So far as *The Mourning Bride* is concerned, it continued to be neither
greatly popular nor grossly neglected. Before the opening of Lincoln's
Inn Fields in 1714 it was third among Congreve's plays, *Love for Love*
and *The Old Batchelor* greatly overshadowing it. During the period
from 1714–15 to 1728–29 it was in fourth place, but it returned to third
place during the eight seasons from 1729–30 to 1736–37, although by only
a narrow margin over *The Way of the World.* During this period it continued to be greatly exceeded in frequency of performance by *Othello,
Hamlet, The London Merchant,* and *Tamerlane,* but it was much
closer to *Cato, Macbeth, Oroonoko,* and *The Orphan.* In fact, it had
been growing in popularity while *King Lear, Aurengzebe, All for Love,
Oedipus,* and *The Distrest Mother* had declined.

The relation of Congreve's comedies to each other and to *The Mourning Bride* may be seen most clearly in a table of their performances:

	Old Batchelor	Double Dealer	Love for Love	Mourning Bride	Way of the World
1700/1–1713/4	26	1	44	7	1
1714/5–1728/9	89	34	83	35	42
1729/30–1736/7	67	29	78	46	45
Totals	182	64	205	88	88

In the third of these periods *Love for Love* and *The Old Batchelor*
ranked fairly high among the comedies. *The Beggar's Opera,* of course,
easily led, with more than twice as many performances as *Love for Love.*
Slightly more popular than *Love for Love* were *The Provoked Husband,
The Beaux Stratagem,* and *The Committee.* In the general range of
The Old Batchelor and *Love for Love* were such diverse comedies as
The Constant Couple, The Busy Body, The Recruiting Officer, and
Rule a Wife and Have a Wife. The Way of the World compared well
with *The Double Gallant, The Provoked Wife, The Relapse,* and *The
Tender Husband.* Comparable to *The Double Dealer* were *The Coun-
try Wife, The Rover, She Would and She Would Not,* and *Volpone.*

Whatever truth there may have been in Colley Cibber's contention
that whenever two or three theaters competed they were compelled to
resort to pantomime and spectacle, it is nevertheless clear that increased
competition had its effect upon plays as well. During the eight years of

three-theater rivalry, Congreve's plays continued to grow in frequency of performance and there was no very clear suggestion that they were in any danger of losing their growing reputation. In fact, during those eight seasons their share in the repertory increased to 5.5 per cent, the best showing they had made so far in the century. And competition had so benefited them that from comparative obscurity *The Double Dealer* and *The Way of the World* had come into an established place in the repertory since the opening of Lincoln's Inn Fields in 1714–15.

CHAPTER V

THE LICENSING ACT TO GARRICK AS MANAGER, 1737–1747

With the passage of the Licensing Act and the closing of all the play-houses except Drury Lane and Covent Garden, the theatrical scene lost much of its vigor. Soon the visits of foreign comedians ceased. Henry Fielding turned his talents elsewhere. Competition dwindled to that between two legally secure companies. Even the summer seasons, when the young actors were usually in control, were for a time eliminated. Undoubtedly the Licensing Act made the managers more cautious; some new plays were forbidden by the Lord Chamberlain and the first licensed play to be acted was received with a hostility which expressed the views of many people toward the Act itself. With most of the literary and theatrical journals suspending publication, the daily papers contented themselves with "puffs" of forthcoming plays or generalities to the effect that a play had been acted "with universal applause." The years between the Licensing Act and the debut of David Garrick in the autumn of 1741 were, in many ways, very dull when compared with those of the previous decade, although there were some interesting developments. John Rich, for example, in 1737–38 rather suddenly developed a taste for Shakespeare and brought onto the stage several of the dramatist's partially neglected plays.

Through these four seasons, Congreve's plays not only retained their high level of stage prosperity but advanced to a still larger share in the offerings of the theaters. In fact, this period marked the peak of their vogue in the playhouses. Every one of them was acted at least once somewhere in London during each season from 1737–38 through 1740–41. Although each play had its normal fluctuations, only *The Mourning Bride* declined seriously in frequency of performance. The momentum of their increasing popularity carried them through the difficult period of the beginning of governmental regulation.

For three years following the Licensing Act *The Old Batchelor* made only routine appearances. In 1737–38 Covent Garden gave it once, Drury Lane twice. The theaters reversed themselves in the next season: Drury Lane, 1; Covent Garden, 2. A year later it was Drury Lane's 3 to the rival's 1. Not since 1713–14, when Drury Lane had no competitor, had there been as few as 3 performances in one season, and not since 1726–27 as few as 4. In 1740–41, however, *The Old Batchelor,* with 11 performances, began a period of greater vogue than it had experienced for some years. Seven of these performances occurred in Covent Garden, whose company Rich had considerably strengthened. The principal cause of the revival, however, was the return of Colley Cibber at a special benefit on January 12, 1741, for William Chetwood, once a prompter for Drury Lane and now a prisoner in the King's Bench. According to a pamphlet, Cibber stated that he had given his "Promise to play the Part of *Fondle Wife* in *the Old Batchelor* . . . for a Friend's Friend in distress, but not daring to hope that so short a Part would be strong enough to fill the House for him, I fancied an Epilogue upon so particular a Subject might make People a little more curious to come to it." [1] It was an "Epilogue upon Himself," [2] and the receipts (£234) were so good and the reception was so favorable that he was "encouraged . . . to repeat it a second and third Night, for [his] *own* Profit." [3] Newly supporting Cibber were Lacy Ryan, once associated with Fielding in the Haymarket, as Bellmour, and Peg Woffington as Laetitia. Mrs. Woffington, eight years earlier one of Madame Violante's Lilliputians in Dublin and London, had recently made a very successful debut in Covent Garden as Sylvia in *The Recruiting Officer*. According to Davies, Cibber, now seventy, professed himself Mrs. Woffington's "humble admirer" and "his great delight . . . to play Nykin, or Fondlewife in the Old Batchelor, to her Cocky, or Letitia, in the same play." [4] After Cibber withdrew, *The Old Batchelor* was given four more times, with Hippisley resuming Fondlewife.[5]

This resurgence of the comedy was assisted by performances in a third playhouse. Gaining the tacit consent of the authorities, Henry Giffard, whom some regarded as having ingratiated himself with the Lord Chamberlain by offering evidence leading to the Licensing Act, reopened Goodman's Fields in the autumn of 1740. He resorted to a legal

[1] *The Egotist: or Colley upon Cibber* (Dublin, 1743), p. 40.

[2] The epilogue was printed in *The Egotist*, pp. 41–43, and in the *Apology*, ed. Lowe, II, 265–266.

[3] *The Egotist*, p. 40. The receipts on the two nights Cibber acted for his own benefit were: Jan. 13, £171 3s 6d; Jan. 14, £118 8s. Shenstone, who saw one of these performances, mentioned that Cibber in the epilogue "does not only make a bare confession, but an *ostentation* of all his follies. . . . I do not wonder he pleased extremely; but to a considering man there is something strangely disagreeable, to hear a scandalous life recommended by one of his age, and as much satisfaction shewn in the review of it, as if it had been a perfect galaxy of virtues. An Athenian audience would have shewn their different sentiments on this occasion. But I am acting the part of Jeremy Collier, and indeed in some degree of an hypocrite, for I confess I was highly pleased with him myself." *Letters of Shenstone*, pp. 14–15.

[4] *Memoirs of the Life of Garrick*, I, *309.

[5] For the late performances the receipts usually did not equal those for the first three: Jan. 19, £105 5s; March 10, a benefit for Hippisley (Fondlewife), £203 14s; April 11, a benefit for Bencraft, £124 11s; April 15, £38 11s.

technicality which he probably could not have utilized without the consent of the government. He announced that the theater would offer a concert in two parts, with an interval of two hours during which a play would be offered "gratis." For several years this stratagem succeeded, and an occasional manager of booths or other theaters copied Giffard's scheme. Giffard presented *The Old Batchelor* within a week after he opened Goodman's Fields. Quite naturally the Giffards, as Bellmour and Laetitia, were the principals. Among the fairly talented actors associated with him were Paget (Heartwell), Blakes (Sharper), Oates (Sir Joseph), and Jack Dunstall (Bluff). There were others of whom London had heard little: Crofts (Vainlove), Julian (Fondlewife), Sowden (Setter), and Mrs. Middleton (Belinda). He staged the comedy twice, as did Drury Lane.

Unlike *The Old Batchelor, The Double Dealer* varied little during these four seasons. Although Drury Lane never exhibited it as frequently as in 1735–36 (13 performances), it was acted 4 times in each of the three succeeding years. The cast, though changing frequently, was not weakened. In 1737–38,[6] for example, Charles Macklin replaced Berry as Lord Froth, and in the next year three actors, all capable, played Brisk: Theophilus Cibber, Cross, and Woodward. Yet in 1740–41, after offering it 28 times in five years, Drury Lane omitted it. From 1735 to 1739, during the peak of Drury Lane's revival, Covent Garden let *The Double Dealer* go almost unacted. When Drury Lane's interest in it began to lessen, Rich returned it to his stage on February 26, 1739, with performances on 3 successive evenings. Hippisley, Ryan, Chapman, and Mrs. Hallam resumed their former roles and were joined by Hale (Mellefont), Bridgwater (Lord Touchwood), and Rosco (Maskwell). Mrs. Horton, "in Comedy, without a Rival," [7] played Lady Froth, and Mrs. Vincent, whom Chetwood thought "a very promising young Actress," [8] played Cynthia. In 1739–40 the company offered the comedy 4 times, with Theophilus Cibber, who had left Drury Lane in another of his many changes from theater to theater, as Brisk; in 1740–41, with no competition, Covent Garden offered the comedy only twice.

[6] In the summer of 1738 a London company acting in Canterbury gave *The Double Dealer* there, apparently its first performance in that city (Rosenfeld, *Strolling Players*, p. 230).

[7] *History of the English Stage* (1741), pp. 164–165. In *An Apology for the Life of Mr. T. C., Comedian,* there was an extended account of her powers: "Mrs. *H . . t . . n,* though past the *heyday* of her *Beauty,* yet betrays so little decay of Youth, that an *inexpressible Somewhat* in her Air, Face, and Mein throws out such a Glow of Health and Chearfulness, that, on the Stage, few Spectators that are not past it, can behold her without *Desire;* and, in the Fullness of my Heart, I may venture to confess, that the *Desirable* is so predominant in her that my Soul has a *Taste* or *Tendre* for Mrs. *H . . t . . n*" (p. 141).

[8] *General History of the Stage,* p. 229.

Love for Love did steadily better between 1737 and 1741. It was given in 1737–38 4 times, all at Drury Lane. In the next season not only was it acted 5 times there, with Macklin succeeding Miller as Ben and Woodward following Macklin as Jeremy, but Rich also offered it for the first time since 1719–20. It was not a real revival, however, for he gave it late in the season and only once (May 2, 1739), as a benefit for Mr. and Miss Oates. In 1739–40 he again presented it only once, and he never really pushed the play for in the next thirteen years he gave it only 4 times, whereas Drury Lane gave it frequently every season. Yet Rich's cast, though frequently changing, was not without considerable merit. Thomas Walker, still basking in his *Beggar's Opera* fame, acted Scandal. Thomas Chapman, "much and justly admired in parts of absurd impudence, of bold impertinence, and pert foppery," played Tattle. The amusing Hippisley, "of lively humour and droll pleasantry, which he often pushed to their full extent [and at his] first appearance . . . was always received with a loud laugh and a burst of applause," [9] assumed Foresight. The principal actress was Mrs. Horton (Mrs. Foresight), and Miss Oates, who shared in the benefit on May 2, 1739, acted Prue. The contrast to Covent Garden's single offering of it in 1739–40 lies in Drury Lane's 8 presentations. In the next season Covent Garden omitted it, but Goodman's Fields, reopened by Giffard, offered it 3 times to Drury Lane's 5. As before, the Giffards were the principals of the cast.

In 1737 the bitter quarrels over the Licensing Act brought *The Way of the World* into attention again. Although these disputes were basically political, there were literary ramifications. One result of attacks upon the Act by the *Craftsman* and defense of it by the *Daily Gazetteer* in the summer of 1737 was that *The Way of the World* was dragged into the controversy. When the *Craftsman* asserted that the London stage was less libertine than that of the ancient Greeks, especially less so than Greek comedy, the *Gazetteer* (July 16, 1737) cited *The Way of the World* as eloquent proof to the contrary. The periodical stated that it had made "an *Examen*" of the comedy, choosing it because Congreve wrote it after having "been disciplined by Mr. *Collier*" and because it had recently been played and "the Ladies have not forborn shewing themselves in the Front-Boxes, while Mrs. *Fainall* and Mrs. *Marwood*, two of the top Characters, two Women living and glorying in Adultery, were inculcating the Practice of it on the Stage." All the characters, for that matter, were immoral, and the wit not so great as the "smaller Judges" claim, for the "Traps laid for Jests in it, are like the Traps laid for Claps in Tragedy." The writer added that "that

9 Davies, *Memoirs of the Life of Garrick*, i, 30–32.

Sort of Trap-Wit being forced and affected, and consequently out of Nature, loses its Character in a Species of Poetry, which is the Posture of human Life and raises Laughter without Pleasure." These remarks, which might have precipitated an enlightening discussion of the wit and morality of Congreve's comedies as they were viewed in 1737, came to no conclusion. Apparently no one asked for the "Examen" which the writer promised, and the argument went no further. This castigation of the comedy had no discernible effect upon the current vogue of the play. For two seasons after the Licensing Act it was acted 3 times yearly in Covent Garden and 5 times in 1739–40, with 1 performance yearly in Drury Lane. There were no major changes in the casts, though Peg Woffington, for her own benefit, acted Millamant once in 1740–41, interrupting temporarily Mrs. Horton's success in that role. Mrs. Woffington did not frequently play Millamant until 1749.

Unlike the comedies, *The Mourning Bride* fared rather poorly during the four seasons following the Licensing Act and did not have a good season again until 1750–51. In 1737–38 Covent Garden offered it 3 times to Drury Lane's 2, a season not equalled during the ten years. In Covent Garden Stephens played the King for his own benefit (April 19, 1738). After a sensational first season (1734–35), he had been acclaimed by some as superior to either Cibber or Quin, but he never quite fulfilled that promise. In Drury Lane several players from Goodman's Fields joined the cast: Havard as Gonsalez, Thomas Wright as Garcia, and Mrs. Giffard as Almeria. Apparently these changes disturbed the company, for *An Apology for the Life of Mr. T. C., Comedian* reported that Fleetwood dismissed some regular members to make way for the players from Goodman's Fields. "This gave new Uneasiness to the old Stock, for we look'd on them in a contemptible Light; and when the Season came on, and Parts were cast to these *exotic* Actors, still more and more murmuring Taunts and Jealousies arose. The Master favour'd several of these additional Recruits in a particular Manner. . . . This still made more Faction in our State, till at last it was divided into two Parties, the *Riff-Raffs,* and the *Scabs*" (p. 108). This point of view was presumably Theophilus Cibber's, who was again involved in disagreements with the manager and who soon left the company. In 1740–41 Giffard again reopened Goodman's Fields but offered the tragedy only once, for the last time in that theater. Although Giffard had given it during five seasons only, his offerings accounted for nearly a tenth of the total *The Mourning Bride* achieved in the eighteenth century.

At the end of 1740–41 London could not know, of course, that it was approaching a new dramatic age. There had been during the third and fourth decades so many changes—in the types of plays, number of theaters, rise and decline of playhouses, visits of foreign comedians, rise of novelty in ballad opera and pantomime, and governmental censorship—that nearly every year had its variation or novelty. The advent of David Garrick was to be a far more substantial landmark, for never again was the theatrical world quite the same. Although he did not immediately perform any miracles or revolutionize theatrical practice, he nevertheless brought a new concept into acting and ultimately as a great actor who was also a manager he exerted an unmistakable influence during the thirty-five years of his stagecraft. Congreve's plays did not escape this influence. In the forty years preceding his debut, they had gained steadily in popularity until in the four years preceding Garrick they comprised 6.2 per cent of the total offerings of the theaters, a quite remarkable achievement. Now they faced a test, for a new actor, who must select his roles according to his preferences and talents in the light of the theatrical requirements of his day, frequently alters the repertory and public taste by his creation of a large following.

David Garrick made his bow to London under the guidance of Henry Giffard, who, though never a great manager, was an influential man in diverse ways. He shared in producing the Licensing Act. He provided stimulating competition for the older playhouses, but his unmistakable claim upon posterity lay in his giving Garrick his first opportunity to act in London. After he had come to London and established himself as a wine merchant, Garrick had shown an intense interest in the theatrical world. He had spent much time with Charles Macklin, a vigorous Irishman whose liking for the stage kept him on it until he was past ninety. Under this influence Garrick acted in a burlesque *Julius Caesar* at the home of Edward Cave, publisher of the *Gentleman's Magazine*. He wrote *Lethe*. He acted Harlequin one evening in a pantomime in Goodman's Fields when the usual performer was ill. By the spring of 1741 Garrick and Giffard apparently were close acquaintances. In the following summer Giffard took Garrick with him as a member of his strolling company, and in Ipswich Garrick acted before a paying audience as Aboan in *Oroonoko,* his blackened countenance and assumed name of Lyddall presumably being a sufficient disguise should the venture prove unsuccessful.

Garrick and Giffard returned to London by autumn and Giffard began his second season of "gratis" plays at Goodman's Fields. On October 19 Garrick acted Richard III for his first dramatic role there and received a reception which the *Daily Post* described as "the most extraordinary and great that was ever known." Garrick quickly won the town, and by spring he had an immense though not universal following. Gray wrote on May 24, 1742, that Garrick was one whom "the Town are horn-mad after; there are a dozen Dukes of a night at Goodmans-fields sometimes, & yet I am stiff in the opposition." [10] Two nights later Horace Walpole wrote that "all the run is now after Garrick, a wine-merchant, who is turned player, at Goodman's Fields." In Garrick's acting Walpole saw "nothing wonderful . . . but it is heresy to say so." [11] In spite of such doubting voices, Garrick became a great actor. It was he who, more than any one else in his century, brought to the stage an ease and naturalness in tone, voice, and manner which made London conscious of the archaic and unreal quality of the highly declamatory, formal style of his predecessors.

Garrick appeared in a great many roles during his first season, but he acted in only two of Congreve's plays. *The Old Batchelor* came first (Jan. 5, 1742); *The Way of the World* followed (Jan. 27). Although Garrick possibly was not a brilliant success in either, his presence raised performances of *The Old Batchelor* to 11 in Goodman's Fields alone, with 3 at Covent Garden and 1 at Drury Lane. Acted first on January 5, it was repeated 8 times at Goodman's Fields in that month and twice later. Garrick acted Fondlewife, whose humor he may have overplayed,[12] but the town attended and applauded. In this role Garrick did not please at least one of his friends, Thomas Newton, who wrote him on January 18, "I am not fond of your acting such parts as Fondlewife," and went on to explain, "You who are equal to the greatest parts, strangely demean yourself in acting anything that is low and little." No matter how well Garrick might do such a part, Newton argued, there was an "abundance of people who hit off low humour" and there was not half the merit in excelling them as in playing "the hero in Tragedy, and the fine gentleman in Comedy." [13] On the stage with Garrick were Henry Giffard as Heartwell, William Giffard as Bellmour, Elizabeth Hippisley, daughter of the famous comedian, as Sylvia, and Mrs. Yates, the first wife of the actor Richard Yates, as Lucy. Two promising actresses, Mrs. Dunstall and Mrs. Bambridge, were Araminta and Belinda.

Although Giffard had previously offered *The Old Batchelor, Love for Love,* and *The Mourning Bride,* he had never before this season ventured *The Way of the World.* It was offered first on January 27, 1742, midway in the season, with Garrick as Witwoud. It apparently

[10] *Correspondence of Thomas Gray,* I, 205.
[11] *The Letters of Horace Walpole,* ed. Mrs. Paget Toynbee (Oxford, 1903), I, 228–229.
[12] Percy Fitzgerald, *The Life of David Garrick* (London, 1899), p. 266.
[13] *The Private Correspondence of David Garrick* (London, 1831), I, 5–6.

was not extremely well received, for it was repeated on the next night and then only twice more before the end of the season, a great contrast to the eleven performances of *The Old Batchelor*. Garrick never played in the comedy again. As a whole, however, the cast was excellent. Henry and William Giffard acted Mirabell and Fainall, with Mrs. Giffard as Millamant. John Dunstall, a promising young actor, appeared as Sir Wilful, and Richard Yates, beginning a successful career, acted Petulant, with Mrs. Yates as Mrs. Marwood. Mrs. Bambridge, who later was engaged by Rich, acted Mrs. Fainall, and two daughters of John Hippisley—Jane and Elizabeth—acted Foible and Mincing.[14] This production of *The Way of the World*, Giffard's only venture with it, did not offer serious competition to Covent Garden, which presented it 6 times and closed its season with the comedy on June 2.[15] Perhaps Giffard picked an inauspicious moment to stage it, for in the next few years it entered one of its periodic declines in favor.

Although Garrick did not appear in any other of Congreve's plays, Giffard continued to stage *Love for Love* without him. It was given at Goodman's Fields 3 times, with Henry Giffard as Valentine on two evenings and William Giffard in the role on the other evening, but Mr. and Mrs. Richard Yates as Ben and Mrs. Foresight were their only genuine support. At Covent Garden the comedy was given only once (March 27, 1742) as a benefit for Bridgwater, who acted Ben for that night only. The cast was greatly changed. Scandal was played by Oliver Cashel, whom Macklin had brought from Bristol to Drury Lane, from which he quickly changed to Covent Garden. That night was also the debut of Georgiana Bellamy, who acted Prue for her first appearance as an actress. Although she was reputedly only fifteen, her youth and high spirit did not win her immediate acclaim and the comedy benefited little from the publicity she gave it. In Drury Lane the comedy had 6 performances, and even there the cast frequently changed. Young Cibber, after an absence of two years, again played Tattle. Upon the death of Milward, Havard succeeded to Valentine. Jeremy was acted by Neale, whom Shenstone, writing on January 21, 1741, praised highly; after naming Cibber, who rarely acted, and Mrs. Clive as the best performers in London, Shenstone added one more, "in *compliance* with my *own* taste *merely;* and that is Mr. Neal, a fellow who, by *playing*

---

14 A few years later one of the semi-amateur companies which occasionally occupied Goodman's Fields gave *The Way of the World* in the spring of 1746 as a benefit for Furnival, the principal actor. Little is known concerning the performance.

15 It was acted at Bristol in the summer of 1742 as a benefit for John Hippisley, the manager of Jacob's Wells Theater, Bristol. It brought the good sum of £55 6s 6d (Rosenfeld, *Strolling Players*, p. 214).

the fool, had gained my particular *esteem.*" [16] In the same year Johnson, now seventy-seven, relinquished Foresight, a part he had held
since 1708.

The Double Dealer and *The Mourning Bride* were far less popular
than Congreve's other plays. The comedy was given three times by
Rich, who, losing Theophilus Cibber to Drury Lane, had secured four
players from the opposition, three of whom played in the comedy:
Henry Woodward and Thomas Chapman alternating as Brisk, and
Mrs. Pritchard again playing Lady Touchwood. In Drury Lane the
comedy made but one appearance. The tragedy was even less in favor.
Neither Drury Lane nor Goodman's Fields offered it, and Rich gave
it but twice. Perhaps the retirement of Mrs. Porter caused Rich soon
to abandon the tragedy, for he did not offer it for several seasons. Even
Drury Lane gave it only once between 1739–40 and 1750–51, but it was
not alone among tragedies in receiving less appreciation. *The Unhappy Favorite, All for Love,* and *Oedipus* had fallen to fewer than
two performances a season, and *Oroonoko,* though more frequently
staged, was less popular than it had been.

Garrick's great success in his first season had shown the managers
of the other playhouses that something would have to be done. It
was, to their minds, perhaps not unreasonable to allow a man like
Henry Giffard to operate a third theater, but it was certainly insup-
portable to watch the town flock to Goodman's Fields at the expense
of the patent houses. After all, it was open only by sufferance, and the
older houses had the letter and power of the law on their side. As a
result, Garrick was engaged at Drury Lane, and Giffard was allowed
to continue his management—but without his star performer. Giffard,
a man not easily discouraged, made the best of the situation and, as
he had done in 1736–37, took his company to the older but larger
playhouse in Lincoln's Inn Fields, where he continued to offer Congreve's plays, although not so successfully as in the previous season.
Garrick being gone, Theophilus Cibber, who "generally mixed so much
of false spirit and grimace in his acting, that he often displeased the
judicious spectator," [17] played Fondlewife for the first time. Mozeen,
"a very improving Actor" in Chetwood's opinion, played Sharper, and
Mrs. Chetwood, whose husband thought her "an agreeable *Actress,*
when the Part suited her Voice," [18] was Lucy. On February 28, 1743,
Giffard offered a condensation of the play called *Fondlewife and Laeti-*

---

[16] *Letters of Shenstone,* p. 16.
[17] Davies, *Memoirs of the Life of Garrick,* I, 31.
[18] *General History of the Stage,* pp. 193, 130.

tia as a benefit for Cibber, with Heartwell, Vainlove, Sir Joseph, Fondle-wife, and Laetitia as the only parts advertised. He also gave *Love for Love* twice, one performance being a benefit for the widow and four children of William Milward, who had died the year before. At the end of the season Giffard made his peace with the other houses and joined the company at Drury Lane.

The engagement of Garrick at Drury Lane did not lead to a broad-ening of his interest in Congreve's plays or an increase in performances. On the contrary, the five plays dwindled from 41 performances in 1741–42 to 22 in the next year, with Garrick acting only in *The Old Batchelor*. And the withdrawal of Garrick from Goodman's Fields re-duced performances of Congreve's plays there from 18 to 4. For several years, in fact, Garrick appeared only in *The Old Batchelor*. This state of affairs was not necessarily due to a reluctance on his part toward playing Congreve. Part of the difficulty lay in his relationship to other actors at Drury Lane. If he, a newcomer there, undertook parts long in the possession of other actors, he ran the risk of rousing jealousies and creating factions. Of Garrick's hesitation to take roles in which he supplanted persons belonging to his own company, Davies wrote: "Per-haps he was not entirely pleased with his representations of those parts; it is still more probable, that he did not wish either to offend, or risque a competition with, either Woodward or Macklin." [19] With respect to *The Old Batchelor,* in fact, his principal colleague, Charles Macklin, was also his major rival. For five performances Garrick acted Fondle-wife, one of his correspondents writing him that he "could not help thinking it a good deal over-acted, especially in that sort of feeble trot you seemed to affect so much. A part over-acted ever makes the actor look foolish." [20] Macklin played Bluff on these occasions, but near the end of the season, when Garrick absented himself because his salary was grossly in arrears, Macklin played Fondlewife. As Bluff, Macklin re-placed the aged Ben Johnson, who had retired in the previous year. At Covent Garden James Quin, whose histrionic powers had been sharply contrasted against Garrick's naturalness, played Heartwell four times, but the true rivalry between the two actors lay in tragedy, not comedy. As a counter-attraction to Garrick, Rich had engaged Mrs. Cib-ber, who had not been seen in London since 1738, to play Laetitia. With eleven performances and one condensation, *The Old Batchelor* had a good season.

[19] *Memoirs of the Life of Garrick*, I, 53–54.

[20] *Private Correspondence of Garrick*, I, 27. The letter is dated Dec. 4, without year; it would probably be 1742, for only in that year did Garrick act Fondlewife on Dec. 3.

For the next few years the theaters were somewhat unsettled, a condition which continued until 1747–48, when Garrick assumed the
management of Drury Lane. There were many disturbing elements.
Not only did the rise of Garrick disturb the status quo, but Garrick and
Macklin had serious quarrels, and Garrick's brilliance affected Quin's
popularity with the public. In addition, financial conditions within
Drury Lane (and sometimes in Covent Garden) were unsatisfactory,
eventually so much so, in fact, that Fleetwood sold his share of the
patent. After great success in Drury Lane Garrick became ill during
1745 and spent part of the autumn and winter in Dublin. When he
returned, he joined Covent Garden. Many other actors shifted from
company to company as the two houses jostled each other in their
moves for dominance. These were also less satisfactory years for Congreve's plays. Nearly all of them declined in popularity, and some—
particularly *The Mourning Bride* and *The Way of the World*—were
so infrequently given as to represent a very small portion of the repertory. During Garrick's association with Drury Lane, a theater which
had always been more devoted to Congreve than had Rich's theaters,
the young actor made no effort to undertake new roles in Congreve's
plays, and because he dominated the scene, his choice of parts to a
great degree determined the vogue of plays. A survey of the fortunes
of each play from 1743–44 through 1746–47 will clarify the changes
that came over their reception in the theaters.

The Old Batchelor was clearly declining in favor, though still rather
frequently given. From 15 performances in 1741–42, it dropped to 12
in the next year, and to 7 in 1743–44. The decline was accelerated by
dissension within Drury Lane late in 1743. Both Macklin and Garrick
had quarrelled with Fleetwood, the manager, and by the opening of
the winter season neither had settled his grievances and their absence
greatly weakened the casts. By December, however, Garrick had reached
an agreement with Fleetwood, but Macklin had not, and believed himself deserted by Garrick. The two were then at odds. As a result, *The
Old Batchelor* suffered and was given there only three times, with a
different Fondlewife each night. In December it was Theophilus Cibber, whose "Fondlewife is true Comedy"; [21] in January it was Colley
Cibber, who returned to play that part and Sir John Brute; and in
April it was Garrick. From Goodman's Fields, which was again closed,
came Henry Giffard and his wife to play Bellmour and Belinda.[22]

[21] *The Present State of the Stage in Great Britain and Ireland* (London, 1753), p.
54.

[22] *The Old Batchelor* was acted at Smock Alley, Dublin, in the summer of 1743,
with Theophilus Cibber as Fondlewife, Giffard as Bellmour, and Mrs. Giffard as
Laetitia. John Genest, *Some Account of the English Stage* (Bath, 1832), x, 320.

Bridges played Heartwell, and Peg Woffington, Laetitia. For the next ten years the comedy was seen less and less frequently, even though in 1744–45 Macklin, his grievances aired and adjusted, played Fondle-wife again. In that season and the next it was given 6 performances a year, but in 1746–47 Drury Lane relinquished the comedy altogether, for the first time since 1707–08. The previous breaks in its continuity —in 1709–10 and 1733–34—had been caused by internal quarrels which disrupted the company and each interruption had been for a season only. The omission in 1746–47, however, was more important, for it was not caused by any crisis within the company and it was not acted there again for seven seasons. From 15 performances in 1741–42 it dropped to 2 in 1746–47.[23]

Even an extraordinary season in Covent Garden during 1746–47 failed to aid *The Old Batchelor.* Garrick had been engaged by Rich, and Quin and Mrs. Cibber re-engaged. Quin and Garrick, exponents of widely differing conceptions of acting, met on the same stage and proved a great attraction. As one periodical recorded, *"Rich* [has] got *Quin, Garrick,* Mrs. *Cibber,* and Mrs. *Pritchard* to the new House. The Consequence has been, that the Stage was never, in my Memory, so fashionable; not even in the Time of Mrs. *Oldfield*'s highest Fame. A good Taste both of Acting and of Plays themselves, is much more general than I ever expected to have seen it; and those who are skilled in such Matters, tell me, that *Rich* will be a greater Gainer this Season than has been known for these many Years."[24] This "good Taste," however, did not extend to an enthusiasm for Congreve. Although Quin and Garrick acted together in several plays—their first appearance together as Horatio (Quin) and Lothario (Garrick) in *The Fair Penitent* was a sensation—they did not appear together in *The Old Batchelor.* Although they had both previously acted in that comedy and their appearance in it would no doubt have been immensely interesting, they made no attempt to appear in it or in any other of Congreve's dramas.

From 1743–44 to 1746–47, when *The Double Dealer* remained pretty much Rich's property, it varied considerably in frequency of performance. Rich gave it 11 times to Drury Lane's 1, yet occasionally, as in 1743–44, Covent Garden's offerings declined to a single performance. The principal addition to the cast was Catherine Clive, a "natural

---

[23] The Haymarket on April 22, 1747, offered a condensed version of *The Old Batchelor* called *The Credulous Husband,* with only Fondlewife, Bellmour and Laetitia advertised. In the summer of 1747 Macklin took the Drury Lane company to Norwich, where he acted Fondlewife (Rosenfeld, *Strolling Players,* p. 61).

[24] *The Museum, or The Literary and Historical Register,* II (Feb., 28, 1747), 382.

Actress," [25] as Lady Froth. Coming from Drury Lane, where, during a quarrel between Garrick and Fleetwood, she had offended both men, she now supplanted Mrs. Cibber as Rich's principal actress. In 1746–47 Quin reappeared after a year's absence to resume Maskwell. *The Museum* stated that, perhaps stimulated by Garrick, Quin, who previously as "the Head of the Fraternity; but a very different Man from what he is at present, and meerly a bad Copy of *Booth*," was much "improved, beyond what you will really imagine." The writer was uncertain whether "Time or Emulation has had the greatest hand in improving him," but "he has got more Variety, and much more Spirit. He was always a tolerably just Speaker; but then he was hardly anything more; he recited, rather than acted." [26] With Quin in the leading role, the comedy was acted 4 times.

During the four years preceding Garrick's assumption of the management of Drury Lane, *Love for Love* was Congreve's most popular play. In 1743–44 the disbanding of Giffard's company brought him to Drury Lane as Valentine and William Giffard there as Scandal. Of Richard Yates (Ben) it was in 1759 observed: "I never saw so good a Ben in my life." In 1744–45 Mrs. Giffard joined the cast as Angelica, and a season later Mrs. Clive reappeared there as Prue, although her "figure and her years are indeed against her in Miss Prue and Hoyden"; nevertheless, "her performance is just and pleasing even in these, as in every thing she undertakes to perform." [27] And Samuel Foote thought her "the best Actress in her Walk, that I, or perhaps any Man living, has seen. She also is peculiarly happy in hitting the Humours of Characters in low Life. The awkward Forwardness of a Country Girl, the ridiculous affected Airs of a Lady's Woman, or the pert Behaviour of an intriguing Chambermaid." [28] Even so, *Love for Love,* like *The Old Batchelor,* was not so frequently acted as it had been, although during 1744–45 a new company appeared in Goodman's Fields and gave the comedy 5 times, with Townley and Miss Houghton as Valentine and Prue. In the next year it was given but 2 times there, and in 1746–47 but once.

Similarly, *The Way of the World* declined greatly from its high level of 10 performances in 1741–42. From then to the close of the fifth

[25] Chetwood, *General History of the Stage*, p. 126.

[26] *The Museum* (Feb. 28, 1747), p. 382. In the summer of 1746 Rosco chose *The Double Dealer* for his benefit at Jacob's Wells Theater, Bristol, where it brought £50 (Rosenfeld, *Strolling Players*, p. 214).

[27] *General View of the Stage* (1759), pp. 272, 288.

[28] *The Roman and English Comedy Consider'd and Compar'd* (London, 1747), pp. 41–42.

decade it was acted every season except one, but often only twice and never more than three times. It was almost exclusively the property of Covent Garden, being given only once at Drury Lane. The amateur company at Goodman's Fields managed to offer it once in 1745–46.[29] And the account of *The Mourning Bride* during these years was neither spirited nor long. It had one performance (Oct. 15, 1743), when Drury Lane offered it, with Delane once more appearing as Osmyn.[30]

The period between 1737 and 1747 was, on the whole, a critical one for Congreve's plays, though the crisis had not sufficiently developed by the end of that period to indicate clearly what their future was to be. In the years before Garrick's debut Congreve's plays accounted for 6.2 per cent of the repertory; in the six seasons from 1741–42 to 1746–47 their share declined to about 5 per cent, a good share in itself but a substantial falling off from that of the previous period. During the six seasons Garrick had appeared in two of the comedies. To one, *The Old Batchelor,* his presence had resulted in a decisive stimulation, but his acting in *The Way of the World* had not genuinely aided it. Garrick had not appeared in the other plays, perhaps because he was not greatly interested in doing so, perhaps because he could not do so without displacing some of his fellow actors from their customary roles. Whatever the cause, the plays had declined. But Garrick in the autumn of 1747–48 was to be the manager of Drury Lane. Perhaps Garrick would have greater freedom to choose roles in Congreve's plays if he wished to do so. At least, Congreve devotees of the mid-century could hope so.

29 On Sept. 8, 1744, *The Way of the World* was acted at Westbury. See *The Purefoy Letters, 1735–1753* (London, 1931), II, 380. It was also acted at Edinburgh on Feb. 24, 1749 (Dibdin, *Annals of the Edinburgh Stage,* p. 62).

30 *The Mourning Bride* was given in Edinburgh on March 6, 1744 (Dibdin, *Annals of the Edinburgh Stage,* p. 55) and at York during 1745 (Rosenfeld, *Strolling Players,* p. 137).

CHAPTER VI

THE AGE OF GARRICK, 1747–1776

In 1747 David Garrick undertook the most ambitious venture of his career. On April 9 he purchased from James Lacy a half interest in Drury Lane and on September 15 the two managers opened with *The Merchant of Venice*. For the occasion Samuel Johnson contributed a prologue which set the tone for a reformation of taste and theatrical practice. On the whole, Garrick had a good season. He had engaged some of the best talent available, and he also brought to Drury Lane one of his successes of the previous year, *The Suspicious Husband*. During the first years of his management, there was, however, little change in the status of Congreve's plays. In his first managerial season Garrick offered only *Love for Love,* and it did not reach the stage until late, January 12, 1748; it was repeated twice in the spring. In the next season Garrick added *The Double Dealer,* but neither it nor *Love for Love* was a marked success.

In fact, from 1747–48 through 1749–50 these were the only Congreve plays offered in Drury Lane, and they were eclipsed by other pieces, both old and new. In 1748–49, for example, *Romeo and Juliet* was revived for 19 performances, yet Garrick's revival of *The Double Dealer* produced only 3 performances of it as contrasted with twice as many in Covent Garden. Drury Lane retained, however, its customary superiority with *Love for Love,* 10 performances to one. During 1747–48 Isaac Sparks acted Sir Sampson. Although Chetwood had not seen him, he had been informed, "by very good Judges, that he performs the Character of Sir *Sampson Legend* . . . to the utmost Perfection." [1] Havard played Valentine, and Mills assumed Scandal, Havard's previous part. Mrs. Pritchard replaced Mrs. Giffard as Angelica. During these years Garrick, however, did not attempt a part in *Love for Love*.

In Covent Garden all five of Congreve's plays were offered during one or another season from 1747–48 through 1749–50, but performances were not numerous. In fact, it is surprising that Rich managed to do as well as he did, for 1747–48 was one of his weakest seasons. Not only had Garrick left him, but Quin, irritated at the public's open admiration of his rival, had retired in disgust to Bath. Rich had only Theophilus Cibber, Ryan, Foote, and Mrs. Horton against Drury Lane's

[1] *General History of the Stage,* p. 221.

Garrick, Mrs. Cibber, Mrs. Clive, Mrs. Woffington, Macklin, Mrs. Macklin, Delane, Mrs. Pritchard, and Yates. The odds were so heavy against
Rich that several times his theater was nearly empty and performances
were cancelled. Rich was most successful with *The Old Batchelor*,
which was given 3 times in 1747–48 and 2 times in each of the succeeding two seasons. Samuel Foote, who had played Fondlewife in *The
Credulous Husband* a year before, took the place of Hippisley, who
died early in 1748. By the next season Covent Garden was strengthened,
for Quin, mollified, returned to play Heartwell, and Peg Woffington,
once more under Rich's management, acted Laetitia, although her
greatest success lay in Shakespearean plays and Rowe's *Lady Jane Gray*.
The Old Batchelor was repeated there in 1750–51, but in 1751–52, for
the first time since 1706–07, it was not given anywhere in London. Probably Covent Garden omitted it because Peg Woffington, restless again,
had gone to Dublin. The vogue of *The Old Batchelor* was dwindling,
however.

During the three seasons beginning with 1747–48 *The Double Dealer*
did fairly well, with 3 performances in Drury Lane and 6 in Covent
Garden. Although Rich omitted it in 1747–48, when his company was
at its weakest, he restored it for a single performance in 1748–49. Peg
Woffington acted Lady Touchwood for the first time, and Georgiana
Bellamy played Lady Froth. Theophilus Cibber (Brisk) had also returned to Rich's company, but it was probably Mrs. Woffington's presence which increased performances in 1749–50 to 5. Congreve's other
plays fared less happily in Covent Garden. *Love for Love* was given only
once during the three years. *The Mourning Bride* also had a single performance,[2] a benefit (April 3, 1750) for Mrs. Horton, who acted Zara for
her last appearance in the tragedy. The receipts (£67 9s 6d) were very
low, especially for a performance honoring an actress retiring after thirty-
five years even though she now had an outmoded manner. In the next
year Mrs. Pritchard, who spoke naturally and simply, succeeded her in
many tragic roles. The benefit was also a debut for Sparks in the role
of the King, a part which he held for some years, although one writer
thought that he "requires something of agitated passion in Tragedy,
[which] he sometimes overdoes."[3] Years later the *Dramatic Censor* (II,
413), which considered the King a dreadful role, stated that the "highest merit that can be attained is to pass through him inoffensively, and
in this view we have seen Mr. SPARKS." Almeria was acted by Miss Bellamy, and Osmyn was acted by a "Gentleman," following Delane's

[2] It was given at Bath on March 21, 1748, and on Feb. 19, 1750 (Rosenfeld, *Strolling
Players*, pp. 181–182).
[3] *General View of the Stage*, p. 302.

death. In spite of recasting the tragedy, Rich did not offer it again for five years. And *The Way of the World,* with only 3 performances in as many years, fared poorly also.

Quite clearly Garrick's assumption of the management of Drury Lane had not brought a genuine renewal of appreciation for Congreve's plays. From 1747–48 to 1749–50 Drury Lane offered only 13 performances of the five plays, as compared with 18 at Covent Garden. As a result, the dramas, which had had 41 performances in 1741–42, dwindled to 16 in 1743–44, and to 8, 11, and 12 in the three seasons beginning with 1747–48. In view of the steadily rising vogue which they had experienced in the preceding thirty years, this was a discouraging reversal of popularity. Fortunately in 1750–51 there were genuine revivals of two of them—*The Mourning Bride* and *The Way of the World.* Both came on at Drury Lane, where Garrick, hitherto neglecting Congreve, presumably was responsible for the restorations, although he acted only in the tragedy. Both plays received sufficient impetus to maintain themselves on the stage for several years thereafter.

The Way of the World appeared first (Nov. 15, 1750) and was acted 10 times in Drury Lane,[4] its best showing there thus far. Although the cast was mainly new, it was not wholly so. Henry Woodward (Witwoud) had previously amused London: "If frequent peals of laughter be a test of merit, Mr. Woodward deservedly enjoys the favour of the town." [5] Mrs. Pritchard (Millamant) [6] and Mrs. Clive (Mrs. Marwood), undertaking these roles for the first time, had previously appeared in the comedy. Newly cast were William Havard (Fainall), Palmer (Mirabell), Ned Shuter (Petulant), who later changed to Sir Wilful when he was engaged at Covent Garden. Yates' Sir Wilful was one of the "still stronger proofs of his abilities." [7] The receipts, which ranged between £50 and £180, averaged better than £110 and were higher in the later part of the season. The comedy continued to do well, with 7 and 5 performances in Drury Lane in 1751–52 and 1752–53.

The revival of *The Mourning Bride* was preceded by competitive runs of *Romeo and Juliet*—Garrick, Woodward, and Miss Bellamy at Drury Lane; Barry, Macklin, and Mrs. Cibber at Covent Garden—for twelve consecutive nights. When Drury Lane staged Congreve's tragedy, how-

---

[4] It was acted once at Covent Garden during this season, and in the spring at Norwich (Rosenfeld, *Strolling Players,* p. 80).

[5] *General View of the Stage,* p. 263.

[6] Mrs. Pritchard succeeded several famous Millamants—Mrs. Oldfield, Mrs. Heron, Mrs. Clive, Mrs. Horton, and Mrs. Woffington—and from 1760 to her retirement in 1768 "the town was charm'd . . . with her representation" (Davies, *Memoirs of the Life of David Garrick,* II, 179).

[7] *General View of the Stage,* p. 272.

ever, Covent Garden did not present a competitive cast for it. The performance of *The Mourning Bride* on December 3, 1750, was the first of 13 in that season, a very successful recovery from the relatively dormant state of the play in recent years. No doubt it was the opportunity to see Garrick act Osmyn which gave the tragedy its drawing power. The *Dramatic Censor* (1770) reported of him: "Mr. GARRICK, we think, in the soliloquies, and the scene with Heli, outstripped every competitor; but the Moorish habit proved rather too much for his figure, and the amorous passages did not flow from him with . . . natural sincerity" (II, 414). Tate Wilkinson, who saw a performance sometime during the year, stated that Garrick was not in his "secret opinion so enchanting as Barry." [8]

Although Drury Lane had not offered the tragedy for several years, some of the performers, particularly Edward Berry (King), Havard (Gonsalez), and Mrs. Bennet (Leonora), had previously played those roles. The *Dramatic Censor* had special praise for Havard, and Davies stated that "such was the soundness of his judgment, and so respectable his character, that he never met with any marks of displeasure from the public." [9] Most of the performers, however, were new to their parts. Garcia was attempted by Palmer, who should, according to one critic, "quit the Buskin; for though he is a just speaker, yet he is apt sometimes to run into a puerility of tone, which quite enervates his performance; however, his daily improvements encourage us to hope, that he has not reached his utmost perfection." The same writer had praise for Mrs. Pritchard, who was adding Zara as well as Millamant to her roles: "She fills the stage well, her appearance is commanding, and her middle voice clear, intelligible, and melodious. . . . No woman supports better the dignity of Tragedy." [10] With this opinion Churchill in *The Rosciad* (1761) agreed:

> When Congreve's favour'd pantomime to grace,
> She comes a captive queen of Moorish race;
> When love, hate, jealousy, despair and rage,
> With wildest tumults in her breast engage,
> Still equal to herself is Zara seen;
> Her passions are the passion of a Queen. [ll. 809–814]

In general agreement was Samuel Foote, who declared that she "is peculiarly happy in a good Voice, a pleasing Figure, and a correct Judgment." [11] Tate Wilkinson, who saw her play in 1750, said that her

[8] *Memoirs of His Own Life* (York, 1790), I, 38.
[9] *Memoirs of the Life of Garrick*, II, 204.
[10] *General View of the Stage*, pp. 277, 284.
[11] *The Roman and English Comedy Consider'd*, p. 43.

"Zara struck me with admiration," [12] and Davies thought she gave the role importance "by her action, as well as speaking." [13] The *Dramatic Censor* (II, 416) was more reserved, expressing the belief that although she was "majestic," she was also "rather too corpulent. . . . The amorous passages were indeed not so harmonious as might be wished, but in the jealousy she made ample amends." Mrs. Pritchard had now the distinction of acting in all five of Congreve's plays. In the supporting cast was Miss Bellamy as Almeria, whom Wilkinson thought "very inferior" to Mrs. Cibber.[14] The receipts for each of the first six nights approximated £180, a very good figure; for the next four they declined from £170 to £100, and then rallied, reaching £212 on one night.

Although Garrick continued to act Osmyn, performances declined to two in each of the next two seasons. Only one incident enlivened these performances. Catherine Clive, for her own benefit (March 22, 1753), acted Zara. Although her action enabled her to join the list of performers who had appeared in all of Congreve's plays, everyone agreed that, even as an experiment, she should not attempt a tragic role: "Her talents are wholly of a humorous turn. She knows it, and is right in not attempting the serious in Comedy, nor the sublime in Tragedy, as her performance in that case would certainly be attended with a ludicrous disadvantage." [15] That was what happened: "For her own benefit, the comic Clive put on the royal robes of Zara; she found them too heavy, and very wisely never wore them afterwards." [16] The *Dramatic Censor* (II, 416) underlined her deficiencies in the role: "We remember to have seen Mrs. CLIVE make a laughable assault upon Zara, which was nearer burlesque than could well be imagined. Had it not been to excite curiosity upon her night, it would have been one of the most unpardonable attempts that ever was made: exclusive of a voice dreadfully unfit for serious speaking, her person rendered all the King's amorous compliments ludicrous."

During Drury Lane's excellent revivals of the two plays Covent Garden failed to produce the tragedy from 1750–51 through 1753–54. *The Way of the World* was not neglected in Covent Garden, but it was acted only 6 times there to 22 performances in Drury Lane from 1750–51 through 1752–53. During this period it was the only Congreve play performed in both theaters. In 1751–52, with 4 performances in Covent Garden, the comedy had several major changes in the cast. Ridout began a decade of acting Fainall; Dyer replaced Theophilus Cibber as

[12] *Memoirs*, I, 38.
[13] *Memoirs of the Life of Garrick*, II, 178.
[14] *Memoirs*, I, 38.
[15] *General View of the Stage*, p. 288.
[16] Davies, *Dramatic Miscellanies*, III, 210.

Witwoud; and Cushing played Petulant, a part he retained for several years. Mrs. Marwood was played by Mrs. Elmy, whom Chetwood characterized as having a weak voice but meaning very well,[17] and Wilkinson, who had received dramatic tutoring from her, loyally stated that her "merit in Octavia, Lady Grace, or Mrs. Marwood" would never be "erased from my mind." [18] During 1752–53 Rich relied greatly upon Mrs. Bland, who played Millamant, a part she had inherited from Mrs. Woffington. After Hippisley's death, Macklin, upon whom Rich also greatly depended, acted Sir Wilful until Ned Shuter undertook the role. To one writer it seemed that "Mr. Shuter's performance in the comic way is nearer to nature than most of the Comedians on our Stage. His chief excellence lies in old men. The setness and risible turn of his features diffuse a peculiar humour thro' all the parts he plays in low Comedy." [19]

The other three comedies had little success during these three years. *The Old Batchelor,* given only in Covent Garden, had but 3 performances. In 1752–53 Laetitia was assigned to Mrs. Bland, whose "person was rather of the *en bonne point,* but tall, and a good set of features, but by no means elegant: She possessed what was all sublime and precious to Mr. Rich, a fine head of jetty black flowing locks." [20] Rich also continued to offer *The Double Dealer* without competition, and with 7 performances in three years it was much more frequently performed than was *The Old Batchelor.* In 1750–51 the Macklins acted Sir Paul, who had been excellently played by Hippisley for twenty-five years, and Lady Plyant. Chetwood named Lady Plyant as one role in which he had not seen Mrs. Macklin's equal in his thirty years in the theaters: She "knows the Power of her own Talents, and always shines with unborrow'd Light, without the Danger of being eclipsed." In 1751–52 Mrs. Woffington was replaced by Mrs. Elmy, who in Chetwood's opinion had more spirit off stage than on, and from Ireland came Luke Sparks (Maskwell), whom Chetwood placed in the second rank of actors.[21] *Love for Love* did slightly better than *The Old Batchelor* during the three seasons, but it was in a period of infrequent performance. At no time during the previous forty years had it been acted so few times in three years.[22]

[17] *General History of the Stage,* p. 147.
[18] *Memoirs,* I, 82.
[19] *General View of the Stage,* p. 300.
[20] Tate Wilkinson, *The Wandering Patentee* (1795), I, 123.
[21] *General History of the Stage,* pp. 190, 147, 220. On July 23, 1750, *The Double Dealer* was acted, apparently for the first time, in New York, and again in the following season, on Feb. 4, 1751. See G. C. D. Odell, *Annals of the New York Stage* (New York, 1927), I, 35, 40.
[22] *Love for Love* was played at Bath on July 16, 1750, and again in 1751–52. In

After the impressive revivals of *The Way of the World* and *The Mourning Bride* in 1750–51, they lost some of their frequency of performance in the next two years and there was no real change in the status of the other plays. Then in 1753–54 *The Old Batchelor* and *Love for Love,* in their turn, received a great deal more attention. It could hardly be said that the 1750's were returning Congreve's plays to their former dominant position; rather, they entered upon a phase of individual dominance. If there was a pattern to their changing status, it was a revival of one or another with considerable success, followed by a decline in performances and, possibly, disappearance from the stage for a while. In four successive seasons, beginning with 1750–51, *The Way of the World* was acted 11, 11, 6, and 5 times; *The Mourning Bride,* 13, 2, 2, and 0. In 1753–54, *The Old Batchelor* was acted 10 times (9 in Drury Lane), more than in all of the preceding five years, and then declined to 3 performances in 1754–55. In 1753–54 *Love for Love* was given on 7 evenings, more times than in all of the previous three years. On the other hand, *The Mourning Bride,* acted 17 times in the past three years, went unacted, but in 1754–55 was revived for 10 performances. In 1753–54 *The Double Dealer* was missing altogether. Such variations had become the lot of Congreve's plays.

Samuel Foote was primarily responsible for the revival of *The Old Batchelor* and the good showing of *Love for Love* in 1753–54. Foote had acted previously in *The Old Batchelor,* but this was his first attempt at Fondlewife in Drury Lane, which was offering the comedy for the first time in seven years.[23] Foote's friends rallied to the occasion, and the *Gray's Inn Journal* (Oct. 27), ever cordial to him, stated that he had "appeared in the Character of *Fondlewife,* in which Part he discovered by several nice Strokes that humorous Insight into Nature, for which he is remarkable." On November 3 it reported that "Mr. *Foote* has again drawn together a very splendid and numerous Audience, by his appearing in the Character of *Fondlewife,* which whole Incident is represented by this Performer and Mrs. *Pritchard,* with as much Pleasantry as has been known on the Stage." Even Tom Davies, who thought it was Foote's "intimacy with people of the first rank" which "contributed to support him in his feeble attempts upon [the] masterly characters" of Congreve, stated that Foote "had luckily remembered that great master of acting, Colley Cibber. In the course of the first scene he drew the attention of the audience, and merited, and gained much applause; but,

---

1753–54 it was acted three times there, but the receipts for the comedy at a benefit for Dancer were so low that he was given another benefit (Rosenfeld, *Strolling Players,* pp. 183, 190, 199).

[23] It was also offered at Simpson's Theater in Bath during 1753–54 (Rosenfeld, *Strolling Players,* p. 199).

in the progress of the part, he forgot his exemplar and degenerated into buffoonery." [24] Although the comedy had not been given there for some time, the cast was in the main experienced. Mrs. Pritchard, whose "chief Excellence certainly lay in the natural, sprightly, and what are called the *higher Characters in Comedy*," [25] played Laetitia. Richard Yates—once Setter—now personated Bluff; Blakes played Setter instead of Sharper, with Havard exchanging Vainlove for Sharper. Henry Woodward, long absent from the play, resumed Sir Joseph, and in Davies' opinion he had a look so "serious and composed" that one would hardly expect him to play the "affecter of gaiety, the brisk fop, and pert coxcomb. But the moment he spoke, a certain ludicrous air laid hold of his features, and every muscle of his face ranged itself on the side of levity." Not only in Sir Joseph but also in Brisk, Tattle, and Witwoud, he "was extremely entertaining, and kept the audience perpetually and merrily attentive." [26]

It was undoubtedly Foote who dominated the revival, for when he went to Covent Garden in 1754–55, Drury Lane omitted the comedy. Under Rich's management it was given three times, then once more in 1755–56, when Ryan, who had been in the cast since 1741, played Bellmour for the last time. A writer observed that Ryan had "been long, and deservedly, a favourite of the town; but *being now sunk into the vale of years,* claims indulgence as much as he formerly did applause." Sparks as Heartwell was praised by the same writer.[27] Yet this sequence of 14 performances in three seasons virtually marked the end of *The Old Batchelor* as a really popular play until it was revived in 1776.[28]

After Foote had appeared as Fondlewife in Drury Lane on October 24, 1753, he undertook Ben in *Love for Love* on January 16, 1754, with Maria Macklin acting Prue for the first time. Having lauded Foote

---

[24] *Memoirs of the Life of Garrick*, I, 190–191. In *The Rosciad* Churchill agreed with Davies' principal point: "His strokes of humour, and his bursts of sport/Are all contain'd in this one word, *Distort*."

[25] Victor, *History of the Theaters*, III, 124.

[26] *Memoirs of the Life of Garrick*, I, 265–266. The receipts indicate that Foote at first attracted good audiences, with the first three performances averaging £175. The next three slumped to an average of £130, and the next three to £95.

[27] *General View of the Stage*, pp. 299, 302.

[28] *The Old Batchelor* came upon the stage a few more times before its revision in 1776, but in the twenty years after 1755 it was very infrequently acted. In 1756–57 Foote acted Fondlewife once at Drury Lane with very discouraging receipts, £60. Two years later Drury Lane ventured it for another performance, and in the next three years Covent Garden gave it twice. Then it went unacted from 1762 to 1768, when the Haymarket offered it during four consecutive summers—1769 to 1772—and again in the summer of 1775. Even so, it was acted only 8 times in five summers. During these years it and *The Double Dealer* were the least frequently given of Congreve's plays, a great change from the early years of the century when *The Old Batchelor* was more popular than any other of the five dramas.

as Fondlewife, Murphy found him equally praiseworthy in "the humorous and diverting part of *Ben*." Foote performed the part with "great Pleasantry" and "shewed by his Manner and his Looks, that he has entered into the Secret of the Character, tho' it was visible at the same Time, that his Powers were greatly suppressed by his Sollicitude for his first Appearance in a new Character." Murphy added that Miss Macklin, "though perhaps better qualified for spirited genteel Comedy . . . , acquitted herself with great Applause in a part in which Mrs. *Clive* has displayed so many inimitable Strokes of Humour." [29] Davies, as usual, dissented, stating that "it will scarce be credited, that for three nights the boxes were crowded, to see Foote murder the part of Ben; for his acting bore no resemblance to nature and character. He was even destitute of what no man could suppose him to want, a proper confidence in his own abilities; for sure his Ben was as lifeless a lump of insipidity as ever a patient audience was presented with; it was not even a lively mistake of humour." [30] Although the receipts for the first five performances averaged £140, in time it became apparent that, whereas Foote never gave genuine satisfaction as Ben, Miss Macklin was highly regarded as Prue.

Near the end of the same season, on May 13, 1754, Covent Garden revived *Love for Love* after having omitted it for five years. This revival gave the comedy sufficient impetus to keep it on that stage during each of the next eight years. Many parts were assigned to new performers. William ("Gentleman") Smith, who had joined Covent Garden in 1752–53, played Valentine. *A General View of the Stage* offered the judgment that "Mr. Smith's figure is very pleasing; and his performance very tolerable: his voice is agreeable, but he wants variety, and speaks always in the same tone" (p. 302). He held the role for several years. Dyer played Tattle, a part in which he had made his debut in 1742 when a strolling player in southern Ireland.[31] Sir Sampson was acted by Jack Dunstall, once a member of Giffard's company in Goodman's Fields. As a comedian his talents lay "between the rustic and the splenetic—not reaching to the highly voluptuous in character." [32]

During the eight to ten years following Garrick's purchase of a portion of the Drury Lane patent, the fluctuations in the popularity of Congreve's plays indicate that they had entered upon another phase of their stage vogue. In the forty years preceding 1747 the five plays had

[29] *Gray's Inn Journal*, Jan. 19, 1754.

[30] *Memoirs of the Life of Garrick*, I, 190. *Love for Love* was also acted twice in this season in New York, on Oct. 22 and Dec. 20 (Odell, *Annals of the New York Stage*, I, 60, 64).

[31] *Theatrical Biography* (London, 1772), II, 48.

[32] *Memoirs of Mrs. Siddons* (Philadelphia, 1893), p. 104.

established themselves in the repertory, gained steadily in their share of the total number of performances, and held among themselves a moderately consistent standing. After 1747 their frequency of performance became spasmodic rather than consistent, and their place in the repertory was kept at a moderately popular level only by one play's having a good revival to offset a decline in another play's vogue. A table of their performances during the ten years following 1747 will show how much variation there was not only between the plays individually but also in the vogue of each one.

Season	Old Batchelor		Double Dealer		Love for Love		Mourning Bride		Way of the World		Total
	DL	CG	DL	CG	DL	CG	DL	CG	DL	CG	
1747–48		3			3	1				1	8
1748–49		2	2	1	4					2	11
1749–50		2	1	5	3			1			12
1750–51		1	2		1		13		10	1	28
1751–52			4		1		2		7	4	18
1752–53		2	1		3		2		5	1	14
1753–54	9	1			6	1			3	2	22
1754–55		3	4		2	3	6	4	3	6	31
1755–56		1	3		2	5	7	2		3	23
1756–57	1		3	3		4	6	2		4	23

The seasons of 1753–54 and 1754–55 show the strikingly varying fortunes of the plays. In 1753–54 *The Old Batchelor* and *Love for Love* were more popular than *The Way of the World,* with the other two not appearing at all. In the next season the situation was almost exactly the reverse. *The Mourning Bride* and *The Way of the World* did quite well, *The Double Dealer* reappeared, and the other two comedies declined considerably. *The Old Batchelor* was gradually disappearing from the stage, whereas *The Mourning Bride* and *The Way of the World,* in the past much less frequently performed, were assuming a much more substantial role in the playhouses.

After being omitted in 1753–54, *The Mourning Bride* reappeared in both playhouses, and for six consecutive seasons it was offered competitively. During the next twenty years it never failed to make at least one appearance yearly.[33] Possibly some of its appeal lay in a cast which, though its principals occasionally varied, was always good. When Drury Lane offered it 6 times in 1754–55, the appearance of Maria Macklin for her first attempt at Almeria was the principal event. Although one writer considered her more especially suited to comedy, he had

[33] Early in 1754 *The Mourning Bride* was acted in York, with Frodsham ("The York Garrick") as Osmyn in a performance for his own benefit. It was repeated there the following season (Rosenfeld, *Strolling Players,* pp. 146–147).

"seen her in some scenes of Tragedy wherein she had been capitally great, particularly Almeria." [34] The *Dramatic Censor* (II, 415) was more reserved in its praise, stating that she "by the instruction of, and playing with Mr. GARRICK, supported Almeria through a considerable run, with much credit, and really struck out several beauties; but her feelings, though correct in tragedy, always wanted the animation of expression; her voice was too thin and contracted." During the same season Covent Garden gave the tragedy 4 times, with Mrs. Barrington (Leonora), Mrs. Bellamy (Almeria), and Sparks (King) retaining their roles. Peg Woffington, who had played Zara in Dublin in 1751–52, now played it in Covent Garden and joined the growing list of performers who had appeared in all of Congreve's plays. Davies stated that Cibber had "taught her to recite so pompously, that nature and passion were not seldom sacrificed to a false glare of eloquence," [35] and the *Dramatic Censor* (II, 416) found her not wholly satisfactory: "Mrs. WOFFINGTON's figure and deportment were well adapted to the captive Queen; but the violent, as well as tender passions, grated abominably in her dissonant voice." It was even more critical of Thomas Sheridan, who, returning to Covent Garden after an absence of ten years, undertook Osmyn: "We have seen Mr. SHERIDAN make Gothic attempts upon this part, for which he had not a single requisite: an insufficiency of figure, dissonance of expression, and limitation of voice, conjoined to overshadow every grace of merit" (II, 414). Although he and Mrs. Woffington played together with fair success, his engagement was not renewed at the end of the season.

Following these revivals, *The Mourning Bride* was acted frequently for several years. In 1756–57 it was offered 9 times as against 10 for the year before. Spranger Barry, fresh from a successful season in Dublin where he had acted Osmyn on March 14, 1755,[36] played the same part in place of the departed Sheridan. On May 3, 1756, for her own benefit, Miss Phillips, who had played Zara in *Zara* not long before for her debut, attempted Zara in *The Mourning Bride* for her fourth stage part, and it was given twice more in Covent Garden in 1756–57 with a similar cast. In Drury Lane the tragedy was more successful, even though after 1754–55 Garrick no longer acted Osmyn except on extraordinary occasions. It was given there 7 times in 1755–56,[37] with Arthur Murphy, the dramatist, appearing there for the first time as Osmyn.

---

[34] *General View of the Stage*, p. 286.

[35] *Memoirs of the Life of Garrick*, I, *309.

[36] Genest, *Some Account of the English Stage*, x, 398.

[37] In 1755–56 Mrs. Dancer, who later acted Zara in London, played the role at York. The tragedy was also given at Bath in that year (Rosenfeld, *Strolling Players*, p. 203).

Richard Cross, the prompter of Drury Lane, characterized Murphy's acting as "Indiff—tho' great Applause." [38] He kept the role most of the season, although Garrick, by command of the Prince of Wales, acted Osmyn on January 9, 1756.

In the following season, 1756–57, Mossop, returning to Drury Lane, replaced Murphy and made his own first appearance as Osmyn on November 17, 1756. Victor believed that Mossop had begun his career in Dublin with "only one theatrical Requisite, a strong, full, harmonious Voice," but being young, Mossop used his basically good theatrical sense to make himself an admirable actor.[39] Davies considered him inferior only to Barry and Garrick, and "in parts of vehemence and rage he was almost unequalled; and in sentimental gravity, from the power of his voice, and the justness of his conceptions, he was a very commanding speaker." [40] As Osmyn "in the first act, wherein he is brought in prisoner, his countenance and comportment strongly indicated the passions of his mind; and in his manner of replying to the King . . . there was a proper mixture of rage, grief, and contempt for the person by whom he was addressed. Though tenderness is not his fort, in the scenes with Almeria, he had a sufficiency; and his confusion on being discovered with her by Zara, was kept up with well-marked propriety." [41] The *Dramatic Censor* (II, 414) offered a contrasting opinion that "Mr. MOSSOP is much too mechanical and boisterous, he cannot shake off the bashaw," a view which Churchill (*Rosciad,* ll. 579–580) shared: "In cold-wrought scenes the lifeless actor flags; / In passion, tears the passion into rags." Later Miss Rosco did Zara indifferently, with the *London Chronicle* (Feb. 8–10, 1757) adding: "This Character requires a Mrs. Pritchard or a Mrs. Gregory; and an unexperienced actress could not adventure upon a more dangerous part." The manager apparently agreed, for she is supposed never to have made a second appearance in Drury Lane and Mrs. Pritchard resumed the part.

In 1757–58 Drury Lane again experimented with casting Zara, assigning it (Jan. 10) to Mrs. Glen, for her second appearance in Drury Lane. Her inept performance prompted Cross to remark that "Mrs Glen did Zara (bad)!" When she repeated the part a week later, his comment was expressively emphatic: "Mrs Glen did Zara—Oh!" [42] At the next performance the manager restored Mrs. Pritchard to the part, which she kept until 1765, only three years before her death. During this period

---

[38] This quotation and subsequent ones from Cross' Diary are used by the kind permission of the Folger Shakespeare Library.

[39] *History of the Theaters,* I, 148.

[40] *Memoirs of the Life of Garrick,* II, 225.

[41] *General View of the Stage,* pp. 269–270.

[42] Diary (Folger Library).

the tragedy had only a perfunctory existence in Covent Garden. Acted twice in 1757-58, when Rich was having a run of poor attendance, it was given on October 21 as a benefit for Mrs. Mayo, who acted Zara for her second appearance, with receipts of £144 7s. On December 2 it was given for the benefit of a hospital, with better receipts, £190 10s.

At much the same time (1754-55) that *The Mourning Bride* reappeared in both theaters, *The Double Dealer* was restored, but only in Covent Garden. It was not a great success. Its 4 performances must be credited principally to the return of Mrs. Woffington to act Lady Plyant, a new role for her. Davies stated that those who saw her remembered with pleasure "her whimsical absurdity of passion, and her awkwardly assumed prudery." [43] Two years later (1756-57) Drury Lane revived the comedy for the first time in six years. On October 29, 1756, Miss Barton, later (as Mrs. Abington) one of the great actresses of the century, played Lady Plyant for her debut. Richard Cross, who as prompter of Drury Lane had seen many youthful attempts, reported that "Miss Barton for her first appearance did Lady Plyant pretty well." [44] There were two other important additions: Mossop as Maskwell, and Foote as Sir Paul. In a review (*London Chronicle*, Feb. 19-22, 1757) of a later performance, Mossop was judged as wanting "nothing but being accustomed to the Walks of Comedy, to qualify him to be very successful in many Characters in common Life," a point which was emphasized because "his Deportment is rather constrained in Maskwell; though it is but Justice to say, his Utterance is throughout the Part very just, graceful, and pleasing; he has likewise conceived the character well." As to Foote's acting there were the usual sharp differences of opinion. Davies was, as always, very critical: "His Sir Paul Plyant was worse, if possible, than his Ben; . . . in the Knight, he gave a loose to the most ridiculous burlesque, and the vilest grimace. However, the people laughed heartily, and that he thought was a full approbation of his grotesque performance." [45] *A General Review of the Stage* gave an extended appreciation of Foote's merits in the role (pp. 273-274):

. . . this is a cast in which he is happy in exerting his judgment, and displaying his admirable talents for humor; the . . . part is, in his hands, a new creation. With him it appears in a light very different from any thing that I had ever seen presented by any other actor. He renders the ridicule of it so striking, without trick or grimace, that he not only commands the applause of the

[43] *Memoirs of the Life of Garrick*, I, *308.

[44] Diary (Folger Library). As Mrs. Abington, Miss Barton in later years appeared in most of Congreve's plays. Of her debut the *Thespian Dictionary* (1802) reported that "she was received with unbounded applause."

[45] *Memoirs of the Life of Garrick*, I, 191.

judicious, but of the *million*. In the third Act he keeps up finely all the awe in which Sir Paul stands of his wife. His admiration of her wit and person here, where she compliments Mr. Careless, and his silent action, as well as his humorous manner of throwing in half lines of rapture and affection, add considerably to the scene. His performance in the fourth Act of this Play is true Comedy; his reading of the letter is masterly; and his change of looks from despondency to joy, at supposing lady Pliant's excuse true, and the whole of what is past a contrivance of Careless to abuse him, is easy, natural, and spirited, and free from any strokes of mimicry: it is nature finely copied. A Stoic would burst with laughter to see the air of gravity and wisdom which he assumes, when Careless advances to inform him of his proceeding with his lady, and his only saying—*Indeed*— *Well, Sir*—*I'll dissemble with him a little*—so strongly indicate Sir Paul's views; his hope of catching Careless in a lye; his subsequent satisfaction at being deceived; and his manner of going off, are just, spirited, in character, and in nature.

It is difficult to reconcile two such divergent views. Let the arbiter be Cross, the prompter, who added a pertinent note concerning a performance of *The Double Dealer* on November 1, 1756: "Mr Foote brings sad houses." [46]

During the same season (1756–57) *The Double Dealer* had three performances in Covent Garden. With Foote, who had been there in the preceding season, bringing "sad houses" at Drury Lane, Ned Shuter took over his role of Sir Paul. Although Mrs. Woffington was still young, she made her last appearance, for she had become seriously ill and was forced to retire in the spring of 1757. Mrs. Green, returning to Covent Garden after an absence of two years, played Lady Froth on October 18, 1756. Nevertheless, *The Double Dealer,* like *The Old Batchelor,* was rapidly declining in favor. In 1757–58 it was acted only once, in Drury Lane.[47] In 1758–59 both houses played it, Drury Lane again but once, Covent Garden three times. Ryan, quite old and now retired, returned to Covent Garden on October 26, 1758, to play Careless for that night only. After this season the comedy was unacted for two years. On October 14, 1761, Drury Lane again offered it, after which it disappeared for twelve years, its longest absence from the stage since its revival in 1714–15.

While *The Mourning Bride* and *The Double Dealer* were being revived in 1754–55, *The Way of the World* reversed its downward trend in frequency of performance. After 11 performances in 1750–51 it had declined to 5 in 1753–54; then in 1754–55 it rose to 9. Probably it was the advent of Shuter as Sir Wilful which assisted the comedy to its

[46] Diary (Folger Library). Cross also recorded an anecdote concerning the evening's performance, an incident which was elaborately related in Davies' *Dramatic Miscellanies*, III, 193.

[47] During 1758–59 Foote was in Edinburgh, where he acted, among other parts, Sir Paul Plyant.

6 performances in Covent Garden, twice as many as it had in Drury Lane. Yet this substantial increase did not continue. In 1755–56 it had only 3 performances, all of them in Covent Garden. In 1756–57 it appeared 4 times there, with Mrs. Green, returning to Rich's management after an absence of two years, as Foible. In 1757–58 Drury Lane restored the comedy, but for 2 performances only, with nearly all of the women's roles changed. Relinquishing Mrs. Marwood, Mrs. Clive undertook Lady Wishfort, in which Richard Cross thought her unsatisfactory: "Mrs. Clive Lᵞ Wishfort (bad) for Mrs. Clive." [48] Her personal popularity, however, brought receipts of £310 for her benefit.

During this period *Love for Love* was only moderately popular. In 1754–55 [49] Covent Garden offered it 3 times, with Ned Shuter "far from being a bad Ben"; [50] Boaden considered his "humour . . . broad and voluptuous." [51] He retained the part to his death in 1776. Ridout (Scandal) and Barrington (Jeremy) were new to the cast, and Mrs. Woffington, who had acted Mrs. Frail in Dublin,[52] played the same role in Covent Garden. The comedy was offered there 5 times in 1755–56,[53] with Mrs. Woffington, perhaps as an experiment, acting Angelica on one night, although her usual role continued to be Mrs. Frail. During each of these two seasons Drury Lane gave the comedy only twice, a very small number for a theater which had for many years made *Love for Love* one of its major attractions; and in 1756–57 Drury Lane omitted it for the first time since 1741–42.

From the first appearance of Garrick to the mid-1750's there has been little upon which to form a judgment concerning the status of Congreve's plays except their frequency of performance, the box office receipts, and the preferences of actors for parts in its plays. None of these factors offers very conclusive evidence of their popularity, although the fluctuations in the number of performances suggests a less sustained demand for the plays than had been present previously. During this period most of what appeared in the periodicals concerning plays were "puffs," some of them inserted into the daily papers by the managers of the theaters. Even the brief reviews of plays, such as those by

[48] Diary (Folger Library). *The Way of the World* was chosen to open the new theater in Norwich on Jan. 31, 1758. It and *Love for Love* seem to have been equally popular on the Norwich circuit (Rosenfeld, *Strolling Players*, pp. 91, 94).

[49] In 1754–55 *Love for Love* was acted at Canterbury by Smith's company, with Mr. and Mrs. Eden as Legend and Mrs. Frail (Rosenfeld, *Strolling Players*, p. 252).

[50] *General View of the Stage*, p. 301.

[51] *Memoirs of Mrs. Siddons*, p. 45.

[52] She had played Mrs. Frail there on Feb. 11, 1752, with Theophilus Cibber as Tattle and Sheridan as Valentine (Genest, *Some Account of the English Stage*, x, 378).

[53] *Love for Love* was also acted at Bath with Thomas King as Tattle (Rosenfeld, *Strolling Players*, p. 202).

Arthur Murphy in the *Gray's Inn Journal*, were as much concerned with
the merits of performers as with the plays. The actor, not the play,
was usually the center of attraction, and it was true also that changes
in the personnel of the companies greatly affected the offerings which
each playhouse decided to present. The movements of actors from
theater to theater had a great deal to do with the fortunes of particular
plays. From early 1757, however, dramatic criticism became more firmly
established, and the reviews thereafter offer information not only upon
actors and their roles but also upon contemporary opinion of plays.
As C. H. Gray has indicated,[54] the founding of the *London Chronicle*
in 1757 was a major event in the history of English dramatic criticism.
Established by Robert Dodsley, the paper appeared three times weekly,
beginning on January 1, 1757. Before the end of that month it began
a series of reviews, the first of which continued until April. In December a new series was projected, but not until October 1758 did the
critical articles attain continuity and volume. Not all of Congreve's
plays were reviewed at length, but the opinions expressed in this journal throw some light upon current appraisal of his works.

The first Congreve play to receive extended comment in the autumn
of 1758 was *Love for Love*, which was acted at Covent Garden on October 13. The reviewer stated that, were he to offer his personal opinion,
he would argue "that this is the best comedy either antient or modern,
that ever was written to please upon the stage," and that "while the
most superficial judges admire it, it is impossible but the nicest, and
most accurate, must approve." As proof of its excellence he stated
that it "is written strictly up to the rules of the drama" yet "has all that
variety of character and incidents, which is pleaded in their excuse
by those who deviate from them." Does it have any faults? "Oh, says
somebody, it has too much Wit." Surely, the critic replied, that fault
was so rare that it could be excused, and Congreve "was richer in wit
. . . of the true sterling kind, than any man whatsoever." The character of Jeremy, in fact, "is one of the wittiest that ever was writ." In
addition, Congreve took care "never to violate Nature," which he set
off "to advantage" rather "than disguise her." No writer, he added,
"marked his characters so strongly, or so highly finished them." In closing, the reviewer complained that he could not understand why a "certain manager"—presumably Garrick—gave so little attention to *Love
for Love*.

Nothing in the review would lead its readers to suppose that *Love*

---

[54] *Theatrical Criticism in London to 1795* (New York, 1931), p. 128. For a discussion
of Murphy as the probable author of these reviews, see H. H. Dunbar's *The Dramatic
Career of Arthur Murphy* (New York: MLA, 1946), pp. 38–40, 305–310.

for Love had lost its appeal for mid-century spectators. In fact, the reviewer's complaint concerning Garrick's indifference to it implies that he saw no reason for the comedy's not being so important an element in Drury Lane's repertory as it had been in the regime of Cibber, Wilks, and Booth. He was equally enthusiastic about the performers and took particular notice of Ross, who acted Valentine for the first time and who performed the part "better, than I ever saw it done by any one else. Indeed, genteel comedy seems to be his *fort:* not that I would be thought to insinuate as if he had it not in his power to make himself considerable in any part . . . but he has so much of the gentleman about him in every respect, that he appears . . . more like himself." [55] In the cast "Collins takes the superstitious, credulous old fool upon him, in the character of *Foresight,* with great justness; and no body can see Shuter in the part of *Ben,* without being put in a good humour."

Later in the autumn the *London Chronicle* (Nov. 14–16) gave *The Way of the World* its first extensive criticism in many years. The reviewer considered it a "comedy, which for poignancy of wit; delicacy of humour; regularity of conduct; propriety of manners; and continuity of character; may (if ever work might) be reckoned a finished piece." The critic undertook to explain Congreve's basic assumptions by stating that the dramatist "had too intimate an acquaintance with human nature not to know that the generality of mankind have a much greater share of vices, than virtues, in their composition"; because this was true, it was the "business of a comic poet to turn the most glaring side outward." As a result, Congreve created Fainall and Mirabell, whose "justness" of characterization the actors display, yet who are, the reviewer urged as the principal point in their favor, merely "a couple of well-bred rascals." Mirabell "indeed seems to be immoral upon principle; his vices are shewn as an ornament to his character." Fainall was more grossly "vicious." Although the reviewer believed that Congreve intended to display them as "fools," he quoted Pope's "Tell me if Congreve's fools be fools indeed" to reinforce his statement that they might not properly be termed fools; they might, then, be called coxcombs. "And since the best things degenerated become the worst, why may we not say that an impertinent wit is the most disagreeable of fools." In spite of his perplexity concerning the relation of wit and characterization in the comedy, the writer attempted an involved proof that Congreve's handling of the materials was much superior to that

[55] *A General View of the Stage* (1759) also thought well of Ross, who "is a good figure, and has an elegance on the Stage which must recommend him in genteel Comedy, in which cast he has lately given strong proofs of his genius" (p. 300). In 1770, however, the *Dramatic Censor* thought that by his own "matchless neglect" Ross had seriously declined in acting power (II, 488).

of Betterton in *The Amorous Widow,* which, he stated, came from the
same French original as did *The Way of the World.* In conclusion, he
repeated the tradition that the comedy had had a "cold reception" at
its première, but he was glad to see that since then London audiences
"have acquired a juster notion of its value" and that there was a crowded
audience at the performance on November 13, 1758.

The reviewer was also generous in his praise of the performers. William O'Brien, acting Witwoud for the first time, gave promise of becoming a "great actor," for he had a "peculiar tone of voice very fit for
doing justice to a part of this kind." Mrs. Clive had either improved
her impersonation of Lady Wishfort or found a critic more susceptible
to her charms than the prompter had been in the previous spring, for
he found Lady Wishfort an excellent character with "nothing wanting but what can only be given by such an actress as Mrs. Clive." He
thought that Mrs. Clive, by recognizing that Lady Wishfort was a
"ridiculous woman of quality," improved upon other actresses who
apparently dressed themselves "like mad women, and acted in the
strain of an old nurse." Mrs. Clive did not need "such pityful expedients. Accordingly she dresses the part in the pink of the present mode,
and makes more of it than any actress ever did." Mrs. Yates acted Mrs.
Marwood incomparably well. As Sir Wilful, Yates "hardly ever opened
his mouth, but he set the house in a roar." The critic was least complimentary to Mrs. Pritchard, for he considered Millamant not a proper
role for her because of the "strong tincture of affectation" in it "which
is so foreign to Mrs. Pritchard's disposition, one of whose beauties is
ease, and a close attention to nature. . . . Notwithstanding which, her
life and spirit is such, that, since Mrs. Woffington's retirement from the
stage, I do not see any actress, besides herself, in any degree equal to
it." [56] The critic concluded that "from the great satisfaction [the spectators] expressed at the whole performance, it is evident, that however
fond the town may be of those fantastical representations (which old
Cibber aptly enough compares to dram drinking) it is evident I say
that their tastes are not yet so vitiated, but they have still a relish for
some wholesome entertainments." [57]

These reviews of the two comedies were the most extensive critiques
of Congreve's plays during 1758–59. In spite of the critic's concern over
the immorality of the plays, his appraisal was genuinely favorable. In

[56] Mrs. Pritchard kept the part for more than twenty years. According to Davies,
"Notwithstanding the fulness of her figure, and her advanced age, the town was
charm'd to the last with her representation of Congreve's delightful portrait of wit,
affectation, and good-nature, in Millamant" (*Memoirs of the Life of Garrick,* II, 179).

[57] The receipts for the first evening (£121 18s 6d) suggest only moderate attendance,
but they rose steadily: £144 1s; £164 18s; £155 18s 6d.

fact, he was far more severe morally with *The Twin Rivals, The Provoked Wife,* and *The Careless Husband,* and he was greatly offended by *The London Cuckolds,* generally considered one of the most objectionable plays on the stage. On other grounds he disapproved of *The Rover* and *The Fair Quaker,* and in general Congreve came off well under his inspection. There appeared, however, to be no significant relationship between these reviews and the frequency with which the plays were performed. None of Congreve's plays reviewed in 1758-59 apparently appeared more frequently because of the praise given them, nor did their stage performance run visibly counter to the critic's opinion. Yet nearly all continued the decline in frequency of performance which had been underway for several seasons, and never again was their popularity to be as high as it had been around 1750.

Not until 1768-69, in fact, did the status of the plays change appreciably. Until then the three active Congreve plays had unspectacular and variable stage histories which are much less interesting than is the story of their rise. Rarely was one offered in both theaters in the same season, yet only one of the three failed to appear somewhere each year. What kept them on the stage was, in part, their long tradition of being in the repertory and being good theater. In addition, of course, there was a large number of actors who were experienced in the roles and who could win praise for their conception of the parts. What often caused the variation in frequency of performance was the movement of actors from one house to another. The plays followed the actors, and since the plays were familiar to most of the spectators, their interest often lay in the acting rather than in the play itself.

The course of *Love for Love* was typical. During 1758-59, when the *London Chronicle* reviewed it, the comedy was acted 3 times in Covent Garden only. Performances of it there in the next three years totalled only 5. In fact, in 1760-61 *Love for Love* was the only Congreve play offered by Rich, who was managing Covent Garden for his last season; and when, in 1762-63, Covent Garden omitted *Love for Love,* not one of Congreve's dramas was offered there, a state of affairs which had not existed in Rich's company since he opened Lincoln's Inn Fields in 1714. On April 9, 1760, after an absence of three seasons, *Love for Love* reappeared in Drury Lane. In the considerably altered cast was Burton (Sir Sampson), who played frequently "in the serious cast of elderly men in Comedy; and as he is a respectable citizen-like figure, and no stranger to his author's meaning, he never displeases." [58] King, who had played Tattle in Bath in 1755-56, acted it here. Miss Pope, who had made her debut as an actress only that autumn, acted Prue and

[58] *General View of the Stage,* p. 291.

prompted Churchill to state that "Cheer'd by her promise, we the less deplore / The fatal time when Clive shall be no more" (*Rosciad,* ll. 701–702). Although it was acted 3 times in 1759–60, Drury Lane omitted it in the following season,[59] only to revive it again in 1762–63, when it had 2 performances, followed by 2 more in the next year. In the autumn of 1763, after Garrick had gone to the Continent, leaving George Colman and George Garrick in charge, Miss Cheney made her debut as Prue with sufficient success to raise performances to five and to retain the part for several years. Her first appearance (Oct. 1) was received with cautious optimism by the prompter, who thought she played "with Spirit" and had a good figure, though she was inexperienced. She got "great Applause" and the prompter thought she might "make an Actress." [60] The *St. James' Chronicle* (Oct. 1–4) commented upon the "generous Encouragement" which the English audiences always lend to initial "Efforts of Genius" and the warm reception Miss Cheney received. The writer also saw "a spirited Simplicity in her Manner, and an innocent Vivacity in her Countenance, admirably calculated for Success on the Stage." Indeed, Miss Cheney was worthy to be "set . . . down in the Table of Theatrical Consanguinity as a younger Sister to the sprightly and elegant Miss Pope."

In the same season (1763–64) Covent Garden played the comedy once after having omitted it in the previous year. Although Miss Macklin (Angelica) and Miss Elliot (Prue), two promising actresses, played those roles for the first time, the infusion of new blood did not give the comedy much additional vigor. In 1764–65 it was acted 6 times (4 in Covent Garden) and in 1765–66 but once. An argument in the *Public Ledger* (Sept. 25, 1765) in favor of contemporary versus Restoration dramatists made the point that "Congreve's Love for Love will perhaps draw half a house once or twice in a season; whereas there is scarce a production of an author now living . . . but that will bring a crouded audience half a dozen times in the course of a winter." Although the writer underestimated the audiences,[61] he accurately stated the frequency of the comedy's appearances. After a performance in 1765–66, it had 2 in the

59 On March 8, 1762, *Love for Love* was acted in New York, apparently for the first time since 1753 (Odell, *Annals of the New York Stage,* I, 90).

60 Notes on the playbill in the Huntington Library. For the full entry see Dougald MacMillan, *Drury Lane Calendar, 1747–1776* (Oxford, 1938), p. 97. Isaac Reed, who saw the performance, agreed that "She was recd. with Applause." See *Isaac Reed Diaries, 1762–1804,* ed. Claude E. Jones (Berkeley, 1946), p. 20.

61 The receipts for Miss Cheney's debut on Oct. 1, 1763, were £187 16s 6d, a sum about average thus far in that season. A few days later the comedy attracted a similar sum, but the later performances averaged only about £130. Isaac Reed saw a performance of *Love for Love* at the Richmond Playhouse on Sept. 8, 1764. See *Isaac Reed Diaries,* p. 25.

next season.[62] Then, for the first time since the opening decade of the century, it failed to make an appearance anywhere in London during two seasons (1767–68 and 1768–69).

A similar decline affected *The Way of the World* between 1758–59 and 1767–68. Although it was acted more frequently during that period than was *Love for Love,* a reversal of their usual relationship, *The Way of the World* also disappeared from the stage in 1768–69. Had it not been for a long-delayed revival of *The Double Dealer* in that season, no comedy by Congreve would have appeared on the London stages. The decline in the status of *The Way of the World* began after the good showing (6 performances in Drury Lane, 2 in Covent Garden) it made in 1758–59. In the next season [63] it was given 5 performances, 4 of them in Drury Lane, and the single performance at Covent Garden was its last there for five years. Drury Lane continued, however, to present it: 3 times in 1760–61, 2 in 1761–62, 1 in 1762–63,[64] and 1 more in 1763–64. In the next winter, on December 18, 1764, Drury Lane offered Thomas King, who had been brought from Dublin, as Witwoud in place of O'Brien. Davies thought King "a very pleasing representer of Witwou'd," with an "articulate volubility" resembling that of Chapman in the same role.[65] But the 2 performances in Drury Lane that season were eclipsed by Covent Garden's revival of it for 6 performances. This was the last season in the century to present the comedy 8 times.

In 1765–66 there was the customary relapse after a revival. The comedy had a single performance in Drury Lane, where Mrs. Abington, after an absence of five years, acted Millamant. According to Davies,

[62] *Love for Love* was acted in Philadelphia on Feb. 27, 1767. See T. C. Pollock, *The Philadelphia Theater in the 18th Century* (Philadelphia, 1933), p. 92. That the growing reluctance to offer Congreve's comedies without alteration had already reached America was evident in a note which stated that because Congreve deviated from the rules "a more refined Age, and chaste Stage require," the reviver had expunged "every Passage that might be offensive either to Decency or good Manners" (p. 92).

[63] *The Way of the World* was acted in the Crow Street Theater, Dublin, on Oct. 3, the opening night of the 1759–60 season. In the cast were performers who later played in it in London: Mrs. Kennedy (Mrs. Marwood) made her debut in Drury Lane in that role on Oct. 10, 1760.

[64] On this day (Nov. 26, 1762) Edward Gibbon went to Drury Lane in the morning and watched rehearsals of Mallet's *Elvira* and of *The Way of the World,* which was given that night. He stated that he could not help noticing "the surprising versatility of Mrs. Pritchard's talents, who rehearsed, almost at the same time, the part of a furious Queen in the Green-room, and that of a Coquette on the stage; and passed several times from one to the other with the utmost ease and happiness." He went that night to see *The Way of the World. Gibbon's Journal,* ed. D. M. Low (New York, n.d.), pp. 185–186.

[65] *Dramatic Miscellanies,* III, 221.

she had a person "formed with great elegance," a "graceful" address, and an "animated and expressive" look. By means of the "superiority of her taste" and the "goodness of her understanding," she "skilfully modelled and adapted" Congreve's "Millamant of past times to the admired coquette and the lovely tyrant of the present day." [66] The vagaries of the comedy, as well as the decline of *Love for Love,* created a controversy in the *Public Ledger* (Sept. 25, 1765) over the wit of Congreve's plays. After pointing out that *Love for Love* scarcely drew a good house once yearly, the writer added that the coolness of the public did not check the enthusiasm of those few who were, to his way of thinking, inordinately fond of Congreve. To emphasize his irritation with Congreve idolaters, he cited their excessive praise of a detail: " 'What (cry these elaborate judges of the Drama) is all the merit of the present hour to the single stroke of Congreve's in the Way of the World, where Witwou'd says that Petulant and he sputter at each other like a pair of roasting apples.—Ah!—that's a flight of genius, infinitely beyond any thing which our authors nowadays can possibly pretend to; and is in reality worthy every thing that has been produced since the beginning of the present century.' " Angered by this idolatry, the writer declared that there had been an over-emphasis upon wit and that, when it was used to "gloss over the illiberal effusions of a licentious imagination," every "benevolent mind must consider it with an equal mixture of concern and contempt."

Attacks upon the wit, and especially upon the immorality, of Restoration writers became more heavily concentrated in the 1760's, and some comedies—for example, Wycherley's *The Plain Dealer* and *The Country Wife*—were being revised to cater to the somewhat squeamish taste of the public. Although alteration of Congreve's plays did not occur for several years, the change in taste and the constant attacks upon the dramas of Wycherley, Vanbrugh, Farquhar, and Congreve had a growing effect upon the vogue of their plays. *The Way of the World,* like *Love for Love,* was nearing a break in its yearly appearances. In 1766–67 it was given 3 times in Covent Garden, followed by a performance at Richmond on June 27, 1767. In 1767–68, when *Love for Love* failed to appear, *The Way of the World* was acted but once. Missing from the stage in 1768–69, it failed to appear for the first time since 1749–50, a break which was followed by 11 performances in 1750–51. How greatly it had declined in recuperative power showed in the fact that, after the omission in 1768–69, it did not reappear until 1770–71, when it had only 2 performances.

During the years between 1758 and 1768 *The Mourning Bride* held

[66] *Memoirs of the Life of Garrick,* II, 169.

the stage better than did the comedies, but it was not greatly popular. After being omitted in 1753–54, it was on the stage every season through 1776–77, but during most of that time it was acted only two or three times yearly. Like the comedies, it had moderate success in the mid-1760's and then declined in popularity. The process took longer for the tragedy, yet the decline was steady: from 10 performances in 1754–55 to 9 in the next season, then 8, then 6, and, in 1758–59, 5. Two-thirds of these performances occurred in Drury Lane, where it was played 4 times in 1758–59, with Packer acting Selim (Sept. 19, 1758) for his first appearance in Drury Lane. For two nights Berry, who to the irritation of the *Dramatic Censor* (II, 413) "rumbled him out in a most disgusting manner," acted the King; then the part went to Davies, who retained it in the next season, when the tragedy had 3 performances in Drury Lane. Charles Holland, who had been trained by Garrick, played Osmyn for the first time. According to Davies, his "ear was perfectly good; he . . . had a moderate share of sensibility. By a constant attention to the voice, manner, and action of Mr. Garrick, he did not displease when he represented some of that performer's most favourite characters." [67] According to the *Dramatic Censor* (II, 414) he "stiffened his deportment into a degree of aukwardness, and tortured the tones of his voice into an irksome degree of dissonance," and Churchill said of him that "with truly tragic stalk / He creeps, he flies,—a hero should not walk" (*Rosciad*, ll. 323–324) and implied that Holland was Garrick at "second-hand" (l. 336).

In the meantime *The Mourning Bride* was having only a perfunctory existence in Covent Garden, where it was offered mainly for special benefits. The two performances in 1757–58 were on behalf of an actress and a hospital. A single performance in 1758–59 aided a "Widow in distress," with Almeria by Mrs. Bellamy, who "has all the softness of her sex, and that sweet sensibility which gives the most affecting pathos to the tender parts in Tragedy. . . . Parts of violence are too strong for her powers." [68] At the same time Miss Nossiter, recently returned to Covent Garden, acted Zara for the first time. The single performance in 1759–60 was again a benefit, this time for the "Unhappy Sufferers by the late *dreadful Fire* that happen'd *in* King's Street, *Covent Garden*"; receipts rose to the extraordinary sum of £870 18s.[69]

In 1761–62 *The Mourning Bride* made a slight recovery: 3 performances in Drury Lane and 1 in Covent Garden. In Drury Lane Mrs.

[67] *Memoirs of the Life of Garrick,* II, 91.
[68] *General View of the Stage,* p. 303.
[69] It was acted at Canterbury in the winter of 1760–61 (Rosenfeld, *Strolling Players,* p. 259).

Yates continued to act Almeria except on November 14, 1761, when Mrs. Hopkins, late of the Norwich company, received favorable comment from the *Court Magazine* (Nov.) for her playing of Almeria, "which, considering the disadvantage of a first night, and the fears inseparable from a new performer, who executed with no little share of propriety and tenderness; and discovered herself mistress of a genius that must make her a valuable acquisition to a theatre." In Covent Garden the single performance was another benefit for citizens suffering from a fire, with the play omitted there in the following season.[70] It continued, however, to be acted two to four times yearly for several seasons.[71] Not until 1765–66 were there important changes in the cast. In Drury Lane Keene acted Perez, a role he kept for several years. Succeeding Mrs. Pritchard, who retired after thirty seasons, Mrs. Fitzhenry attempted Zara on January 20, 1766, not very successfully. In 1766–67 Covent Garden gave the tragedy its single performance of the season.[72] On its return to Drury Lane in 1767–68,[73] Mrs. Barry played Zara, but in 1768–69 she acted Almeria to Mrs. Hopkins' Zara. The *Dramatic Censor* (II, 417), censuring Congreve for writing the part, declared that Mrs. Hopkins "makes rather a better figure in Zara, yet is bad enough, Heaven knows." During 1768–69 J. Aickin acted the King, though "why he should be imposed upon Mr. J. AICKIN, we cannot conceive" (II, 413). And on September 26 Mrs. W. Barry made such a poor attempt at Almeria that the prompter supposed she must be under the influence of liquor.[74] Havard retired in May 1769, concluding thirty-one years as Gonsalez.

The late 1760's were not good years for Congreve's plays, and during the ten years preceding Garrick's retirement in 1776 they made no real progress toward a genuine restoration of popularity. In 1761–62 all five had been acted in London. For many years after that only *Love for Love, The Way of the World,* and *The Mourning Bride* could be seen by devotees of Congreve. In 1767–68 only *The Mourning Bride* and *The Way of the World* were staged, and in 1768–69 only the tragedy appeared during the regular season, with *The Old Batchelor* being

---

[70] *The Mourning Bride* was acted in Edinburgh during 1761–62, with John Jackson, a newcomer there, as Osmyn (Dibdin, *Annals of the Edinburgh Stage,* p. 113).

[71] On Dec. 22, 1763, it was acted at Charleston, S.C., for apparently its first performance in America, and repeated on April 9, 1764, with *Love for Love* also played there on Feb. 27, 1764. See Eola Willis, *The Charleston Stage in the XVIII Century* (Columbia, S.C., 1924), p. 44.

[72] *The Mourning Bride* made its first appearance in Philadelphia in 1766–67, being acted twice, and was repeated two seasons later (Pollock, *Philadelphia Theater,* pp. 89, 96, 104).

[73] Apparently it had its first performance in New York on Dec. 30, 1767 (Odell, *Annals of the New York Stage,* I, 121).

[74] Prompter's note on the playbill, Huntington Library.

offered at the Haymarket in the summer. Within a decade the plays had come close to disappearing from the stage. Although their status improved slightly after 1768–69, the change was not sufficient to offer any assurance that they would be retained indefinitely.

The annals of the plays from 1769 to 1776 are not lively ones. *The Old Batchelor* was to be seen only in the summer at the Haymarket,[75] for what was once the second most popular of the comedies was now least in favor. *The Double Dealer* did slightly better. In 1769, when David Ross was negotiating with George Colman the Elder for a new contract, he suggested that he would like to "get up" *The Double Dealer*, with Yates as Lord Touchwood, Woodward as Brisk (whom Ross called Brush), and Shuter as Sir Paul.[76] Nothing came of the suggestion at that time, but in 1772–73 the comedy was restored. With two performances in Drury Lane, it had a relatively new cast: Samuel Reddish as Maskwell; William Parsons, Lord Froth; King, Sir Paul; Miss Young, Lady Plyant. William Dodd (Brisk), whom Boaden considered "one of the most perfect actors that I have ever seen," was "the prince of pink heels, and the soul of empty eminence. As he tottered rather than walked down the stage, in all the protuberance of endless muslin and lace in his cravats and frills, he reminded you of the jutting motion of the pigeon. His action was suited to his figure." [77] Mrs. Abington, who as Miss Barton had played Lady Plyant in 1756–57, acted Lady Froth. Georg Christoph Lichtenberg, a foreign patron of the London theaters, said of Mrs. Abington on January 10, 1775, that in "comedy, and above all when the manners of the first circles . . . are to be parodied, she is unique on the English Stage." [78] She was supported by Mrs. Hopkins as Lady Touchwood. On April 14, 1773, the comedy was acted for the last time before it, like Congreve's other dramas, underwent revision for the revivals of 1775 and 1776.

During the years preceding Garrick's retirement, the other two comedies were more often seen, with *Love for Love* holding the stage more steadily than *The Way of the World*. After 1768–69,[79] when neither was acted, *Love for Love* returned to Drury Lane in 1769–70, for 5 perform-

[75] It was given at Edinburgh on Jan. 3, 1771, with Foote as Fondlewife (Dibdin, *Annals of the Edinburgh Stage*, p. 156).

[76] Letter of Sept. 9, 1769, in *Posthumous Letters from Various Celebrated Men, Addressed to Francis Colman and George Colman, the Elder* (London, 1820), pp. 147–149.

[77] James Boaden, *Memoirs of the Life of John Philip Kemble, Esq.* (London, 1825), I, 55.

[78] *Lichtenberg's Visits to England*, tr. and annotated by Margaret L. Mare and W. H. Quarrell (Oxford, 1938), pp. 68–69.

[79] *Love for Love* was again given in New York on June 19, 1769 (Odell, *Annals of the New York Stage*, I, 151). It was acted in Philadelphia on May 10, 1770, and Jan. 13, 1773 (Pollock, *Philadelphia Theater*, pp. 112, 120).

ances, a rather good showing. Parsons' acting of Foresight was a high-light of the performances: "Parsons, by a happy attention to all the minutiae of his cast, shews a finished picture of doteage, avarice, or whatever infirmity of passions he would represent;—the *tottering knee* . . . the *plodding look,* nay, the *taking out the handkerchief,* all proclaim him a finished actor in this walk. What can, for instance, be a finer illustration of *Sir Sampson Legend's* account of him in the character of *Old Foresight* . . . where he asks, 'On what old nail, now, my Nostradamus, are you poring?' than Parsons shews you at that time in his face and attitude." [80] This performance also served to introduce Dodd as Tattle, who had been appraised for Garrick by his friend, Dr. John Hoadley, after seeing Dodd in several parts: "My . . . opinion of him in general is, that his *person* is good enough, but his motion is too much under restraint and form. . . . He has a white *calf-like* stupid face, that disgusted me much till I heard him speak and throw some sensibility into it. His voice is good, and well heard everywhere; and he seems sensible, alive, and attentive to what is going on, and properly so." [81] In spite of a good cast, the comedy managed but a single performance in 1770–71 and another in 1771–72. At that time (Nov. 14, 1771), Mrs. Robinson, succeeding Mrs. W. Barry, played Angelica, doing the part indifferently.[82]

That performance was reviewed at length in the *Public Ledger.*[83] Much of the criticism was a restatement of the objections Lord Kames had made of the tendency of the comedy toward being a "conversation piece," although the review added that "the Plot of this Comedy is contrived with great ingenuity, and is pleasingly intricate; the Characters are strongly drawn; the Language is masterly; and the Wit brilliant." These virtues, however, were overbalanced by the "vein of licentiousness, so dangerous in its tendency, and so unsuitable to the present professed chastity of the times," that the comedy has to be "consigned to oblivion." This curious incongruity between praise and condemnation was ridiculed by "Longinus" in the *General Evening Post* (Nov. 23–26), who remarked that the reviewers emphasize "that the *characters* of *Love for Love* are *strongly* (that is *well*) drawn; that the *language* is *masterly,* and the wit *brilliant;* yet that upon the *whole* humanity and virtue require, from the *predominant* quality of *licentiousness,*" that the comedy be withdrawn from the stage. The writer asked, "To speak dramatically, how is it possible for characters to be

---

80 *Theatrical Biography* (London, 1772), I, 101.

81 *Private Correspondence of Garrick,* I, 184. Dodd later acted Brisk in *The Double Dealer* and Witwoud in *The Way of the World.*

82 See MacMillan, *Drury Lane Calendar,* p. 157.

83 As reprinted in the *Theatrical Review,* I, 190–194.

well drawn, which are wholly improper for exhibition? How is it possible, for language to be *masterly*, which is not proper to be heard; or for wit to be *brilliant*, which calls for an instant banishment from our theaters?" Although no one offered a decisive answer to this type of query, the age showed its general agreement with the moral attack by offering the comedy less and less frequently. After this season, Drury Lane did not again play it until 1776 and Covent Garden rarely gave it more than once yearly until then.[84]

The fortunes of *The Way of the World* were also declining. Like *Love for Love*, it was absent from the stage in 1768–69 and did not appear again until 1770–71. Acted twice then, it was seen only in Drury Lane, with Mrs. Abington as Millamant. Excellent as she was, she could not sustain the play, and in the following season it was given only in Covent Garden, which had not presented it for four years. Its revival there was also short-lived, for the performance on April 4, 1772 (a benefit for Dyer, who acted Witwoud) was its last appearance there before its revision. It was not well received, the *Public Ledger* emphasizing that although it was the best of Congreve's comedies and possessed wit and many "high-finished Characters," it had such an "abominable vein of Licentiousness" that it was "scarcely fit to be exhibited" at that time.[85]

Although Covent Garden relinquished *The Way of the World* in 1772, Drury Lane continued to offer it infrequently: once in 1773–74, for the benefit of Mrs. Abington, with Yates acting Sir Wilful for his first appearance in Drury Lane in seven years, and twice in 1775–76. By this time the lines were becoming clearly drawn between those who demanded its expulsion or revision and those who thought it had sufficient wit to warrant its retention. Criticism of the performance on October 7, 1775, illustrates the conflicting views. A writer for the *Morning Post* argued that, because the play was licentious, if it had to be performed ("and indeed, it would be high treason against wit to lay it on the shelf"), then "let the delicate and critical taste of a Garrick, or some other dramatic writer, root out these poetical excrescences." Once corrected, *The Way of the World* would "stand the severest test of criticism, and be acknowledged by the most polished hearers, to be an ornament to the British Stage." The *Morning Chronicle* defended the play, stating that "Congreve has given as much wit and spirit to one act of this play as would serve to set up twenty such spinning poets as Cumberland, &c." In the same spirit the *Gazetteer* inveighed against

---

[84] It was acted at Liverpool on Sept. 8, 1773, with Palmer as Ben and Mrs. Mattocks as Angelica (Genest, *Some Account of the English Stage*, v, 385).

[85] As rptd. in *Theatrical Review*, ii, 162.

"Sentimental Comedy," which "has so vitiated the taste of the town, that it ceases to be a matter of surprise why Congreve's pieces are not more frequently laid before the public. This great Master of the Drama, were he to rise, and take a view of our modern *sermon like pieces*, would blush for his countrymen, and scarcely desire to exist . . . among the play-makers that infested the stage since Murphy."

Each review gave an account of the performance. Yates (Sir Wilful) was praised by all, having been received "with the heartiest plaudits" (*Post*), "with great marks of approbation" (*Chronicle*), and "with much judicious applause" (*Gazetteer*). All agreed that his acting had much improved. Praise of Mrs. Abington, however, was somewhat reserved.[86] The *Post* stated only that her performance "was very decent." The *Chronicle* observed that although she was "undoubtedly an admirable comic actress," she did not show her *"usual* powers"; and the *Gazetteer* noted a "want of that *spirit* best calculated to call her powers into action: her delivery was tediously formal." Very probably she simply was not at her best that night. To the *Gazetteer*, King (Witwoud) was "as entertaining and full of spirits as usual." For some performers, however, there was sharp reproof. The *Chronicle* rebuked Reddish for not playing Fainall well and Jefferson (Mirabell) for being "so shamefully imperfect as to receive strong marks of the disapprobation of the audience." [87] It was Mrs. Greville (Mrs. Fainall) on whom the *Gazetteer* was most severe. "Mrs. Greville, to convince the town that she could keep a secret, whispered it only to a few friends in the pit. This lady behaves as if she were a Princess in disguise, that had been ousted of her dominions, and took up with her present profession until she was restored; her indifference is intolerable, and should be noticed by her employer." Only one phase of the comedy was greatly discussed: a cantata by Dr. Arne which, introduced into the third act, comprised fifteen minutes of the performance. The *Post* called it an "egregious absurdity," especially since it was of the "gravest cast" and since Dr. Arne must have thought he was writing a "dirge for Romeo and Juliet, rather than some strains for one of the liveliest comedies in the English language."

86 Lichtenberg thought Mrs. Abington inferior to Mrs. Yates and Mrs. Barry in "majesty of demeanour and the expression of tender emotion," but superior "in a talent for convincing the innermost heart of the spectators that she does not feel herself to be acting a part, but presenting reality in all its bitter truth" (*Lichtenberg's Visits to England*, p. 33).

87 Ordinarily nothing was so likely to arouse the ire of a late-18th-century audience as the inability of an actor to remember his lines. The audience took it as a mark of disrespect, as though the actor were a servant who had been negligent in his duties to a master. Jefferson apparently did not take this censure to heart, for at the next performance, three weeks later, the prompter noted that he was "hissed."

It was perhaps no more than a coincidence that the *Post* should have suggested that the "delicate and critical taste of a Garrick . . . root out these poetical excrescences" from the comedy, but there was only one more performance of *The Way of the World* before someone removed some of the offending passages. It was offered in its pre-revision state for the last time on October 27, 1775.

Before its revision, *The Mourning Bride* was acted each season, but never more than three times a year. There were occasional changes of importance in the cast. On October 8, 1770, when Joseph Inchbald attempted Osmyn, a part which Holland had long sustained, there was general agreement that his venture was not successful. The *Dramatic Censor* (II, 414) stated he presented himself "with a very slender degree of credit," being the worst in the role since Sheridan. The *Town and Country Magazine,* more charitable, referred to him as the "Garrick of the Norwich Company" but stated that Inchbald "did not meet with the success his friends expected, for tho' his voice and figure are agreeable, his feeling and deportment did not entitle him to rank as a first rate actor upon a London stage." [88]

Concerning a performance on September 28, 1771, the *Public Ledger* printed a long review. There was a history of the tragedy, and there was also an account of the scene, plot, and subject, as though these topics might be unfamiliar to readers. The writer stated that "the Story is pleasingly told, and the Incidents very affecting," but that it had "too much of the Bombast, and too little of Nature, to merit any great degree of praise." He found, however, "many instances of a fine taste in the Sentiments, though they are sometimes rather strained and artificial." He also criticized the tragedy for its failure to respect the unities, especially in the last act. As to the performers, he thought Reddish (Osmyn) and Miss Younge (Almeria) acted "with great attention and sensibility." He believed that J. Aickin was insufficiently "accustomed to the Language of Tragedy" to play the King well, and he wished that Leonora had been in the hands of "a better Actress than Mrs. *Johnston,* who seems but little acquainted with any Language." [89] Later (April 11, 1772) Almeria was played by Mrs. Barry, in the opinion of Lichtenberg (p. 31), "the greatest, or at least the most versatile," of the London actresses. Three seasons later Almeria was performed by Mrs. Yates, whom Lichtenberg designated (p. 14) as the "first actress in the high tragic style at Garrick's playhouse," [90] and on another oc-

[88] Oct. 1770, p. 546. Isaac Reed saw a performance of *The Mourning Bride* at Chesterfield on Sept. 12, 1771. See *Isaac Reed Diaries,* p. 72.

[89] As rptd. in the *Theatrical Review,* I, 22–24. The review was also reproduced in the *General Evening Post,* Oct. 1–3, 1771.

[90] Lichtenberg was especially impressed by her gestures, for she was "so skilled

casion he named her (p. 32) as the second actress—Mrs. Barry as the first —in the tragic style in England. By this time the tragedy was nearing revision. It had only a few performances during the closing years [91] of Garrick's management, the last under his guidance taking place on December 30, 1775. Drury Lane then omitted it for three seasons.

Looking backward, it is evident that great changes had occurred in the status of Congreve's plays during Garrick's regime. Two of the comedies—*The Old Batchelor* and *The Double Dealer*—had almost ceased to appear even before Garrick retired. *Love for Love,* usually the most popular of the comedies, had fallen upon evil days. *The Mourning Bride* and *The Way of the World,* though not extremely popular, had held the stage better than the other plays. To what extent Garrick as actor and manager influenced these changes it is not easy to say, but certain facts are very evident. Let them appear first in a table of performances of the five plays in the two theaters in three units representing roughly equal portions of Garrick's career as manager:

Period	Old Batchelor		Double Dealer		Love for Love		Mourning Bride		Way of the World	
	DL	CG	DL	CG	DL	CG	DL	CG	DL	CG
1747/8–1756/7	10	15	6	23	25	14	36	9	28	24
1757/8–1766/7	1	2	3	3	14	19	23	12	22	16
1767/8–1775/6	0	0	2	1	7	5	20	1	6	1
Totals	11	17	11	27	46	38	79	22	56	41

So far as *The Old Batchelor* is concerned, with the exception of one season, it rarely appeared in Drury Lane after Garrick became manager. It was not, however, much more frequently performed in Covent Garden. Because *The Double Dealer* had not really been a stock piece in Drury Lane, its vagaries have less relationship to Garrick. With *Love for Love,* however, it is a different matter. For many years it had been one of Drury Lane's most successful plays, and Garrick inherited a genuine tradition of favoring *Love for Love.* Under him the comedy

---

in the management of her arms, that from this woman alone could be made an abstract of the art of gesticulation" (p. 14). Mrs. Yates seems not, however, to have been happy in the role. On Nov. 16, 1775, Garrick wrote her after he had learned that she wished to quit the role because it was not *"fit"* for her. Garrick asked: "But why is it unfit, if it is the capital part of the play, and always performed by the first actresses?" On Nov. 17 she wrote: "In respect to Almeria, I think it a part unworthy of a capital actress." Although she did not elaborate her objections, she agreed to play "it a few nights" to oblige Garrick (*Private Correspondence of Garrick,* II, 110–111).

[91] It was acted at Liverpool on Aug. 30, 1773 (Genest, *Some Account of the English Stage,* V, 385).

was not greatly more popular at Drury Lane than at Covent Garden, and it averaged fewer than two performances a season under Garrick's regime. That was a great decline in its vogue. In contrast, Garrick seems considerably responsible for the increased vogue of *The Mourning Bride*. Not only did he give it a very successful revival in 1750–51 by taking the leading role himself, but the tragedy was offered more than three times as often under his management than at Covent Garden. In fact, it was acted in Drury Lane more frequently than any other of Congreve's plays. As for *The Way of the World*, it was second in popularity between 1747 and 1776, yet honors for its improved status must be divided between the two theaters, although Garrick's playhouse gave it with slightly greater frequency. On the whole, it is quite clear that only one of Congreve's plays did greatly better under Garrick's management, and *The Old Batchelor* and *Love for Love* lost ground steadily. Had Garrick been willing or able to undertake roles in more of Congreve's plays, they might not have declined so much or perhaps not at all.

Chapter VII

THE DECLINE OF THE PLAYS

In the spring of 1776, when Garrick retired in a grand finale of his best parts, there was no Congreve role among them. Congreve's plays had clearly lost their former high place in the repertories. Not one of of them had had more than five performances in a single season since 1764–65, when *Love for Love* and *The Way of the World* had had their last really genuine shares in the repertory. *The Old Batchelor* and *The Double Dealer* had been so nearly neglected that any Londoner who wished to see either one would have had to scan the playbills closely to catch their infrequent performances.

Congreve's plays were not, however, the only ones which were neglected. By the middle of the century Wycherley's *The Country Wife* and *The Plain Dealer,* once fairly popular, had disappeared. Each was replaced by a revision which, particularly for *The Country Wife,* changed its character and content. Etherege's comedies had left the stage much earlier, although *The Man of Mode* made a single appearance in 1765–66, over ten years after its previous performances. Other playwrights of the late seventeenth and early eighteenth centuries had proved not wholly enduring writers. Cibber's comedies, for example, were no longer really substantial parts of the repertory. Other comedies—*A Bold Stroke for a Wife, The Busy Body, The Confederacy, The Spanish Fryar,* and *The Tender Husband*—appeared occasionally rather than steadily.[1] Many of the older tragedies—*The Mourning Bride, Cato, The Distrest Mother,* and *Lady Jane Gray*—also appeared infrequently.

During the late years of Garrick's career, an indifference, if not antagonism, toward many old plays had developed. It appeared in the many arguments concerning the propriety of performing plays which seemed outmoded or morally objectionable in theme or manner or simply in need of revision to make them entertaining to an age different from the one for which the dramas had been written. This indifference was not, however, universal. There were many individuals who deplored the decay of the stage and who wished to see their old favor-

---

[1] Although there is no complete calendar of performances in the middle of the century, the lists in MacMillan's *Drury Lane Calendar* show what happened to many of these plays in Drury Lane during Garrick's regime.

ites restored to a dominant place in the repertories. Often this desire seemed to rise from nostalgic glimpses backward to the days of Betterton or the age of Cibber and his fellow managers, or from recollections of the superb handling by great but departed actors of characters in the plays of Wycherley, Congreve, Vanbrugh, and Farquhar.

Thus, at the same time that the older plays were disappearing, there was a movement to restore them, in altered form if need be. If it was not feasible or wise to revive them in all their original glory, a compromise could be achieved. Perhaps a new sparkle could be given tarnished plays by a rewriting which would remove the blemishes and heighten their dramatic virtues. Garrick, in fact, did a good deal of such revising. It was not limited to Shakespeare's plays, although these received much of his attention. He brought out, in 1754-55, a new alteration of *The Chances*. It was he who brought out in 1766-67, a year after John Lee had altered Wycherley's *The Country Wife,* a new version of the same comedy as *The Country Girl.* In 1770-71 he revised Dryden's *King Arthur.* As Garrick neared retirement, other adapters turned dramatic tinkers. George Colman in 1775-76 presented a slightly successful version of Ben Jonson's *The Silent Woman,* and in the same season Charlotte Lennox turned *Eastward Hoe* into *Old City Manners.*

It is hardly surprising that Congreve's plays should undergo similar treatment. Actually there was no single precedent to dictate just what form the revision should take. Some plays—for example, *The Country Wife*—had been thoroughly rewritten, with some characters eliminated and new ones created. In others—*The Plain Dealer,* for example—the changes had been less extensive. The revisions of Congreve's plays followed a relatively consistent pattern: the expunging of "exceptionable passages" without really significant change in the plot or characterization. This process usually involved the removal of words, phrases, sometimes whole speeches, but it rarely—except in some portions of *The Mourning Bride*—included the elimination of a sequence of speeches or an entire scene. It was a purifying by the cutting of detail rather than by genuine rewriting. The first of Congreve's plays to appear in this new fashion made its appearance shortly before Garrick's retirement. It was *The Double Dealer,* revived on March 5, 1776, at Covent Garden. It was advertised (inaccurately) as not acted there for twenty years, but the important fact was that it was "Written by Congreve, and now carefully revised and corrected, by expunging the exceptionable Passages." Thomas Sheridan apparently was mainly responsible for the alterations.

The reception of this revision set the pattern for judgments of the later ones. As might have been foreseen, the age could not agree upon the absolute necessity for rewriting or upon the virtues of the revisions. The *Gazetteer and New Daily Advertiser* (March 6, 1776), pleased to see the comedy revived, expressed the hope that it would be "more frequently brought to view than it has been of recent years." The writer acknowledged that the elimination of expressions "too loose and indelicate for the present times" had been necessary but thought that the play still "abounds with wit, character, and fable." Disagreeing, the *St. James' Chronicle* (March 5–7) disapproved of both the revival and the revision. Never having had "any great Opinion of the Play," the reviewer could not see that it had been improved by the "Corrections" made by Sheridan. On the whole, he thought the effect of the comedy to be as detrimental morally as it had been previously, if not actually worse. Expressing his "Abhorrence of Indecency," he nevertheless stated that if somewhat indecent plays had to be exhibited, "let it be in the original *naive* Manner of Congreve, and not in the Puritanical punning Manner of Tuesday Night; every Indecent Idea in the Commerce of the Sexes was continually kept in the Minds of the Audience; and yet the Wit which would have atoned for them was squeezed out by the leaden Hand of Mr. Sheridan." [2]

On the stage Maskwell was played by the alterer, who impressed neither reviewer. The *Gazetteer* stated that "by attempting ease, (which is far from natural to him)" Sheridan hurt the "proper sequence of the character." The *Chronicle,* much less kind, declared that Sheridan "would perform Harlequin just as well as he does Maskwell. He lays his hands before him; weighs and pronounces his Words like a Schoolmaster, in a Character which should be all Ease, Pliability, and Insinuation." Although the *Gazetteer* praised Booth as Lord Froth, it thought that he wanted spirit; the *Chronicle* believed, however, that he acted the part "as Congreve designed it." Both critics felt that Lee Lewes (Brisk) wanted "gentlemanly deportment," the *Gazetteer* adding that he was imperfect in his lines. The reviewers agreed that William T. Lewis (Careless) had little to do but did that little very well. Wroughton (Mellefont), praised by the *Gazetteer,* was judged by the *Chronicle* as not "sufficiently gentleman-like." Quick (Sir Paul) showed to the *Gazetteer* more originality than was his custom; to the *Chronicle*

---

[2] This statement, with its somewhat confused moral outlook, was discussed by a writer ("Reformation") in a letter to the same paper (March 19–21) in which he desired to "assist the writer with some essential Observations." Irritated by the critic's high-handedness, especially by the shafts directed at Sheridan, "Reformation" stated: "He abhors the Indecency of the Piece; yet desires to see it in its Original State of Indelicacy; rather than reformed by the Man he enviously points at. Mr. Sheridan's known Power forbids me to offer any Defence against the erring Shafts of this Rifler. What he means by 'squeezing Wit with a leaden Hand,' is a deep Secret to himself."

he appeared as "extravagant and ranting" as was Congreve in creating the part. To Isabella Mattocks (Lady Plyant) the *Chronicle* gave the same reserved compliment it had offered Quick; to the *Gazetteer* she was an "undescribable comic character," a phrase meant in praise, for she "showed her judgment in correcting the obscurities of the author without injuring the force of his wit." To the *Gazetteer* Mrs. Green, regarded by Davies as one of the best comic actresses of her day,[3] "showed how Lady Froth should be acted," an opinion with which the *Chronicle* disagreed; it asserted that she had "nothing about her of the Woman of Fashion, and was unfit for Lady Froth." Lady Touchwood, performed by a "Gentlewoman" for her first appearance on any stage, brought from both critics the judgment that, although she was "received with indulgence," she ought not to appear again.

This alteration did not lead to frequent offerings of *The Double Dealer*. The performance on March 5, 1776, was the only one of that season, the event being a benefit for Sheridan. During the next summer the Haymarket offered it, with John Palmer as Maskwell and Samuel Foote as Sir Paul, a part he had played before. None of the Covent Garden cast, however, appeared in the play. Early in the winter (Dec. 17, 1776) it was staged at Covent Garden as a benefit for the Theatrical Fund, a philanthropic enterprise for "decayed actors." Charles Macklin, now advanced in age, played Sir Paul, which he had acted as early as 1742, and Maria Macklin, who retired at the end of the season, acted Lady Plyant for the first time. Two performances in Covent Garden during 1776 were the only ones for *The Double Dealer* during the regular seasons until 1781–82.

Despite the unsuccessful revival of *The Double Dealer* in the spring of 1776, both Covent Garden and Drury Lane made a concerted effort to restore Congreve's other plays in altered versions in the autumn and early winter of 1776–77. Before the opening of 1777 the three other comedies and *The Mourning Bride* had reappeared in the two theaters. According to contemporary opinion, Sheridan, upon inheriting the management, restored these plays upon Garrick's advice. Davies, in fact, had little doubt that Sheridan acted under Garrick's guidance in "retrenching some licentious expressions, and connecting, by some slight additions, character and sentiment" in Congreve's plays. In Davies' opinion, Sheridan thus "saved those excellent plays from oblivion, which the extreme delicacy of a refined age, whose ears are become exceedingly chaste, could not endure." [4]

First to appear was *The Way of the World*, which was modified by

[3] *Dramatic Miscellanies*, III, 193.
[4] *Memoirs of the Life of Garrick*, II, 324.

removing those details most distasteful to audiences of that time. It was Covent Garden which revived it (Nov. 2, 1776), but that performance was not followed there by another one for over six years. According to the *Gazetteer and New Daily Advertiser* (Nov. 4) there was a "very thin house," [5] a fact which the reviewer lamented. He accounted for it by the fact that "the taste of the town has been considerably vitiated by a combination of some dull, sentimental scribblers, and low-witted poets, who have hitherto monopolized the literary emoluments of the stage, and committed continual rape of the Muses with impunity." As a result, "the palates of an English audience can have no more relish for the true attic salt of the incomparable Congreve." The *Morning Chronicle* stated, however, that the licentiousness of Congreve's comedies still remained a barrier to their appreciation. Despite Congreve's genius, "we may warrantably observe, that the line in Dr. Johnson's famous Prologue, spoken by Mr. Garrick, on opening Drury-Lane Theatre in 1747, is particularly applicable to Congreve's pieces, 'Intrigue was plot, obscenity was wit.' . . . Hence, we find the brilliant productions of Congreve . . . almost inadmissible, from the prudish coyness of modern audiences." Although the comedy had not been offered at Covent Garden since 1772–73, not all of the cast was new. Wroughton, retaining Fainall, was "equal" to the part (*Chronicle*). Lewis, new to Mirabell; Woodward, acting Petulant for the last time; and Lee Lewes, as Witwoud, similarly sustained their roles. There was special praise for Jack Dunstall, who did Sir Wilful "so much justice, that now that Shuter is dead, we place him second to Yates in that character." To the *Chronicle* Wilson, playing Waitwell, "over-acted" the part, "particularly while he personated Sir Rowland," a tendency apparently prevalent among most performers in that role. Mrs. Barry, making her first appearance as Millamant, "never comes before us without deserving our praise; she played Millamant in such a stile, as to defy censure; but she did not excite that involuntary applause which in tragedy she generally extorts. In fact, there is a better Millamant now on the stage." Mrs. Mattocks as Mrs. Marwood "looked and spoke the very character Congreve drew." In contrast, "Mrs. Pitt *bawled* out Lady Wishfor't with more applause than she deserved, while Mrs. Whitefield was content with whispering the words of Mrs. Fainall."

Seven weeks after Covent Garden's revival of *The Way of the World*, Drury Lane offered its revision of the comedy and repeated it five times that season, the receipts for the first four performances averaging nearly £200. This performance brought from the *St. James' Chronicle* (Dec. 31,

---

[5] Receipts of £185 4s (Egerton MS., Brit. Mus.) suggest a better than "thin" audience.

1776–Jan. 2, 1777) a spirited attack upon the whole system of resur-
recting old plays, altering them, and offering them on the stage. The
writer warned the managers that they were in danger of being called
"Resurrection-Men," whose "Business is with Bodies which should lie
in their Graves." Until recently "Congreve had been dead of Las-
civiousness and Debauchery . . . and it was the Opinion of that Part
of the Public which regards the Rites of Religion and the Customs of
Decency" that his plays should "never be dug up to the Annoyance
and Prejudice of the World. The Managers, however, having neither
Wit themselves; nor Interest to produce *living* Subjects, are imitating
their Brethren the *Resurrection-Men,* and are almost wholly employed
in raising the Dead." The writer admitted that the play had been produced "with Care, and performed with almost the whole strength of
the Company," a view shared by most of the other dramatic reviewers.
In the *Gazetteer* (Jan. 1, 1777) it was pointed out that "no play whatever can afford a more rational entertainment than Congreve's pieces,
especially when performed as the Way of the World was last night";
and the *Chronicle* agreed that it was well acted. In fact, there was
general agreement that this was probably the finest of Congreve's plays,
a reversal of the opinion prevalent seventy-five years earlier. A correspondent to the *St. James' Chronicle* (Jan. 11–14) selected "The Scene
between Fainall and Marwood in the second Act" as "a Master-piece
of fine writing. An accidental Quarrel between two artful Characters
discovers their own intrigues, and helps to carry on the Plot in a Manner the most artless and simple Imaginable; this I will venture to say
is a favourite Scene with all true Judges of Dramatic Poetry."

Although Drury Lane had not frequently offered *The Way of the
World* in recent years, few performers were new to their parts. Samuel
Reddish, continuing as Fainall, was praised, and Richard Yates (Sir
Wilful) and Mrs. Abington (Millamant) were deemed so excellent by
the *Chronicle* that their acting alone made the play "well worth the
attention of every lover of the drama. Nothing could be more elegant
and highly finished" than Mrs. Abington's manner, "nothing more
natural and truly characteristic than Yates'"; they seemed worthy of
being esteemed "the first actor and actress in the comic line now upon
the stage." The *St. James' Chronicle* concurred in this commendation
of Yates but stated that Mrs. Abington as Millamant "was sometimes
childishly affected, and forgot that this amiable Tyrant, with all her
Foibles, is a woman of fine Understanding." If Mrs. Abington felt that
this judgment was damning with faint praise, she could balance it
with the *Gazetteer*'s observation that all of its praise "cannot but fall
short of her merit." Among the newcomers, Smith, as Mirabell, was

commended by the *Gazetteer* and *Morning Chronicle,* but a correspondent to the *St. James' Chronicle* observed that "Mirabel was rather a well looking Man than a graceful and easy Gentleman. He understands the Meaning of his Author, but gives it too loudly." King (Witwoud) and Baddeley (Petulant) were complimented, the *Gazetteer* stating that "Mr. Baddeley was a real Petulant." Parsons as Waitwell was guilty of a common failing when he was "rather too extravagant" in impersonating Sir Rowland before Lady Wishfort (*Morning Chronicle*). The *St. James' Chronicle* stated that Miss Sherry (Mrs. Marwood) was "so far above Mediocrity, that I think the Part has not received equal Justice in the Performance since Mrs. Pritchard acted it," and to be compared with Mrs. Pritchard was praise indeed. With most of the performers more than merely adequate, the comedy remained for several years in good standing.

For fourteen years *The Old Batchelor* had been neglected by the two patent theaters. As the vogue for revising Congreve swept the playhouses in 1776, it too was taken up and on November 19, two weeks after *The Way of the World* had been revived, it appeared in Drury Lane. The comedy had also undergone "pruning" of the "obscenities" or "luxuriant passages" by Sheridan, who had become manager of Drury Lane in the autumn of 1776. As was true of the other revisions, *The Old Batchelor* was both welcomed and frowned upon. The *Morning Post and Daily Advertiser,* for example, stated that Sheridan had not used his "pruning-knife" sufficiently, for he had retained some "undramatic, wild shoots, which still weakened the bearing branches." These forced "the representation to an unnatural length;—several scenes in the first, and second act, remain still insufferably long, and in many parts, totally uninteresting.—We think there is full *seasoning* enough left behind even now; at any rate *Bellmour*'s pressing *Laetitia* a second trip into her bed-chamber we think might very well have been dispensed with." The *New Morning Post and General Advertiser* (Nov. 27) praised the alterer for doing the best that could possibly be done "to *accommodate* so capital a comedy to the present *taste* of the town." Taking a middle path, the *Morning Chronicle* (Nov. 20) stated merely that the revisions had been made necessary by changing tastes.

As more and more revisions appeared, the reviews became more greatly concerned with the method and wisdom of the alterations. Other reviews of *The Old Batchelor* reflected the uncertainty of the age concerning the problem. For example, the *Gazetteer and New Daily Advertiser* (Nov. 20) reported that the comedy was revived with "many judicious alterations, and even witty improvements, which were highly relished by the most sensible part of the audience, and generally ensured the success of the piece, in spite of the modern *Colliers,* and of all the sentimental scribblers, who will certainly not fail to frown at several humorous strokes, with which this excellent comedy is abundantly furnished." At the other extreme, the *St. James' Chronicle* (Nov. 19–21) argued that not only was the practice of reviving old plays a mistaken one but that *The Old Batchelor* in particular was detrimental to the public good. It pointed out that the comedy had been neglected for sixteen years because of its obscenity but that contemporary dramatists possessed such a "Lack of Wit" that they have turned "to an avowed Piracy on the Works of former Times." Revising *The Old Batchelor* was a serious error, for it was "unfit for Representation before an Audience, who would wish to see any Thing like Decency and Honour in the Commerce of the Sexes." The Prologue, "which was well written, and well spoken," was judged the "best Justification" which could be made for the revival, but it would be "despised by those who wish to see our Publick Entertainments, not as Means of preparing the Audience for Debauchery, but as Means to retard and prevent that Licentiousness to which we are so inclined."

Once the play had been performed, the argument continued for several weeks. Because the *St. James' Chronicle* had taken a firm stand against the revival, it received several letters, most of which agreed with the reviewer. "Flint" (Nov. 23–26) did not wholly condemn the revival but pointed out that the "Design of this Play is to represent People as vicious as Nature and Passion can make them, without the least reserve of the Poet in Favour of Virtue, or even decent Manners." Although he considered the plot "highly improbable and absurd," in "Wit, Humour, Pleasantry, and Character, few comedies come near it." "Theatricus" (Nov. 30–Dec. 3) expressed his surprise that, of Congreve's four comedies, this one should be chosen for revival, for it had "ever been esteemed the most indelicate of the four." Two weeks later (Dec. 14–17) a correspondent reproved women for flocking to Congreve's plays and added that this revival was a mark of the "highest Dishonour to the present Age." In a similar vein "A Polite Man of the World" wrote to the *Morning Post and Daily Advertiser* (Dec. 11) that, though he was "what the world and the women call a devilish impudent fellow," he was shocked at the "many indelicate speeches" still present in *The Old Batchelor.* He also experienced both pleasure and pain at seeing "a blush tinge the cheeks of many of my fair Friends; with pleasure,—as it proved Dame Modesty had not taken leave of *all* the sex, as some would insinuate; with pain,—because I was convinced they must experience very disagreeable sensations during the whole performance." He urged the managers to "make some few more alterations in the play," one of which he specified: "I would recommend also to Mr. *Fondlewife* the substituting some other pretty appellation for his Deary . . . anything but *Cockey.*"

The newspapers also participated in one of those lively engagements between actor and audience which enlivened theatergoing in the eighteenth century. At the revival of *The Old Batchelor* Samuel Reddish (Vainlove) brought the wrath of the town upon himself by being, as all the reports agreed, shamefully imperfect, so much so that the *Morning Chronicle* reported that Reddish interrupted the last scene to explain that he had taken the part on short notice "to *strengthen* the play" and had had only two rehearsals. Not inclined to treat Reddish lightly, the *Chronicle* pointed out that *The Old Batchelor* was six weeks in preparation, that for four of these Reddish was advertised to play Vainlove, and that, although the comedy was rehearsed seven times, Reddish attended only two rehearsals. For the next performance of the comedy there was in prospect one of those riotous evenings when the spectators would not permit a play to begin until the recreant player made his apologies. Reddish apparently knew the temper of the town and did not appear, Vernon taking his place. Even so, the *Chronicle* (Nov. 21) did not let the town forget Reddish's fall from grace: "The representation was much benefitted from Mr. Vernon's not only perfectly reciting the words of Vainlove, but restoring a considerable portion of what Mr. Reddish had the preceding evening *suo periculo* cut out, in violation of character, and while they were willing to applaud the man who had necessarily cleared the ground, as the Pioneer of Decency, neither hoped nor imagined that a principal figure in Congreve's group was to be annihilated by the destructive hand of a capricious and opinionated actor." On the following day the *Morning Post and Daily Advertiser* thundered at Reddish for his insolence in being so brazenly imperfect, and the *Chronicle* printed a communication from Reddish justifying his conduct. On the next day Reddish defended himself in another letter to the *Morning Post,* but he did not return to the cast.

Naturally, the cast had greatly changed from that of 1758. Still present, however, was Richard Yates, who won praise for his Fondlewife. The *Morning Post* pronounced him "exceedingly great" and the *Chronicle* stated that he "exhibited one of the most correct and comic pieces of acting we ever saw," an opinion shared by the *Gazetteer* and *St. James' Chronicle.* Among the newcomers, Bensley played Heartwell, for which the *Post* and *St. James' Chronicle* thought him well suited, but the *Gazetteer* deemed him weak. Farren as Sharper received lukewarm praise. The *Post* argued that "Mr. Moody's *Bluff* was too Bobadilian;

an error perhaps more chargeable on Congreve than on the actor," but the *St. James' Chronicle* coupled him with Yates as receiving highly deserved applause. Miss Essex, playing Sylvia for the first time, was judged by all as acting rather poorly, the *Gazetteer* softening the verdict slightly by adding, "She has a very engaging figure, and is not a contemptible actress." After Miss Hopkins replaced her for the second performance, the *St. James' Chronicle* admitted that Miss Essex "had hardly a Requisite as an Actress, but pretty sparkling Eyes." To the *Post* some of the actresses had been miscast. Mrs. Abington (Laetitia), in its judgment, should have played Belinda, which was taken by Miss Younge. Although no other review suggested an exchange of roles, the *St. James' Chronicle* was not satisfied with the acting of either: "Miss Young in Belinda wants every Thing but Sprightliness and a Conception of her Part; she is so destitute of Feminine Softness, that she should never be the Object of a tender Passion. . . . But Mrs. Abington was herself only at Times in Laetitia. We never before observed Mrs. Abington on the Stage seemingly inattentive to her Part."

Absent from the winter stages for nearly fifteen years, *The Old Batchelor* was only a moderate success at this revival. It had 8 performances, with receipts averaging £190 for the first 5 evenings. Yet it did not firmly establish itself in the theaters, for it was acted only 8 times in the next four seasons and it never had more than 3 performances in any one. Its long absence (1762 to 1776) from the regular theaters and its weak showing between 1776 and 1780 suggest that even a revision could not make the comedy sufficiently acceptable to enable it to prosper. The revised version had only 15 performances in Drury Lane and ended its career there with an appearance on May 10, 1782.

Following shortly upon the revival of *The Old Batchelor* came one of *Love for Love*, also newly revised by Thomas Sheridan. Offered at Drury Lane on November 29, 1776, it proved to have slightly more appeal with 9 performances during the season [6] as against 8 for *The Old Batchelor*. The receipts for the two plays were, on the average, very nearly the same, and the critical reception showed a very similar disagreement over the wisdom of revising and reviving the play. The *Gazetteer and New Daily Advertiser* received it with the statement "that never were plays that could afford a more rational entertainment than Congreve's pieces, especially *Love for Love* . . . but it is not food fit for every one's palate." The writer clarified his point by adding that reviving Congreve's comedies was "the highest compliment that Mr. Sheridan could pay to the public." The *St. James' Chronicle* (Nov.

[6] It was acted at Bath, Feb. 1, 1777 (Genest, *Some Account of the English Stage*, v. 623).

30–Dec. 3) expressed a pleasure that "the Managers took such Pains in reviving this admirable Play" and asserted that "no Man understood Human Nature more philosophically than Congreve. His Wit is easy, his Humour genuine, and his Sense profound." On the other hand, attentive readers of the *Morning Post and Daily Advertiser,* remembering that it had asserted that Sheridan had failed to use his "pruning-knife" sufficiently on *The Old Batchelor,* could not have been surprised to learn that the alterer had made the same mistake with *Love for Love.* Pointing out that the alterations were "trifling," the reviewer emphasized that "the dish, even in its present state, is served up in a style, savoury enough, to prevent the most high-fed glutton from starving.—Tho' the bed-chamber of Miss Prue is now converted into a closet, the manner in which *Tattle* and she enter it, and remain in it, till the Nurse comes, who is at first refused admittance, is rather too strong for some modern stomachs." Yet the writer stated that the "first three acts went off with a brilliancy proportioned to its true attic wit, and fine dramatic situations," although the closing two acts, "affording little more than scenes of ill-woven perplexities, hung fire, and consequently fell short of the former both in effect, and applause." No doubt, much of London shared the disapproval of the reviewer as well as the delicate sentiment of Fanny Burney's heroine upon witnessing *Love for Love:* "though it is fraught with wit and entertainment I hope I shall never see it represented again; for it is so extremely indelicate—to use the softest word I can—that Miss Mirvan and I were perpetually put out of countenance, and could neither make any observation ourselves nor venture to listen to those of others." [7]

The cast included the best talent of the company, some of whom continued former parts. Samuel Reddish, who had acted Valentine since 1769, was apparently more perfect in his lines than he had been in *The Old Batchelor,* for, according to the *Gazetteer,* he "found commendation" in the audience. William Parsons, who had played Foresight since 1769, was deemed "inimitable" (*Gazetteer*). Boaden thought that his "Foresight was a perfect thing" [8] and Davis considered him "born a comic actor; the tones of his voice and the muscles of his face proclaim it; nobody can forbear laughing, either *with* him, or *at* him, whenever he opens his mouth." Davies thought, however, that "If he would be more simple and chaste in drawing Old Foresight's character, and not imitate the action of a sailor pulling up his trowsers so often, he would not, perhaps, gain so much loud applause, but he would find more judicious approvers." [9] Mrs. Abington, playing her accustomed

7 *Evelina,* ed. Sir Frank Mackinnon (Oxford, 1930), p. 97.
8 *Memoirs of the Life of Kemble,* i, 62.
9 *Memoirs of the Life of Garrick,* ii, 325.

Prue, presented a "specimen of her wonted excellence" (*Gazetteer*),[10] and Davies, remembering how well she played characters of high life, saw with pleasure that she "rendered Miss Prue as naturally rude and diverting, as if she had been mistress of no other style in acting than rustic simplicity." Thomas King, acting Tattle for the first time, "made all he could of it," according to the *Gazetteer*, which preferred him in Scandal, his usual part, and Davies apparently agreed, for he wrote that "King's Tattle was as entertaining as a shallow debauchee could be made by a good actor." Richard Yates, now sixty, did Ben "strict justice" (*Gazetteer*) and played the part "with all the vigour, humour and spirit of a man of thirty." [11] Of those new to the play, Robert Bensley (Scandal) was considered by Boaden "the ablest representative" of that type of character.[12] John Moody (Sir Sampson) was thought by Davies to be well suited in "figure, voice, and manner," but needed to convey "a little more of the gentleman in acting this sarcastic knight." [13] To the *Gazetteer* Miss Pope "appeared the real Mrs. Frail"; Miss Younge (Angelica) and Mrs. Sherry (Mrs. Foresight) completed the cast.

The *London Magazine* (XLIV, 621) was probably not far wrong in its summation of these revivals. They had been brought on because of promises made to the public and the "attempt, in the language of the treasury, deserved 'our hearty commendations.' " Nevertheless, "the parts were not judiciously cast, nor was the whole strength of the company put forth. *Love for Love,* and *The Old Batchelor* brought some tolerable houses, but on the whole, both the town and the managers were disappointed." The failure of *The Old Batchelor* to be acted frequently in later years suggests that the town was disappointed in it, but *Love for Love* did better. It managed to appear in Drury Lane during nearly every season to the end of the century, although its success in Covent Garden was extremely limited.

Among the revisions of Congreve's plays, *The Mourning Bride* came last both in time and in success. The altered version first appeared in Covent Garden on December 18, 1776, its first performance there since September 21, 1767. Like the comedies, the tragedy was shortened, but the omissions were more extensive than those for the comedies.

---

[10] On May 4, 1780, the *Morning Post and Daily Advertiser,* comparing the merits of Mrs. Abington and Miss Younge, stated that one of the characters in which Mrs. Abington was unrivalled was Prue (the other, Hoyden): "Mrs. Abington's great merit in these parts is her vivacity, and her happy manner of delivering a *double entendre;* nor will she, I hope, think it an ill compliment in my declaring she utters a *bon mot* of that sort more expressively enchanting, than any contemporary or predecessor, (Kate Clive excepted). A third beauty in Mrs. Abington's playing is her *affectation* —I mean where it is necessary."

[11] Davies, *Memoirs of the Life of Garrick,* II, 325–326.

[12] *Memoirs of the Life of Kemble,* I, 59.

[13] *Memoirs of the Life of Garrick,* II, 325.

For some reason *The Mourning Bride* [14] did not catch on. Not only was it acted only once during the season, but it did not again appear in London until almost two years later. It was not until Mrs. Siddons assumed Zara in 1783 that the tragedy appeared more regularly. Although *The Mourning Bride* had not been staged at Covent Garden for a decade, not all of the performers were new to their parts. As he had done in 1767, Clark performed the King. Although Mrs. Ward was advertised as playing Zara for the first time, the manager must have overlooked the fact that she had acted it once in 1767. The Osmyn was Lewis, whom Boaden considered weak in tragedy.[15] The Almeria was Mrs. Hartley,[16] whom Lichtenberg considered "remarkable" in some respects, but he qualified his judgment by adding that her "great reputation is founded less on her art than on her exquisite form, which verges on ideal beauty." [17] Among the other newcomers were Thompson (Perez), Fearon (Alonzo), Hull (Gonsalez), L'Estrange (Heli), Robson (Selim), and Miss Ambrose (Leonora), not an exceptionally strong cast. The low receipts of £103 17s may have been a decisive factor in the play's not appearing again for some time.

In view of the concerted effort to re-establish Congreve's plays, it is not surprising that they had their best season in many years. Only *The Double Dealer* and *The Mourning Bride,* with a single performance each, did poorly. The other three had a much better showing: *Love for Love,* 10 performances; *The Old Batchelor,* 8; *The Way of the World,* 7. Not since 1761–62 had all five appeared in the same season; not since 1754–55 had there been 27 performances in one year. The season of 1776–77 alone, however, could not fully determine how genuinely the plays could be re-absorbed into the repertory, for it was only natural that, revised and recast, the plays should be well publicized and much discussed. No doubt, the managers pushed the plays. Had they held the same frequency of performance for several successive seasons, there would be evidence that the revival was genuine and that Congreve's plays, previously neglected, were gratefully received by a public which had actually missed them. The fact that the plays failed

14 It had been played at Liverpool on Sept. 6, 1776, as a benefit for Mrs. Hunter (Zara), with Osmyn by Lewis and Almeria by Mrs. Hartley, who later appeared in that role in Covent Garden (Genest, *Some Account of the English Stage,* v, 538).

15 *Memoirs of the Life of Kemble,* I, 70–71.

16 On June 14, 1774, Robert Jephson had written Garrick his impressions of Mrs. Hartley when Garrick was thinking of engaging her. Jephson thought that she had a "very fine" figure and "unexceptionable" features, although "her countenance is neither marked nor engaging." He believed that she had modelled herself upon Mrs. Yates, but unless she was instructed by Garrick, she would "rise but slowly, if ever, above an uninteresting mediocrity" (*Private Correspondence of Garrick,* I, 635).

17 *Lichtenberg's Visits to England,* pp. 35–36.

to hold the position they achieved during 1776–77 made that season a turning-point in their vogue. Had the plays caught on, they might well have continued into the nineteenth century as an important part of the repertory. But few of them held the stage after 1777 with real success. *The Old Batchelor* remained active for only five more years and eight performances. The *Double Dealer*, after a single performance in 1776–77, did not appear again until 1781–82. The other three were staged more frequently, but not one of them had an unbroken seasonal appearance to the end of the century. By 1790–91 *The Way of the World* had almost ceased to appear, and during 1793–94, for the first time in many years, not one of Congreve's plays appeared anywhere in London during the winter season. That had not happened since 1701–02.

For several years after 1776 the principal fact concerning the five plays as a group was their decline. In 1776–77 five of them had 27 performances. Not until 1781–82 did all five again appear in the same season, and never again in the century did the total of their performances reach even 20. In 1777–78 there was a precipitous decline to 6 performances of three plays. After that there was a rally, but 16 performances in a single season was the best showing they made. Yet there was spirited discussion of the plays, more than there had been for many years. In part, this was the result of the growth of dramatic departments in the newspapers and the custom of reviewing every night's offering. The increased attention resulted also from a desire on the part of reviewers and correspondents to speculate on the causes of the plays' decline in popularity.

In the four seasons following the revivals there was not, however, very much to invite discussion. In 1777–78 three plays shared the 6 performances. *The Old Batchelor* had good receipts: October 9, £185 16s, and May 17, £287 5s. *Love for Love* did nearly as well: March 5, £192 8s 6d, and April 6, a benefit for Dodd (Ben), £248 7s 6d. On January 23 *The Way of the World* had moderately good receipts, £199 6d. On May 27 it was offered as a benefit for Mr. and Mrs. Thomas Davies, both of whom had theatrical connections. A not very successful actor, Davies later failed as a publisher. His fellow-actors gave him a benefit, at which he acted Fainall for his first appearance in fifteen years but with somewhat disappointing receipts of £198 9s 6d. Boaden, an admirer of Davies, could say of him only that his "countenance was Garrick's, with all its fire quenched." [18] In 1778–79 the plays did slightly

[18] *Memoirs of Mrs. Siddons*, p. 95. In the previous summer (Aug. 20, 1777) *The Way of the World* was acted at Liverpool as a benefit for Mrs. Wilson (Millamant), with Clinch as Fainall, Wilson as Sir Wilful, and Mrs. Siddons as Mrs. Marwood (Genest, *Some Account of the English Stage*, v, 627).

better. *The Old Batchelor* had but a single performance, it is true, but *The Mourning Bride* reappeared; and both *Love for Love* and *The Way of the World* more than doubled their performances of the previous year. The tragedy was given in Drury Lane, its first perform-ance there since the late revision. J. Aickin (King) and Packer (Gon-salez) repeated roles which they were to retain to the end of the cen-tury. Davies (Garcia), Wrighten (Alonzo), Hurst (Heli), and Fawcett (Selim) had their usual parts. Miss Younge, who had previously played both Almeria and Zara, took the former role; and Mrs. Farren, for her first appearance in six years, was Zara. Nevertheless, these two per-formances had as little effect in re-establishing the tragedy as had Covent Garden's one in 1776–77, for it was omitted in 1779–80. During 1778–79 *Love for Love,* with 5 performances, averaged receipts of £166; *The Way of the World,* with 4 performances, £202.

Performances of three plays were fewer during 1779–80: 10 in the regular season, with *Love for Love* given once at the summer Hay-market. *The Old Batchelor* had 1 performance; *Love for Love,* 3; *The Way of the World,* 6. In 1780–81 there was a slight improvement, with four plays presented for 12 performances. *The Old Batchelor* had its best showing in several years, with 3 performances, but the receipts on the first two nights averaged slightly less than £100. *Love for Love* appeared twice, with only slightly better receipts, £145 on the average. *The Mourning Bride* was given once by each house. At Drury Lane, where Mrs. Crawford played Almeria,[19] a performance early in the season brought only a fair £157 16s. At Covent Garden it appeared late in the season as a benefit for Brandon, with very good receipts, £289 6s. *The Way of the World* had 5 performances. After several seasons of infrequent performances, Congreve's plays in 1781–82 took a brief new lease on popularity. For the first time since 1776–77 and for the last time in the century, all five appeared in the same season. Even so, it was not a very substantial gain, for the total of performances was only 15, and the plays declined again in the following seasons.

The seasons of 1781–82 marked the return of *The Double Dealer* to Covent Garden for 3 performances, all benefits, with good attendance. John Henderson acted Maskwell, and Elizabeth Inchbald, who had joined Covent Garden the year before and who later turned to play-writing, played Lady Touchwood, with Mrs. Mattocks as Lady Plyant

19 What Mrs. Crawford's fortunes in London might have been we do not know, but, as Genest pointed out (VI, 213), she left London soon after the opening of 1781–82 and went to Ireland, a step which Genest called the "most imprudent . . . that ever was taken." Her departure made an opening for Mrs. Siddons, who might other-wise have remained at Bath. When Mrs. Crawford returned to London, she en-countered the superior talent of Mrs. Siddons at her best.

and Miss Younge as Lady Froth. The comedy did not appear again, however, for two years. The other three comedies fared unequally. *The Old Batchelor* had but 1 performance, and *Love for Love* was, for the first time in many years, given only a single performance (Nov. 6), with modest receipts, £173 13s. *The Way of the World* was more successful, with 6 performances, apparently its peak, for during three seasons it had been given that many times but no more. The receipts varied greatly. On October 13, when Miss Farren acted Millamant, they were only £91 15s 6d, a very small sum. On January 9, when Mrs. Abington returned to play Millamant, they rose to £207 13s 6d, and on February 6 were nearly as good, £204 14s. Except at a benefit late in the season, attendance again fell off, although Mrs. Abington, a very popular comedienne, continued as Millamant. It was in this season that Charles Lamb, for his third visit to a theater, saw *The Way of the World:* "I think I must have sat at it as grave as a judge; for, I remember, the hysteric affectations of good Lady Wishfort affected me like some solemn tragic passion." [20] *The Mourning Bride,* with 4 performances, was more frequently seen than it had been in years; it was given at Covent Garden, where it had not appeared since 1765–66. The four performances brought fairly substantial receipts: £196 3s, 6d, £231 17s, £277 11s 6d (a benefit for Miss Younge, who acted Zara), and £140 17s. [21]

Once again the plays faded into the background for several seasons. Although J. P. Kemble began a long and successful careeer with his debut as Hamlet in Drury Lane (Sept. 30, 1783), he failed then to undertake parts in any of Congreve's plays. Just as Garrick's failure early in his career to give more than moderate attention to Congreve's plays had weakened their status within the repertory, so Kemble's lack of interest in them undoubtedly kept them in the background. For two years both *The Old Batchelor* and *The Double Dealer* went unacted. Even *Love for Love* had no genuine success. Acted once in 1782–83 and 3 times in 1783–84, it then went unacted for a season, the first time since 1768–69. Following its success with *The Way of the World* in recent years, Drury Lane unaccountably dropped it in 1782–83. Covent Garden kept it on the stage, however, for 3 performances, its first appearance there since 1776. Mrs. Barry again played Millamant, and three others—Wroughton (Fainall), Lewis (Mirabell), and Lee

20 "My First Play," *Works of Lamb,* ed. MacDonald, I, 199.

21 *The Mourning Bride* had an even better season at Bath. Acted first on Oct. 6, 1781, it presented Mrs. Siddons as Zara, with Dimond as Osmyn and Miss Scrace as Almeria. Later it was given as a benefit for Mrs. Siddons, who shortly became the sensation of London, and the tragedy had 7 performances that season (Genest, *Some Account of the English Stage,* VI, 233–237).

Lewes (Witwoud)—repeated roles they had had six years earlier. Richard Yates, for his first appearance in Covent Garden, acted Sir Wilful (which he had often played in Drury Lane) on one evening. The situation was reversed in 1783–84, when Covent Garden omitted the comedy and Drury Lane restored it for 4 performances.

It was *The Mourning Bride,* however, which received the greatest attention in 1782–83 and 1783–84. Not only was it acted five times in the first season, but both theaters played it. More important, Mrs. Siddons, the idol of the late eighteenth-century stage, made her first London appearance in many years and acted Zara there for the first time. Her success in Zara and other roles eclipsed that of any other player during the year. In Covent Garden, Mrs. Yates, a distinguished actress, courted comparison by playing Almeria, an act whose "baseness" Boaden disapproved. Yet, he was "impressed with the majestic grandeur of her person, and the musical enchantment of her declamation, that, in this imperial tragedy of Congreve's, I cordially agree with our critic, that her fourth act, and her last scene . . . were all of them in the 'highest style of sublime tragedy.' " [22] To challenge Mrs. Siddons in 1782–83 was, indeed, to be courageous. After her somewhat unimpressive debut at Drury Lane as Portia in *The Merchant of Venice,* she had toured the provinces and made great progress. Greatly acclaimed in London, she acted on eighty evenings, playing Isabella 22 times, Jane Shore 14, Calista 14, and Belvidera 13. On her first benefit Boaden estimated the receipts at £800, a tremendous sum. Her acting of Zara on March 18, 1783, was her second benefit of that season, on which she received "expressions of admiration from persons of rank and talent," [23] and by Her Majesty's command she was appointed reading preceptress to the young princesses. Although Mrs. Siddons did not frequently act Zara, she immediately became the standard by which excellence in the role was judged. Three performances of Zara in a year were, however, her greatest attention to the role, and it never became one of her choice parts.

Boaden's complaint that Mrs. Yates imprudently courted comparison with Mrs. Siddons seems hardly borne out by the facts, for in 1782–83 Mrs. Yates' two performances in *The Mourning Bride* occurred before Mrs. Siddons acted in the tragedy in London. Possibly Mrs. Yates wished to establish herself before Mrs. Siddons could make her Zara *the* standard, but Mrs. Yates did not act Almeria after January 15 and Mrs. Siddons did not play Zara until March 18. In 1784–85 Mrs. Siddons had a new rival when Covent Garden gave the tragedy once to Drury

[22] *Memoirs of Mrs. Siddons,* pp. 202–203.
[23] *Memoirs of the Life of Kemble,* I, 118.

Lane's three performances. For the single performance Mrs. Crawford, who in 1781–82 had left London for Dublin, returned to play Almeria. Because she brought better attendance than Covent Garden had known for some time, the manager saw in her a possible rival to the great actress at Drury Lane. In comparing the two performers, Boaden summarized the opinions of many spectators: " 'If the flights of Crawford,' said they, 'are higher, Siddons continues longer on the wing. If of Crawford's fire, the blaze is brighter, of Siddons's the heat is more regular and constant. The one often surpasses expectation, and the other never falls below it. Crawford is heard with frequent astonishment, and Siddons with perpetual delight.' " To Boaden the actresses belonged to different schools of acting, for "what was unimpassioned in the dialogue was somewhat rapidly given by Mrs. Crawford, who evidently reserved herself for striking effects." Mrs. Siddons, however, "seemed to consider that every thing in the part she played required the utmost care; and that where declamation was not to be lifted by passion, it was to charm by a kind of tender and melancholy music, disposing the soul to the superior effects when they arose." [24] Although box office receipts are often misleading, those for the only performance in Covent Garden were £182 7s, lower than those for any performance of the tragedy in Drury Lane: £240 17s 6d, £224 17s, and £249 7s 6d.

During 1784–85 it was *The Double Dealer*, however, which made the best showing, especially since *Love for Love* was not acted at all. *The Double Dealer* was staged at Drury Lane, which had not acted it since 1772–73, 8 times, the largest number of performances for any of the comedies since the 9 appearances of *Love for Love* in 1776–77. Yet only once during the first 6 performances did the receipts rise much above £110. A few performers—King (Sir Paul), Dodd (Brisk), and Packer (Lord Touchwood)—had acted their roles before. John Palmer, who was noted for Joseph Surface as one of his three hundred parts, acted Maskwell, except on April 4, when John Philip Kemble played it for the first time. Elizabeth Kemble, sister of Stephen Kemble, played Lady Touchwood for the first time. Miss Pope, who was celebrated for pert chambermaids and elderly ladies, was Lady Froth, and Miss Farren, later the Countess of Derby, acted Lady Plyant.

The success of *The Double Dealer*, mild as it may have been, exceeded that of the other Congreve plays during 1784–85. *The Way of the World* appeared but once at each theater, its poorest showing since 1777–79. Mrs. Abington, formerly of Drury Lane, was now the Millamant of Covent Garden; according to the *Public Advertiser,* reviewing the performance on November 11, 1784, "Millamant, the last and high-

[24] *Memoirs of the Life of Kemble,* I, 129–131.

est-polished character of Congreve's pen . . . would have lain on the
shelf, or (what would be perhaps of more discredit to our taste) would
be but *ill represented,* were it not for the peculiar talents of Mrs. Abington, who . . . restores the character all its original value. To enter into the particulars of her performance would not be doing her justice.—Fine acting, like fine writing, should be felt by general impressions." Wroughton (Mirabell), Lewis (Witwoud), and Mrs. Bates (new
to Mrs. Marwood) were also praised, but the reviewer thought that
when Farren as Fainall "begins to familiarize his dialogue a little
more, and speak less *declamatory,* he will do better." The writer concluded that the "rest of the characters were as well sustained as perhaps
the strength of the company would admit of it—but where is the whole
of a *Dramatis Personae* that can do strict justice to the language of
Congreve? An author who is in some respects getting obsolete, from
our being so long used to *other kind of writers.*"

By the mid-1780's the vogue of Congreve's plays followed no clear
pattern, and it must have been difficult for either the managers or spectators to predict the fortunes of any one of them. No one could easily
foresee that, after the eight performances of *The Double Dealer* in
1784–85, it would not be acted at all in the next season, or that *Love
for Love,* absent during 1784–85, would reappear for only a single
performance in 1785–86. Unacted at Covent Garden for ten years, it was
staged there on January 28, 1786, probably because it offered a good
part for Mrs. Brown, who had been brought from York to rival Mrs.
Jordan, Drury Lane's rising star. On January 28 Mrs. Brown played
Prue for the first time, and, according to Boaden, "was seen with considerable pleasure, as an actress, who had claims to figure, face, and
voice." [25] A party formed to applaud her, but, failing to surpass Mrs.
Jordan, she soon retired from the contest. Tate Wilkinson thought
that Mrs. Brown, who had great faith in her own powers, "forgot what
an audience *never* will, and that was, that Mrs. Jordan at that time was
very young, an article for superiority which few performers confess." [26]
Like *Love for Love, The Way of the World* had but a single performance. *The Mourning Bride* had three performances, with Mrs. Siddons playing Zara but once and Covent Garden offering Mrs. Warren
(Almeria) and Miss Brunton (Zara) as ineffectual competitors to the
incomparable Mrs. Siddons.

In 1786–87 it was *Love for Love* which unexpectedly was a considerable success. Acted 9 times in Drury Lane and 3 in Covent Garden, it

25 *Memoirs of the Life of Kemble,* I, 317.
26 *The Wandering Patentee,* II, 166.

had its best season since 1732–33 and its second best in the century. In Covent Garden the cast was centered in Mrs. Brown, whose attempt to rival Mrs. Jordan enabled *Love for Love* to achieve its 3 performances there, for when Mrs. Brown relinquished the part in the next season, the comedy was unacted in Covent Garden for ten years. Similarly, Drury Lane's success with it was due to the virtuosity of Mrs. Jordan, who acted Prue for the first time. According to Boaden, who was very partial to her, she found that the "getting up of 'Love for Love' afforded her, in Miss Prue, a character exactly suitable to her style of acting, and which kept its hold upon the public mind"; her performance in Act I was "inimitably natural." [27] Although the reviews did not always accord her first place among contemporary actresses, London in general welcomed her warmly. During this season the most interesting comments upon the comedy appeared in the *World*, whose dramatic reviews, eccentric in style and biased in favor of Kemble (Valentine), were presumably written by Charles Este.[28] On February 15, 1787, the *World* discussed both the comedy and the acting:

Tho' it cannot easily be acknowledged with Addison, that *Love for Love, is* the best play in the world, and as such to be followed with equal eagerness, by those who have seen it, and those who have not, yet so many are its charms, in vivacity of dialogue, and strength of character, that the representation is amusing, tho' far from safe.

With something more than abatement in the article of the moral praise, for the '*callida junctura,*' and probability are no where visible. We sat this comedy with much contentment!

In the acting, there is abundant merit. The Valentine of *Kemble,* is perfect in all its parts. The ease, the elegance, the strong sense, and feeling of the character came up, as Congreve would let them. *Parsons* in *Foresight,* is second to nothing, but *Parsons* in *Corbaccio:* he is the only player in the cast, who boasts as sure acceptance, from the Stage Box to the Shilling Gallery! Dodd . . . was heard with pleasure. And *Ben,* never pleasant, and now wrong, as out of all probable date, yet forced into something better than sufferance, by the skill of *King.*

Miss *Farren*'s comedy yields to none—her dress, one mass of un-relieved *white sattin,* did not aid her triumph. Miss *Pope* and Mrs. *Jordan* are not to be dismissed but as the best representatives of Miss Prue and Mrs. Frail.[29]

A month later the *World* stated of another performance of *Love for Love:* "Better acted—worse attended—it never was. . . . For the praise

[27] *Mrs. Jordan* (New York, n.d.), I, 99–100.
[28] Gray, *Theatrical Criticism in London to 1795,* pp. 259–260.
[29] Lamb agreed wholeheartedly with the *World* regarding Kemble: "No man could deliver brilliant dialogue—the dialogue of Congreve or of Wycherley—because none understood it—half so well as John Kemble. His Valentine . . . was, to my recollection, faultless" ("On the Artificial Comedy of the Last Century," *Works,* I, 290).

—Parsons has the largest claim, tho' *Kemble, Dodd, King, Pope, Jordan,* and *Farren,* are also to be much at large. Each day determines anew, that *Kemble* must be eminent in comedy."

After its success in 1786–87, *Love for Love* proved again the erratic course of Congreve's comedies in this period by declining to two performances. On October 15, 1787, Bannister, Junior, acted Tattle for the first time but "did not retain the character which Dodd so ably portrayed, nor did his playing it affect, in any degree, his general reputation, or his position at the theater." [30] After the second performance, the *World* (Nov. 15) repeated almost by rote its stand that *Love for Love,* "if good for nothing else, may serve to exemplify towards content, and prove the preference of present manners and opinions, over those that are past. Scenes, which now, every body knows enough, not to admire for their structure, and to despise for their tendency, were once the subject of unqualified praise. Even ADDISON himself . . . mentions *Love for Love* as a play so good—that no one should omit seeing it . . . when judgment was thus perverted with *Addison,* what must it have been with all who were under him." In 1786–87 and 1787–88 the other Congreve plays varied little from their recent records, *The Way of the World* being given only once each season. *The Mourning Bride* did slightly better in 1786–87: 2 performances in Covent Garden, 1 in Drury Lane. Concerning a performance at Drury Lane on May 19, the *World,* which rarely lost an opportunity to emphasize the weakness of the play, was almost ecstatic in praise of Mrs. Siddons:

Mrs. SIDDONS
To enquire what beauty is—must be the question of a man who cannot see—He who asks what dignity is, cannot have seen Zara by Mrs. Siddons:—The dignity of empire, and personal charm; that is, intrepid, and would be commanding.

And yet it is, in spite of all that astonishing acting can do for it, signifying nothing. Sound without cause, and fury without effect. If Zara's passions outstript the wind, they neither interest the mind, nor impress the heart.

The play is very worthless. That it is a pantomime, is not its greatest fault. Inasmuch as it offends manners no less than taste; and bursts with ribaldry more than nonsense.

And yet such is the force of talents—that against this obstacle and others, with Fahrenheit at Summer heat, and all the acting about her, below freezing—such is the force of talents—there was a full house, and much applause.

In 1787–88 *The Double Dealer,* "According to the last, and much approved Alterations," which differed only in details from previous editings, made its last return to the eighteenth-century stage. Although it had three performances, perhaps its disappearance was due to the low

[30] John Adolphus, *Memoirs of John Bannister, Comedian* (London, 1839), I, 208.

receipts, which on the first two nights averaged only £110. Its reception
was a mixed one. The *World* and the *Public Advertiser* lamented its
indecency, the *World* (Nov. 30) emphasizing that if Congreve's comedies "astonish often, and too often captivate *in their dialogue,* as being *intellectual* . . . the *tendencies* are to be lamented as perverse—
the *structure* slighted as unreal—Sometimes the plan is absurd. Here,
the story, in any system of life, is impossible." It added that, if the
comedies had been "as active on right principles" as on wrong ones,
"Pity would not, with intellectual anguish, now be drooping over [Con-
greve's] fame." Nevertheless, as "a performance, the Stage was complete. In all the lower parts, there was an excellence of an upper order.
In the leading characters of the Play, the excellencies were yet higher.
It was genius working upon genius. The varieties were exact: and the
exactness was that which referred to spirit as well as truth." The *Public
Advertiser* (Dec. 1), seeing the mixture of wit and immorality, stressed
its moral stand by asking, "but without a *moral tendency,* what advantage can possibly be derived from visiting the theatre?" The *Morning Herald* was more cordial, however, and lamented that the comedy
had not "that attendance which its merits demand." It ranked *The
Double Dealer* "in contrast of characters, happiness of conduct, and
brilliancy of wit" as better than any "modern Comedy, *but one.*"

To Kemble (Maskwell), the *World,* ever partial to the Kembles, gave
its highest praise: "In execution, as well as conception, his *Double
Dealer* yields to no acting, past or present." The *Advertiser* praised him
for playing well opposite Mrs. Taylor (Lady Touchwood), who acted
"with great *judgment, energy,* and *execution*—their last scene in particular was a masterly piece of performance; and were the author alive,
would probably receive his thanks for it." The *Herald,* however, thought
that a "little more flippancy, with less solemnity, would have made his
Maskwell—not only what we shou'd approve, but what we shou'd
applaud." Wroughton as Careless was "airy, pleasant, and sensible"
(*Advertiser*). The *World* praised Suett (Lord Froth) and Miss Pope
(Lady Froth) and gave greater applause to Miss Farren (Lady Plyant),
the *Herald* agreeing that "more discrimination or better applied, we
could not possibly desire." Bannister, attempting Brisk, was, to the
Advertiser, good but unequal to Dodd, his predecessor. His biographer,
who condemned the play for its immorality, thought Kemble's masterly
performance as Maskwell so overshadowed the others that Bannister
had little opportunity to show his talents in Brisk. When the play was
repeated on December 21, the *World* referred to it as having "wit im-
properly applied" and after failing at its première, "never rose much
afterwards." Yet by "the artifice of acting, and no acting was ever more

perfect than KEMBLE's, this outrage upon Decency and Probability, may, now and then lift up its head and laugh . . . It is, on the whole, among the most perfect comic acting of its time." A performance on May 30, 1788, brought down the curtain on the last eighteenth-century appearance of *The Double Dealer*.

In the next season (1788–89) it was *The Old Batchelor* which had its last eighteenth-century performance. Covent Garden played the comedy twice late in the season, with receipts of £213 5s and £136 13s. Most of the cast was new, although three principals—Mrs. Abington (Laetitia), Mrs. Pope (Belinda), and Farren (Sharper)—had played those roles in one theater or another. The *World* (March 6, 1789) pointed out that it was a vigorous play to come from an author only twenty years old but that it was also "often so obsolete, uncouth, and disgusting to modern manners, that not many people have ever seen it, and fewer still will see it again," a very accurate prediction, for the performance on March 12 was its last in the century. The *World* stated that the acting "to be mentioned with any praise, is Mrs. POPE, LEWIS, and above all, BLANCHARD, in *Sir Joseph*—and that, indeed, with *Bluff*, is the most amusing part of the play."

Although this revival of *The Old Batchelor* was a failure, *Love for Love* had eight performances, not quite so many as it had had two seasons before, but an excellent showing. Acted at Drury Lane by a strong company, it had good receipts early in the season. The *World* (Oct. 13, 1788) selected Ben and Prue for its disapproval: "As for *Ben*, and yet more Miss *Prue*, it is such obsolete vulgarity, it could do nothing but disgust, even if BANNISTER and Mrs. JORDAN could be better than they are." The *Morning Chronicle*, however, stated that the "novelty of the evening was young Bannister in Ben, which he performed excellently, particularly in his first scene with Miss Prue, and the quarrel that afterwards takes place between him and Mrs. Frail." Bannister apparently made a considerable change in the portrayal of Ben, a part which Adolphus thought was "not well calculated for the display of his powers," because Ben had been "sketched by the poet as being all rough, coarse, and unmannered." Previous actors—Shuter and Edwin—had made Ben a character of "extreme low life," but in "the hands of Bannister it assumed a form somewhat new, and greatly improved. . . . In the dialogue, the grossness used in speaking to and of Miss Prue was veiled, as far as it could be, by the light and joyous manner of the performer: when he was duped by Mrs. Frail, he did not show himself a helpless self-calf . . . but vented his homely reproaches against her inconstancy with a justness of feeling, and manliness of deportment, which rescued him from every thing approaching to contempt." [31] Lamb also wrote of Bannister as Ben, especially of the scene in which the sailor, returning home, talks with his father. "Here is an instance of insensibility which in real life would be revolting. . . . But when you read it in the spirit with which such playful selections and specious combinations rather than strict *metaphrases* of nature should be taken, or when you saw Bannister play it, it neither did, nor does wound the moral sense at all. For what is Ben—the pleasant sailor which Bannister gives us—but a piece of satire—a creation of Congreve's fancy—a dreamy combination of all the accidents of a sailor's character. . . ." [32] On another occasion Lamb contrasted two performers of Foresight. Parsons emphasized the "old man, the doater," and the astrologer, whereas Munden "dropped the old man, the doater —which makes the character—but he substituted for it a moon-struck character, a perfect abstraction from this earth, that looked as if he had newly come down from the planets." [33]

These changing portrayals probably had a good deal to do with the ability of some of the comedies to keep their slender hold upon the stage. The *Morning Chronicle,* analyzing a performance of *Love for Love* in December, argued that the comedy might not have succeeded if it had been written in its coarse vein during the late years of the century, for its immorality was a deterrent to contemporary appreciation. It had survived, however, because of "the characteristick wit and humour, with which it is replete" and "the powerful aid it has generally received from the abilities of some of the best performers." Adolphus, writing many years later of Bannister's playing of Ben, made a similar point: "Yet, with all the wit which sparkles in every line of the play . . . many persons felt uncomfortable and dissatisfied when the performance was ended.—Why?—Because there is not a spark of virtue or honour in any person in the whole drama." The saving element was "the grace it could derive from the ability of such performers" as Bannister.[34]

During the same season (1788–89) *The Way of the World* made two appearances, both in Drury Lane, which in recent years had nearly monopolized the comedy. The principal event was the appearance of Kemble as Mirabell on November 12, 1788. According to Boaden, "he certainly stood well in the place of Smith; but the house was thin, though Miss Farren graced her own Millamant." [35] The receipts were very small, £81 11s. Both the *Morning Chronicle* and *World* agreed

[31] *Memoirs of Bannister,* I, 204–205.
[32] "On Some of the Old Actors," *Works,* I, 279.
[33] "The Death of Munden," *Works,* III, 95–96.
[34] *Memoirs of Bannister,* I, 207–208.
[35] *Memoirs of the Life of Kemble,* I, 419.

that the play had been poorly attended; the *World,* referring to its presumed failure at its première, lamented: "Worse than all be serv'd / In Childhood murder'd, and when murder'd starv'd." It added that the excellent dialogue coupled with brilliant acting should have produced much better attendance. Both reviews compliment Miss Farren (Millamant). The *World* naturally praised Kemble greatly, but the *Chronicle* thought his performance "wanted more *nerve* and warmth of colouring," for he often "by endeavouring to be chaste and correct is too cold and languid." *The Mourning Bride,* given twice in Covent Garden and once in Drury Lane, presented the *World* with a fine opportunity to express its continued dislike of the play and also a contrast between the fine acting at Drury Lane and the wretched performance at Covent Garden. Of the latter it remarked: "To have a bad Tragedy is one thing —to act it badly is another: so combined, they produced the pleasantest effect possible, and a merrier Tragedy we never witnessed. To these effects, GARDINER, Mr. HULL, and a Mute, contributed all they could." A few weeks later its appearance at Drury Lane, with Kemble as Osmyn and Mrs. Siddons as Zara, was a vastly different one:

CONGREVE'S PANTOMIME

For if the *Mourning Bride* was a Play, and at all adequate to the Merit of Mrs. SIDDONS and KEMBLE, in the playing it, this narrative would undo us.— The Paper, without restrictions, could not hold it.

Sir JOSHUA, the first night of Mrs. SIDDONS in Zara, pronounced it a *chef d'oeuvre!*—and who like him to be judge of taste and grace! But if *emotion* be sought for by the Spectator, it is not in *Zara* it can be found. Of such powers as Mrs. SIDDONS, it is a waste, when they do not soften the temper, or amend the mind.

The season of 1788–89, with 15 performances, was the last one in the century in which Congreve's plays had a considerable share. Four were on the stage then, but only two in 1789–90: *Love for Love* and *The Way of the World.* The two playhouses offered the latter competitively for the first time in five years. When Drury Lane offered it (Sept. 15, 1789), with Mrs. Goodall as Millamant, the receipts were only £110 8s 6d, and possibly the small returns prompted Drury Lane to omit it until 1800. In Covent Garden it was acted before Their Majesties on January 13, 1790, with receipts of £407 4s 6d, for royalty nearly always brought a full house. For the second performance (Jan. 20) they were substantial, £235 13s. It was probably Mrs. Abington as Millamant which attracted a good audience; nevertheless, the comedy did not reappear in Covent Garden until 1797–98. After 8 performances in 1788–89 *Love for Love* declined to 5 in 1789–90. On the first night (Oct. 3, 1789) Parsons made his first appearance of the season and "drew, THEATRI-

CALLY, an excellent House" (*World*). Miss Prideaux made her first Drury Lane appearance as Prue and, according to Kemble, "proved herself the worst Actress that ever was seen." [36] The *World* ambiguously stated that she "gained something like applause in it—if that be the criterion of good acting." On her second appearance as Prue, the *Prompter* (Nov. 9) stated: "We feel hurt to direct our readers against her, as to her appearance and acting; it is but justice to say, and we must say it, that a more disgustful figure cannot be pictured; surely the manager can find a better Miss Prue." At the next performance Mrs. Jordan resumed Prue. Both the *World* and *Prompter* spoke highly of Parsons, the *World* referring to him as a "prodigy of excellence" and the *Prompter* calling him "the oddest compound of drollery and astrological calculations, we were ever witness to.—We think Parsons the most humorous in such characters of any actor we have, not excepting Edwin."

By 1790 *The Old Batchelor* and *The Double Dealer* had ended their eighteenth-century careers. *The Way of the World,* not entirely vanquished, was to appear in only one season (for three performances) in the last decade of the century. Of the remaining two plays, neither appeared during every season from 1790 to 1800. *Love for Love* was absent in 1793–94, and *The Mourning Bride* missed four seasons. In 1793–94 there was no performance of a Congreve play in either Drury Lane or Covent Garden, an event which had occurred but once (1701–02) since the beginning of the century. During the last decade the plays appeared so irregularly that their course may be most easily followed in an account of the stage history of each play during the decade. *Love for Love* was the most frequently performed, with 27 performances in ten years but with never more than 5 in any season. It was almost exclusively to be seen in Drury Lane, with only one performance in the rival theater. With the play itself presumably familiar to most of the audience, the reviews usually devoted their attention to the actors. A long account in the *Morning Chronicle* of a Drury Lane performance on October 15, 1796, offers a glimpse into the modes of acting then current:

On Saturday CONGREVE's witty Comedy of *Love for Love* was performed at Drury-lane Theatre, when Mr. KING for the first time stood forward in the character of *Sir Sampson Legend,* which by his comic exertion and judicious colouring, he contrived to render one of the most pleasant of the *dramatis personae.* It is some novelty to see an actor broad awake in *Sir Sampson,* the wily Knight having been in a deep sleep at the Theatre for some years past, and it is also a novelty to see an actor of Mr. KING's acknowledged merit condescending to

36 Brit. Mus. Add. MS. 31972.

play such a character as *Sir Sampson Legend,* which has not hitherto been considered as a part in the play worth the employ of the talents of a Comedian, who stood high in the estimation of the public. . . .

KEMBLE was interesting and easy in *Valentine,* and Miss FARREN peculiarly arch and entertaining in *Angelica.* Mrs. POPE's *Mrs. Frail* was uncommonly lively, and R. PALMER's *Tattle* proved, that he is capable of being a most unexceptionable substitute for the deceased DODD. J. BANNISTER's *Ben* produced its usual effect, and excited many hearty laughs from the Galleries. . . . SUETT, generally speaking, is a good and successful Comedian, but we could not help regretting the loss of poor PARSONS, who was particularly whimsical in *Old Foresight.* SUETT wanted eccentricity both in nature and appearance; his wig was too formal for a man, whose mind is described as wholly occupied by the idle pursuits of star-gazing, divination, and the interpretation of dreams. Miss MELLON was the *locum-tenens* of Mrs. JORDAN, and played *Miss Prue* more than tolerably well.

Although *The Mourning Bride* did not fare so well as *Love for Love,* it was more frequently seen than the other comedies. Like *Love for Love,* the tragedy was almost exclusively the property of Drury Lane, but it never appeared more than twice a season there. Acted once in 1790–91, it was omitted in the next season. In 1792–93 it was staged twice in Drury Lane, once in Covent Garden. In Drury Lane the tragedy won comment chiefly because of Kemble as Osmyn and Mrs. Siddons as Zara. The *Thespian Magazine* (Dec. 1792, p. 166) declared that Kemble "is undoubtedly the best Osmyn on the stage," a not very magnificent compliment since Pope of Covent Garden had played it only once. Kemble was judged well suited to "that firmness of sentiment and action that characterizes the unfortunate prince." On the second performance the critic (March 1793, p. 218) again praised Kemble and complimented Mrs. Siddons for "finely" acting "the haughty Zara." Four more performances of the tragedy occurred before the end of the century, with Mrs. Siddons and Kemble the chief ornaments of the cast and probably the principal reasons for presenting it. The *Morning Chronicle,* reviewing a performance on October 12, 1795, stated that the tragedy had become fashionable again, for "every time Mrs. SIDDONS has appeared she has attracted a crouded House." The review lamented, however, seeing "her exquisite abilities employed on *The Mourning Bride.*" Imperfect as the tragedy seemed, it was "rendered . . . interesting and agreeably" by Mrs. Siddons, and Kemble "did all that was possible for Osmyn."

Only one other of Congreve's plays made an appearance in the 1790's: *The Way of the World.* In 1797–98 Covent Garden, which rarely offered any Congreve play in the closing years of the century, staged it three times. The receipts generally were substantial, but the *Monthly Review* (IV, 299), reporting the performance on October 28, stated that the "cast . . . exhibited the comic strength of the company to great advantage;

but the flat reception it met with, proves that *wit* is not the grand *desideratum* of modern audiences. Congreve would have no chance with the dramatists of the present day." This melancholy verdict seems borne out by the status of the plays in the twenty-four seasons following the retirement of Garrick. Revised and revived in 1776, *The Old Batchelor* and *The Double Dealer*, in terms of performances, hardly warranted the effort, for neither reached twenty performances in twenty-four years. *Love for Love*, as it nearly always had been in the past, proved more enduring and had the nearest claim to genuine appreciation. Having grown fairly steadily in esteem, *The Way of the World* was second in frequency of performance between 1776 and 1800. *The Mourning Bride* was a fair third, but had it not been for Kemble and Mrs. Siddons, it might well have been as neglected as *The Old Batchelor* and *The Double Dealer*. The five plays were certainly no longer a substantial part of the repertory. All in all, there is a curious parallel between their status from 1741 to 1776 and their vogue from 1776 to 1800. In 1741, when Garrick entered the theatrical scene, they were very nearly at their peak, and although they held their position fairly well for a while, by the end of Garrick's career, they were a very insubstantial part of the repertory. In 1776, at the beginning of another new regime, they rose suddenly to a rather large share in the theatrical offerings but soon declined into an erratic and unpredictable frequency of performance. There was to be little change in their status in the early nineteenth century.

Chapter VIII

AFTERMATH

Although the close of the eighteenth century marks the chronological limit of this study, there remain some elements of the vogue of Congreve's plays still to be considered. The first is an outline, necessarily brief, of their status in the nineteenth and twentieth centuries, for their appearances did not automatically cease on the closing day of the eighteenth century, and it is of interest to see what eighteenth-century influences extended into the following decades. There is also a need to examine the relative popularity and the standing of the plays in relationship to each other during the eighteenth century. Finally, there need to be examined the factors which caused their fluctuations in vogue during the century.

Not all of the plays appeared in the early nineteenth century. *The Old Batchelor* left the stage in 1789 and did not appear again for many decades. Among the remaining four, *The Double Dealer* had the briefest history. Acted on February 27, 1802, the comedy presented Kemble as Maskwell and Charles Kemble as Mellefont. Supporting them were some members of the cast of 1787–88, particularly King (Sir Paul), Suett (Lord Froth), Pack (Lord Touchwood), and Miss Pope (Lady Froth). Apparently this revival, with only one performance, was a failure, a contention borne out by a review in the *Monthly Mirror* (XIII, 202). The reviewer stated that this was one of the comedies which, with Wycherley's plays and others from the Restoration age, "ought never again to be revived." In fact, the audience on this night "with difficulty suppressed its indignation," and the writer thought it to be to the "credit of the times" that the "audience was not numerous." Should another performance be attempted, he hoped that the audience would "testify the most decided reprobation of a play to which no female can listen without emotions of shame, and which must excite the utmost abhorrence in every virtuous mind." The reviewer would not even compliment the performers, "because, to play the scenes of the *Double Dealer,* with the effect intended by the author, requires a degree of effrontery which we will not impute to any actor, particularly to the females, by praising their performance." Arguing that the "whole mass" of the play was "infectious" and defied "any attempt at reform or qualification," the writer rejected the usual plea that its wit might "atone for its indecency."

This was a particularly harsh view of the comedy, yet its failure to appear again suggests that the reviewer was not stating an isolated opinion.

The Way of the World fared slightly better in the early nineteenth century. After being absent for some years, it reappeared in the late months of 1800 with some new deletions and other minor revisions by Kemble. In a comment upon the printed version, the December *Monthly Mirror* (x, 386) observed that many "of the indelicate passages . . . are omitted, and others softened, in such manner as to be no longer very objectionable on the score of morality." Acted on November 22, the performance was reviewed by the same journal (x, 395–396). Pointing out that he had already commended Kemble's curtailments, the reviewer stated that he could "not speak so favorably of the representation of this excellent comedy, which, with the exception of two or three characters, was but indifferently performed. Congreve, who is chiefly supported by his *dialogue,* must have the benefit of very superior acting indeed, or nothing can keep him from flagging."

It was not until 1842, during a revival of Congreve, that *The Way of the World* had many performances, but its twelve appearances in that season did not enable it to remain on the stage thereafter. A review in the *Times* (Dec. 19) contrasted *The Way of the World* and *Love for Love,* also being revived. In the latter there is "a perpetual torrent of dashing repartee—a representation of an artificial state of things; but nevertheless coarse and strong. The profligates of *Love for Love* are not ill-natured profligates." But in *The Way of the World* there is "quite another set" of "rogues and—ladies, whose predicate we suppress, who edify us by their very subtle contrivances and their very admirable dialogue." Referring to *The Way of the World* as "the most artificial of artificial comedies," the reviewer called it also "one of the greatest comedies that ever was written. A calm quiet knowledge of a state of society in which heart has no place, in which unclouded intellect reigns alone, is fully displayed in this wonderful production." According to the review, the comedy was acted in "a pretty strict adherence to the original," although there were obviously some considerable changes of which the reviewer did not approve. "In the first place, Mrs. Marwood, Fainall's mistress, was converted into a dull and heavy gentleman, who was assigned to Mr. Stuart, and the speeches intended for an indignant woman were made to croak harshly from the throat of a sort of heavy 'Snake.'" The other change was made "to preserve Mrs. Fainall's reputation, and render her merely the subject of a wrongful persecution on the part of her husband. This change was no more felicitous than the other."

Mrs. Siddons and Kemble were mainly responsible for the attraction which *The Mourning Bride* held for early nineteenth-century audiences. In fact, writing of a performance at Drury Lane on January 28, 1802, the *Monthly Mirror* (VIII, 131) stated that "The *Zara* of Mrs. Siddons, which is decidedly one of her very best characters, attracted an overflowing audience on this evening." The writer thought that she never played it better; "indeed nothing can possibly go beyond it." Of a performance on October 15, 1807, in Covent Garden, at which Mrs. Siddons was then engaged, the same journal reported that Mrs. Siddons was "excellent throughout, but in the scene with *Osmyn,* in the prison she was wonderfully fine. Mr. Kemble wore his Moorish dress with all its advantage, and played with great ability; but in tragedy Mrs. Siddons' star has so much the ascendant, as to eclipse every other within the sphere of its lustrous action." That the tragedy itself was no longer greatly valued appeared in the admission of the writer that it "displays as much inflated language, or what Aristophanes calls *prose on horseback,* as can be produced in any tragedy equally successful." [1] With so much of its vogue dependent upon Mrs. Siddons, the tragedy could not long survive her departure from the stage.

The only Congreve play genuinely in vogue during these years was *Love for Love.* Unlike the others, it had several seasonal cycles, each lasting two or three years. After it was omitted in 1793–94, it appeared at least once each season through 1803–04. Omitted in 1804–05, it returned in the next season at Drury Lane, which alone had offered it thus far in the new century, and was more frequently acted than it had been for five years. After 1808–09 there was again a gap until Covent Garden, in September of 1812, staged it. Once again it lapsed until 1815–16. During this season, Hazlitt, reviewing for the *Examiner,* saw it and thought it "in wit and elegance, perhaps inferior to *The Way of the World;* but it is unquestionably the best acting of all his plays." Although it "abounds in dramatic situation, in incident, in variety of character," Hazlitt thought it better reading "in the closet" than upon the stage. He felt that "many of the finest traits of character were lost" in the acting. With these qualifications, he "hardly ever saw a richer or more powerful piece of comic acting" than Munden in Foresight. "It was done to the life, and indeed somewhat over; but the effect was irresistible. His look was planet-struck, his dress and appearance like one of the signs of the Zodiac taken down. We never saw any thing more bewildered. Parsons, if we remember right, gave more imbecility, more of the doating garrulity of age, to the part, and blundered on with a less determined air of stupidity." Harley as Tattle was "very entertaining," particularly his "indifference in the scene where he breaks

[1] N.S. II (Oct. 1807), 288 (misnumbered 260).

off his engagement with Miss Prue." In the love catechism "he was less successful: he delivered his lessons to his fair disciple with the air of a person giving good advice, and he did not seem to have a proper sense of his good fortune." In general, Hazlitt was less pleased with the other actors. "Mr. Dowton did not make much of Sir Sampson Legend. He looked well, like a hale, hearty old gentleman, with a close bob-wig, and bronze complexion—but that was all." As Prue, Mrs. Mardyn "was a little hard and coarse" and did not make Prue "fond and yielding enough." [2]

After this season performances of *Love for Love* became more sporadic. Played in 1815–16, it then went unacted until 1819–20. Not until 1825–26 and 1826–27 was it again staged, and then in 1842 it was revived. Although it did not do quite so well as *The Way of the World,* it was more frequently performed than it had been in a long time. The reviewer in the *Times* (Nov. 21, 1842) was somewhat critical of Congreve, who "revelled in his knowledge of his little world, but he displayed that knowledge more by the apophthegms he put into the mouths of his characters, than by what they did and felt. His language could not sink into commonplaces, for he felt a requisition to be witty, and by this one element of wit alone he created an atmosphere neither real nor ideal, but something between both." In addition, his "characters are broadly and hastily sketched, his plots are confused and miserably inartificial, he does not awake a spark of interest for one of his people, and yet by this vast power of wit . . . he has produced dramas which, with all their deficiencies as dramas, stand a marvel for succeeding generations." Like *The Way of the World,* revived a month later, *Love for Love* had been adapted "to modern delicacy." The major "alterations were the omission of Scandal's intrigue with Mrs. Foresight, of Angelica's coarse dialogue with her uncle in the second act, and a softening of the catastrophe of Miss Prue's love-scene with Tattle." *Love for Love* made another brief appearance in 1848, but there was nothing then to compare with the twenty performances of it and *The Way of the World* in 1842.

In the present century a good many revivals of the plays have occurred, some under the auspices of societies or of repertory companies and some in the commercial theaters. In April 1904 the Mermaid Society presented *The Way of the World* at the Court Theater in London, and it was given again in November at the Royalty Theater.[3] During World War I the Stage Society and the Phoenix Society began a

[2] *A View of the English Stage* (London: George Bell & Sons, 1906), pp. 159–161.
[3] Harold Child, "Revivals of English Dramatic Works, 1919–1925," *Rev. of Eng. Studies,* II (1926), 186.

cycle of Congreve which eventually brought all five plays upon the stage. The first to appear was *The Double Dealer* (May 14–15, 1916).[4] A year later *Love for Love* was given at the Aldwych (April 15–16, 1917), followed by *The Way of the World* (May 12 and 14, 1918) at the King's Hall. Several years later [5] the two other plays were acted: *The Old Batchelor* at the Regent Theater (June 1–2, 1924) and *The Mourning Bride* at the Scala (Nov. 22, 1925).

In more recent years some of the plays have been given in both New York and London, but only a few of the performances can be noted here. Apparently the longest run for a Congreve play in many years was attained by *The Way of the World* when it was presented by the Cherry Lane Players at the Cherry Lane Theater, a rather small house, in New York on November 17, 1924, for 120 performances. In the following spring *Love for Love* appeared at the Greenwich Village Theater, another small playhouse in New York, for 47 performances beginning on March 31, 1925. *Love for Love* was repeated that autumn in Daly's Theater. During 1927 *The Way of the World* was acted at Wyndham's Theater in London,[6] and in New York the Players' Club gave it at the Guild Theater for 8 performances during the week of June 1–6, 1931.[7] In 1934 *Love for Love* was staged at Sadler's Wells, London,[8] and, interspersed with scenes from *The Way of the World,* at the Country Playhouse in Westport, Connecticut, on June 29, 1936. For 8 performances during June 3–8, 1940, the Players' Club gave *Love for Love,* with a distinguished cast including Cornelia Otis Skinner, Barry Jones, Peggy Wood, Dorothy Gish, and Bobby Clark, at the Hudson Theater.[9] During War II *The Way of the World* was given in London at the Mercury Theater late in 1942 [10] and *Love for Love* at the Haymarket late in 1944.[11] In New York John Gielgud produced *Love for Love* at the Royale Theater for a limited engagement beginning May 26, 1947, and *The Way of the World* was part of the Old Vic repertory

[4] For the Stage Society and Phoenix Society revivals, see Montague Summers, *The Restoration Theater* (London, 1934), Appendix III.

[5] *Love for Love* was again revived at the Lyric, Hammersmith, on March 20 and 22, 1921 (Summers, Appendix III), and *The Way of the World* at the Maddermarket Theater in Norwich in March, 1923 (Child, p. 186). *The Way of the World* was also acted at the Lyric, Hammersmith, on Feb. 7, 1724. See Nigel Playfair, *The Story of the Lyric Theater, Hammersmith* (London, 1925), pp. 227–228.

[6] See a review in the *Spectator,* Nov. 26, 1927.

[7] See the New York *Times,* June 2, 1931.

[8] Reviewed in the *Spectator,* March 16, 1934.

[9] See the New York *Times,* June 4, 1940.

[10] See a review in the *Spectator,* Dec. 4, 1942, and *New Statesman and Nation,* Nov. 28, 1942.

[11] See a review in the *Spectator,* Oct. 27, 1944.

at the New Theater in the early months of 1948–49, with Dame Edith Evans as Lady Wishfort.

In the earlier chapters there have been presented two substantial phases of the reputation of Congreve's plays: the critical appraisal in the century and a half from the première of *The Old Batchelor* to Macaulay's review of Hunt's edition of the plays, and the stage history of the dramas from 1693 to the end of the eighteenth century. There is another phase of the reputation of the plays which appears in their frequency of performance and their popularity relative to each other during the eighteenth century. Of the five plays, *Love for Love* received, on the whole, more unqualified praise than any other and it was beyond any doubt the most popular on the stage. It was acted approximately 435 times in the century—the statistics in this section are all given in approximate figures—and that figure represents a third of the performances of all of Congreve's plays. It was also acted in more seasons than any other play; according to the extant records, it was missing from the stage during only eight of the hundred years.

The Old Batchelor was second in frequency of performance, its greatest vogue occurring in the first half of the century. In fact, by the time Garrick became manager of Drury Lane in 1747, the vogue of *The Old Batchelor* was nearly ended, for, of its 300 performances in the century, 250 occurred before 1747. Yet it had two periods in which it was more frequently acted than *Love for Love:* between 1714–15 and 1728–29, when it was the only Congreve play offered in both Drury Lane and Lincoln's Inn Fields; and during the six seasons following the debut of Garrick in 1741–42, when Garrick acted in it but not in *Love for Love.*

The Way of the World, third in popularity, was the principal example among the five of a play which rose from a cool initial reception to considerable popularity. It was very infrequently acted during the first two decades of the century, but once it had achieved a genuine revival, it steadily improved its position. By the middle of the century it was third in frequency of performance, and for a brief period it was the most frequently acted of the five. With 285 performances in the century, it was only slightly below *The Old Batchelor.*

The Double Dealer, with 150 performances, was the least successful of all. In no period was it eminently appreciated, although the twelve seasons from the opening of Goodman's Fields in 1729 to the debut of Garrick in 1741 marked its most successful period. Its better showing then was due to a long run in Drury Lane during 1735–36. Like *The*

Old Batchelor, The Double Dealer was most frequently seen in the first half of the century, its vogue being concentrated between 1718–19 and 1758–59, when 135 of its 150 performances were given.

The Mourning Bride, with 245 performances, stood fourth among the plays, considerably above *The Double Dealer,* slightly below *The Way of the World.* Not until 1718–19 did it do much better than two performances a season, and between 1714 and 1729 it ranked with *The Double Dealer* as the least frequently performed. Gaining moderately in frequency of performance, it reached its high point in the fifteen years following 1747. During that period it was acted more often than any other of Congreve's plays except *The Way of the World.* For the rest of the century *The Mourning Bride* appeared less frequently than *Love for Love,* slightly more often than *The Way of the World.*

A more illuminating comparison concerns the stage vogue of *The Mourning Bride* and that of other tragedies. Before the opening of Goodman's Fields in 1729 Congreve's tragedy had been acted about 40 times since 1700, as had *All for Love, The Distrest Mother, The Indian Emperor,* and *Richard III.* All of these were much less frequently performed than *Cato, Julius Caesar, Oroonoko,* and *Tamerlane,* with 100 performances each, and were even less frequently seen than *Hamlet* or *Macbeth,* in the 125 to 150 class. By 1741, when Garrick made his debut, *The Mourning Bride,* with 100 performances, had gained on *All for Love* (65), *Aurengzebe* (30), or *Lady Jane Gray* (30). It had fallen further behind *Julius Caesar* (150), or *Cato, Oroonoko,* and *Othello* (around 170 each). These, of course, lagged behind *Macbeth* and *Hamlet* (200–250).

At this point *The Mourning Bride* may well be contrasted with *Richard III,* which had an important place in Garrick's early repertory. In the first six seasons of Garrick's acting career, *The Mourning Bride* was acted 3 times, *Richard III* nearly 100. In the nine seasons following 1747, Congreve's play did much better, with nearly 40 performances, but *Richard III* had almost twice as many, and *Romeo and Juliet,* an important vehicle for both Garrick and Barry, had about 150 performances in the fifteen years following 1741. In the ten seasons beginning with 1756–57 *The Mourning Bride* had nearly the same number of performances as in the preceding nine years, but it was exceeded by *The Fair Penitent, Macbeth,* and *Othello,* each in the neighborhood of 50 performances; *Hamlet* and *Jane Shore,* with better than 60 each; *Richard III,* nearly 80; and *Romeo and Juliet,* more than 100. By the end of the century *The Mourning Bride,* with 245 performances, held a middle position among the tragedies, along with *Cato* and various versions of the Earl of Essex theme. Slightly below Congreve's tragedy was *The Distrest Mother,* but above it were at least twelve tragedies which were on the stage during most of the century. Shakespeare's plays greatly exceeded it, especially *Hamlet, Macbeth, Othello, Romeo and Juliet,* and *Lear.* Neither did Congreve's tragedy compete successfully with Rowe's best, for *Tamerlane, The Fair Penitent,* and *Jane Shore* had a greater vogue. Among Restoration tragedies *The Mourning Bride* made a better showing. Although Otway's *The Orphan* and *Venice Preserved* ranked above it, *Caius Marius* and the lesser Otway dramas failed to approach it in frequency of performance, and *All for Love, Aurengzebe, The Indian Emperor,* and *Oedipus* were distinctly below it.

Perhaps a more illuminating illustration of the vogue of Congreve's plays appears in the following table. It is a statement of the share which Congreve's plays had in the repertory during the principal theatrical periods of the century: the percentage of performances of his plays to those of all plays (excluding operas and plays in foreign languages) in the regular and summer seasons, with the exception of the summer offerings at the Haymarket in the last forty years of the century when that theater emphasized primarily farces.

Seasons		The share which Congreve's plays had in the repertory
1700/1–1704/5	The opening five seasons	2.1%
1705–6–1709–10	Five seasons of competitive playing at Drury Lane and the Queen's Theater	2.7%
1710/1–1713/4	Four seasons during most of which Drury Lane had a monopoly	4.0%
1714/5–1719/20	Six seasons of competitive playing between Drury Lane and Lincoln's Inn Fields	4.7%
1720/1–1728/9	Nine seasons of competition before the opening of a third major theater	5.1%
1729/30–1736/7	Eight seasons of competition: Drury Lane, Lincoln's Inn Fields, and Goodman's Fields	5.5%
1737/7–1740/1	Four seasons following the Licensing Act and preceding the debut of David Garrick	6.2%
1741/2–1746/7	Six seasons from the debut of Garrick to his assumption of the management of Drury Lane	5.0%
1747/8–1755/6	The first third of Garrick's career as actor-manager	5.2%
1756/7–1765/6	The middle seasons	3.6%
1766/7–1775/6	The last third of Garrick's career	1.3%
1776/7–1783/4	Eight seasons following Garrick's retirement	3.4%
1784/5–1791/2	The next eight seasons	2.4%
1792/3–1799/00	The closing eight seasons of the century	1.0%

The stage history of Congreve's plays makes it apparent not only that they shared the normal fluctuations inherent in a repertory system but that they also experienced fairly well defined cycles of popularity both as individual plays and as a group. Essentially they were at their best during the first forty years of the eighteenth century. Their very substantial vogue then was founded upon an advantageous theatrical environment which created an appreciation for the natural virtues of the dramas. In the first place, the majority had a very warm reception at their premières; for at least three of them contemporaries spoke of "extraordinary" success, and it is doubtful that *The Double Dealer* or *The Way of the World* had initial failures except by contrast with the more cordial and universal reception of the others. Such a warm welcome, even when cooled by the disapproval of the Collierites, elevated the plays to an enviably high position among spectators and actors. In addition, they were cast with the finest performers of the 1690's—Betterton, Dogget, Mrs. Barry, and Mrs. Bracegirdle, for example—and for several seasons in the next century these players lent their excellence and prestige to the plays and set a standard for the younger actors. To emulate these performers (Cibber's conscious imitation of Dogget is a case in point) and to acquire their roles became goals of the youthful thespians, a situation which brought the more popular plays more and more frequently to the stage. By the second decade Robert Wilks, especially accomplished in acting "fine gentlemen," Colley Cibber, celebrated for foppish roles, and Anne Oldfield, brilliant in high comedy, not only equalled the excellence of Betterton, Dogget, and Mrs. Bracegirdle, but in their turn became the standard for the next generation.

As the number of theaters increased with the opening of Lincoln's Inn Fields in 1714 and Goodman's Fields in 1729, competition fostered the continued offering of the genuinely popular plays and the trial of those less frequently seen. As a result, *The Old Batchelor* and *Love for Love* were to be seen in two and sometimes three theaters simultaneously, and the other three plays, much less frequently performed before 1714, were successfully added to the repertory. There is probably no clearer indication of the high regard for Congreve's plays than their continually larger share in the repertory in spite of the many other revivals and the constant addition of new plays. By the late 1720's all of his dramas were offered with sufficient regularity that they should have been familiar, scene by scene, to regular theatergoers, and public interest in them was focussed more and more upon the actors and their conception of Congreve's characters. Commentators suggest that the audience not only relished the plays but also the varied portrayals by Wilks, Cibber, Hippisley, Giffard, Harper, Mrs. Oldfield, Miss Younger, Mrs. Giffard and the host of others who appeared in one or another of the dramas. Then, too, plays written in the late seventeenth century were sufficiently close in time, manners, topicality, and dramatic as well as acting tradition to offer the spectator a familiar and recurring pleasure.

After the Licensing Act of 1737 theatrical conditions changed. Competition was reduced. Wilks, Booth, and Mrs. Oldfield were dead; Cibber had retired. Although their influence lingered, the rise of Garrick and his followers created new styles of acting and a different theatrical atmosphere. Congreve's plays now had to compete not only with a continually larger body of plays in the repertory but with a tremendous increase in Shakespearean performances, with Garrick playing many roles in Shakespeare's plays. Garrick had a decisive role in another respect. He did not bridge the gap between the old days and the new by taking and retaining roles in all of Congreve's plays. In his first season he played in *The Old Batchelor* and *The Way of the World,* but did not long retain a part in either. He did not perform at all in *The Double Dealer* or *Love for Love.* Several years after his debut he acted Osmyn in *The Mourning Bride,* but again he did not long sustain the part. When a brilliant and enterprising actor fails to take an active interest in a group of plays, particularly in a repertory system and more particularly when he as manager of a leading playhouse does not continue its tradition of presenting a particular body of plays, they are unlikely to continue a past success unless there is a tremendous public demand for them. (In fairness to Garrick, it should be pointed out again that he was possibly not well suited to many roles in Congreve's plays and that he was in danger of creating dissension and jealousy by assuming roles which had long "belonged" to another actor.) At much the same time, unfortunately, the age was being told again and again, particularly in the newspapers and magazines, that late seventeenth-century drama was highly licentious and unworthy to be presented before a more delicate and sentimental age. Congreve's plays, as well as many others written in the late 1600's, were acted less and less frequently until by the time of Garrick's retirement (1776) they had a smaller share in the repertory than they had had at the beginning of the century.

Nevertheless, there were spectators and critics who desired to see the plays remain on the stage. As a result, they were revised and revived in 1776, but not with enduring success. Once again, as in Garrick's early years, no great actor or group of actors gave them the prestige and the audiences the pleasure to be had from original and vitalizing reinterpretations of roles no longer so familiar as they had once been. In addition, the revisions were not genuinely satisfactory. They were intended to achieve a happy compromise by retaining the best of Congreve and removing the objectionable elements. The alterations did not, however, wholly eliminate the licentiousness which the age deplored, yet, in removing portions, the revisers could not easily escape rendering the comedies insipid and lifeless. Neither the admirers nor detractors of Congreve were satisfied with versions which did not constitute a really intelligent and able revival, and the public responded rather indifferently. There is evidence in the reviews that the plays seemed dated in spirit, tone, topicality, and characterization. Probably the late eighteenth century had not yet achieved that stage in the cycle of literary revolutions which finds the drama of a fairly distant period interesting, lively, and enchanting. (The present century seems more genuinely appreciative of late seventeenth-century drama than did the audiences from 1760 to 1800.) Congreve's plays were not uniquely exposed to those conditions nor uniquely neglected. That they retained some semblance of popularity in the late years of the eighteenth century seems due principally to their being valuable vehicles for leading actors—Sheridan, Kemble, Mrs. Jordan, and Mrs. Siddons—and to their having a small core of appreciative spectators. But neither factor could sustain them indefinitely, and in the years from 1785 to 1815 their appearances were sporadic and dwindling. Finally they were no longer performed. Nevertheless, three generations of theatergoers had enjoyed them immensely, and our own day has derived from them a pleasure not unlike that which audiences experienced in the years when Congreve himself was alive.

APPENDIX I

THE REVISIONS OF THE PLAYS

As has been apparent in Chapter VII, all of Congreve's plays were changed in some degree when they were restored to the stage in 1776. There were other revisions during the late years of the century. His plays were not, in the strict sense, rewritten; rather, they were somewhat superficially revised by the elimination or rephrasing of lines. Hence an account of the revisions is—except for *The Mourning Bride* —principally a matter of indicating the nature of the alterations which the adapters made.[1]

The Old Batchelor

Before the alterations in the last quarter of the century, *The Old Batchelor* had occasionally been the source of several short pieces created out of it. On July 7, 1703, Drury Lane offered "Select Scenes" from the comedy but did not indicate what portions were staged. On December 11, 1705, it offered one act only; on February 28, 1706, it presented the fourth act as one of several short pieces. Occasionally during the first half of the century Tony Aston offered scenes from the comedy as part of a medley which he acted in theaters or taverns. There was also given in Lincoln's Inn Fields, on February 28, 1743, a shortened version called *Fondlewife and Laetitia;* and the Haymarket, on April 22, 1747, offered another version entitled *The Credulous Husband.* Although *The Old Batchelor* was not the only play from which such cuttings were made, it was the only one by Congreve to be presented so often by parts.

By 1776, however, two acting versions incorporating alterations had been printed. One represented the comedy as offered in the summer Haymarket, where it was staged occasionally from 1769 to 1775. In this version the changes are negligible.[2] For example, in IV, iii, Fondlewife, alone, remarks that he is going to "reason" with himself and wonders

---

[1] For the sake of convenience, references to Congreve's plays are to the two volumes in the "World's Classics": *Comedies by William Congreve* (1925) and *The Mourning Bride, Poems, and Miscellanies* (1928), both edited by Bonamy Dobree.

[2] *The Old Batchelor . . . Marked with the Variations in the Manager's Book, at the Theatre-Royal in the Hay-Market* (London: Printed for T. Davies; T. Lowndes; T. Caslon; W. Nicoll; and S. Bladon, 1776).

why he married; he decides that he did so because "she was beautiful and tempting, and because I was obstinate and doating." These statements were retained but his next remark was deleted: "so that my Inclination was (and is still) greater than my Power."

The other version,[3] which represents the acting copy for Drury Lane in 1776 and thereafter, shows more extensive changes. The elements eliminated are chiefly detail, not scenes or characters whose removal would alter the plot or the spectator's conception of the *dramatis personae*. They were clearly undertaken to remove licentious remarks and to condense the play, although the motive of purifying the play was clearly the stronger. To list all the phrases and passages marked for removal would be to compile an anthology of lines in which there was language or idea which the late century termed "indelicate." It seems desirable, therefore, merely to indicate the nature of the eliminations.

In the opening scene of Act I several objectionable phrases were excised. For example, in Bellmour's speech beginning, "Never—Her Affections," the reviser struck out: "and blushing like the Virgin Morn when it disclos'd the Cheat, which that trusty Bawd of Nature, Night, had hid." Similarly, when Bellmour reads the note, he comments upon the "Gusto" which a disguise gives to an "Amour," but all discussion of that pleasure was removed. Vainlove's speech beginning "Never doubt it" and discussing the "Spirit of Cuckoldom" was cut to leave only the opening remark. Scenes ii and iii are intact, but more cuts were made in iv, where the opening remarks of Bellmour were reduced by half. In the same scene Sharper's first speech ("That's because he always sets out in foul Weather") and every remark through to Sharper's speech of "She had need have a good share of Sense to manage so *Capricious* a Lover" were marked for omission.

In Act II there was less censoring. Toward the end, when the Music-Maker enters to offer a song, the song itself has been removed. The dialogue was changed to permit Araminta to ask the others to "walk into the next room," where she will "entertain . . . with a song, to divert the discourse." As a rule, most of the songs in all the comedies were marked for omission.

In Act III there were more changes. Occasional phrases were cut from the opening portion, but it was Scene x which suffered the most ex-

[3] *The Old Batchelor . . . As Performed at the Theatre Royal in Drury-Lane. Regulated from the Prompt-Book, By Permission of the Managers, by Mr. Hopkins, Prompter* (London: John Bell, 1776). For nearly all the plays there are variant editions purporting to be the version used in the playhouses. They differ occasionally in the phrase eliminated but not in the principle of revision. They suggest that it was difficult for the age to agree upon what was objectionable and what was not.

cisions. In the dialogue between Heartwell and Sylvia, the following passage, which was eliminated, typifies the portions which were cut:

Silv. Never tell me that, I know it is not chang'd by my self; for I love you, and would marry you.

Heart. I'll have my Beard shav'd, it shan't hurt thee, and we'll go to Bed—

The opening remarks between Lucy and Sylvia at the start of Scene xi were also eliminated.

In Acts IV and v there were occasional cuts, but none of very great length. In Scene i of Act IV Bellmour's second speech—"I wonder why all our young Fellows should glory in an Opinion of Atheism; when they may be so much more conveniently lewd under the Coverlet of Religion"—was marked for removal, very possibly because of the protests against the licentious language and the anti-religious quality in some of Congreve's characters. Otherwise, throughout the remaining scenes of Acts IV and v, the nature of the alterations was much the same as in the earlier acts—the cutting of any material which seemed contrary to the delicacy or morals of the age. No large portions, however, were taken from the play. The cuts were chiefly of phrases, occasionally of a whole speech or a song, and, less frequently, two or three remarks in sequence.

The Double Dealer

The revised version of *The Double Dealer* was first given in Covent Garden in the spring of 1776, the revisions being made by Thomas Sheridan.[4] The changes made in it are, in essence and spirit, similar to those in *The Old Batchelor*. The advertisements of the performances of this revised version specified that the comedy had been "revised and corrected" mainly by removing the "exceptionable" passages. Those elements appear to have been not only those which represented a greater freedom of expression in regard to the relations of the sexes than the late eighteenth century permitted, but also those which represented to that period various degrees of swearing. In every act there was considerable expunging of such details, but, as with *The Old Batchelor*, there was insufficient alteration to affect the characterizations or plot.

An early excision in Act I suggests an intent to remove language which was not necessarily suggestive of immorality but rather reflective of an undesirable freedom of language. In Scene iii Mellefont's second speech begins, "O, I would have no room for serious Design." He continues that

---

[4] Two editions represent the acting versions at Covent Garden: (1) *The Double Dealer* (London: Printed for W. Lowndes; T. Davies; T. Lowndes; T. Caslon; W. Nicoll; and S. Bladon, 1777). (2) *The Double Dealer* (London: Printed for W. Lowndes; J. Nicholls; W. Nicoll; S. Bladon; and J. Barker, 1788).

he would have "Noise and Impertinence" to keep Lady Touchwood's head from working. The next remark was omitted: "For Hell is not more busie than her Brain, nor contains more Devils, than that Imagination." That type of expression was not, as a rule, removed from *The Old Batchelor,* in the revision of which Sheridan apparently did not participate. Similarly, in Careless' speech, in the same scene, beginning, "Exquisite Woman!" the words in parentheses in the following statement were omitted: "But what (the Devil) does she think, thou hast no more Sense, than to get an Heir (upon her Body) to disinherit thy self." In Scene vi Lady Touchwood, upbraiding Maskwell, warns him after saying, "Death, do you dally with my Passion?" In the midst of her outburst she swears "by the Eternal Fire," a phrase which Sheridan cut. Licentious passages were, of course, omitted also. For example, in Scene iii, Careless remarks of Lady Touchwood, "Was there ever such a Fury!" a remark which was retained; but the conclusion of that speech —" 'tis well Nature has not put it into her Sex's Power to ravish" —was omitted, as were many other similar ones.

In Act ii similar expunging was made. The song was removed from Scene iii, with Mellefont's speech preceding and announcing the song, and in iii, x, the song by Lord Froth was deleted along with all reference to it. The other cuttings in those acts were mainly like those in Act i, remarks too "free" in language, such as Lord Touchwood's "No, no, no,—Damnation!" which was removed.

Several consecutive speeches were at times removed in Act iv. In Scene i the dialogue between Cynthia and Mellefont was considerably shortened, with Cynthia's fourth speech (beginning "My Mind gives me it won't") and the two remarks following it being wholly eliminated. In Scene iii, in the conversation between Sir Paul and Cynthia, near the end of the scene, Cynthia's speech, "I don't blush, Sir," Sir Paul's reply, and Cynthia's retort were expunged. Act v was less disturbed, the excisions generally being limited to phrases (such as Maskwell's "by Heav'n" in his first speech in Scene i). One excision (v, xvii) apparently was made to achieve less interrupted action. When Lady Touchwood and Maskwell are being overheard by Cynthia and Lord Touchwood, the reviser eliminated Cynthia's "How, my Lord!" and Lord Touchwood's reply, "Pray forbear all Resentments for a while, and let us hear the rest." The removal of such remarks, which could hardly be construed as licentious, simplified the acting of that scene.

In 1802 J. P. Kemble made a further alteration of *The Double Dealer.*[5] His revision was no more a genuine rewriting than was Sheri-

---

[5] *Congreve's Double Dealer. A Comedy. Revised by J. P. Kemble* (London: Printed and Published by C. Lowndes, Drury Lane, 1802).

dan's, for there was no great difference in their methods or in the parts eliminated. Probably Kemble worked from the Sheridan revision, for there is considerable agreement between them with respect to omissions. There are, however, a few differences which seem to be due to varying tastes in the alterers, one of whom disliked phrases which the other did not find seriously objectionable. For example, in I, iii, Mellefont remarks that Lady Touchwood had "this Morning . . . surpriz'd me in my Bed," a statement unaltered by Sheridan but changed by Kemble to "in my own chamber." In a passage previously quoted, Sheridan omitted the words given in parentheses: "But what (the Devil) does she think, thou hast no more Sense, than to get an Heir (upon her Body) to disinherit thy self"; Kemble omitted "the Devil" but retained "upon her Body." Otherwise, Kemble's Act I is approximately the same as Sheridan's.

In Act II Kemble retained a few portions which Sheridan had rejected. In Scene iv Mellefont interjects "What can this mean!" between remarks by Sir Paul and Lady Plyant, a phrase which Sheridan had removed but Kemble restored. Kemble also retained a remark at the end of Scene iv which Sheridan had omitted, Sir Paul's "I'm sure if ever I should have Horns, they would kill me; they would never come kindly, I should die of 'em, like a Child, that was cutting his Teeth—I should indeed, *Thy*—therefore come away." Kemble omitted the song in Act II but retained that in III. Throughout the remaining portions of the play, Kemble's procedure was much the same. Occasionally he removed an element not expunged by Sheridan, but he more often made restorations than fresh cuttings.

Love for Love

The alterations in *Love for Love,* although not markedly different, are slightly more extensive than those for the first two comedies. Even so, they do not alter the structure or character of the play, although they soften its tone. Because it was frequently performed in both patent theaters in the late years of the century, several editions of the altered versions exist. They differ in details only. Usually, the same passages are marked for elimination, with an occasional disagreement concerning how much of a passage is to be expunged. Because it would serve no useful purpose to list all the variations, the discussion will be limited to the kinds of changes made in *Love for Love.*

In Act I there are, relatively speaking, few excisions. The closing two speeches by Valentine and Jeremy in Scene i were omitted. In Scene ii Scandal's speech beginning, "Rail? At whom?" was cut by omitting the words in parentheses: "No, turn Pimp, Flatterer, Quack,

Lawyer, (Parson, be Chaplain to an Atheist, or Stallion to an old Woman), any thing but Poet." In Scene iv Valentine's first speech was considerably cut, the second half being omitted, and most versions left out the last speeches of both Scandal and Valentine. In Act ii the omissions were of details rather than of extended passages. In Scene iii Angelica's rather coarse remarks beginning with "Will you? I care not," and the Nurse's speech immediately following were marked for omission on the stage. In Scenes ix and x several phrases uttered by Mrs. Frail, Prue, and Mrs. Foresight were excised, some of them, such as Mrs. Foresight's "Oh, damn you Toad," being incidental to the main point of the dialogue.

Much more extensive revisions were made in Act iii. Scene iii, in which Tattle, Valentine, Scandal, and Angelica converse, was almost wholly deleted. Only the first eight speeches, none of them long, were left. After Scandal's "I shall receive no Benefit from the Opinion: For I know no effectual Difference between continued Affectation and Reality," every remark, including the song, was removed. Nearly all of Scene x was cut. Although Sir Sampson's "Hoity toity" speech was retained, there was inserted a short summary of the principal portions of the scene so that the gist of the matter would be known. Scenes xi, xii, xiii were entirely removed. In Scene xiv, Scandal's first speech was left out, but the next six exchanges of dialogue were retained, after which all but the closing remarks were eliminated. In Scene xv Ben's song was kept, although portions of the dialogue preceding and following it were marked for omission.

Act iv was left much more nearly intact. Not until Scene xii were more than a few phrases removed, but in Scene xii several exchanges of dialogue were marked for cutting. In Scene xvi the song "I tell thee, Charmion" joined the other rejected lyrics. Relatively little was expunged from the rest of the act. The closing act of the play was also relatively untouched. In Scene ii Angelica's speech beginning with "She that marries a Fool" was removed, as was also Sir Sampson's comment upon it. In Scene vi Prue's longest remarks to Foresight were reduced by omitting the second half. But there was no elimination of whole scenes as in Act iii.

The Mourning Bride

The alterations made in *The Mourning Bride* were fairly extensive during the late eighteenth and early nineteenth century, perhaps because it offered a somewhat different problem from that of the comedies. In them the principal defect which prompted revision was the presence of "exceptionable elements." As E. B. Potter has pointed out in an excellent account of the revisions of the tragedy,[6] that was but one of the motives which the adapters had in mind when they tried to make Congreve's tragedy conform to the taste of a new age. Whatever passages were thought unsuitable morally were, of course, removed. Another purpose was to eliminate from the tragedy those passages which were open to criticism because of bombast or morbidity of sentiment.[7] An example of this type of excision is the speech which Almeria makes in Act v, Scene xi:

> O I foreknow, foresee that Object.
> Is it at last then so? is he then dead?
> What dead at last, quite, quite, for ever dead?
> There, there I see him; there he lies, the Blood
> Yet bubbling from his Wounds—O more than Savage!
> Had they, or Hearts, or Eyes, that did this Deed?
> Could Eyes endure to guide such cruel Hands?
> Are not my Eyes guilty alike with theirs,
> What thus can gaze, and yet not turn to Stone?
> —I do not weep! The Springs of Tears are dry'd;
> And of a sudden I am calm, as if
> All things were well; and yet my Husband's murder'd!
> Yes, yes, I know to mourn! I'll Sluce this Heart,
> The Source of Woe, and let the Torrent loose.
> —Those Men have left to weep! they look on me!
> I hope they murder all on whom they look.
> Behold me well; your bloody Hands have err'd,
> And wrongfully have slain those Innocents:
> I am the Sacrifice design'd to bleed;
> And come prepar'd to yield my Throat—they shake
> Their Heads in sign of Grief and Innocence!
> > (*They point at the Bowl on the Ground.*
> And point! what mean they? Ha! a Cup. O well
> I understand what Medicine has been here.
> O noble Thirst! yet greedy, to drink all—
> —O for another Draught of Death—What mean they?
> > (*They point at the other Cup.*
> Ha! point again? 'tis there, and full, I hope.

<hr/>

[6] *PMLA*, LVIII (1943), 996–999.

[7] The attitudes underlying the changes may be seen in the preface to the revised version in Bell's *British Theater* (1791): "As the language and sentiment of this tragedy exemplify very forcibly every fault in dramatic composition, it may not be disserviceable to Letters to extend the brevity of our mentions for this article. CONGREVE's imagination was naturally vivid, luxuriant, and rapid.—He heaps up, when the *impetus* is upon him, an accumulation of glitter and gawd, extravagant and mistimed.—For passion his common substitute is splendor; yet so unequal are his powers, that he has frequently scenes of alternate inanity and bombast—of creeping imbecility and soaring extravagance." The note offered examples of Congreve's faults.

> Thanks to the liberal Hand that fill'd thee thus;
> I'll drink my glad Acknowledgment—

In one of the early revisions after Garrick's retirement [8] this passage was considerably cut. The first two lines of it remain; the next seven are omitted, lines which to the late century may well have seemed not only bombast but too much dwelling upon horror. The rest of the passage is nearly intact, though the question "What mean they?" and "Ha! point again?" before and after the second stage direction were removed.[9]

In the 1777 version representing the text used in Drury Lane and Covent Garden, a great deal of this type of cutting is evident. For example, in I, i, several speeches have been cut or omitted, partly to eliminate Almeria's highly emotional outbursts and partly to speed the action. In Leonora's third speech in that scene, a reference to past events was omitted by removing these lines:

> that then, in spite of Hate,
> Revenge, and that Hereditary Feud
> Between *Valentia's* and *Granada's* Kings.

Almeria's next remarks, beginning *"Alphonso! O Alphonso!"* which serve principally to express Almeria's state of emotion, are wholly gone. Once Almeria has made known to Leonora that Alphonso and Almeria had early been married, Almeria says:

> Alas! What have I said?
> My Grief has hurry'd me beyond all thought,
> I wou'd have kept that secret; though I know
> Thy Love and Faith in me deserve all Confidence.

With this fact clear to the audience, the rest of Almeria's speech and all of her two succeeding ones, which do not advance the action, have been removed. A few speeches later, Almeria's statement beginning, "O no! Time gives Encrease to my Afflictions," has been removed. The effect of these cuttings is to permit Almeria to state salient points but to shorten or remove her anguished exclamations.

By this type of cutting, the adapter shortened the play by at least a fifth. Not only did that give the action a swifter pace but it also en-

[8] *The Mourning Bride. A Tragedy. As it is Acted at the Theatres-Royal in Drury-Lane and Covent-Garden. By Mr. Congreve* (London: Printed for J. Wenman . . . 1777).

[9] In *The Mourning Bride . . . Marked with the Variations in the Managers Books, at the Theatre-Royal in Drury-Lane* (London: Printed for T. Lowndes, T. Caslon, S. Bladon, and W. Nicoll, 1776) exactly the same portions are marked for omission on the stage. In *The Mourning Bride . . . Taken from the Manager's Book, at the Theatre-Royal, Covent-Garden* (London: sold by RACHEL RANDALL, 1787), the omissions have been increased by adding " 'tis there, and full, I hope."

abled the adapter to remove "extravagances" and "luxuriances" without fundamentally changing the plot or characterizations. Not seeking to make a new play out of Congreve's materials, the adapter apparently aimed to present the story as Congreve conceived it but to simplify it and to purify it of passages which the age found objectionable.

This process of cutting was not confined to Almeria's remarks. Throughout the play the adapter has shortened many scenes by having a few lines of a speech take the place of the whole speech. For example, in Act ii, Scene viii, Osmyn soliloquizes before Zara's entrance. In Congreve's version Osmyn's soliloquy runs to fifteen lines. In the 1777 revision only the first three lines are retained, and they have been made to follow closely upon Osmyn's speech at the end of the preceding scene. When Zara enters (Scene ix) Congreve gave her a speech of sixteen lines, a passage shortened (through removing lines in the middle of it) to nine lines. None of these changes genuinely affected the substance of the scene.

In his article Potter has given further examples of the process of shortening the play and has pointed out two other motives underlying the adaptation. One involves an alteration of the stage directions to conform to current stage practice. The other, which is even more evident in the later revisions, is a strengthening of the role of Zara at the expense of other parts. In all the adaptations there is a much more thorough revision than was accorded any of the comedies, probably because contemporary criticism had objected to a great many of the long and ranting speeches in the tragedy but had not found that kind of defect in the comedies.

The Way of the World

The alterations in *The Way of the World* are very similar to those in the other comedies, changes accomplished principally by the elimination of detail or by slight variations in the phrasing. There is also the same tendency to omit the songs. Because the Drury Lane and Covent Garden stage versions in 1776 and succeeding years are very similar, it seems sufficient merely to offer an example of the type of change commonly made in *The Way of the World*. In I, ii, when the Footman is asked if the marriage has taken place, Congreve has him reply: "Married and Bedded, Sir: I am Witness." In some revisions the reply is changed to "Incontestibly, sir: I am witness."

In 1802 J. P. Kemble made a new alteration of the comedy. In general, his method and revisions do not differ markedly from those of the previous Drury Lane and Covent Garden revisions, although he does not agree consistently with either of the preceding ones. For example, Kemble followed Drury Lane in retaining the Footman's "Married and Bedded, Sir" which Covent Garden had changed to "Incontestibly, sir." In the last speech in the same scene Kemble followed Covent Garden. When Mirabell says, "That's well. Do you go home again, d'ye hear, and adjourn the Consummation 'till farther Order," Covent Garden had omitted "and adjourn the Consummation 'till farther Order," but Drury Lane had retained it. Kemble also made some independent changes. In IV, xi, he changed Witwoud's "Come, Knight —Pox on him" to "Come, Knight, Plague on him." In Scene xiv Foible says, "What a washy Rogue art thou," which Kemble changed to "What a poor rogue art thou."

These changes, like those in the comedies generally, were intended to purify the pieces even though the alterations often made the dialogue more conventional and less characteristic of the speakers. A degree of vitality was lost. And the fact that the various adapters did not always agree upon what should be eliminated illustrates the age-old dilemma of the moralists who differ as to what is morally dangerous. Kemble's sometimes following Drury Lane, occasionally agreeing with Covent Garden, and at other times making independent changes suggest the difficulty, if not futility, of the process.

This is not to say that Congreve's plays should not have been revised at all, for each age must decide in what form it will present the drama of preceding centuries. Yet the type of alteration which the late eighteenth century practised was not very satisfactory. By eliminating a phrase here or a speech there or a song somewhere else, an adapter apparently expected to transform an unacceptable play into an acceptable one. Uncertain as to whether the plays were morally sound or not, the age apparently believed that a little pruning of their luxuriances would remove all objections to them.

PERFORMANCES OF CONGREVE'S PLAYS, 1700–1701
TO 1799–1800

This appendix contains a list of performances of the five plays in the London theaters to the early nineteenth century and in some of the outlying theaters, such as those at Richmond and Twickenham, in the first sixty or so years of the century before those playhouses developed into well-established repertory companies. These listings have come from the advertisements in the London newspapers (chiefly in the Burney collection in the British Museum) and from playbill collections in the British Museum, in the Enthoven Library at the Victoria and Albert Museum, and in the Huntington Library. They have been checked with two manuscript compilations: the Latreille Calendar (British Museum) and the Winston Calendar (Folger Shakespeare Library). It is not wholly certain, of course, that all of these performances occurred, for the playbills and newspaper advertisements represent intended performances; in addition, last-minute changes in the casts, of which we often know only a few examples, must have happened frequently. In each season the cast for the first performance at a particular theater is given in full (often by reference to a previous listing); for the successive performances at the same theater during a season only the changes from the previous performances are listed. (In the late part of the century the playbills do not always advertise the full cast.) The receipts are from notation in the various manuscript calendars and on playbills and, in the later years of the century, from treasurers' account books, chiefly in the British Museum. These abbreviations have been used: CG—Covent Garden; DL—Drury Lane; GF—Goodman's Fields; HAY—Little Haymarket; LIF—Lincoln's Inn Fields; QUEEN'S—Queen's Haymarket.

The Old Batchelor

1700–01. DL: March 25.
1702–03. DL: Nov. 19. July 7 ("Select Scenes" only).
1703–04. DL: Oct. 13. Nov. 18 (Heartwell—Griffin).
1704–05. DL: Sept. 26 (no cast). Oct. 26 (Bluff—Estcourt). Jan. 15 (Fondlewife—Dogget; Bluff—Estcourt).

1705–06. DL: Oct. 22 (no cast). Dec. 11 (one act only). Jan. 14. Feb. 28 (Act IV only).

1707–08. DL: March 15 (Heartwell—Betterton; Bellmour—Wilks; Vain-love—Booth; Sharper—Mills; Sir Joseph—Bullock; Bluff—Estcourt; Setter—Fairbank; Laetitia—Mrs. Barry; Belinda—Mrs. Rogers; Ara-minta—Mrs. Bradshaw; Sylvia—Mrs. Bicknell; Lucy—Mrs. Saunders).

1708–09. DL: Dec. 30 (as March 15, 1708, except Bluff—Johnson; Fon-dlewife—Cibber; Laetitia—Mrs. Knight; Sylvia—Mrs. Porter). April 28 (Bluff—Estcourt; Belinda—Mrs. Cross; Sylvia—Mrs. Bicknell).

1709–10. QUEEN'S: Dec. 8 (Heartwell—Betterton; Fondlewife—Dog-get). March 9 (Heartwell—Betterton). July 6 (Bellmour—Wilks; Laeti-tia—Mrs. Oldfield).

1710–11. DL: Nov. 27 (Heartwell—Keene; Bellmour—Wilks; Sharper —Mills; Sir Joseph—Bullock; Bluff—Johnson; Fondlewife—Dogget; Laetitia—Mrs. Knight; Belinda—Mrs. Rogers; Araminta—Mrs. Brad-shaw; Sylvia—Mrs. Bicknell; Lucy—Mrs. Saunders). May 5 (Laeti-tia—Mrs. Oldfield; Lucy omitted).

1711–12. DL: Oct. 24 (as Nov. 27, 1710, except Vainlove—Booth; Bluff —Estcourt; Setter—Norris; Laetitia—Mrs. Oldfield; Sylvia—Miss Willis). May 13 (Bellmour—Wilks; Sir Joseph—Bullock; Bluff— Johnson; Fondlewife—Dogget; Setter—Norris; rest omitted).

1712–13. DL: Oct. 10 (as Nov. 27, 1710, except Vainlove—Booth; Setter —Norris; Sylvia omitted). Dec. 17 (Laetitia—Mrs. Oldfield; Belinda— Mrs. Mountfort). April 10.

1713–14. DL: Oct 5 (no cast). Dec. 30. May 28.

1714–15. DL: Sept. 23 (Laetitia—Mrs. Oldfield; rest omitted). Nov. 11. Jan. 8. Feb. 16 (no cast). LIF: Jan. 4 (Heartwell—Keene; Bellmour— J. Leigh; Vainlove—Husband; Sir Joseph—Bullock, Sen.; Bluff— Hall; Fondlewife—C. Bullock; Setter—Spiller; Laetitia—Mrs. Kent; Belinda—Mrs. Cross; Araminta—Mrs. Rogers; Sylvia—Miss Schoold-ing; Lucy—Mrs. Hunt). Feb. 4 (no cast). March 12 (Heartwell— Keene). April 2 (no cast).

1715–16. DL: Oct. 14 (no cast). Nov. 8. Feb. 27. April 20. LIF: Nov. 7 (Heartwell—Keene). June 5 (no cast).

1716–17. DL: Oct. 12 (Bellmour—Wilks; Vainlove—Booth; Sharper— Mills; Sir Joseph—Bowen; Bluff—Johnson; Fondlewife—Cibber; Set-ter—Norris; Laetitia—Mrs. Oldfield; Belinda—Mrs. Mountfort; Ara-minta—Mrs. Porter; Sylvia—Miss Willis; Lucy—Mrs. Saunders). Jan. 28 (Heartwell—Bickerstaff). April 25 (Sir Joseph—Miller). LIF: Nov. 29 (no cast).

1717–18. DL: Nov. 15 (Laetitia—Mrs. Oldfield; rest omitted). Jan. 27 (as Oct. 12, 1716, except Heartwell—Bickerstaff; Sir Joseph omitted).

May 3 (Sir Joseph—Miller). LIF: Oct. 15 (as Jan. 4, 1715, except Sharper—Cory; Fondlewife—Bullock, Jun.; Laetitia—Mrs. Thurmond; Belinda—Mrs. Rogers; Araminta—Mrs. Bullock; Lucy omitted). Nov. 23 (Sylvia—Mrs. Robertson). Jan. 23 (Heartwell—Keene; rest omitted).

1718–19. DL: Oct. 28 (as Oct. 12, 1716, except Heartwell—Bickerstaff; Sir Joseph—Miller; Belinda—Mrs. Bicknell; Araminta omitted). Jan. 26 (Araminta—Mrs. Garnet). April 14 (Fondlewife—Norris). May 19 (Heartwell—Thurmond; Setter omitted; Laetitia—Mrs. Thurmond). LIF: April 29 (no cast).

1719–20. DL: Oct. 1 (Laetitia—Mrs. Oldfield; rest omitted). Dec. 10. Feb. 2 (no cast). June 2 (Heartwell—Thurmond; Bellmour—Wilks; Vainlove—Booth; Sharper—Mills; Sir Joseph—Miller; Fondlewife—Cibber; Setter—Norris; Laetitia—Mrs. Oldfield; Belinda—Mrs. Bicknell; Araminta—Mrs. Garnet; Lucy—Mrs. Saunders).

1720–21. DL: Sept. 13 (as June 2, 1720, except Heartwell—Bickerstaff; Laetitia—Mrs. Thurmond; Sylvia—Miss Willis). Nov. 8 (Bluff—Johnson). Dec. 14 (Heartwell—Thurmond; Bluff—Shepard). March 7 (Bluff—Johnson; Laetitia—Mrs. Oldfield; Sylvia—Miss Tenoe). April 29. BIRD CAGE ALLEY: Nov. 28 (no cast).

1721–22. DL: Oct. 12 (Heartwell—Thurmond; Bellmour—Wilks; Vainlove—Booth; Sharper—Mills; Sir Joseph—Miller; Bluff—Johnson; Fondlewife—Cibber; Setter—Norris; Laetitia—Mrs. Oldfield; Belinda—Mrs. Bicknell; Araminta—Mrs. Younger). Dec. 7 (Vainlove—Watson). April 25. LIF: Jan. 13 (Heartwell—Quin; Bellmour—Walker; Vainlove—Ryan; Sharper—Egleton; Sir Joseph—Bullock; Bluff—Hall; Fondlewife—Aston; Setter—Spiller; Laetitia—Mrs. Seymour; Belinda—Mrs. Bullock; Araminta—Mrs. Rogeir; Sylvia—Miss Stone; Lucy—Mrs. Egleton; Betty—Miss Hutton). 15. 18. 31. April 10 (no cast). May 18 (Sylvia—Mrs. Purden; rest as Jan. 13).

1722–23. DL: Sept. 20 (as Oct. 12, 1721, except Heartwell omitted; Vainlove—Watson; Lucy—Miss Tenoe). Jan. 2 (Belinda—Mrs. Horton). April 19 (Heartwell—Harper). LIF: Nov. 7 (as Jan. 13, 1722, except Sharper—Leigh; Fondlewife—Hippisley; Setter—Morgan; Araminta—Mrs. Cross; Sylvia—Miss Purden; Betty—Miss Bullock). Dec. 19.

1723–24. DL: Oct. 1 (Heartwell—Harper; Bellmour—Wilks; Vainlove—Watson; Sharper—Mills; Sir Joseph—Miller; Bluff—Johnson; Fondlewife—Cibber; Setter—Norris; Laetitia—Mrs. Oldfield; Belinda—Mrs. Horton; Araminta—Mrs. Younger; Sylvia—Mrs. Lindar; Lucy—Miss Tenoe). Dec. 18 (no cast). March 2. May 20 (Laetitia—Mrs. Thurmond; Sylvia—Mrs. Wetherilt; rest as Oct. 1, 1723).

LIF: March 23 (Heartwell—Quin; Bellmour—Walker; Vainlove—
Ryan; Sharper—Leigh; Sir Joseph—Bullock; Bluff—Hall; Fondle-
wife—Hippisley; Setter—Spiller; Laetitia—Mrs. Cantrell; Belinda—
Mrs. Sterling; Araminta—Mrs. Cross; Sylvia—Miss Purden; Lucy—
Mrs. Egleton). May 28 (Sharper—Orfeur; Lucy—Mrs. Taylor).

1724–25. DL: Sept. 17 (as Oct. 1, 1723, except Araminta—Mrs. Heron).
Oct. 23 (no cast). Feb. 22. May 19 (Laetitia—Mrs. Thurmond; Sylvia
—Miss Tynte; rest as Sept. 17, 1724). LIF: Jan. 4 (as March 23, 1724,
except Laetitia—Mrs. Bullock; Belinda—Mrs. Butcher; Araminta—
Mrs. Parker; Sylvia—Mrs. Legar). May 17 (Sharper—Egleton; Sir
Joseph—Morgan; Araminta—Mrs. Moffet).

1725–26. DL: Sept. 7 (as Oct. 1, 1723, except Setter—Oates; Araminta—
Mrs. Heron). Nov. 16. Feb. 14 (no cast). May 3 (Araminta—Mrs.
Porter; rest as Sept. 7, 1725). LIF: Dec. 1 (no cast). Feb. 7. May 4
(Heartwell—Quin; Bellmour—Walker; Vainlove—Ryan; Sharper—
Diggs; Sir Joseph—Egleton; Bluff—Hall; Fondlewife—Hippisley;
Setter—Spiller; Laetitia—Mrs. Bullock; Belinda—Mrs. Younger;
Araminta—Mrs. Moffet; Sylvia—Mrs. Legar; Lucy—Mrs. Egleton).
26 (Sir Joseph—Bullock; Setter—Norris; Sylvia—Mrs. Rice).

1726–27. DL: Sept. 10 (Heartwell—Harper; Bellmour—Wilks; Vainlove
—Watson; Sharper—Mills; Sir Joseph—Miller; Bluff—Johnson; Fon-
dlewife—Cibber; Setter—Oates; Laetitia—Mrs. Oldfield; Belinda—
Mrs. Horton; Araminta—Mrs. Butler; Sylvia—Miss Lindar; Lucy—
Miss Teno). Nov. 7 (no cast). Jan. 3 (Fondlewife—Cibber; Laetitia—
Mrs. Oldfield; rest omitted). LIF: Nov. 7 (no cast).

1727–28. DL: Sept. 19 (as Sept. 10, 1726). Dec. 6 (Lucy—Mrs. W. Mills).
Feb. 21. April 9. LIF: Nov. 20 (no cast). May 11 (as May 4, 1726, except Sharper—Milward; Sir Joseph—Bullock; Araminta—Mrs. Berriman).

1728–29. DL: Sept. 26 (as Sept. 10, 1726, except Lucy—Mrs. Mills).
Nov. 27 (Fondlewife—Cibber; Laetitia—Mrs. Oldfield; rest omitted).
Jan. 24 (as Sept. 10, 1726, except Araminta—Mrs. Heron; Sylvia—
Mrs. Cibber; Lucy—Mrs. Mills). March 17. LIF: Dec. 31 (as May 4,
1726, except Sharper—Milward; Sir Joseph—Bullock; Setter—Chap-
man; Araminta—Mrs. Buchanan). April 14 (no cast).

1729–30. DL: Oct. 9 (Heartwell—Harper; Bellmour—Wilks; Vainlove—
Watson; Sharper—Mills; Sir Joseph—Miller; Bluff—Johnson; Fon-
dlewife—Cibber; Setter—Oates; Laetitia—Mrs. Oldfield; Belinda—
Mrs. Horton; Araminta—Mrs. Butler; Sylvia—Mrs. Cibber; Lucy—
Mrs. Mills). Dec. 12. LIF: Sept. 24 (Heartwell—Quin; Bellmour—
Walker; Vainlove—Ryan; Sharper—Milward; Sir Joseph—Bullock;
Bluff—Hall; Fondlewife—Hippisley; Laetitia—Mrs. Bullock; Sylvia

—Mrs. Legar; Lucy—Mrs. Egleton). April 13 (Sir Joseph—Ray). GF: Nov. 17 (Heartwell—W. Giffard; Bellmour—Giffard; Vainlove —Minns; Sharper—W. Williams; Sir Joseph—W. Bullock; Bluff— Pearce; Fondlewife—Penkethman; Setter—Collett; Laetitia—Mrs. Seal; Belinda—Mrs. Giffard; Araminta—Mrs. Clark; Sylvia—Mrs. Mountfort; Lucy—Mrs. Thomas). Dec. 19 (Vainlove—Huddy; Bluff —Penkethman; Fondlewife—Burney). Feb. 16 (Araminta—Mrs. Purden). June 1 (Sir Joseph—R. Williams; Laetitia—Mrs. Haughton; Araminta—Miss Vaughan).

1730–31. DL: Sept. 17 (as Oct. 9, 1729, except Sharper—Miller; Sir Joseph—Th. Cibber; Laetitia—Mrs. Thurmond; Belinda—Mrs. Haughton). Nov. 9 (no cast). Jan. 12. LIF: Nov. 17 (no cast). Feb. 23. May 5 (as Sept. 24, 1729, except Sir Joseph—Ray; Setter—Chapman; Belinda—Mrs. Younger; Araminta—Mrs. Cantrell). GF: Dec. 1 (Heartwell—W. Giffard; Bellmour—Giffard; Vainlove—Rosco; Sharper—W. Williams; Sir Joseph—W. Bullock; Bluff—Huddy; Fondlewife—Penkethman; Setter—Collett; Laetitia—Mrs. Haughton; Belinda—Mrs. Giffard; Araminta—Miss Smith; Sylvia—Mrs. Mountfort; Lucy—Mrs. Thomas). Jan. 19 (Vainlove—Bowman; Fondlewife—Morgan).

1731–32. DL: Sept. 25 (as Oct. 9, 1729, except Sir Joseph—Th. Cibber; Laetitia—Mrs. Butler; Belinda and Araminta omitted). Nov. 25 (no cast). Jan. 7. LIF: Nov. 20 (no cast). Feb. 24. March 20. May 9 (as Sept. 24, 1729, except Sir Joseph—Ray; Setter—Chapman; Belinda —Mrs. Younger; Araminta—Mrs. Hallam; Sylvia—Miss Holliday). GF: Nov. 20 (as Dec. 1, 1730, except Sharper—Havard; Sir Joseph —Bullock; Bluff—Morgan; Fondlewife—Norris; Laetitia—Mrs. Giffard; Belinda—Mrs. Roberts; Araminta—Mrs. Haughton; Sylvia— Mrs. Purden; Lucy—Mrs. Morgan). Jan. 27 (Sir Joseph—Miller). 28.

1732–33. DL: Oct. 3 (Heartwell—Harper; Bellmour—W. Mills; Vainlove—Watson; Sharper—Mills; Sir Joseph—Th. Cibber; Bluff— Johnson; Fondlewife—Cibber; Setter—Oates; Laetitia—Mrs. Thurmond; Belinda—Mrs. Horton; Araminta—Mrs. Butler; Sylvia—Miss Raftor). Dec. 8 (Sir Joseph—Miller; Belinda—Mrs. Heron). Feb. 6 (no cast). April 27. LIF: Nov. 22 (Heartwell—Quin; Bellmour— Walker; Vainlove—Ryan; Sharper—Milward; Sir Joseph—Neale; Bluff—Hall; Fondlewife—Hippisley; Setter—Chapman; Laetitia— Mrs. Bullock; Belinda—Mrs. Younger; Araminta—Mrs. Cantrell; Sylvia—Miss Holliday; Lucy—Mrs. Egleton). CG: Feb. 2 (as at LIF, Nov. 22, except Sylvia—Mrs. Laguerre). April 27. GF: Oct. 6 (Heartwell—W. Giffard; Bellmour—Giffard; Vainlove—Rosco; Sharper—

Havard; Sir Joseph—Bullock; Bluff—Morgan; Fondlewife—Norris; Setter—Collett; Laetitia—Mrs. Giffard; Belinda—Mrs. Roberts; Araminta—Mrs. Christian; Sylvia—Mrs. Hamilton; Lucy—Mrs. Morgan). Nov. 13 (Sir Joseph—R. Wetherilt; Laetitia—Mrs. Thurmond; Belinda—Mrs. Giffard). 14. 20. Jan. 12, May 10 (Lucy—Miss Wherrit).

1733–34. CG: Oct. 9 (as at LIF, Nov. 22, 1732, except Sharper—Salway; Sylvia—Mrs. Laguerre; Lucy—Mrs. Stevens). Jan. 17 (Araminta—Mrs. Templer). GF: Sept. 17 (as Oct. 6, 1732, except Heartwell—Hyde; Sir Joseph—R. Wetherilt; Laetitia—Mrs. Thurmond; Belinda—Mrs. Giffard; Araminta—Mrs. Haughton). Jan. 28 (Heartwell—W. Giffard; Bluff—Huddy; Fondlewife—Penkethman; Setter—Woodward; Lucy—Mrs. Wetherilt). HAY: Oct. 25 (Heartwell—Harper; Bellmour—W. Mills; Vainlove—A. Hallam; Sharper—Milward; Sir Joseph—Miller; Bluff—Johnson; Fondlewife—Griffin; Setter—Oates; Laetitia—Mrs. Heron; Belinda—Mrs. Butler; Araminta—Mrs. Shireburn; Sylvia—Miss Oates; Lucy—Mrs. Grace). Feb. 8.

1734–35. DL: Oct. 3 (Heartwell—Quin; Bellmour—W. Mills; Vainlove—Salway; Sharper—Milward; Sir Joseph—Miller; Bluff—Johnson; Fondlewife—Griffin; Setter—Oates; Laetitia—Mrs. Thurmond; Belinda—Miss Holliday; Araminta—Mrs. Cantrell; Sylvia—Mrs. Pritchard; Lucy—Mrs. Charke). Dec. 16 (Lucy—Mrs. Sherburn). Feb. 26 (Fondlewife—C. Cibber). CG: May 1 (Heartwell—Bridgwater; Bellmour—Walker; Vainlove—Ryan; Sharper—Marshall; Sir Joseph—Neale; Bluff—Mullart; Fondlewife—Hippisley; Setter—Chapman; Laetitia—Mrs. Bullock; Belinda—Mrs. Horton; Araminta—Mrs. Templer; Sylvia—Miss Norsa; Lucy—Mrs. Stevens). GF: Nov. 1 (no cast). Jan. 11 (Heartwell—W. Giffard; Bellmour—Giffard; Vainlove—Rosco; Sharper—Havard; Sir Joseph—Wetherilt; Bluff—Hardy; Fondlewife—Penkethman; Setter—Hamilton; Laetitia—Mrs. Giffard; Belinda—Mrs. Hamilton; Araminta—Mrs. Haughton; Sylvia—Miss Tollet; Lucy—Mrs. Woodward). Feb. 18 (Setter—Woodward). April 11.

1735–36. DL: Sept. 25 (as Oct. 3, 1734, except Lucy—Mrs. Cross). Dec. 2. Jan. 28 (Lucy—Mrs. Grace). March 5. CG: Nov. 7 (as May 1, 1735). May 24 (Sylvia—Miss Binks). GF: Nov. 21 (as Feb. 18, 1735, except Sir Joseph—Ray; Bluff—Lyon; Fondlewife omitted; Setter—Hamilton). Feb. 11 (Fondlewife—Penkethman).

1736–37. DL: Nov. 3 (as Oct. 3, 1734, except Vainlove—Este; Araminta—Mrs. Cross; Sylvia and Lucy omitted). Dec. 6. Feb. 22. CG: Jan. 10 (as May 1, 1735, except Laetitia—Mrs. Horton; Belinda—Mrs.

Bellamy; Sylvia—Miss Binks). LIF: Jan. 4 (no cast). YORK BUILD-
INGS: Dec. 1 (no cast).

1737–38. DL: Sept. 15 (Heartwell—Quin; Bellmour—Mills; Vainlove
—Havard; Sharper—Wright; Sir Joseph—Miller; Bluff—Johnson;
Fondlewife—Griffin; Setter—Macklin; Laetitia—Mrs. Clive; Belinda
—Miss Holliday; Araminta—Mrs. Pritchard; Sylvia—Mrs. Brett;
Lucy—Mrs. Marshall). May 16 (Belinda—Mrs. Hamilton; Lucy—
Mrs. Grace). CG: May 18 (Heartwell—Bridgwater; Bellmour—
Walker; Vainlove—Ryan; Sharper—Hale; Sir Joseph—Yates; Bluff
—Mullart; Fondlewife—Hippisley; Setter—Chapman; Laetitia—
Mrs. Horton; Belinda—Mrs. Bellamy; Araminta—Mrs. Elmy; Sylvia
—Mrs. Vincent; Lucy—Mrs. Mullart).

1738–39. DL: Oct. 17 (as Sept. 15, 1737, except Sir Joseph—Th. Cibber;
Belinda—Mrs. Pritchard; Araminta omitted; Sylvia—Mrs. Chet-
wood; Lucy—Mrs. Grace). (May 12: Dismissed). CG: Nov. 28 (as
May 18, 1738, except Sir Joseph—Neale; Laetitia—Mrs. Marten;
Araminta omitted). Jan. 16.

1739–40. DL: (Advertised for Oct. 25, possibly not given). Nov. 1
(as Sept. 15, 1737, except Sir Joseph—Woodward; Belinda—Mrs.
Mills; Sylvia—Mrs. Chetwood). Feb. 2 (Lucy—Mrs. Macklin). March
18 (Fondlewife—Macklin; Setter—Chapman). CG: Sept. 17 (Heartwell—Bridgwater; Bellmour—Gibson; Vainlove—Ryan; Sharper—
Hale; Sir Joseph—Neale; Bluff—Rosco; Fondlewife—Hippisley; Setter—James; Bransby—Bencraft; Laetitia—Mrs. Horton; Belinda—
Mrs. Bellamy; Araminta—Mrs. Cross; Sylvia—Mrs. Vincent; Lucy—
Mrs. Mullart).

1740–41. DL: Sept. 25 (Heartwell—Quin; Bellmour—Mills; Vainlove—
Havard; Sharper—Wright; Sir Joseph—Woodward; Bluff—John-
son; Fondlewife—Macklin; Setter—Chapman; Laetitia—Mrs. Clive;
Belinda—Mrs. Mills; Araminta—Mrs. Pritchard). Nov. 17 (Sylvia—
Mrs. Wright). CG: Jan. 12 (as Sept. 17, 1739, except Bellmour—
Ryan; Bluff—Mullart; Fondlewife—C. Cibber; Laetitia—Mrs. Wof-
fington; Araminta—Mrs. Cross; Lucy omitted). 13. 14 (Vainlove—
Gibson). 19 (Fondlewife—Hippisley). March 10 (Heartwell—Rosco).
April 11 (Heartwell—Bridgwater; Setter—Oates). 15 (Heartwell—
—Bridgwater; Bellmour—Ryan; Sharper—Hale; Fondlewife—Hip-
pisley; Laetitia—Mrs. Woffington; rest omitted). GF: Oct. 21 (Heart-
well—Paget; Bellmour—Giffard; Vainlove—Crofts; Sharper—Blakes;
Sir Joseph—Oates; Bluff—Dunstall; Fondlewife—Julian; Setter—
Sowden; Laetitia—Mrs. Giffard; Belinda—Mrs. Middleton. April
28 (Setter—Snow).

1741–42. DL: March 27 (Heartwell—Delane; Bellmour—Mills; Vain-

love—Havard; Sharper—Ridout; Sir Joseph—Th. Cibber; Bluff—
Johnson; Fondlewife—Macklin; Setter—Turbutt; Barnaby—Leigh;
Laetitia—Mrs. Clive; Belinda—Mrs. Mills; Araminta—Mrs. Cross;
Sylvia—Mrs. Ridout). CG: Sept. 25 (Heartwell—Bridgwater; Bell-
mour—Ryan; Vainlove—Gibson; Sharper—Hale; Sir Joseph—
—Woodward; Bluff—Mullart; Fondlewife—Hippisley; Setter—
Chapman; Barnaby—Clarke; Laetitia—Mrs. Horton; Belinda—Mrs.
Pritchard; Araminta—Mrs. James; Sylvia—Mrs. Vincent; Lucy—
Mrs. Mullart). Nov. 30 (Bluff—Rosco; Setter—James; Araminta—
Mrs. Hale). Jan. 11 (Setter—Chapman; Araminta—Mrs. James).
GF: Jan. 5 (Heartwell—Giffard; Bellmour—W. Giffard; Vainlove—
Blakes; Sharper—Marshall; Sir Joseph—Yates; Bluff—Paget; Fon-
dlewife—Garrick; Setter—Peterson; Barnaby—Clough; Laetitia—
Mrs. Giffard; Belinda—Mrs. Bambridge; Araminta—Mrs. Dunstall;
Sylvia—Miss Hippisley; Lucy—Mrs. Yates; Betty—Miss Vallois). 6.
7. 8. 9. 11 (Sharper—Blakes; Vainlove—Dighton). 12. 13. 20. Feb.
24. May 10 (Sylvia—Miss E. Hippisley).

1742–43. DL: Nov. 1 (as March 27, 1742, except Sharper—Hallam; Sir
Joseph—Neale; Bluff—Macklin; Fondlewife—Garrick; Setter—
Yates; Lucy—Mrs. Bennet; Betty—Miss Minors). 13. Dec. 3. April
11. 22 (Sharper—Blakes; Belinda—Mrs. Pritchard). May 9 (Bluff—
Morgan; Fondlewife—Macklin; Belinda—Mrs. Mills). CG: Oct.
6 (as Sept. 25, 1741, except Heartwell—Quin; Bluff—Rosco; Barnaby—Bencraft; Laetitia—Mrs. Cibber; Belinda—Mrs. Horton; Araminta—Mrs. Hale; Betty—Miss Hillyard). Nov. 12. Dec. 9. May 2
(Bluff—Marten; Vainlove—Carr). LIF: Dec. 30 (Heartwell—Giffard;
Bellmour—W. Giffard; Vainlove—Dighton; Sharper—Mozeen; Sir
Joseph—Peterson; Bluff—Dunstall; Fondlewife—Th. Cibber; Setter—Julian; Laetitia—Mrs. Giffard; Belinda—Mrs. Butler; Araminta—Mrs. Dunstall; Sylvia—Mrs. E. Giffard; Lucy—Mrs. Chetwood). Jan. 17. Feb. 28: Fondlewife and Laetitia (an abridgment).

1743–44. DL: Dec. 1 (Heartwell—Bridges; Bellmour—Giffard; Vain-
love—Havard; Sharper—Blakes; Sir Joseph—Neale; Bluff—Morgan;
Fondlewife—Th. Cibber; Setter—Yates; Barnaby—Green; Laetitia
—Mrs. Woffington; Belinda—Mrs. Giffard; Araminta—Mrs. Cross;
Sylvia—Mrs. Ridout; Lucy—Mrs. Bennet; Betty—Mrs. King). Jan.
5 (Fondlewife—C. Cibber). April 4 (Fondlewife—Garrick). CG:
Nov. 21 (Heartwell—Bridgwater; Bellmour—Ryan; Vainlove—Gib-
son; Sharper—Hale; Sir Joseph—Woodward; Bluff—Rosco; Fondle-
wife—Hippisley; Setter—Chapman; Barnaby—Bencraft; Laetitia—
Mrs. Horton; Belinda—Mrs. Walker; Araminta—Mrs. Hale; Sylvia
—Mrs. Vincent; Lucy—Mrs. Mullart; Betty—Miss Hillyard). Dec.

21 (Heartwell—Quin). March 28 (Bluff—Marten). April 28 (Vainlove—Anderson; Bluff—Rosco; Belinda—Mrs. Clive).

1744–45. DL: April 19 (as Dec. 1, 1743, except Bluff—Taswell; Fondlewife—Macklin; Barnaby—Leigh). CG: Nov. 7 (as Nov. 21, 1743, except Heartwell—Quin; Barnaby—Bencraft; Laetitia—Mrs. Pritchard; Belinda—Mrs. Hale; Araminta—Mrs. Vaughan; Betty omitted). Jan. 11 (Belinda—Mrs. Clive; Araminta—Mrs. Hale; Betty—Mrs. Bland). May 3 (Lucy—Mrs. Bland; Betty—Mrs. Vaughan). GF: Jan. 15 (no cast). 16.

1745–46. DL: Sept. 24 (as Dec. 1, 1743, except Heartwell—Sparks; Bellmour—Mills; Bluff—I. Sparks; Fondlewife—Macklin; Barnaby omitted; Belinda—Mrs. Mills; Araminta—Mrs. Bennet; Lucy—Mrs. Macklin). Jan. 28 (Bellmour—Giffard; Sylvia—Miss Minors). CG: Dec. 12 (as Nov. 21, 1743, except Barnaby omitted; Laetitia—Mrs. Pritchard; Belinda—Mrs. Horton; Sylvia—Miss Hippisley; Lucy—Mrs. Bland; Betty—Mrs. Vaughan). GF: Nov. 19 (Heartwell—Furnival; Bellmour—Cushing; Vainlove—Blakey; Sharper—Lee; Sir Joseph—Kennedy; Bluff—Paget; Fondlewife—Hallam; Setter—L. Hallam; Servant—Shepard; Laetitia—Mrs. Cushing; Belinda—Mrs. Bambridge; Araminta—Mrs. Hallam; Sylvia—Mrs. Phillips; Lucy—Mrs. Williamson; Betty—Mrs. Dove). 20. Feb. 18 (no cast).

1746–47. CG: Nov. 26 (as Nov. 21, 1743, except Heartwell—Quin; Sharper—Ridout; Barnaby—Vaughan; Laetitia—Mrs. Pritchard; Belinda—Mrs. Horton; Sylvia—Miss Hippisley; Lucy—Mrs. Bland; Betty—Mrs. Vaughan). March 2 (Sylvia—Mrs. Vincent). HAY: April 22 (The Credulous Husband: Fondlewife—Foote; Bellmour—Lee; Laetitia—Mrs. Hallam).

1747–48. CG: Dec. 15 (Heartwell—Bridgwater; Bellmour—Ryan; Vainlove—Gibson; Sharper—Ridout; Sir Joseph—Th. Cibber; Bluff—Rosco; Fondlewife—Foote; Setter—James; Laetitia—Mrs. Bland; Belinda—Mrs. Storer; Araminta—Mrs. Hale; Sylvia—Miss Hippisley; Lucy—Mrs. Dunstall). Feb. 1 (Fondlewife—Collins; Laetitia—Mrs. Horton; Lucy—Mrs. Bland). May 5.

1748–49. CG: Sept. 30 (as Dec. 15, 1747, except Heartwell—Quin; Bluff—Marten; Fondlewife—Arthur; Setter—Bencraft; Laetitia—Mrs. Woffington; Belinda—Mrs. Horton; Araminta—Miss Copen; Sylvia—Mrs. Ridout). Nov. 21 (Sir Joseph—Cushing; Araminta—Mrs. Hale; Lucy—Mrs. Phillips).

1749–50. CG: Oct. 6 (Heartwell—Quin; Bellmour—Ryan; Vainlove—Gibson; Sharper—Ridout; Sir Joseph—Cushing; Bluff—Marten; Fondlewife—Arthur; Setter—Bencraft; Laetitia—Mrs. Woffington; Belinda—Mrs. Horton; Araminta—Mrs. Barrington; Sylvia—Mrs.

Ridout; Betty—Miss Allen). Nov. 29 (Setter, Bluff, Barnaby, and Betty omitted).

1750–51. CG: Nov. 19 (as Oct. 6, 1749, except Setter—Dyer; Barnaby—Hacket; Belinda—Mrs. Elmy; Lucy—Mrs. Dunstall).

1752–53. CG: Dec. 14 (Heartwell—Bridgwater; Bellmour—Ryan; Vainlove—Usher; Sharper—Ridout; Sir Joseph—Cushing; Bluff—Marten; Fondlewife—Arthur; Setter—Bencraft; Laetitia—Mrs. Bland; Belinda—Mrs. Elmy; Araminta—Mrs. Barrington; Sylvia—Mrs. Ridout; Lucy—Miss Pitt). Jan. 31 (Barnaby—Paddick; Betty—Miss Allen).

1753–54. DL: Oct. 24 (Heartwell—Berry; Bellmour—Palmer; Vainlove—Jefferson; Sharper—Havard; Sir Joseph—Woodward; Bluff—Yates; Fondlewife—Foote; Setter—Blakes; Laetitia—Mrs. Pritchard; Belinda—Miss Haughton; Araminta—Mrs. Davies; Sylvia—Mrs. Cowper; Lucy—Mrs. Bennet). 27. 30. Nov. 2. 12. 30. Dec. 15. Jan. 29. Feb. 22 (Belinda—Mrs. Mills). CG: Oct. 17 (as Dec. 14, 1752, except Bluff—Dunstall; Barnaby—Paddick; Sylvia—Mrs. Vincent; Betty—Miss Allen).

1754–55. CG: Oct. 14 (as Dec. 14, 1752, except Heartwell—Sparks; Vainlove—Gibson; Fondlewife—Foote; Barnaby—Paddick; Laetitia—Mrs. Bellamy; Sylvia—Mrs. Baker; Betty—Miss Allen). Nov. 12. May 12 (Sir Joseph—Costollo; Bluff—Stevens; Setter—Bennet).

1755–56. CG: Feb. 9 (Heartwell—Sparks; Bellmour—Ryan; Vainlove—Gibson; Sharper—Ridout; Sir Joseph—Cushing; Bluff—Marten; Fondlewife—Foote; Setter—Bencraft; Barnaby—Bennet; Laetitia—Mrs. Bellamy; Belinda—Mrs. Elmy; Araminta—Mrs. Barrington; Sylvia—Mrs. Baker; Lucy—Mrs. Pitt; Betty—Miss Allen).

1756–57. DL: Oct. 14 (as Oct. 24, 1753, except Vainlove and Sharper omitted).

1758–59. DL: Oct. 27 (as Oct. 24, 1753, except Vainlove—Packer; Sir Joseph—Yates; Bluff—Taswell; Sylvia—Miss Barton).

1759–60. CG: April 29 (as Feb. 9, 1756, except Bellmour—Smith; Fondlewife—Collins; Setter—Bennet; Barnaby—Holtom; Laetitia—Mrs. Hamilton).

1761–62. CG: April 21 (Heartwell—Dunstall; Bellmour—Smith; Vainlove—Mattocks; Sharper—Hull; Sir Joseph—Cushing; Bluff—Marten; Fondlewife—Shuter; Setter—Dyer; Barnaby—Holtom; Laetitia—Mrs. Ward; Belinda—Mrs. Vincent; Araminta—Mrs. Barrington; Sylvia—Mrs. Abeg; Lucy—Mrs. Pitt).

1768–69. HAY: Aug. 25, 1769 (Heartwell—Sowden; Bellmour—Aickin; Vainlove—DuBellamy; Sharper—Kearny; Sir Joseph—Hamilton; Bluff—Sharper; Fondlewife—Foote; Setter—Vandermere; Laetitia

—Mrs. Gardner; Belinda—Mrs. DuBellamy; Araminta—Mrs. Dyer; Sylvia—Mrs. Jefferies; Lucy—Mrs. Reade). 28.

1769–70. HAY: Aug. 24, 1770 (as at Hay, Aug. 25, 1769, except Sharper —Smith; Bluff—Sparks; Belinda—Mrs. McGeorge; Lucy—Mrs. White). Sept. 7. 14.

1770–71. HAY: Sept. 2, 1771 (Heartwell—Gardner; Bellmour—Aickin; Vainlove—Robson; Sharper—Didier; Sir Joseph—Woodward; Bluff —Gentleman; Fondlewife—Foote; Setter—Vandermere; Laetitia— Mrs. Gardner; Belinda—Mrs. Granger; Araminta—Mrs. Collins; Sylvia—Mrs. Didier; Lucy—Mrs. White; Betty—Mrs. Farrell).

1771–72. HAY: Sept. 8, 1772 (as at Hay, Sept. 2, 1771, except Sharper— Fenton; Sir Joseph—Weston; Setter—Dance; Barnaby—Jacobs; Be- linda—Miss Ambrose; Araminta—Miss Platt; Sylvia—Miss Went- worth; Lucy and Betty omitted).

1774–75. HAY: Sept. 18, 1775 (Heartwell—Fearon; Bellmour—Aickin; Vainlove—Baker; Sharper—Love; Sir Joseph—Whitfield; Bluff— Williams; Fondlewife—Weston; Setter—Everard; Barnaby—Jacobs; Laetitia—Mrs. Gardner; Belinda—Miss Ambrose; Araminta—Miss Platt; Sylvia—Mrs. Palmer; Lucy—Mrs. Whitfield).

1776–77. DL: Nov. 19 (Heartwell—Bensley; Bellmour—Smith; Vain- love—Reddish; Sharper—Farren; Sir Joseph—King; Bluff—Moody; Fondlewife—Yates; Setter—Baddeley; Laetitia—Mrs. Abington; Be- linda—Miss Younge; Araminta—Mrs. Baddeley; Sylvia—Miss Essex; Lucy—Miss Pope). 20 (Vainlove—Verson; Sylvia—Miss P. Hopkins). 22. 27. Dec. 7. 11. Feb. 11. April 12.

1777–78. DL: Oct. 9 (as Nov. 19, 1776, except Vainlove—Vernon; Laetitia—Miss Pope; Araminta—Mrs. Robinson; Sylvia—Miss P. Hopkins; Lucy—Mrs. Wrighten). May 18.

1778–79. DL: Nov. 28 (as Nov. 19, 1776, except Vainlove—Vernon; Laetitia—Miss Pope; Sylvia—Mrs. Brereton; Lucy—Mrs. Wrighten).

1779–80. DL: March 4 (as Nov. 19, 1776, except Vainlove—Davies; Laetitia—Miss Pope; Belinda—Miss Farren; Araminta—Mrs. Sharp; Sylvia—Mrs. Brereton; Lucy—Mrs. Wrighten).

1780–81. DL: Dec. 19 (as Nov. 19, 1776, except Vainlove—Vernon; Laetitia—Miss Pope; Belinda—Miss Farren; Araminta—Mrs. Sharp; Sylvia—Mrs. Brereton; Lucy—Mrs. Wrighten). Jan. 27. May 22.

1781–82. DL: May 10 (as Nov. 19, 1776, except Vainlove—Packer; Laetitia—Miss Pope; Belinda—Miss Farren; Araminta—Mrs. Sharp; Sylvia—Mrs. Brereton; Lucy—Mrs. Wrighten).

1788–89. CG: March 5 (Heartwell—Ryder; Bellmour—Lewis; Vain- love—Macready; Sharper—Farren; Sir Joseph—Blanchard; Bluff— Cubitt; Fondlewife—Quick; Setter—Bernard; Barnaby—Milburne;

Laetitia—Mrs. Abington; Belinda—Mrs. Pope; Araminta—Miss Chapman; Sylvia—Mrs. Mountain; Lucy—Miss Stuart). 12.

The Double Dealer

1703–04. LIF: Nov. 29 (no cast).

1718–19. LIF: Oct. 18 (Maskwell—Quin; Sir Paul—Pack; Careless—Ryan; Brisk—C. Bullock; Mellefont—Leigh; Lord Touchwood—Cory; Lord Froth—Spiller; Lady Touchwood—Mrs. Rogers; Lady Froth—Mrs. C. Bullock; Lady Plyant—Mrs. Knight; Cynthia—Mrs. Seymour). 20. Nov. 18 (no cast). Dec. 4.

1719–20. LIF: March 7 (Lady Froth—Mrs. Bullock; rest omitted). 10 (no cast). May 11 (Maskwell—Quin; Sir Paul—Pack; Careless—Ryan; Brisk—C. Bullock; Mellefont—Leigh; Lady Touchwood—Mrs. Giffard; Lady Froth—Mrs. Bullock).

1720–21. LIF: Nov. 2 (as May 11, 1720, except Sir Paul—Griffin; Lady Touchwood—Mrs. Seymour; Lady Froth—Mrs. C. Bullock; Lady Plyant—Mrs. Giffard; Cynthia—Mrs. Purden). 25 (Lord Froth—Egleton). May 2.

1721–22. LIF: Dec. 12 (Maskwell—Quin; Sir Paul—Phipps; Careless—Ryan; Brisk—C. Bullock; Mellefont—Walker; Lord Touchwood—Boheme; Lord Froth—Egleton; Lady Touchwood—Mrs. Seymour; Lady Froth—Mrs. Bullock; Lady Plyant—Mrs. Egleton; Cynthia—Mrs. Rogeir). Jan. 8. April 20 (Brisk—Egleton; Lord Froth—Spiller).

1722–23. LIF: Oct. 24 (as Dec. 12, 1721, except Brisk—Egleton; Lord Froth—Spiller). April 4 (Sir Paul—Hippisley; Lord Froth—Morgan).

1723–24. LIF: Jan. 20 (no cast). Feb. 8. 22. April 13. June 3 (as Dec. 12, 1721, except Sir Paul—Hippisley; Brisk—Egleton; Lord Froth—Spiller; Lady Touchwood—Mrs. Egleton; Lady Froth—Mrs. Cross; Lady Plyant—Mrs. Knight; Cynthia—Mrs. Cantrell).

1724–25. LIF: Jan. 5 (no cast). 16 (Maskwell—Quin; Sir Paul—Hippisley; Careless—Ryan; Brisk—Egleton; Mellefont—Walker; Lord Touchwood—Boheme; Lord Froth—Spiller; Lady Touchwood—Mrs. Parker; Lady Froth—Mrs. Bullock; Lady Plyant—Mrs. Egleton; Cynthia—Mrs. Legar).

1725–26. LIF: Nov. 2 (as Jan. 16, 1725). Feb. 9 (no cast). 26. May 10 (Lord Touchwood—Ogden; Lord Froth—Morgan; rest as Jan. 16, 1725).

1726–27. LIF: Oct. 10 (no cast). Dec. 9. April 19 (Maskwell—Quin; Sir Paul—Hippisley; Careless—Ryan; Brisk—W. Bullock; Mellefont—Walker; Lord Touchwood—Ogden; Lady Touchwood—Mrs. Berri-

man; Lady Froth—Mrs. Bullock; Lady Plyant—Mrs. Cook; Cynthia
—Mrs. Rice).

1727–28. LIF: Jan. 5 (no cast). April 4 (Maskwell—Milward; Sir Paul—
Hippisley; Careless—Ryan; Brisk—Chapman; Mellefont—Walker;
Lord Touchwood—Boheme; Lord Froth—Spiller; Saygrace—H.
Bullock; Lady Touchwood—Mrs. Berriman; Lady Froth—Mrs.
Bullock; Lady Plyant—Mrs. Egleton; Cynthia—Mrs. Legar).

1728–29. LIF: Jan. 25 (no cast). March 10 (as April 4, 1728, except
Maskwell—Quin; Lord Touchwood, Lord Froth, and Saygrace
omitted). April 12.

1729–30. LIF: Oct. 25 (no cast). Jan. 13. April 25.

1730–31. LIF: Oct. 19 (Maskwell—Quin; Sir Paul—Hippisley; Careless
—Ryan; Brisk—Chapman; Mellefont—Walker; Lord Touchwood—
Boheme; Lady Touchwood—Mrs. Berriman; Lady Froth—Mrs. Bul-
lock; Lady Plyant—Mrs. Egleton; Cynthia—Miss Holliday). Jan. 19
(Cynthia—Miss Legar). Feb. 26 (no cast).

1731–32. LIF: Nov. 6 (no cast). Jan. 19 (as Oct. 19, 1730, except Lord
Touchwood omitted; Lady Touchwood—Mrs. Hallam). April 28
(no cast).

1732–33. CG: Feb. 8 (Maskwell—Quin; Sir Paul—Hippisley; Careless—
Ryan; Brisk—Chapman; Mellefont—Walker; Lord Touchwood—
Milward; Lord Froth—Neale; Saygrace—Houghton; Lady Touch-
wood—Mrs. Hallam; Lady Froth—Mrs. Bullock; Lady Plyant—Mrs.
Egleton; Cynthia—Mrs. Laguerre).

1733–34. CG: Nov. 16 (as Feb. 8, 1733, except Lord Touchwood—Aston;
Lady Plyant—Mrs. Cantrell).

1735–36. DL: Oct. 11 (Maskwell—Quin; Sir Paul—Griffin; Careless—
W. Mills; Brisk—Th. Cibber; Mellefont—Milward; Lord Touchwood—Winstone; Lord Froth—Berry; Lady Touchwood—Mrs. Butler; Lady Froth—Mrs. Clive; Lady Plyant—Mrs. Cantrell; Cynthia—
Miss Holliday). 14. 16. 18. 20. 29. Nov. 8. 28. Dec. 12. Jan. 29. March
22. April 8. May 14. CG: April 13 (Maskwell—Bridgwater; Sir
Paul—Hippisley; Careless—Ryan; Mellefont—Walker; Lord Froth
—Paget; Lady Touchwood—Mrs. Hallam; Lady Froth—Mrs. Bullock; Lady Plyant—Mrs. Mullart; Cynthia—Miss Norsa).

1736–37. DL: Nov. 6 (as Oct. 11, 1735, except Lady Plyant—Mrs. Thurmond). 25. Feb. 4. May 10 (no cast).

1737–38. DL: Oct. 31 (as Oct. 11, 1735, except Careless—Mills; Lord
Froth—Macklin; Lady Plyant—Mrs. Roberts; Cynthia—Mrs. Mills).
Jan. 10. Feb. 14. May 10 (Brisk—Cross).

1738–39. DL: Sept. 19 (as Oct. 11, 1735, except Careless—Mills; Lord
Froth—Macklin; Lady Plyant—Mrs. Roberts; Sylvia—Mrs. Mills).

Oct. 28 (Brisk—Cross). Jan. 11 (Brisk—Th. Cibber). May 15 (Brisk—Woodward). CG: Feb. 26 (Maskwell—Rosco; Sir Paul—Hippisley; Careless—Ryan; Brisk—Chapman; Mellefont—Hale; Lord Touchwood—Bridgwater; Lord Froth—Neale; Lady Touchwood—Mrs. Hallam; Lady Froth—Mrs. Horton; Lady Plyant—Mrs. James; Cynthia—Mrs. Vincent). 27. 28. May 3 (Cynthia—Mrs. Bellamy).

1739–40. DL: Oct. 19 (as Oct. 11, 1735, except Careless—Mills; Brisk—Chapman; Lord Froth—Macklin; Lady Plyant—Mrs. Roberts; Cynthia—Mrs. Mills). Dec. 19. Feb. 9. CG: Sept. 12 (as Feb. 26, 1739, except Brisk—Th. Cibber; Saygrace—Arthur; Lady Touchwood—Mrs. Cross). Nov. 24 (Lady Touchwood—Mrs. Hallam). May 14 (Lady Touchwood—Mrs. Cross). 20.

1740–41. CG: Sept. 29 (as Feb. 26, 1739, except Brisk—Th. Cibber; Saygrace—Arthur; Lady Touchwood—Mrs. Cross). April 8.

1741–42. DL: March 29 (Maskwell—Berry; Sir Paul—Macklin; Careless—Mills; Brisk—Th. Cibber; Mellefont—Havard; Lord Touchwood—Winstone; Lord Froth—Neale; Lady Touchwood—Mrs. Butler; Lady Froth—Mrs. Clive; Lady Plyant—Mrs. Macklin; Cynthia—Mrs. Mills). CG: (Nov. 23, possibly given). Nov. 28 (Maskwell—Rosco; Sir Paul—Hippisley; Careless—Ryan; Brisk—Woodward; Mellefont—Hale; Lord Touchwood—Bridgwater; Lord Froth—Mullart; Saygrace—Lascelles; Lady Touchwood—Mrs. Pritchard; Lady Froth—Mrs. Horton; Lady Plyant—Mrs. James; Cynthia—Mrs. Vincent). Dec. 21 (Brisk—Chapman). March 16.

1742–43. CG: Oct. 19 (as Nov. 28, 1741, except Maskwell—Quin; Lord Froth—Gibson; Lady Touchwood—Mrs. Woodward). Nov. 17.

1743–44. DL: April 23 (Maskwell—Berry; Sir Paul—Yates; Careless—Mills; Brisk—Th. Cibber; Mellefont—Havard; Lord Touchwood—Winstone; Lord Froth—Neale; Saygrace—Turbutt; Lady Touchwood—Mrs. Cross; Lady Froth—Mrs. Mills; Lady Plyant—Mrs. Roberts; Cynthia—Mrs. Ridout). CG: Jan. 7 (as Nov. 28, 1741, except Maskwell—Quin; Lord Froth—Gibson; Saygrace omitted; Lady Froth—Mrs. Clive; Lady Plyant—Mrs. Mullart).

1744–45. CG: Jan. 18 (as Nov. 28, 1741, except Maskwell—Quin; Brisk—Th. Cibber; Lord Froth—Gibson; Saygrace omitted; Lady Froth—Mrs. Clive; Lady Plyant—Mrs. Mullart). March 4. 9. May 21 (Brisk—Chapman; Lady Plyant—Mrs. James).

1745–46. CG: Dec. 6 (as Nov. 28, 1741, except Brisk—Th. Cibber; Lord Froth—Gibson; Saygrace omitted). Jan. 17.

1746–47. CG: Dec. 22 (Maskwell—Quin; Sir Paul—Hippisley; Careless—Ryan; Brisk—Woodward; Mellefont—Havard; Lord Touchwood—Bridgwater; Lord Froth—Gibson; Lady Touchwood—Mrs.

Pritchard; Lady Froth—Mrs. Horton; Lady Plyant—Mrs. James; Cynthia—Mrs. Vincent). March 5 (Mellefont—Havard). 31. May 6.

1748–49. DL: Dec. 21 (Maskwell—Berry; Sir Paul—Yates; Careless—Mills; Brisk—Woodward; Mellefont—Havard; Lord Touchwood—Winstone; Lord Froth—Neale; Saygrace—James; Lady Touchwood—Mrs. Pritchard; Lady Froth—Mrs. Clive; Lady Plyant—Mrs. Pitt; Cynthia—Mrs. Willoughby). Jan. 18. CG: April 5 (Maskwell—Quin; Sir Paul—Collins; Careless—Ryan; Brisk—Th. Cibber; Mellefont—Ridout; Lord Touchwood—Bridgwater; Lord Froth—Gibson; Saygrace—Paget; Lady Touchwood—Mrs. Woffington; Lady Froth—Miss Bellamy; Lady Plyant—Mrs. Hale; Cynthia—Mrs. Ridout).

1749–50. DL: Nov. 27 (as Dec. 21, 1748, except Lord Froth—Shuter). CG: Oct. 16 (as April 5, 1749, except Brisk—Cushing; Saygrace—Redman; Lady Froth—Mrs. Vincent; Lady Plyant—Mrs. Barrington). 31. Dec. 13. Jan. 22. April 19 (Lady Froth—a Gentlewoman).

1750–51. CG: Oct. 20 (as April 5, 1749, except Sir Paul—Macklin; Brisk—Dyer; Saygrace—Redman; Lady Froth—Mrs. Vincent; Lady Plyant—Mrs. Macklin). Jan. 28 (Cynthia—Mrs. Barrington).

1751–52. CG: Nov. 21 (as April 5, 1749, except Maskwell—Sparks; Sir Paul—Macklin; Brisk—Dyer; Saygrace—Redman; Lady Touchwood—Mrs. Elmy; Lady Froth—Mrs. Vincent; Lady Plyant—Mrs. Macklin). Jan. 13. March 2. April 16.

1752–53. CG: Dec. 19 (Maskwell—Sparks; Sir Paul—Macklin; Careless—Ryan; Brisk—Dyer; Mellefont—Ridout; Lord Touchwood—Bridgwater; Lord Froth—Arthur; Lady Touchwood—Mrs. Bland; Lady Froth—Mrs. Vincent; Lady Plyant—Mrs. Macklin; Cynthia—Mrs. Ridout).

1754–55. CG: Nov. 28 (Maskwell—Sparks; Sir Paul—Shuter; Careless—Smith; Brisk—Dyer; Mellefont—Ridout; Lord Touchwood—Anderson; Lord Froth—Gibson; Lady Touchwood—Mrs. Hamilton; Lady Froth—Mrs. Bellamy; Lady Plyant—Mrs. Woffington; Cynthia—Mrs. Baker). Dec. 4 (Lady Touchwood—Mrs. Elmy). Jan. 18 (Lady Froth—Mrs. Green). May 16 (Lady Froth—Mrs. Bellamy; Lady Touchwood—Mrs. Hamilton).

1755–56. CG: Nov. 7 (as Nov. 28, 1754, except Lord Touchwood—Arthur; Lady Touchwood—Mrs. Woffington; Lady Plyant—Mrs. Barrington). March 1 (Sir Paul—Foote; Lady Plyant—Miss Nossiter). 4.

1756–57. DL: Oct. 29 (Maskwell—Mossop; Sir Paul—Foote; Careless—Palmer; Brisk—Woodward; Mellefont—Havard; Lord Touchwood—Davies; Lord Froth—Blakes; Saygrace—Clough; Lady Touchwood—Mrs. Pritchard; Lady Froth—Mrs. Clive; Lady Plyant—a Gentlewoman; Cynthia—Mrs. Davies). Nov. 1. Feb. 19 (Lady Plyant—Miss Barton). CG: Oct. 18 (as Nov. 28, 1754, except Lady Touchwood—Mrs. Woffington; Lady Froth—Mrs. Green; Lady Plyant—Miss Nossiter). Dec. 8 (Lady Froth—Mrs. Vincent). Jan. 17 (Lady Froth—Mrs. Green).

1757–58. DL: Oct. 18 (as Oct. 29, 1756, except Lady Plyant—Miss Barton).

1758–59. DL: Nov. 17 (as Oct. 29, 1756, except Brisk—O'Brien; Lady Plyant—Miss Barton). CG: Oct. 26 (as Nov. 28, 1754, except Careless—Ryan; Lady Plyant—Miss Nossiter). March 6 (Careless—Smith). May 25 (Lady Touchwood—Mrs. Elmy; Lady Plyant—Mrs. Barrington).

1761–62. DL: Oct. 14 (Maskwell—Davies; Sir Paul—Yates; Careless—Palmer; Brisk—O'Brien; Mellefont—Havard; Lord Touchwood—Packer; Lord Froth—Blakes; Lady Touchwood—Mrs. Pritchard; Lady Froth—Mrs. Clive; Lady Plyant—Miss Haughton; Cynthia—Mrs. Davies).

1772–73. DL: March 23 (Maskwell—Reddish; Sir Paul—King; Careless—Palmer; Brisk—Dodd; Mellefont—Brereton; Lord Touchwood—Packer; Lord Froth—Parsons; Saygrace—Wright; Lady Touchwood—Mrs. Hopkins; Lady Froth—Mrs. Abington; Lady Plyant—Miss Younge; Cynthia—Miss Platt). April 14.

1775–76. CG: March 5 (Maskwell—Sheridan; Sir Paul—Quick; Careless—Lewis; Brisk—Lee Lewes; Mellefont—Wroughton; Lord Touchwood—Clarke; Lord Froth—Booth; Lady Touchwood—a Gentlewoman; Lady Froth—Mrs. Green; Lady Plyant—Mrs. Mattocks; Cynthia—Mrs. Jackson). HAY: Sept. 2, 1776 (Maskwell—Palmer; Sir Paul—Foote; Careless—Aickin; Brisk—Whitfield; Mellefont—L'Estrange; Lord Touchwood—Fearon; Lord Froth—Parsons; Lady Touchwood—Miss Sherry; Lady Froth—Miss Ambrose; Lady Plyant—Mrs. Gardner; Cynthia—Mrs. Whitfield). 12.

1776–77. CG: Dec. 17 (as March 5, 1776, except Maskwell—Aickin; Sir Paul—Macklin; Lady Touchwood—Mrs. Jackson; Lady Froth—Mrs. Mattocks; Lady Plyant—Miss Macklin; Cynthia—Miss Leeson).

1781–82. CG: March 19 (Maskwell—Henderson; Sir Paul—Quick; Careless—Lewis; Brisk—Lee Lewes; Mellefont—Whitfield; Lord Touchwood—Clarke; Lord Froth—Booth; Lady Touchwood—Mrs. Inchband; Lady Froth—Miss Younge; Lady Plyant—Mrs. Mattocks; Cynthia—Miss Satchell).

1784–85. DL: Dec. 3 (Maskwell—Palmer; Sir Paul—King; Careless—Brereton; Brisk—Dodd; Mellefont—Barrymore; Lord Touchwood—Packer; Lord Froth—Suett; Saygrace—Wright; Lady Touchwood—Miss E. Kemble; Lady Froth—Miss Pope; Lady Plyant—Miss Far-

ren; Cynthia—Miss M. Stageldoir). 8. 16. Jan. 3. 26. Feb. 5. April 4
(Maskwell—Kemble). May 12 (Maskwell—Palmer).

1787–88. DL: Nov. 29 (as Dec. 3, 1784, except Maskwell—Kemble;
Careless—Wroughton; Brisk—Bannister; Lady Touchwood—Mrs.
Taylor). Dec. 21. May 30 (Mellefont—Benson; Cynthia—Miss Col-
lins). In the early nineteenth century it was given at Drury Lane on
February 27, 1802.

Love for Love

1703–04. LIF: April 26 (Ben—Dogget). June 1.

1704–05. QUEEN'S: June 25 (acted wholly by women). 27. 29.

1705–06. QUEEN'S: Nov. 22 (no cast). Jan. 9 (acted wholly by women).

1707–08. DL: Feb. 7 (Sir Sampson—Estcourt; Valentine—Wilks;
Scandal—Booth; Tattle—Pack; Ben—Cibber; Foresight—Johnson;
Jeremy—Bowen; Trapland—Norris; Angelica—Mrs. Oldfield; Mrs.
Foresight—Mrs. Rogers; Mrs. Frail—Mrs. Barry; Prue—Mrs. Bick-
nell; Nurse—Mrs. Willis). March 1 (Ben—Dogget). 2. 20. June 10
(Scandal—Husband; Ben—Cibber; Jeremy—Bickerstaff).

1708–09. DL: Oct. 7 (as Feb. 7, 1708, except Mrs. Frail and Nurse
omitted). March 12 (Mrs. Frail—Mrs. Porter). April 7 (Valentine—
Betterton; Ben—Dogget; Angelica—Mrs. Bracegirdle; Mrs. Frail—
Mrs. Barry; rest omitted).

1709–10. DL: Dec. 3 (Sir Sampson—Leigh; Valentine—Booth; Scandal
—Keene; Tattle—Pack; Ben—Bickerstaff; Foresight—Norris; Jeremy
—Miller; Angelica—Mrs. Bradshaw; Mrs. Foresight—Mrs. Moor;
Mrs. Frail—Mrs. Knight; Prue—Miss Santlow). 5 (Jeremy omitted).
April 20 (Tattle omitted). June 6 (as Dec. 3, 1709, except Nurse—Mrs.
Hunt). QUEEN'S: Sept. 24 (Sir Sampson—Estcourt; Valentine—
Wilks; Scandal—Husband; Tattle—Cibber; Ben—Dogget; Fore-
sight—Johnson; Jeremy—Bowen; Trapland—Bullock; Angelica—
Mrs. Oldfield; Mrs. Foresight—Mrs. Cross; Mrs. Frail—Mrs. Porter;
Prue—Mrs. Bicknell; Nurse—Mrs. Willis). Oct. 18. Dec. 1 (Jeremy
omitted). 28 (Jeremy—Bowen). Jan. 16 (Scandal, Foresight, Mrs. Fore-
sight, Mrs. Frail and Nurse omitted).

1710–11. DL: Feb. 12 (Sir Sampson—Estcourt; Valentine—Wilks;
Scandal—Booth; Ben—Dogget; Foresight—Johnson; Jeremy—
Bowen; Trapland—Norris; Angelica—Mrs. Oldfield; Mrs. Foresight
—Mrs. Rogers; Mrs. Frail—Mrs. Porter; Prue—Miss Santlow).
March 15 (Tattle—Cibber; Nurse—Mrs. Willis). April 12. May 25
(Prue—Mrs. Bicknell). QUEEN'S: Oct. 5 (Sir Sampson—Estcourt;
Valentine—Wilks; Scandal—Husband; Ben—Dogget; Tattle—Cib-

ber; Foresight—Johnson; Jeremy—Bowen; Trapland—Bullock; Angelica—Mrs. Oldfield; Mrs. Foresight—Mrs. Rogers; Prue—Mrs. Bicknell). Nov. 9 (Scandal—Booth; Trapland—Norris; Angelica—Mrs. Bradshaw; Mrs. Frail—Mrs. Porter; Prue—Miss Santlow; Nurse—Mrs. Willis).

1711–12. DL: Sept. 27 (as Feb. 12, 1711, except Tattle—Cibber; Ben omitted; Nurse—Mrs. Willis). Dec. 6 (Sir Sampson—Leigh; Ben—Dogget). Jan. 31 (no cast). April 22. May 9 (as Feb. 12, 1711, except Sir Sampson—Leigh; Angelica—Mrs. Bradshaw; Mrs. Frail—Mrs. Knight).

1712–13. DL: Nov. 27 (Ben—Dogget; rest omitted). Jan. 2. Feb. 13 (Sir Sampson—Leigh; Valentine—Wilks; Scandal—Booth; Tattle—Cibber; Ben—Dogget; Foresight—Johnson; Jeremy—Bowen; Trapland—Norris; Angelica—Mrs. Bradshaw; Mrs. Foresight—Mrs. Rogers; Mrs. Frail—Mrs. Porter; Prue—Mrs. Bicknell; Nurse—Mrs. Willis). March 7. May 25 (Prue—Miss Younger).

1713–14. DL: Oct. 12 (Ben—Dogget; rest omitted). March 11 (no cast). May 26 (as Feb. 13, 1713, except Sir Sampson—Bullock; Ben—Bickerstaff; Angelica—Mrs. Oldfield; Mrs. Foresight—Mrs. Cox; Prue—Miss Younger).

1714–15. DL: Oct. 1 (no cast). Nov. 30 (Ben—Griffith). March 8 (Valentine—Wilks; Scandal—Booth; Ben—Bickerstaff; Foresight—Johnson; Jeremy—Bowen; Trapland—Norris; Angelica—Mrs. Oldfield; Mrs. Frail—Mrs. Porter; Prue—Miss Younger). April 9. LIF: Jan. 12 (no cast). Feb. 2 (Sir Sampson—Bullock, Sen.; Valentine—Leigh; Scandal—Husband; Tattle—Pack; Foresight—a Gentleman; Jeremy—Spiller; Trapland—Bullock, Jun.; Angelica—Mrs. Spiller; Mrs. Foresight—Mrs. Moor; Mrs. Frail—Mrs. Knight; Prue—Miss Schoolding). May 10 (Ben—Mrs. Hunt; rest omitted) .

1715–16. DL: Oct. 28 (no cast). Jan. 9. March 20. May 9 (Sir Sampson—Booth; Tattle—Cibber; Foresight—Johnson; Jeremy—Bowen; Trapland—Norris; Angelica—Mrs. Oldfield; Mrs. Frail—Mrs. Porter; Prue—Miss Younger; Nurse—Mrs. Willis). LIF: April 9 (Ben—a Gentleman). June 6 (no cast). Aug. 10 (Tattle—Thurmond, Jun.)

1716–17. DL: Oct. 9 (Sir Sampson—Leigh; Valentine—Wilks; Scandal—Booth; Tattle—Cibber; Ben—Bickerstaff; Foresight—Johnson; Jeremy—Bowen; Trapland—Norris; Angelica—Mrs. Oldfield; Mrs. Foresight—Mrs. Horton; Mrs. Frail—Mrs. Porter; Prue—Miss Younger; Nurse—Mrs. Willis). Dec. 7 (no cast). March 11. 25 (Ben—Dogget; rest omitted). LIF: Dec. 3 (no cast). May 10 (Ben—Spiller; Sir Sampson—Hall).

1717–18. DL: Nov. 25 (as Oct. 9, 1716, except Prue—Mrs. Santlow).

Feb. 11 (Jeremy—Miller). April 3 (Ben and Jeremy omitted; Prue—Miss Younger). 29 (Jeremy—Miller; Nurse—Mrs. Hunt). LIF: Feb. 22 (no cast). March 18. April 16. RICHMOND: Aug. 9 (Sir Sampson—Bullock, Sen.; Valentine—Leigh; Scandal—Ogden; Tattle—Oates; Foresight—Shepard; Ben—Spiller; Jeremy—Williams; Angelica—Mrs. Spiller; Mrs. Foresight—Mrs. Shepard; Mrs. Frail—Mrs. Finch; Prue—Mrs. Moreau; Nurse—Mrs. Elsam).

1718–19. DL: Oct. 15 (as Oct. 9, 1716, except Jeremy—Miller; Mrs. Foresight—Mrs. Moor). Dec. 22 (Mrs. Foresight—Mrs. Horton; Prue—Miss Santlow). April 11 (Valentine—Wilks; Ben—Miller; Angelica—Mrs. Oldfield; Mrs. Frail—Mrs. Porter; rest omitted). May 27 (no cast). LIF: Oct. 30 (Ben—Burney; rest omitted). May 7 (no cast).

1719–20. DL: Sept. 17 (Valentine—Wilks; Scandal—Booth; Tattle—Cibber; Foresight—Johnson; Trapland—Norris; Angelica—Mrs. Thurmond; Mrs. Frail—Mrs. Porter). Nov. 30 (Sir Sampson—Shepard; Ben—Bickerstaff; Jeremy—Miller; Prue—Mrs. Younger). Feb. 4. May 10 (Ben—Miller; Jeremy omitted). LIF: Nov. 13 (Sir Sampson—Bullock; Valentine—Leigh; Scandal—Ogden; Tattle—Pack; Ben—Morgan; Foresight—Griffin; Jeremy—Spiller; Trapland—Ch. Bullock; Angelica—Mrs. Biggs; Mrs. Foresight—Mrs. Gulick; Mrs. Frail—Mrs. Giffard; Prue—Miss Shore; Nurse—Mrs. Willis; Jenny—Mrs. Knapp). Dec. 15 (Angelica—Mrs. Bullock; Nurse—Mrs. Elsam).

1720–21. DL: Oct. 4 (Sir Sampson—Shepard; Valentine—Wilks; Scandal—Booth; Tattle—Cibber; Ben—Miller; Foresight—Johnson; Trapland—Norris; Angelica—Mrs. Thurmond; Mrs. Foresight—Mrs. Horton; Mrs. Frail—Mrs. Garnet; Prue—Mrs. Younger). Dec. 2 (Mrs. Frail—Mrs. Porter). Feb. 2. April 27. May 23. GREAT BOOTH, SOUTHWARK: Oct. 3 (no cast).

1721–22. DL: Sept. 12 (as Oct. 4, 1720, except Jeremy—Oates; Mrs. Frail—Mrs. Porter; Nurse—Mrs. Willis). Nov. 24 (Angelica—Mrs. Oldfield). Dec. 29. March 6 (Angelica—Mrs. Thurmond). April 18. May 25 (Prue—Miss Seal).

1722–23. DL: Sept. 18 (Sir Sampson—Shepard; Valentine—Wilks; Scandal—Booth; Tattle—Cibber; Ben—Miller; Foresight—Johnson; Jeremy—Oates; Trapland—Norris; Angelica—Mrs. Thurmond; Mrs. Foresight—Mrs. Horton; Mrs. Frail—Mrs. Porter; Prue—Miss Seal; Nurse—Mrs. Willis). Nov. 28 (Prue—Mrs. Younger). Jan. 22 (Prue—Miss Lindar). March 16 (Prue—Mrs. Younger). May 17 (no cast). HAMPSTEAD WELLS: July 22 (Sir Sampson—Bullock; Valentine—Smith; Scandal—Roberts; Tattle—Parker; Foresight—Drew; Ben—Harper; Angelica—Mrs. Spiller; Mrs. Frail—Mrs. Ratcliff).

1723–24. DL: Sept. 17 (as Sept. 18, 1722, except Prue—Miss Lindar). Nov. 25. Dec. 16 (no cast). Jan. 9 (cast as Sept. 17, 1723). April 30.

1724–25. DL: Sept. 15 (as Sept. 18, 1722, except Prue—Miss Lindar). Nov. 25. Feb. 8. May 6 (Prue—Miss Tynte).

1725–26. DL: Sept. 9 (as Sept. 18, 1722, except Prue—Miss Tynte). Nov. 19. March 1. May 9.

1726–27. DL: Oct. 11 (as Sept. 18, 1722, except Scandal—W. Mills; Prue—Miss Tynte; Nurse—Mrs. Wetherilt). Dec. 2. Feb. 10 (Prue— Mrs. Cibber). April 12 (Scandal—Booth).

1727–28. DL: Sept. 26 (as Sept. 18, 1722, except Prue—Mrs. Cibber). Dec. 8 (Scandal—W. Mills). Feb. 15. May 6.

1728–29. DL: Sept. 12 (as Sept. 18, 1722, except Scandal—W. Mills; Mrs. Foresight—Mrs. Heron; Prue—Mrs. Cibber). Dec. 5 (no cast). Jan. 4. March 10 (Mrs. Foresight—Mrs. Horton; rest as Sept. 12, 1728). May 21.

1729–30. DL: Sept. 13 (as Sept. 18, 1722, except Scandal—W. Mills; Mrs. Foresight—Mrs. Heron; Prue—Mrs. Cibber). Dec. 19 (Mrs. Fore-sight—Mrs. Horton). April 18 (Angelica—Mrs. Oldfield; Prue—Miss Raftor). May 1 (Angelica—Mrs. Thurmond; Prue—Mrs. Cibber). 12 (Ben—Griffith). GF: Nov. 5 (Sir Sampson—W. Williams; Valentine— Giffard; Scandal—W. Giffard; Tattle—R. Williams; Ben—Burney; Jeremy—Collet; Angelica—Mrs. Purden; Mrs. Foresight—Mrs. Clark; Mrs. Frail—Mrs. Haughton; Prue—Mrs. Mountfort; Nurse—Mrs. Palmer). 18 (Sir Sampson—Penkethman; Tattle—W. Bullock; Trap-land—Pearce). Dec. 5. Jan. 22 (Foresight—Bardin; Mrs. Foresight— Mrs. Seal). Feb. 14. April 10. May 18 (Tattle—R. Williams; Mrs. Foresight—Mrs. Kirk). RICHMOND: Aug. 6.

1730–31. DL: April 8 (Sir Sampson—Shepard; Valentine—Wilks; Scandal—W. Mills; Tattle—Cibber; Ben—Harper; Foresight—John-son; Jeremy—Oates; Trapland—Griffin; Angelica—Mrs. Thurmond; Mrs. Foresight—Mrs. Horton; Mrs. Frail—Mrs. Porter; Prue—Mrs. Cibber; Nurse—Mrs. Willis). 22 (Prue—Miss Raftor). GF: Sept. 28 (Sir Sampson—Penkethman; Valentine—Giffard; Scandal—W. Gif-fard; Tattle—W. Bullock; Ben—Woodward; Foresight—Bardin; Jeremy—Collett; Trapland—Pearce; Angelica—Mrs. Giffard; Mrs. Foresight—Mrs. Woodward; Mrs. Frail—Mrs. Haughton; Prue—Mrs. Mountfort; Nurse—Mrs. Palmer). Nov. 23 (Mrs. Foresight—Mrs. Thomas). Dec. 14 (Sir Sampson—W. Williams; Ben—Morgan; Prue —Mrs. Morgan). Feb. 8. April 5 (Tattle—Macklin). June 8 (Valen-tine—Smith; Tattle—R. Williams; Angelica—Mrs. Haughton; Mrs. Frail—Mrs. Plomer). HAY: Feb. 26 (Sir Sampson—Jones; Valentine —Furnival; Scandal—Mullart; Tattle—Lacy; Ben—Ayres; Foresight

—Hallam; Jeremy—Reynolds; Trapland—Wathen; Angelica—Mrs. Mullart; Mrs. Foresight—Mrs. Lacy; Mrs. Frail—Mrs. Furnival; Prue—Miss Price; Nurse—Mrs. Nokes).

1731–32. GF: Nov. 11 (Sir Sampson—Smith; Valentine—Giffard; Scandal—W. Giffard; Tattle—Bullock; Ben—Morgan; Foresight—Collett; Jeremy—Rosco; Angelica—Mrs. Giffard; Mrs. Foresight—Mrs. Haughton; Mrs. Frail—Mrs. Roberts; Prue—Miss Tollett; Nurse—Mrs. Palmer). Jan. 20 (Ben—Miller; Trapland—Norris). 21. 24. 25. March 16 (Mrs. Frail—Mrs. Morgan; Prue—Mrs. Roberts). May 10 Prue—Miss Wherrit).

1732–33. DL: Oct. 28 (Sir Sampson—Shepard; Valentine—Bridgwater; Scandal—W. Mills; Tattle—Th. Cibber; Ben—Cibber; Forewright—Johnson; Jeremy—Oates; Trapland—Griffin; Angelica—Mrs. Booth; Mrs. Foresight—Mrs. Horton; Mrs. Frail—Mrs. Heron; Prue—Mrs. Cibber; Nurse—Mrs. Willis). 31. Nov. 2. 6. 25 (Ben—Miller). 27. Dec. 29 (no cast). Jan. 12. April 24 (Ben—Miller; Mrs. Foresight—Mrs. Butler; Prue—Miss Raftor; rest as Oct. 28). May 21 (no cast). GF: Nov. 3 (Sir Sampson—Morgan; Valentine—Giffard; Scandal—W. Giffard; Tattle—Bullock; Ben—Stoppelaer; Foresight—Collett; Jeremy—Rosco; Trapland—Norris; Angelica—Mrs. Thurmond; Mrs. Foresight—Mrs. Haughton; Mrs. Frail—Mrs. Roberts; Prue—Mrs. Hamilton; Nurse—Mrs. Norris). Jan. 20. May 8 (Tattle—Jenkins; Ben—Rosco; Jeremy—James).

1733–34. DL: April 4 (as Oct. 28, 1732, except Valentine—Mills, Sen.; Ben—Miller; Angelica—Mrs. Heron; Mrs. Foresight—Mrs. Grace; Mrs. Frail—Mrs. Butler; Prue—Miss Robinson). May 23 (Angelica—Miss Holliday; Prue—Mrs. Clive). GF: Oct. 22 (Sir Sampson—Morgan; Valentine—Giffard; Scandal—Hulett; Tattle—R. Wetherilt; Ben—Bardin; Foresight—Collett; Jeremy—Rosco; Trapland—Penkethman; Angelica—Mrs. Thurmond; Mrs. Foresight—Mrs. Haughton; Mrs. Frail—Mrs. Roberts; Prue—Mrs. Hamilton; Nurse—Mrs. Wetherilt). Jan. 24 (Sir Sampson—Penkethman; Scandal—W. Giffard; Foresight—Lyon; Trapland—Pearce). March 14 (no cast). April 27. HAY: Sept. 26 (Sir Sampson—Shepard; Valentine—Mills; Scandal—W. Mills; Tattle—Th. Cibber; Ben—Miller; Foresight—Johnson; Jeremy—Oates; Trapland—Griffin; Angelica—Mrs. Heron; Mrs. Foresight—Mrs. Grace; Mrs. Frail—Mrs. Butler; Prue—Miss Robinson). 28. Oct. 1. 24. Nov. 24. Feb. 4. March 4. INNER TEMPLE: Feb. 2.

1734–35. DL: Sept. 7 (Sir Sampson—Harper; Valentine—Milward; Scandal—W. Mills; Tattle—Cibber; Ben—Miller; Foresight—Johnson; Jeremy—Oates; Trapland—Griffin; Angelica—Mrs. Thurmond;

Mrs. Foresight—Miss Holliday; Mrs. Frail—Mrs. Butler; Prue—Mrs. Clive; Nurse—Mrs. Willis). Oct. 30. Jan. 1 (Sir Sampson—Shepard). March 20 (as Sept. 7). May 20 (Sir Sampson—Turbutt; Jeremy—Jones; Mrs. Foresight—Mrs. Elmy). GF: Oct. 7 (no cast). Dec. 20 (Sir Sampson—Penkethman; Valentine—Giffard; Scandal—W. Giffard; Tattle—Wetherilt; Ben—Ray; Foresight—Lyon; Jeremy—Rosco; Trapland—Norris; Angelica—Mrs. Gifford; Mrs. Foresight—Mrs. Haughton; Mrs. Frail—Mrs. Roberts; Brue—Mrs. Hamilton; Nurse—Mrs. Wetherilt). Feb. 7 (Tattle—Jenkins). 20. RICHMOND: Aug. 16.

1735–36. DL: Sept. 4 (as Sept. 7, 1734, except Sir Sampson—Shepard; Tattle—Th. Cibber; Mrs. Frail—Mrs. Cross). Nov. 26 (Mrs. Frail—Mrs. Butler). Feb. 17. April 3. May 7 (Nurse—Mrs. Bennet). GF: Nov. 10 (as Oct. 7, 1734, except Tattle—Woodward). Feb. 6. May 6 (Ben—Norris; Trapland omitted; Prue—Mrs. Woodward).

1736–37. DL: Oct. 30 (as Sept. 7, 1734, except Sir Sampson—Shepard; Tattle—Th. Cibber; Nurse—Mrs. Bennet). Dec. 10 (Buckram—Winstone; Nurse—Mrs. Willis). March 26. May 13 (Nurse—Mrs. Marshall). NEW HAY: March 7 (no cast). LIF: Oct. 23 (as at GF, Oct. 7, 1734, except Tattle—Mrs. Charke; Ben—Oates; Buckram—Hamilton).

1737–38. DL: Aug. 30 (as Sept. 7, 1734, except Scandal—Mills; Tattle—Th. Cibber; Jeremy—Macklin; Angelica—Miss Holliday; Mrs. Foresight—Mrs. Pritchard). Nov. 2 (Angelica—Mrs. Mills). April 13 (Nurse—Mrs. Marshall). May 26 (Sir Sampson—Marten).

1738–39. DL: Nov. 3 (Sir Sampson—Shepard; Valentine—Milward; Scandal—Mills; Tattle—Cross; Ben—Macklin; Foresight—Johnson; Jeremy—Woodward; Trapland—Griffin; Angelica—Mrs. Mills; Mrs. Foresight—Mrs. Pritchard; Mrs. Frail—Mrs. Butler; Prue—Mrs. Clive; Nurse—Mrs. Marshall). Dec. 30. Feb. 23 (Sir Sampson—Turbutt; Tattle—Th. Cibber). April 3. May 30 (Sir Sampson—Shepard; Tattle—Cross; Ben—Ray). CG: May 2 (Sir Sampson—Rosco; Valentine—Hale; Scandal—Walker; Tattle—Chapman; Ben—James; Foresight—Hippisley; Jeremy—Oates; Trapland—Arthur; Buckram—Stevens; Angelica—Mrs. Bellamy; Mrs. Foresight—Mrs. Horton; Mrs. Frail—Mrs. Stevens; Prue—Miss Oates; Nurse—Mrs. Martin).

1739–40. DL: Sept. 4 (as Nov. 3, 1738, except Tattle—Woodward; Jeremy—Oates; Angelica—Mrs. Pritchard; Mrs. Foresight—Mrs. Bennet). Oct. 26 (Tattle—Chapman; Angelica—Mrs. Mills; Mrs. Foresight—Mrs. Pritchard). Nov. 22 (Tattle—Woodward). Jan. 16 (Tattle—Chapman). Feb. 6 (Tattle—Woodward). March 4 (Tattle—Chapman). April 21. May 21. CG: March 25 (Sir Sampson—Rosco;

Valentine—Hale; Scandal—Delane; Tattle—Th. Cibber; Ben—Hippisley; Foresight—Arthur; Jeremy—Oates; Trapland—Smith; Angelica—Mrs. Horton; Mrs. Foresight—Mrs. Woodward; Mrs. Frail—Mrs. Ware; Prue—Miss Bennet; Nurse—Mrs. Marten; Jenny—Miss Horsington).

1740–41. DL: Sept. 9 (Sir Sampson—Shepard; Valentine—Milward; Tattle—Chapman; Ben—Macklin; Foresight—Johnson; Jeremy—Woodward; Trapland—Ray; Angelica—Mrs. Mills; Mrs. Foresight—Mrs. Pritchard; Mrs. Frail—Mrs. Butler; Prue—Mrs. Clive; Nurse—Mrs. Egleton). Dec. 12. Jan. 16. April 28 (Nurse omitted). May 25. GF: Oct. 28 (Sir Sampson—Dunstall; Valentine—W. Giffard; Scandal—Blakes; Tattle—Linnet; Ben—Yates; Angelica—Mrs. Giffard; Mrs. Foresight—Mrs. Dunstall; Mrs. Frail—Mrs. Oates; Prue—Miss Hippisley; Nurse—Miss Jones). Nov. 21 (Jeremy—Vaughan; Trapland—Richards; Mrs. Foresight—Mrs. Oates; Mrs. Frail—Mrs. Dunstall). May 1 (no cast).

1741–42. DL: Sept. 5 (as Sept. 9, 1740, except Scandal—Mills; Tattle—Th. Cibber; Jeremy—Neale; Mrs. Foresight—Mrs. Macklin). Oct. 27 (Trapland—Taswell). Nov. 6 (Trapland—Ray; Mrs. Foresight—Mrs. Cross). Jan. 19 (no cast). April 21 (Valentine—Lowe; Tattle—Cross; Mrs. Foresight—Mrs. Cross; rest as Sept. 5, 1741). May 25 (Valentine—Havard; Prue—Miss Lee). CG: March 27 (Sir Sampson—Marten; Valentine—Hale; Scandal—Cashell; Tattle—Chapman; Ben—Bridgwater; Foresight—Hippisley; Jeremy—Woodward; Angelica—Mrs. Horton; Mrs. Foresight—Mrs. Woodward; Mrs. Frail—Mrs. Pritchard; Prue—Miss Georgiana Bellamy; Nurse—Mrs. Martin; Jenny—Mrs. Bland). GF: Sept. 16 (Sir Sampson—Dunstall; Valentine—Giffard; Scandal—Blakes; Tattle—Peterson; Ben—Yates; Foresight—Julian; Jeremy—Vaughan; Trapland—Clough; Buckram—Crofts; Angelica—Mrs. Giffard; Mrs. Foresight—Mrs. Dunstall; Mrs. Frail—Mrs. Yates; Prue—Miss Hippisley; Nurse—Mrs. Bishop). Dec. 30 (Trapland—Marr). May 6 (Valentine—W. Giffard; Prue—Miss E. Hippisley).

1742–43. DL: Sept. 18 (Sir Sampson—Morgan; Valentine—Havard; Scandal—Mills; Tattle—Neale; Ben—Macklin; Foresight—Arthur; Jeremy—Yates; Trapland—Ray; Angelica—Mrs. Mills; Mrs. Foresight—Mrs. Cross; Mrs. Frail—Mrs. Pritchard; Prue—Mrs. Clive; Nurse—Mrs. Bennet). Nov. 6. Jan. 1 (Buckram—Woodburn). May 11 (Angelica—Mrs. Pritchard; Mrs. Frail—Mrs. Macklin). LIF: Feb. 17 (Sir Sampson—Dunstall; Valentine—Giffard; Scandal—W. Giffard; Tattle—Th. Cibber; Ben—Clough; Foresight—Julian; Jeremy—Peterson; Trapland—Dove; Buckram—Dighton; Snap—Hemskirk;

Angelica—Mrs. Giffard; Mrs. Foresight—Mrs. Dunstall; Mrs. Frail—
Mrs. Butler; Prue—Miss Scot; Nurse—Mrs. Bambridge; Jenny—
Miss Royer). April 11 (Prue—Miss Hippisley). SOUTHWARK: Feb.
18 (Sir Sampson—Marten; Valentine—Gibson; Scandal—Ridout;
Tattle—Woodward; Ben—Yates; Foresight—Arthur; Jeremy—
Vaughan; Trapland—Legar; Buckram—Bencraft; Angelica—Mrs.
Mullart; Mrs. Foresight—Mrs. Dunstall; Mrs. Frail—Mrs. Yates;
Prue—Miss Bradshaw).

1743–44. DL: Sept. 17 (Sir Sampson—Bridges; Valentine—Giffard;
Scandal—W. Giffard; Tattle—Neale; Ben—Yates; Foresight—Tas-
well; Jeremy—Cross; Trapland—Ray; Buckram—Anderson; Angel-
ica—Mrs. Bennet; Mrs. Foresight—Mrs. Woodward; Mrs. Frail—
Mrs. Cross; Prue—Mrs. Ridout; Nurse—Mrs. Egerton). Nov. 14
(Jeremy—Oates; Mrs. Foresight—Mrs. Giffard; Prue—Mrs. George).
Dec. 21 (Valentine—Havard; Angelica—Mrs. Mills). May 5 (Sir
Sampson—Dunstall; Valentine—Giffard; Foresight—Arthur; Jeremy
—Green; Mrs. Foresight—Mrs. Chetwood; Prue—Mrs. Dunstall).

1744–45. DL: Sept. 15 (as Sept. 17, 1743, except Scandal—Havard; Tat-
tle—Hale; Jeremy—Blakes; Buckram—Woodburn; Angelica—Mrs.
Giffard; Mrs. Foresight—Mrs. Cross; Mrs. Frail—Mrs. Woffington;
Nurse—Mrs. Bridges). Jan. 8 (Ben—Macklin). 29 (Prue—Miss Mi-
nors). Feb. 18. May 1 (Valentine—Mozeen; Tattle—Yates; Foresight—
Collins; Jeremy—Neale; Prue—Miss Bradshaw). GF: Dec. 19 (Valen-
tine—Townley; Prue—Miss Houghton). 27 (no cast). Jan. 23. 28.
March 19.

1745–46. DL: Oct. 10 (as Sept. 17, 1743, except Scandal—Mills; Tattle—
Yates; Ben—Macklin; Jeremy—Neale; Buckram—Woodburn; Angel-
ica—Mrs. Giffard; Mrs. Foresight—Mrs. Macklin; Mrs. Frail—Mrs.
Woffington; Prue—Mrs. Ridout; Nurse—Mrs. Bridges). Dec. 30
(Scandal—Havard; Prue—Mrs. Clive). Jan. 16. Feb. 20. CG: Nov. 25
(Sir Sampson—Marten; Valentine—Hale; Scandal—Cashell; Tattle
—Th. Cibber; Ben—Woodward; Foresight—Arthur; Jeremy—James;
Trapland—Hippisley; Angelica—Mrs. Pritchard; Mrs. Foresight—
Mrs. James; Mrs. Frail—Mrs. Hale; Prue—Miss Hippisley; Nurse—
Mrs. Martin). April 18 (Tattle—Chapman; Mrs. Foresight—Mrs.
Vincent). GF: Nov. 21 (Ben—Morgan; Prue—a Gentlewoman). Feb.
3 (Sir Sampson—Paget; Valentine—Cushing; Scandal—Furnival;
Tattle—Kennedy; Foresight—Julian; Jeremy—L. Hallam; Angelica
—Mrs. Hallam; Mrs. Foresight—Mrs. Bambridge; Mrs. Frail—Mrs.
Cushing; Prue—Mrs. Phillips). TWICKENHAM: Sept. 2.

1746–47. DL: Oct. 30 (as Sept. 17, 1743, except Scandal—Mills; Tattle—
Th. Cibber; Ben—Macklin; Jeremy—Neale; Buckram omitted; An-

gelica—Mrs. Giffard; Mrs. Foresight—Mrs. Macklin; Mrs. Frail—Mrs. Woffington; Prue—Mrs. Clive; Nurse omitted). Dec. 4 (Mrs. Foresight—Mrs. Cross; Nurse—Mrs. Bridges). May 14 (Tattle—Cross).
. GF: Nov. 6 (as Feb. 3, 1746, except Foresight—Hallam, Sen.; Tattle—Cartwright; Ben—L. Hallam; Buckram—Dove; Jeremy—Pinner; Mrs. Foresight—Mrs. Beckham; Mrs. Frail—Mrs. Butler; Prue—Miss Maddox; Nurse—Mrs. Dove). RICHMOND: Sept. 28, 1747.

1747–48. DL: Jan. 12 (Sir Sampson—I. Sparks; Valentine—Havard; Scandal—Mills; Tattle—Yates; Ben—Macklin; Foresight—Taswell; Jeremy—Neale; Trapland—Shuter; Buckram—Bransby; Angelica—Mrs. Pritchard; Mrs. Foresight—Mrs. Macklin; Mrs. Frail—Mrs. Woffington; Prue—Mrs. Clive; Nurse—Mrs. Yates). Feb. 12 (Jeremy, Trapland, Buckram, Nurse omitted). May 6 (Buckram—Simon; Mrs. Foresight—Mrs. Bennet; Prue—Miss Minors). CG: March 26 (no cast).

1748–49. DL: Sept. 20 (as Jan. 12, 1748, except Sir Sampson—Taswell; Tattle—Woodward; Ben—Yates; Foresight—Arthur; Trapland—Ray; Mrs. Foresight—Mrs. Cross; Mrs. Frail—Mrs. Elmy; Nurse—Mrs. Pitt). Oct. 27 (Sir Sampson—Bridges; Foresight—Taswell; Nurse—Mrs. James). Jan. 4. Feb. 4 (Trapland—James).

1749–50. DL: Sept. 20 (as Jan. 12, 1748, except Sir Sampson—Bridges; Tattle—Woodward; Ben—Yates; Trapland—Ray; Mrs. Foresight—Mrs. Willoughby; Mrs. Frail—Mrs. Elmy; Nurse—Mrs. Pitt). Nov. 17 (Prue—Mrs. Green). Jan. 18 (Jeremy—Shuter).

1750–51. DL: Oct. 26 (Sir Sampson—Bridges; Valentine—Havard; Scandal—Palmer; Tattle—Woodward; Ben—Yates; Foresight—Taswell; Jeremy—Shuter; Trapland—Ray; Angelica—Mrs. Pritchard; Mrs. Foresight—Mrs. Willoughby; Mrs. Frail—Mrs. Mills; Prue—Mrs. Clive; Nurse—Mrs. Pitt).

1751–52. DL: Sept. 17 (as Oct. 26, 1750, except Sir Sampson—Taswell; Foresight—Shuter; Jeremy—Blakes; Nurse—Mrs. James).

1752–53. DL: Jan. 22 (as Oct. 26, 1750, except Sir Sampson—Taswell; Valentine—Ross; Foresight—Shuter; Jeremy—Blakes; Trapland omitted; Angelica—Miss Haughton; Mrs. Foresight—Mrs. Bennet; Nurse—Mrs. James). Feb. 19. May 16.

1753–54. DL: Jan. 16 (Sir Sampson—Berry; Valentine—Havard; Scandal—Palmer; Tattle—Woodward; Ben—Foote; Foresight—Taswell; Jeremy—Blakes; Trapland—W. Vaughan; Angelica—Mrs. Haughton; Mrs. Foresight—Mrs. Bennet; Mrs. Frail—Mrs. Clive; Prue—Miss Macklin; Nurse—Mrs. James). 18. 21. 25. Feb. 15. May 14 (Ben—Yates; Prue—Miss Minors). CG: May 13 (Sir Sampson—Dunstall;

Valentine—Smith; Scandal—Anderson; Tattle—Dyer; Ben—Cushing; Foresight—Arthur; Jeremy—Wignell; Trapland—Collins; Angelica—Mrs. Bland; Mrs. Foresight—Mrs. Elmy; Mrs. Frail—Mrs. Barrington; Prue—Mrs. Baker; Nurse—Mrs. Pitt).

1754–55. DL: Jan. 15 (as Jan. 16, 1754, except Ben—Yates; Trapland omitted; Nurse—Mrs. Bradshaw). May 15 (Valentine—Ross). CG: Feb. 8 (as May 13, 1754, except Scandal—Ridout; Ben—Shuter; Jeremy—Barrington; Angelica—Mrs. Hamilton; Mrs. Frail—Mrs. Woffington; Prue—Mrs. Green). 15. April 24.

1755–56. DL: Dec. 1 (as Jan. 16, 1754, except Ben—Yates; Trapland— omitted; Nurse—Mrs. Bradshaw). May 24 (Scandal—Davies; Tattle— Palmer). CG: Oct. 10 (as May 13, 1754, except Scandal—Ridout; Ben—Shuter; Jeremy—Barrington; Angelica—Mrs. Hamilton; Mrs. Frail—Mrs. Woffington). Nov. 25 (Angelica—Mrs. Woffington; Mrs. Frail—Mrs. Barrington). Jan. 2 (Angelica—Mrs. Hamilton; Mrs. Frail—Mrs. Woffington). Feb. 27. May 4.

1756–57. CG: Oct. 21 (Sir Sampson—Dunstall; Valentine—Smith; Scandal—Ridout; Tattle—Dyer; Ben—Shuter; Foresight—Arthur; Jeremy—Barrington; Trapland—Collins; Angelica—Mrs. Hamilton; Mrs. Foresight—Mrs. Elmy; Mrs. Frail—Mrs. Woffington; Prue—Mrs. Green; Nurse—Mrs. Pitt). Nov. 19 (Trapland—Bennet; Prue—Mrs. Baker). Jan. 20 (Trapland—Collins; Prue—Mrs. Green). May 9 (Sir Sampson—Marten; Mrs. Frail—Mrs. Barrington).

1757–58. CG: Oct. 12 (as Oct. 21, 1756, except Mrs. Frail—Mrs. Vincent). Dec. 19. May 9.

1758–59. CG: Oct. 13 (as Oct. 21, 1756, except Valentine—Ross; Foresight—Collins; Trapland—Bennet; Mrs. Frail—Mrs. Vincent). Nov. 27. May 23.

1759–60. DL: April 9 (Sir Sampson—Burton; Valentine—Fleetwood; Scandal—Palmer; Tattle—King; Ben—Yates; Foresight—Blakes; Jeremy—Austin; Trapland—Vaughan; Angelica—Miss Pritchard; Mrs. Foresight—Mrs. Pritchard; Mrs. Frail—Mrs. Clive; Prue—Miss Pope; Nurse—Mrs. Bradshaw). 18 (Angelica—Miss Haughton; Mrs. Foresight—Mrs. Bennet). May 12. CG: Dec. 18 (as Oct. 21, 1756, except Valentine—Ross; Foresight—Collins; Trapland—Bennet; Mrs. Frail—Mrs. Vincent).

1760–61. CG: Oct. 14 (Sir Sampson—Dunstall; Valentine—Ross; Scandal—Ridout; Tattle—Dyer; Ben—Shuter; Foresight—Collins; Jeremy —Barrington; Trapland—Bennet; Angelica—Mrs. Hamilton; Mrs. Foresight—Mrs. Elmy; Mrs. Frail—Mrs. Vincent; Prue—Mrs. Green; Nurse—Mrs. Pitt). Dec. 20.

1761–62. DL: Jan. 7 (as April 9, 1760, except Valentine—Havard;

Jeremy—Austin; Angelica—Miss Haughton; Mrs. Foresight—Mrs. Bennet). May 3. CG: Oct. 26 (as Oct. 14, 1760, except Scandal—Clarke). May 21 (Ben—Perry).

1762–63. DL: Nov. 12 (as April 9, 1760, except Valentine—Havard; Jeremy—Parsons; Angelica—Miss Haughton; Mrs. Foresight—Mrs. Bennet). May 16 (Foresight—Parson; Jeremy—Castle; Mrs. Frail—Mrs. Pritchard).

1763–64. DL: Oct. 1 (Sir Sampson—Burton; Valentine—Havard; Scandal—Palmer; Tattle—O'Brien; Ben—Yates; Foresight—Weston; Jeremy—King; Trapland—Vaughan; Angelica—Miss Haughton; Mrs. Foresight—Mrs. Bennet; Mrs. Frail—Mrs. Clive; Prue, a Gentlewoman [Miss Cheney]; Nurse—Mrs. Bradshaw). 6. Nov. 3. 11. Jan. 17 (Jeremy—Baddeley). CG: Feb. 9 (as Oct. 14, 1760, except Scandal—Clarke; Foresight—Bennet; Trapland omitted; Angelica—Miss Macklin; Mrs. Foresight—Mrs. Baker; Prue—Miss Elliot).

1764–65. DL: Oct. 20 (as Oct. 1, 1763, except Tattle—a Gentleman; Foresight—Granger; Jeremy—Baddeley; Angelica—Mrs. Palmer). Dec. 27 (Tattle—Preston). CG: Oct. 3 (Sir Sampson—Dunstall; Valentine—Ross; Scandal—Clarke; Tattle—Woodward; Ben—Shuter; Foresight—Bennet; Jeremy—Dyer; Trapland—Lewis; Angelica—Miss Macklin; Mrs. Foresight—Mrs. Baker; Mrs. Frail—Mrs. Vincent; Prue—Miss Elliot; Nurse—Mrs. Pitt). Nov. 22. Jan. 22 (Prue—Miss Vincent). May 17 (Scandal—White).

1765–66. CG: Nov. 19 (as Oct. 3, 1764, except Scandal—Hull; Mrs. Foresight—Mrs. Burden; Prue—Mrs. Gardner).

1766–67. CG: Dec. 6 (as Oct. 3, 1764, except Trapland—Cushing; Mrs. Foresight—Mrs. Burden). March 5.

1769–70. DL: Dec. 23 (Sir Sampson—Burton; Valentine—Reddish; Scandal—Palmer; Tattle—Dodd; Ben—Moody; Foresight—Parsons; Jeremy—Baddeley; Trapland—Hartry; Buckram—Keen; Officer—Wright; Angelica—Miss Younge; Mrs. Foresight—Mrs. Reddish; Mrs. Frail—Mrs. Jefferies; Prue—Mrs. Abington; Nurse—Mrs. Bradshaw). Jan. 20. Feb. 26. May 14 (Sir Sampson—Sparks; Jeremy—W. Palmer). June 5.

1770–71. DL: Nov. 15 (as Dec. 23, 1769, except Sir Sampson—Love; Jeremy—W. Palmer; Angelica—Mrs. W. Barry).

1771–72. DL: Nov. 14 (as Dec. 23, 1769, except Sir Sampson—Love; Jeremy—W. Palmer; Angelica—Mrs. Robinson; Mrs. Frail—Mrs. Egerton).

1772–73. CG: May 6 (Sir Sampson—Dunstall; Valentine—Ross; Scandal—Hull; Tattle—Woodward; Ben—Shuter; Foresight—Cushing; Jeremy—Dyer; Trapland—Quick; Angelica—Miss Macklin; Mrs.

Foresight—Mrs. Dyer; Mrs. Frail—Mrs. Bulkley; Prue—Mrs. Kniveton; Nurse—Mrs. Pitt).

1773–74. CG: April 5 (as May 6, 1773, except Valentine—Lewis; Scandal—Dyer; Jeremy omitted; Mrs. Foresight—Mrs. Baker; Mrs. Frail—Miss Barsanti; Prue—Mrs. Mattocks). May 6 (Scandal—Hull; Jeremy—Lewes; Angelica—Miss Sherman).

1774–75. CG: May 9 (Sir Sampson—Dunstall; Valentine—Lewis; Scandal—Hull; Tattle—Woodward; Ben—Shuter; Foresight—Quick; Jeremy—Lee Lewes; Trapland—Massey; Angelica—Miss Macklin; Mrs. Foresight—Mrs. Baker; Mrs. Frail—Mrs. Bulkley; Prue—Mrs. Mattocks; Nurse—Mrs. Pitt).

1775–76. CG: April 27 (as May 9, 1775, except Ben—Wilson; Mrs. Foresight—Miss Ambrose).

1776–77. DL: Nov. 29 (Sir Sampson—Moody; Valentine—Reddish; Scandal—Bensley; Tattle—King; Ben—Yates; Foresight—Parsons; Jeremy—Baddeley; Trapland—Waldron; Buckram—Wrighten; Officer—Griffiths; Angelica—Miss Younge; Mrs. Foresight—Mrs. Sherry; Mrs. Frail—Miss Pope; Prue—Mrs. Abington; Nurse—Mrs. Bradshaw). Dec. 3. 5. 9. Jan. 14. 27. Feb. 6. March 22. April 3. CG: Nov. 15 (as May 9, 1775, except Ben—Macklin; Trapland—Cushing; Mrs. Foresight—Miss Ambrose).

1777–78. DL: March 5 (as Nov. 29, 1776, except Valentine—Farren). April 6 (Valentine—Henderson; Ben—Dodd).

1778–79. DL: Oct. 13 (as Nov. 29, 1776, except Valentine—Henderson; Buckram and Officer omitted). Nov. 7. 21 (Valentine—Farren). Jan. 2 (Valentine—Henderson). March 9.

1779–80. DL: Oct. 12 (as Nov. 29, 1776, except Valentine—Farren; Foresight—Waldron; Trapland—Burton; Buckram and Officer omitted; Angelica—Miss Farren). Jan. 5 (Tattle—Dodd; Prue—Mrs. Mattocks). March 14 (Ben—Vernon; Prue—Mrs. Abington). HAY: Sept. 5, 1780 (Sir Sampson—Usher; Valentine—Palmer; Scandal—Bensley; Tattle—R. Palmer; Ben—Wilson; Foresight—Edwin; Jeremy—Baddeley; Angelica—Miss Farren; Mrs. Foresight—Mrs. Lloyd; Mrs. Frail—Mrs. Cuyler; Prue—Mrs. Wilson).

1780–81. DL: Dec. 7 (as Nov. 29, 1776, except Valentine—Farren; Trapland—Burton; Buckram and Officer omitted; Angelica—Miss Farren; Nurse—Mrs. Love). Jan. 12.

1781–82. DL: Nov. 6 (as Nov. 9, 1776, except Valentine—Farren; Buckram and Officer omitted; Angelica—Miss Farren; Nurse—Mrs. Love).

1782–83. DL: May 5 (Nov. 29, 1776, except Valentine—Farren; Ben—Dodd; Buckram and Officer omitted; Angelica—Miss Farren; Mrs. Foresight—Mrs. Ward; Prue—Miss Wheeler; Nurse—Mrs. Love).

1783–84. DL: Nov. 28 (Sir Sampson—Moody; Valentine—Farren; Scandal—Bensley; Tattle—Lewes; Ben—Dodd; Foresight—Waldron; Jeremy—Baddeley; Trapland—Burton; Angelica—Miss Farren; Mrs. Foresight—Mrs. Ward; Mrs. Frail—Miss Pope; Prue—Miss Wheeler; Nurse—Mrs. Love). March 20 (Foresight—Parsons). May 24 (Mrs. Foresight—Mrs. Tidwell; Prue—Miss M. Stageldoir).

1785–86. CG: Jan. 28 (Sir Sampson—Fearon; Valentine—Lewis; Scandal—Farren; Tattle—Wewitzer; Ben—Edwin; Foresight—Quick; Jeremy—Davies; Angelica—Mrs. T. Kennedy; Mrs. Foresight—Mrs. Morton; Mrs. Frail—Mrs. Bates; Prue—Mrs. Brown).

1786–87. DL: Dec. 11 (as Nov. 28, 1783, except Valentine—Kemble; Ben—King; Tattle—Dodd; Trapland omitted; Prue—Mrs. Jordan; Nurse omitted). 18. 21. Feb. 6. 9. 14. March 10. April 23 (Valentine—Whitfield; Ben—Palmer; Mrs. Foresight—Mrs. Ward). May 8 (Valentine—Barrymore; Ben—King; Prue—Mrs. Forester). CG: Nov. 15 (Sir Sampson—Fearon; Valentine—Holman; Scandal—Farren; Tattle—Lewis; Ben—Ryder; Foresight—Quick; Jeremy—Davies; Trapland—Booth; Buckram—Thompson; Buckram—Stock; Angelica—Mrs. Pope; Mrs. Foresight—Mrs. Bates; Mrs. Frail—Mrs. Mattocks; Prue—Mrs. Brown). Dec. 28. Jan. 5.

1787–88. DL: Oct. 15 (as Nov. 28, 1783, except Valentine—Kemble; Tattle—Bannister, Jun.; Ben—King; Foresight—Parsons; Trapland omitted; Prue—Mrs. Jordan; Nurse omitted). Nov. 14.

1788–89. DL: Oct. 11 (Sir Sampson—Moody; Valentine—Kemble; Scandal—Bensley; Tattle—Dodd; Ben—Bannister, Jun.; Foresight—Parsons; Jeremy—Baddeley; Angelica—Miss Farren; Mrs. Foresight—Mrs. Ward; Mrs. Frail—Miss Pope; Prue—Mrs. Forester). 30. Dec. 8. 15 (Valentine—Whitfield; Tattle—R. Palmer; Prue—Mrs. Jordan). Feb. 23. April 13. May 5. June 3.

1789–90. DL: Oct. 3 (as Oct. 11, 1788, except Trapland—Waldron; Buckram—Phillimore; Snap—Jones; Prue—Miss Prideaux; Nurse—Mrs. Booth; Jenny—Miss Tidswell). Nov. 6. Feb. 23 (Foresight—Waldron; Trapland—Burton; Prue—Mrs. Jordan). April 23. May 8 (Valentine—Whitfield).

1790–91. DL: Oct. 12 (as Oct. 11, 1788, except Foresight—Waldron; Trapland—Burton; Prue—Mrs. Jordan). April 12. May 11. June 1.

1791–92. DL: Oct. 25 (as Oct. 11, 1788, except Trapland—Waldron; Buckram—Phillimore; Prue—Mrs. Jordan; Nurse—Mrs. Booth). Dec. 19 (Valentine—Whitfield). April 19.

1792–93. DL: April 25 (as Oct. 11, 1788, except Valentine—Barrymore; Foresight—Suett; Jeremy—Benson; Trapland—Waldron; Buckram—Maddocks; Snap—Fawcett; Prue—Mrs. Jordan).

1794–95. DL: Nov. 7 (as Oct. 11, 1788, except Trapland—Waldron; Buckram—Phillimore; Mrs. Foresight—Mrs. Goodall; Prue—Mrs. Jordan; Nurse—Mrs. Booth; Jenny—Miss Tidswell). 21 (Jeremy—Benson). 28. Jan. 8 (Jeremy—R. Palmer; Mrs. Foresight—Mrs. Collins). April 23 (Foresight—Suett; Mrs. Foresight—Mrs. Goodall).

1795–96. DL: Nov. 5 (as Oct. 11, 1788, except Foresight—Suett; Trapland—Burton; Jeremy—Benson; Buckram—Maddocks; Snap—Fawcett; Mrs. Foresight—Mrs. Goodall; Nurse—Mrs. Booth). Jan. 7. March 8 (Valentine—Whitfield; Scandal—Barrymore; Trapland—Waldron). April 7.

1796–97. DL: Oct. 15 (Sir Sampson—King; Valentine—Kemble; Scandal—Barrymore; Tattle—R. Palmer; Ben—Bannister, Jun.; Foresight—Suett; Jeremy—Wathen; Trapland—Hollingsworth; Buckram—Phillimore; Snap—Maddocks; Angelica—Miss Farren; Mrs. Foresight—Mrs. Goodall; Mrs. Frail—Miss Pope; Prue—Miss Mellon; Nurse—Mrs. Booth; Jenny—Miss Tidswell). Nov. 14 (Prue—Mrs. Jordan). CG: June 13 (Sir Sampson—Davenport; Valentine—Holman; Scandal—Murray; Tattle—Macready; Ben—Haymes; Foresight—Quick; Jeremy—Farley; Trapland—Powell; Buckram—Simmons; Snap—Thompson; Angelica—Miss Chapman; Mrs. Foresight—Mrs. Gilbert; Mrs. Frail—Mrs. Mattocks; Prue—Mrs. Jordan).

1797–98. DL: Nov. 28 (as Oct. 15, 1796, except Tattle—Russell; Buckram—Maddocks; Snap—Wentworth; Angelica—Miss Humphries; Nurse—Miss Tidswell; Jenny—Mrs. Jones).

1798–99. DL: April 8 (as Oct. 15, 1796, except Tattle—R. Palmer; Buckram—Maddocks; Snap—Wentworth; Angelica—Miss Biggs; Mrs. Foresight—Mrs. Sparks; Nurse—Miss Tidswell; Jenny—Mrs. Jones). 16.

1799–00. DL: Oct. 22 (as April 8, 1799). March 22. April 3. June 17 (Valentine—Powell).

Love for Love continued to be performed into the nineteenth century, these performances being given in the first half of the century: DL: April 24, 1801. June 10, 1802. June 3, 1803. Jan. 21, 1804. April 18, 1804. March 8, 1806. April 25, 1806. Dec. 6, 1806. Sept. 26, 1807: Nov. 6, 1807. Dec. 14, 1807. Jan. 28, 1808. Dec. 22, 1808. CG: Sept. 25, 1812. Oct. 23, 1812. Feb. 17, 1813. Feb. 24, 1813. DL: March 1, 1813. CG: March 18, 1813. DL: Jan. 23, 1816. DL: Jan. 25, 1816. CG: Oct. 13, 1819, and twice later in that season. DL: April 17, 1827. DL: Nov. 19, 1842, and seven times later in that season. HAY: June 12, 1848.

The Mourning Bride

1706–07. QUEEN'S: May 28.

1707–08. DL: March 25 (Manuel—Powell; Osmyn—Booth; Gonsalez— Keene; Almeria—Mrs. Bradshaw; Zara—Mrs. Barry; Leonora—Mrs. Porter).

1709–10. DL: Jan. 18 (as March 25, 1708, except Garcia—Cory; Zara— Mrs. Knight; Leonora—Mrs. Cox).

1711–12. DL: March 8 (no cast). May 8 (Manuel—Keene; Osmyn— Booth; Almeria—Mrs. Bradshaw).

1712–13. DL: Nov. 18 (no cast).

1713–14. DL: Nov. 17 (no cast).

1716–17. DL: Dec. 12 (no cast).

1718–19. DL: Jan. 9 (Manuel—Elrington; Osmyn—Booth; Almeria— Mrs. Thurmond; Zara—Mrs. Porter). 12. 13 (Macbeth advertised, but Play Accounts Ms and Winston Ms [Folger Library] give The Mourning Bride). 14. 15. Feb. 10. April 1.

1719–20. DL: Dec. 8 (Manuel—Mills; Osmyn—Booth; Almeria—Mrs. Thurmond; Zara—Mrs. Porter). Jan. 20.

1720–21. DL: Nov. 26 (as Dec. 8, 1719). March 20 (Gonsalez—Thurmond; Garcia—Walker; Alonzo—Williams; Leonora—Mrs. Garnet).

1721–22. DL: April 17 (Manuel—Mills; Osmyn—Booth; Gonsalez— Thurmond; Garcia—Williams; Almeria—Mrs. Thurmond; Zara— Mrs. Porter; Leonora—Miss Seal).

1722–23. DL: Oct. 23 (as April 17, 1722, except Leonora omitted). Dec. 19. May 3 (no cast).

1723–24. DL: Oct. 15 (as April 17, 1722, except Garcia—Bridgwater; Leonora omitted). Jan. 13. March 3 (no cast).

1724–25. DL: Oct. 9 (no cast). Dec. 17. Feb. 23. 25. April 20 (as April 17, 1722, except Alonzo—Watson; Heli—Boman; Selim—W. Mills; Leonora omitted).

1725–26. DL: Oct. 19 (no cast). Jan. 7. Feb. 22. March 29. May 18 (Manuel—Mills; Osmyn—Booth; Gonsalez—Thurmond; Garcia—Williams; Heli—Boman; Selim—W. Mills; Alonzo—Watson; Almeria— Mrs. Thurmond; Zara—Mrs. Porter).

1726–27. DL: Feb. 4 (as May 18, 1726). March 23. May 2.

1727–28. DL: Oct. 6 (Osmyn—Booth; rest omitted).

1728–29. DL: Oct. 5 (Manuel—Mills; Osmyn—Elrington; Gonsalez— Cory; Garcia—Williams; Heli—Boman; Almeria—Mrs. Thurmond; Zara—Mrs. Porter; Leonora—Mrs. Sherburn). Dec. 31.

1729–30. DL: Sept. 27 (as Oct. 5, 1728, except Manuel—W. Mills; Osmyn—Mills). Dec. 15. Jan. 8. Feb. 26. May 15.

1730–31. DL: Sept. 19 (as Oct. 5, 1728, except Manuel—W. Mills; Osmyn—Mills). Nov. 7 (no cast). April 10 (Garcia omitted; rest as Sept. 19, 1730).

1731–32. DL: April 1 (Manuel—W. Mills; Osmyn—Mills; Gonsalez —Cory; Garcia—Bridgwater; Heli—Boman; Almeria—Mrs. Thurmond; Zara—Mrs. Horton; Leonora—Mrs. Sherburn). GF: Dec. 9 (Manuel—Delane; Osmyn—Giffard; Gonsalez—Rosco; Garcia—Bardin; Heli—Havard; Selim—Woodward; Almeria—Mrs. Giffard; Zara —Mrs. Roberts; Leonora—Miss Tollett). 11. 16. April 1 (Manuel— W. Giffard; Osmyn—Delane).

1732–33. DL: Sept. 16 (no cast). GF: Oct. 18 (Manuel—Hulett; Osmyn— Delane; Gonsalez—Rosco; Garcia—Chapman; Alonzo—Jenkins; Heli —Havard; Selim—Woodward; Almeria—Mrs. Thurmond; Zara— Mrs. Roberts; Leonora—Mrs. Purden). 19. 20. 21. 23. Nov. 1. Dec. 21. Feb. 3. 13. April 5 (Leonora—Mrs. Christian). May 5.

1733–34. CG: April 22 (Almeria—Mrs. Buchanan; rest omitted). May 17 (Manuel—Walker; Osmyn—Ryan; Gonsalez—Quin; Garcia— Chapman; Alonzo—Aston; Heli—Hale; Selim—Wignell; Perez— Lacy; Zara—Mrs. Hallam; Leonora—Mrs. Stevens). GF: Sept. 14 (as Oct. 18, 1732, except Leonora—Mrs. Haughton). Nov. 13. 28. Jan. 26. March 26 (no cast).

1734–35. DL: Sept. 28 (Manuel—Mills; Osmyn—Milward; Gonsalez— Quin; Garcia—Cibber; Alonzo—Turbutt; Heli—Este; Selim—Cross; Perez—Winstone; Almeria—Mrs. Thurmond; Zara—Mrs. Butler; Leonora—Mrs. Sherburn). Oct. 1. Nov. 19. Dec. 12. GF: Nov. 22 (as Oct. 18, 1732, except Almeria—Mrs. Giffard; Leonora—Mrs. Haughton).

1735–36. DL: Nov. 12 (as Sept. 28, 1734, except Leonora—Mrs. Cross). Dec. 3. CG: Dec. 17 (Zara—Mrs. Porter; rest omitted). Jan. 28.

1736–37. DL: Nov. 11 (as Sept. 28, 1734, except Manuel—W. Mills; Garcia, Selim, Perez, Alonzo, Heli, and Leonora omitted; Zara— Mrs. Porter). Feb. 24. March 9 (no cast). May 2 (as Nov. 11, 1736, except Zara—Mrs. Butler). CG: March 31 (Manuel—Walker; Osmyn —Delane; Gonsalez—Bridgwater; Garcia—A. Hallam; Alonzo—Aston; Heli—Ridout; Almeria—Mrs. Horton; Zara—Mrs. Hallam; Leonora—Mrs. Stevens). (Feb. 8: Dismissed).

1737–38. DL: Feb. 10 (Manuel—Mills; Osmyn—Milward; Gonsalez— Havard; Garcia—Wright; Almeria—Mrs. Giffard; Zara—Mrs. Butler). April 26 (Zara—Mrs. Roberts). CG: Oct. 19 (as March 31, 1737, except Alonzo, Heli, and Leonora omitted). Jan 21. April 19 (Manuel—Stephens).

1738–39. DL: Nov. 1 (as Feb. 10, 1738, except Heli—Boman). CG: Oct.

28 (as March 31, 1737, except Garcia—Hallam; Alonzo, Heli, and Leonora omitted). Feb. 2 (Manuel—Stephens).

1739–40. DL: May 2 (Manuel—Berry; Osmyn—Milward; Gonsalez—Havard; Garcia—Wright; Heli—Cashell; Selim—Green; Perez—Woodburn; Alonzo—Turbutt; Almeria—Mrs. Giffard; Zara—Mrs. Butler; Leonora—Mrs. Bennet).

1740–41. CG: Jan. 28 (Manuel—Hale; Osmyn—Delane; Gonsalez—Bridgwater; Garcia—Hallam; Alonzo—Arthur; Heli—Stephens; Selim—Gibson; Perez—Rosco; Almeria—Mrs. Horton; Zara—Mrs. Porter; Leonora—Mrs. Cross). Feb. 5 (Perez—Anderson). GF: Nov. 12 (Manuel—Walker; Osmyn—Marshall; Gonsalez—Paget; Garcia—W. Giffard; Almeria—Mrs. Giffard; Zara—Mrs. Steel).

1741–42. CG: Dec. 17 (as Jan. 28, 1741, except Osmyn—Ryan; Garcia—Cashell; Alonzo—Roberts; Leonora—Mrs. Mullart). April 10 (Alonzo—Harrington; Perez—Stevens; Leonora—Mrs. Hale).

1743–44. DL: Oct. 15 (Manuel—Winstone; Osmyn—Delane; Gonsalez—Bridges; Garcia—Giffard; Alonzo—Anderson; Heli—Taswell; Selim—Cross; Perez—Ray; Almeria—Mrs. Giffard; Zara—Mrs. Roberts; Leonora—Mrs. Bennet).

1749–50. CG: April 3 (Manuel—Sparks; Osmyn—a Gentleman; Gonsalez—Bridgwater; Garcia—Gibson; Heli—Bransby; Selim—Bennet; Almeria—Miss Bellamy; Zara—Mrs. Horton; Leonora—Mrs. Barrington).

1750–51. DL: Dec. 3 (Manuel—Berry; Osmyn—Garrick; Gonsalez—Havard; Garcia—Palmer; Alonzo—Burton; Heli—Blakes; Selim—Simson; Perez—Mozeen; Almeria—Miss Bellamy; Zara—Mrs. Pritchard; Leonora—Mrs. Bennet). 4. 5. 7. 8. 10. 11. 12 15. 20 (Gonsalez—Bridges). Feb. 19. April 15. 30 (Almeria—Mrs. Ward). TWICKENHAM: Aug. 20 (Manuel—Cook; Osmyn—Lee; Gonsalez—Phillips; Alonzo—Shepard; Selim—Cross; Perez—Sturt; Almeria—Mrs. Robertson; Zara—Mrs. Lee; Leonora—Miss Davis).

1751–52. DL: March 7 (Manuel—Berry; Osmyn—Garrick; Gonsalez—Havard; Garcia—Palmer; Almeria—Miss Bellamy; Zara—Mrs. Pritchard). April 11 (Leonora—Mrs. Bennet). RICHMOND: Aug. 22 (Manuel—Burton; Osmyn—Davies; Gonsalez—Cross; Garcia—Ackman; Alonzo—Macgeorge; Heli—Blakes; Selim—Master Cross; Perez—English; Almeria—Mrs. Davies; Zara—Miss Ibbot; Leonora—Mrs. Helm). TWICKENHAM: Aug. 25 (as at Richmond, Aug. 22).

1752–53. DL: March 22 (as March 7, 1752, except Zara—Mrs. Clive). May 22 (Heli—Blakes; Alonzo—Burton; Zara—Mrs. Pritchard; Leonora—Mrs. Bennet).

1754–55. DL: Jan. 25 (as March 7, 1752, except Heli—Blakes; Alonzo
—Burton; Selim—Simson; Perez—Mozeen; Almeria—Miss Macklin;
Leonora—Mrs. Bennet). 27. 29. March 22. April 23. May 21. CG: Feb.
20 (Manuel—Sparks; Osmyn—Sheridan; Gonsalez—Ridout; Garcia
—Dyer; Alonzo—Stevens; Heli—Cushing; Selim—White; Perez—R.
Smith; Almeria—Mrs. Bellamy; Zara—Mrs. Woffington; Leonora—
Mrs. Barrington). 22. March 1. April 28 (Osmyn—Smith; Alonzo—
Holtom).

1755–56. DL: Sept. 20 (Manuel—Berry; Osmyn—Murphy; Gonsalez—
Havard; Garcia—Palmer; Alonzo—Burton; Heli—Blakes; Selim—
Simson; Perez—Mozeen; Almeria—Miss Macklin; Zara—Mrs. Pritch-
ard; Leonora—Mrs. Bennet). 30. Oct. 21 (Perez—Walker). Nov. 25.
Jan. 3 (Perez—Mozeen). 9 (Osmyn—Garrick). May 7 (Osmyn—Mur-
phy; Garcia—Walker). CG: March 30 (as Feb. 20, 1755, except Os-
myn—Barry; Alonzo—Anderson). May 3 (Osmyn—Smith; Zara—Mrs.
Phillips).

1756–57. DL: Nov. 17 (as Sept. 20, 1755, except Osmyn—Mossop; Garcia
—Usher). Dec. 6 (Perez—Walker). Jan. 25 (Perez—Mozeen) . Feb. 9
(Selim—Walker; Zara—Miss Rosco). March 29 (Zara—Mrs. Pritch-
ard). May 12. CG: Jan. 14 (as Feb. 20, 1755, except Osmyn—Barry;
Alonzo—Anderson; Perez omitted; Almeria—Mrs. Woffington; Zara
—Mrs. Gregory). March 31 (Perez—R. Smith; Heli—Bennet; Al-
meria—Mrs. Bellamy).

1757–58. DL: Sept. 20 (as Sept. 20, 1755, except Osmyn—Mossop; Garcia—Usher; Selim—Walker). Jan. 10 (Zara—Mrs. Glen). 16. May 1
(Perez omitted; Zara—Mrs. Pritchard). CG: Oct. 21 (as Feb. 20, 1755,
except Osmyn—Smith; Alonzo—Anderson; Almeria—Mrs. Vincent;
Zara—Mrs. Mayo). Dec. 2 (Zara—Mrs. Hamilton).

1758–59. DL: Sept. 19 (as Sept. 20, 1755, except Osmyn—Mossop; Garcia—Austin; Selim—Packer). Dec. 11. March 10 (Manuel—Davies).
May 29 (Osmyn—Smith). CG: Jan. 12 (as Feb. 20, 1755, except Osmyn—Smith; Alonzo—Anderson; Zara—Miss Nossiter).

1759–60. DL: Oct. 4 (Manuel—Davies; Osmyn—Holland; Gonsalez—
Havard; Garcia—Austin; Alonzo—Burton; Heli—Blakes; Selim—
Packer; Perez—Mozeen; Almeria—Miss Macklin; Zara—Mrs. Pritch-
ard; Leonora—Mrs. Bennet). 31 (Alonzo, Heli, Selim, Perez, and
Leonora omitted). April 30. CG: Jan. 4 (as Feb. 20, 1755, except
Osmyn—Smith; Alonzo—Anderson; Heli—Bennet; Selim—Davis;
Almeria—Mrs. Ward; Zara—Mrs. Hamilton).

1760–61. DL: Jan. 28 (as Oct. 4, 1759, except Alonzo, Heli, Selim, Perez,
and Leonora omitted; Almeria—Mrs. Yates). May 6 (Almeria—Mrs.
Palmer).

1761–62. DL: Sept. 21 (Manuel—Davies; Osmyn—Holland; Gonsalez—Havard; Garcia—Kennedy; Almeria—Mrs. Yates; Zara—Mrs. Pritchard). Nov. 14 (Almeria—Mrs. Hopkins). March 6 (Almeria—Mrs. Yates). CG: Oct. 23 (Manuel—Clarke; Osmyn—Smith; Gonsalez—Sparks; Garcia—Dyer; Alonzo—Anderson; Heli—Hull; Selim—Davis; Perez—R. Smith; Almeria—Mrs. Bellamy; Zara—Mrs. Hamilton; Leonora—Mrs. Barrington).

1762–63. DL: Nov. 1 (as Sept. 21, 1761, except Manuel—Love; Garcia—Lee). Feb. 28.

1763–64. DL: Nov. 7 (as Sept. 21, 1761, except Manuel—Love; Garcia—Lee; Alonzo—Ackman; Heli—Castle; Selim—Packer; Leonora—Mrs. Bennet). CG: Oct. 17 (as Oct. 23, 1761, except Garcia—White; Alonzo—Gardner; Almeria—Miss Macklin; Zara—Mrs. Ward). Feb. 6. March 13.

1764–65. DL: Feb. 4 (Manuel—Love; Osmyn—Holland; Gonsalez—Havard; Garcia—Lee; Alonzo—Ackman; Heli—Adock; Selim—Packer; Perez—Fox; Almeria—Mrs. Yates; Zara—Mrs. Pritchard; Leonora—Mrs. Bennet). CG: Oct. 15 (Manuel—Clarke; Osmyn—Smith; Gonsalez—Sparks; Alonzo—Gardner; Heli—Perry; Selim—Davis; Garcia—White; Perez—R. Smith; Almeria—Miss Macklin; Zara—Mrs. Ward; Leonora—Mrs. Barrington). Nov. 19 (Heli—Hull).

1765–66. DL: Dec. 6 (as Feb. 4, 1765, except Heli—Hurst; Perez—Keen; Zara—Mrs. Fitzhenry). 27 (Almeria—Mrs. Palmer). Jan. 20 (Selim—Strange). CG: Oct. 23 (as Oct. 15, 1764, except Manuel—Walker; Gonsalez—Gibson; Heli—Hull; Garcia—Perry; Perez—Wignell).

1766–67. CG: March 2 (as Oct. 15, 1764, except Gonsalez—Gibson; Heli—Hull; Garcia—Perry; Zara—Mrs. Bellamy).

1767–68. DL: Nov. 24 (as Feb. 4, 1765, except Garcia—Aickin; Heli—Hurst; Perez—Keen; Almeria—Mrs. Dancer; Zara—Mrs. Barry; Leonora—Mrs. Johnston). April 23 (Gonsalez—Packer). CG: Sept. 21 (as Oct. 15, 1764, except Gonsalez—Gibson; Heli—Hull; Garcia—Perry).

1768–69. DL: Sept. 26 (Manuel—J. Aickin; Osmyn—Holland; Gonsalez—Havard; Garcia—Aickin; Alonzo—Ackman; Heli—Hurst; Selim—Strange; Perez—Keen; Almeria—Mrs. W. Barry; Zara—Mrs. Hopkins; Leonora—Mrs. Johnston). Jan. 20 (Osmyn—Barry; Gonsalez—Packer; Almeria—Mrs. Barry).

1769–70. DL: Oct. 30 (as Sept. 26, 1768, except Gonsalez—Packer; Garcia—Palmer; Selim—Fawcett; Almeria—Miss Younge). Jan. 22 (Osmyn—Barry; Almeria—Mrs. Barry).

1770–71. DL: Oct. 8 (as Sept. 26, 1768, except Osmyn—Inchbald; Gonsalez—Packer; Garcia—Palmer; Selim—Fawcett; Almeria—Miss

Younge). 11 (Almeria—Mrs. W. Barry). April 29 (Osmyn—Reddish; Almeria—Mrs. Egerton).

1771–72. DL: Sept. 28 (Manuel—J. Aickin; Osmyn—Reddish; Gonsalez —Packer; Garcia—Palmer; Alonzo—Ackman; Heli—Hurst; Selim— Fawcett; Perez—Keen; Almeria—Miss Younge; Zara—Mrs. Hopkins; Leonora—Mrs. Johnston). April 11 (Almeria—Mrs. Barry; Zara— Miss Younge). May 19 (Almeria—Miss Younge; Zara—Mrs. Hopkins).

1772–73. DL: Oct. 24 (as Sept. 28, 1771, except Osmyn—Barry; Garcia—Davies). Jan. 16 (Almeria—Mrs. Barry; Zara—Miss Younge). May 11.

1773–74. DL: Nov. 13 (as Sept. 28, 1771, except Osmyn—Barry; Garcia—Davies; Almeria—Mrs. Barry; Zara—Miss Younge). 29.

1774–75. DL: May 1 (Manuel—Aickin; Osmyn—Smith; Gonsalez— Packer; Garcia—Cautherley; Alonzo—Wrighten; Heli—Hurst; Selim —Fawcett; Perez—Keen; Almeria—Mrs. Yates; Zara—Miss Younge; Leonora—Mrs. Johnston).

1775–76. DL: Nov. 21 (as May 1, 1775, except Osmyn—Grist; Garcia— Davies; Perez—Norris). Dec. 30.

1776–77. CG: Dec. 18 (Manuel—Clarke; Osmyn—Lewis; Gonsalez— Hull; Alonzo—Fearon; Heli—L'Estrange; Selim—Robson; Perez— Thompson; Almeria—Mrs. Hartley; Zara—Mrs. Ward; Leonora— Miss Ambrose).

1778–79. DL: Nov. 16 (as May 1, 1775, except Garcia—Davies; Almeria—Miss Younge; Zara—Mrs. Farren). Jan. 16 (Perez—Phillips).

1780–81. DL: Nov. 1 (as May 1, 1775, except Garcia—Farren; Heli—R. Palmer; Perez—Norris; Almeria—Mrs. Crawford; Zara—Mrs. Ward). CG: May 14 (as Dec. 18, 1776, except Manuel—Hull; Gonsalez— Packer; Alonzo, Heli, Selim, Perez omitted; Almeria—Mrs. Yates; Zara—Miss Younge).

1781–82. CG: Dec. 20 (as Dec. 18, 1776, except Almeria—Mrs. Yates; Zara—Miss Younge). 29. March 18. April 15.

1782–83. DL: March 18 (as May 1, 1775, except Garcia—Farren; Heli— Palmer; Perez—Norris; Almeria—Miss Kemble; Zara—Mrs. Siddons; Leonora—Miss Tidswell). May 24. June 2 (Osmyn—Lewis). CG: Dec. 2 (as Dec. 18, 1776, except Garcia—Whitfield; Selim— Booth; Almeria—Mrs. Yates; Zara—Miss Younge; Leonora—Miss Platt). Jan. 15.

1783–84. DL: Oct. 24 (Manuel—Aickin; Osmyn—Smith; Gonsalez— Packer; Garcia—Farren; Alonzo—Phillimore; Heli—R. Palmer; Selim—Fawcett; Perez—Wilson; Almeria—Miss Kemble; Zara—Mrs. Siddons; Leonora—Miss Tidswell). Feb. 21. April 17. CG: Feb. 5 (as Dec. 18, 1776, except Garcia—Whitfield; Selim—Booth; Almeria —Mrs. Crawford; Zara—Miss Younge; Leonora—Miss Platt).

1784–85. DL: Jan. 14 (as Oct. 24, 1783, except Garcia—Barrymore). Feb. 24. April 26.

1785–86. DL: Sept. 24 (as Oct. 24, 1783, except Garcia—Barrymore). CG: April 19 (Manuel—Hull; Osmyn—Holman, Gonsalez—Gardner; Garcia—Davies; Alonzo—Fearon; Heli—Palmer; Selim—Booth; Perez—Thompson; Almeria—Mrs. Warren; Zara—Miss Brunton; Leonora—Miss Platt). May 4.

1786–87. DL: May 19 (as Oct. 24, 1783, except Garcia—Barrymore; Almeria—Mrs. Ward). CG: Oct. 30 (as April 19, 1786, except Heli—Cubitt; Selim—Macready; Almeria—Mrs. Pope). May 30.

1787–88. CG: March 10 (as April 19, 1786, except Osmyn—Pope; Heli—Cubitt; Selim—Macready; Almeria—Miss Brunton; Zara—Mrs. Pope). May 27 (Heli—Eviatt).

1788–89. DL: Jan. 6 (as Oct. 24, 1783, except Osmyn—Kemble; Garcia—Barrymore; Heli—Benson; Almeria—Mrs. Ward). CG: Dec. 26 (as March 10, 1788, except Heli—Eviatt). June 6.

1790–91. DL: May 14 (as Oct. 24, 1783, except Osmyn—Kemble; Garcia—Barrymore; Heli—Benson; Selim—Williams; Perez—Haynes; Almeria—Mrs. Powell).

1792–93. DL: Feb. 5 (Manuel—Aickin; Osmyn—Kemble; Gonsalez—Packers; Garcia—Barrymore; Alonzo—Phillimore; Heli—Benson; Selim—Caulfield; Perez—Bland; Almeria—Mrs. Powell; Zara—Mrs. Siddons; Leonora—Mrs. Tidswell). May 28 (Alonzo—Maddocks). CG: March 4 (Manuel—Farren; Osmyn—Pope; Gonsalez—Harley; Garcia—Macready; Alonzo—Powell; Heli—Davies; Selim—Eviatt; Perez—Thompson; Almeria—Mrs. Pope; Zara—a Gentlewoman; Leonora—Mrs. Platt).

1794–95. DL: Nov. 29 (as Feb. 5, 1793).

1795–96. DL: Oct. 12 (as Feb. 5, 1793, except Garcia—C. Kemble; Perez—Trueman).

1796–97. DL: Dec. 9 (as Feb. 5, 1793, except Heli—Holland; Perez—Trueman; Mutes—Evans and Webb).

1798–99. DL: May 20 (as Feb. 5, 1793, except Garcia—Holland; Alonzo—Surmount; Heli—Maddocks; Perez—Trueman).

In the early nineteenth century there were these performances: DL: Jan. 28, 1802. Feb. 6, 1802. CG: Feb. 20, 1804. March 15, 1804. May 27, 1805. Oct. 15, 1807. Oct. 25, 1808. Nov. 4, 1808. April 8, 1809.

The Way of the World

1705–06. QUEEN'S: Dec. 17 (no cast).

1714–15. LIF: May 17 (no cast).

1717–18. DL: Jan. 8. 9. 10. 14. 28. Feb. 14 (Fainall—Booth; Mirabell—Wilks; Witwoud—Cibber; Petulant—Boman; Sir Wilful—Penketh-man; Waitwell—Leigh; Lady Wishfort—Mrs. Saunders; Millamant—Mrs. Oldfield; Mrs. Marwood—Mrs. Porter; Mrs. Fainall—Mrs. Horton; Foible—Mrs. Willis; Mincing—Miss Willis). March 18 (no cast). April 18.

1718–19. DL: Dec. 19 (as Feb. 14, 1718). March 3 (no cast). May 12.

1719–20. DL: Nov. 10 (as Feb. 14, 1718, except Petulant, Waitwell, Mrs. Fainall, Foible, and Mincing omitted).

1720–21. DL: March 6 (no cast). April 14 (as Feb. 14, 1718, except Sir Wilful—Miller; Waitwell—Shepard; Foible—Miss Willis; Mincing omitted).

1721–22. DL: March 5 (no cast).

1722–23. DL: Jan. 5 (no cast). 25. April 1.

1723–24. DL: Dec. 20 (no cast). Feb. 5. May 2.

1724–25. DL: Nov. 7 (actors only, not parts). Jan. 27 (Fainall—Booth; Mirabell—Wilks; Witwoud—Cibber; Petulant—Boman; Sir Wilful—Harper; Lady Wishfort—Mrs. Baker; Millamant—Mrs. Oldfield; Mrs. Marwood—Mrs. Porter; Mrs. Fainall—Mrs. Horton; Foible—Miss Willis). April 12. May 13.

1725–26. DL: Nov. 27 (as Jan. 27, 1725). Jan. 25. April 12 (no cast).

1726–27. DL: Dec. 17 (as Jan. 27, 1725, except Fainall—W. Mills; Mrs. Fainall—Mrs. Heron; Foible—Mrs. Wetherilt). March 20 (Fainall—Booth). April 28. June 2 (no cast).

1727–28. DL: Oct. 7 (as Jan. 27, 1725, except Waitwell—Shepard; Lady Wishfort—Mrs. W. Mills; Foible omitted). Dec. 7 (Fainall—W. Mills; Foible—Mrs. Sherburn). Feb. 28. April 6.

1728–29. DL: Oct. 28 (as Jane. 27, 1725, except Fainall—W. Mills; Waitwell—Shepard; Lady Wishfort—Mrs. Mills; Foible—Mrs. Sher-burn). Dec. 19 (no cast). Feb. 10. March 22 (Mincing—Mrs. Walter; rest as Oct. 28, 1728). April 29.

1729–30. DL: Nov. 6 (as Jan. 27, 1725, except Fainall—W. Mills; Wait-well—Shepard; Lady Wishfort—Mrs. Mills; Foible—Mrs. Sherburn). Jan. 5. April 6.

1730–31. DL: Jan. 14 (no cast). Feb. 20. March 29 (Fainall—W. Mills; Mirabell—Wilks; Witwoud—Cibber; Petulant—Boman; Sir Wilful—Harper; Waitwell—Shepard; Lady Wishfort—Mrs. Mills; Milla-mant—Mrs. Horton; Mrs. Marwood—Mrs. Porter; Mrs. Fainall—Mrs. Heron; Foible—Mrs. Sherburn). May 5.

1731–32. DL: Jan. 8 (no cast). Feb. 11 (as March 29, 1731, except Mrs. Marwood—Mrs. Thurmond; Mincing—Mrs. Walker). April 12.

1732–33. DL: Dec. 6 (as March 29, 1731, except Mirabell—Bridgwater;

Mrs. Marwood—Mrs. Butler). 7. Jan. 4. Feb. 1 (Lady Wishfort—Mrs. Mullart). CG: Dec. 7 (Fainall—Quin; Mirabell—Ryan; Witwoud—Chapman; Petulant—Neale; Sir Wilful—Hippisley; Waitwell—Penkethman; Lady Wishfort—Mrs. Egleton; Millamant—Mrs. Younger; Mrs. Marwood—Mrs. Hallam; Mrs. Fainall—Mrs. Buchanan; Foible —Mrs. Stevens). 8. 9. April 23 (Waitwell—Paget).

1733–34. DL: March 26 (as March 29, 1731, except Mirabell—A. Hallam; Lady Wishfort—Mrs. Sherburn; Millamant—Mrs. Heron; Mrs. Marwood—Mrs. Butler; Mrs. Fainall—Mrs. Grace; Foible—Miss Mann). April 30 (Mrs. Fainall—Mrs. Pritchard). CG: Oct. 6 (as Dec. 6, 1732, except Waitwell—Aston; Lady Wishfort—Mrs. Cantrell). March 11 (no cast). HAY: Dec. 5 (Fainall—W. Mills; Mirabell—A. Hallam; Witwoud—Th. Cibber; Petulant—Boman; Sir Wilful—Harper; Waitwell—Shepard; Lady Wishfort—Mrs. Sherburn; Millamant—Mrs. Heron; Mrs. Marwood—Mrs. Butler; Mrs. Fainall—Mrs. Grace; Foible—Miss Mann). 6. Jan. 22. 23.

1734–35. DL: Jan. 20 (as March 29, 1731, except Mirabell—Milward; Witwoud—Th. Cibber; Petulant—Macklin; Lady Wishfort—Mrs. Sherburn; Millamant—Mrs. Heron; Mrs. Marwood—Mrs. Butler; Mrs. Fainall—Mrs. Pritchard; Foible—Miss Mann). Feb. 15 (Lady Wishfort—Mrs. Cross). April 18. CG: Oct. 7 (as Dec. 7, 1732, except Fainall—Walker; Waitwell—Morgan; Lady Wishfort—Mrs. Mullart; Millamant—Mrs. Horton; Mrs. Fainall—Mrs. Templer; Mincing—Miss Binks). Dec. 6 (Mrs. Fainall—Mrs. Buchanan). March 25 (Mirabell—A. Hallam; Lady Wishfort—Mrs. Martin). May 2 (Mirabell—Ryan; Lady Wishfort—Mrs. Mullart).

1735–36. DL: Feb. 5 (Fainall—W. Mills; Mirabell—Milward; Witwoud —Th. Cibber; Petulant—Macklin; Sir Wilful—Harper; Waitwell—Shepard; Lady Wishfort—Mrs. Cross; Millamant—Mrs. Holliday; Mrs. Marwood—Mrs. Butler; Mrs. Fainall—Mrs. Pritchard; Foible—Miss Mann). CG: Oct. 8 (Fainall—Walker; Mirabell—Ryan; Witwoud—Chapman; Petulant—Neale; Sir Wilful—Hippisley; Waitwell—James; Lady Wishfort—Mrs. Mullart; Millamant—Mrs. Horton; Mrs. Marwood—Mrs. Hallam; Mrs. Fainall—Mrs. Buchanan; Foible—Mrs. Stevens; Mincing—Miss Binks). Nov. 21 (Peg—Miss Horsington). Dec. 18. Jan. 31 (no cast). April 5 (as Nov. 21, 1735). May 8 (Mincing and Peg omitted).

1736–37. DL: April 27 (Millamant—Miss Holliday; rest omitted). CG: Oct. 1 (as Oct. 8, 1735, except Peg—Miss Horsington). Nov. 9 (Mrs. Fainall—Mrs. Templer). March 12 (Sir Wilful—Hippisley; rest omitted). May 17 (no cast).

1737–38. DL: May 8 (Fainall—Mills; Mirabell—Milward; Witwoud—

Woodward; Petulant—Macklin; Sir Wilful—Harper; Waitwell—
Turbutt; Lady Wishfort—Mrs. Grace; Millamant—Mrs. Furnival;
Mrs. Marwood—Mrs. Butler; Mrs. Fainall—Mrs. Pritchard; Foible
—Mrs. Bennet; Mincing—Miss Brunette). CG: Oct. 21 (as Oct. 8,
1735, except Waitwell omitted; Mrs. Fainall—Mrs. Templer; Foible
omitted; Peg—Miss Horsington). Jan. 24 (Mincing—Mrs. Vincent).
May 1.

1738–39. DL: Dec. 26 (as May 8, 1738, except Sir Wilful—Turbutt;
Waitwell—Shepard; Millamant—Mrs. Mills; Mincing omitted). CG:
Nov. 11 (Fainall—Walker; Mirabell—Ryan; Witwoud—Chapman;
Petulant—Neale; Sir Wilful—Hippisley; Waitwell—James; Lady
Wishfort—Mrs. James; Millamant—Mrs. Horton; Mrs. Marwood—
Mrs. Hallam; Mrs. Fainall—Mrs. Stevens; Foible—Mrs. Kilby; Peg—
Miss Horsington). Dec. 8. Jan. 19.

1739–40. DL: March 17 (Fainall—Mills; Mirabell—Milward; Wit-
woud—Chapman; Petulant—Macklin; Sir Wilful—Turbutt; Wait-
well—Shepard; Lady Wishfort—Mrs. Macklin; Millamant—Mrs.
Clive; Mrs. Marwood—Mrs. Butler; Mrs. Fainall—Mrs. Pritchard;
Foible—Miss Bennet). CG: Sept. 25 (as Nov. 11, 1738, except Fainall
—A. Hallam; Witwoud—Th. Cibber; Mrs. Marwood—Mrs. Cross;
Mincing—Miss Brunette; Peg omitted). Nov. 27 (Mrs. Marwood—
Mrs. Hallam; Mincing omitted). Dec. 8 (Witwoud—Cross). Feb. 7
(Witwoud—Th. Cibber; Mrs. Marwood—Mrs. Cross; Mincing—Miss
Brunette). April 29 (Mincing omitted).

1740–41. CG: Oct. 27 (as Nov. 11, 1738, except Fainall—Hallam; Wit-
woud—Th. Cibber; Mrs. Marwood—Mrs. Cross; Mincing—Miss
Brunette; Peg omitted). March 2 (Millamant—Mrs. Woffington;
Mincing—Mrs. Vincent). April 27 (Waitwell—Rosco; Millamant—
Mrs. Horton).

1741–42. CG: Jan. 23 (Fainall—Hale; Mirabell—Ryan; Witwoud—
Chapman; Petulant—Woodward; Sir Wilful—Hippisley; Waitwell
—Rosco; Lady Wishfort—Mrs. James; Millamant—Mrs. Horton;
Mrs. Marwood—Mrs. Pritchard; Mrs. Fainall—Mrs. Stevens; Foi-
ble—Mrs. Kilby). 25. March 4 (no cast). April 8 (Mincing—Mrs.
Vincent; rest as Jan. 23, 1742). May 13. June 2. GF: Jan. 27
(Fainall—W. Giffard; Mirabell—Giffard; Witwoud—Garrick; Petu-
lant—Yates; Sir Wilful—Dunstall; Waitwell—Peterson; John—
Vaughan; Lady Wishfort—Mrs. Bishop; Millamant—Mrs. Giffard;
Mrs. Marwood—Mrs. Yates; Mrs. Fainall—Mrs. Bambridge; Foible—
Miss Hippisley; Mincing—Miss E. Hippisley; Betty—Miss Medina;
Peg—Mrs. Vallois). 28. March 1. April 27 (Foible—Mrs. Dunstall;
John, Betty, and Peg omitted) .

1742–43. CG: Oct. 28 (as Jan. 23, 1742, except Mrs. Marwood—Mrs. Woodward; Mincing—Mrs. Vincent). Dec. 17.

1743–44. DL: May 14 (Fainall—Mills; Mirabell—Giffard; Witwoud—Rosco; Petulant—Neale; Sir Wilful—Turbutt; Waitwell—Dunstall; Lady Wishfort—Mrs. Cross; Millamant—Mrs. Woffington; Mrs. Marwood—Mrs. Bennet; Mrs. Fainall—Mrs. Chetwood; Foible—Miss Budgell; Mincing—Miss Cole; Betty—Miss Horsington; Peg—Mrs. King). CG: Sept. 26 (as Jan. 23, 1742, except Lady Wishfort—Mrs. Mullart; Mrs. Marwood—Mrs. Woodward; Mincing—Mrs. Vincent).

1744–45. CG: Dec. 11 (as Jan. 23, 1742, except Waitwell omitted; Lady Wishfort—Mrs. Mullart; Mrs. Fainall—Mrs. Hale; Foible—Miss Hippisley). March 21 (Witwoud—Th. Cibber). RICHMOND: Aug. 17 (Fainall—Cross; Mirabell—Cashell; Witwoud—Chapman; Lady Wishfort—Mrs. Egerton; Millamant—Mrs. Vincent; Mrs. Marwood—Mrs. Horsington).

1745–46. CG: Oct. 2 (as Jan. 23, 1742, except Waitwell omitted; Mrs. Fainall—Mrs. Hale; Foible—Miss Hippisley; Mincing—Mrs. Vincent). Feb. 24. GF: March 20 (no cast). RICHMOND: July 26 (Mirabell—Cashell; Millamant—Mrs. Vincent).

1746–47. CG: Dec. 10 (as Jan. 23, 1742, except Fainall—Cashell; Waitwell omitted; Mrs. Fainall—Mrs. Hale; Foible—Miss Hippisley). Jan. 24. May 11 (Fainall—Davies).

1747–48. CG: April 26 (Fainall—Anderson; Mirabell—Ryan; Witwoud—Cibber; Sir Wilful—Morgan; Petulant—James; Lady Wishfort—Mrs. James; Millamant—Mrs. Horton; Mrs. Marwood—Mrs. Bland; Mrs. Fainall—Mrs. Hale; Foible—Miss Ferguson; Mincing—Miss Morrison).

1748–49. CG: April 7 (Fainall—Ridout; Mirabell—Ryan; Witwoud—Th. Cibber; Petulant—Bencraft; Sir Wilful—Dunstall; Waitwell—Arthur; Lady Wishfort—Mrs. Bambridge; Millamant—Mrs. Woffington; Mrs. Marwood—Mrs. Ward; Mrs. Fainall—Mrs. Hale; Foible—Mrs. Dunstall; Mincing—Miss Copen). 29 (Mincing omitted).

1750–51. DL: Nov. 15 (Fainall—Havard; Mirabell—Palmer; Witwoud—Woodward; Petulant—Shuter; Sir Wilful—Yates; Waitwell—Layfield; Lady Wishfort—Mrs. James; Millamant—Mrs. Pritchard; Mrs. Marwood—Mrs. Clive; Mrs. Fainall—Mrs. Willoughby; Foible—Mrs. Green; Mincing—Miss Minors). 17. 20. 22. Dec. 1. 21 (Fainall—Bridges). Jan. 2. 10. Feb. 1 (Foible—Mrs. Cross). April 27 (Foible—Mrs. Green). CG: May 9 (Fainall—Ridout; Mirabell—Ryan; Witwoud—Dyer; Petulant—Cushing; Sir Wilful—Macklin; Waitwell—Arthur; Lady Wishfort—Mrs. Macklin; Millamant—Mrs. Vincent; Mrs. Marwood—Mrs. Elmy; Mrs. Fainall—Mrs. Barrington;

Foible—Miss Ferguson; Mincing—Miss Houghton). RICHMOND: Aug. 17 (Fainall—Cross; Mirabell—Mattocks; Witwoud—Lee; Petulant—Shuter; Sir Wilful Phillips; Waitwell—Roberts; Lady Wishfort—Mrs. Bambridge; Millamant—Mrs. Lee; Mrs. Marwood—Mrs. Cross; Mrs. Fainall—Mrs. Roberts; Foible—Mrs. Matthews; Mincing—Miss Davis).

1751–52. DL: Sept. 21 (as Nov. 15, 1750, except Waitwell—W. Vaughan). Oct. 28 (Waitwell—Blakes; Foible—Miss Minors; Mincing—Mrs. Toogood). Nov. 23. Dec. 20. Jan. 20. Feb. 5. April 23 (Mincing—Mrs. Simson). CG: Oct. 22 (as May 9, 1751, except Foible—Mrs. Dunstall; Peg—Miss Ferguson). Nov. 19. Feb. 29. April 11. RICHMOND: July 25 (Fainall—Davies; Mirabell—Scrase; Witwoud—Cross; Petulant—Shuter; Sir Wilful—Phillips; Waitwell—Blakes; Lady Wishfort—Mrs. Cross; Millamant—Mrs. Davies; Mrs. Marwood—Miss Ibbot; Mrs. Fainall—Miss Helm; Foible—Mrs. Matthews; Mincing—Miss Davies). TWICKENHAM: Aug. 18 (as at Richmond, July 25, except Mirabell—Cross; Witwoud—Scrase).

1752–53. DL: Oct. 10 (as Nov. 15, 1750, except Waitwell—Blakes; Mrs. Fainall—Mrs. Mills; Foible—Miss Minors; Mincing—Mrs. Toogood). Jan. 20 (Fainall—Davies). 31. Feb. 21 (Mincing omitted). April 28 (Fainall—Havard; Mincing—Mrs. Toogood). CG: Nov. 16 (as May 9, 1751, except Lady Wishfort—Miss Macklin; Millamant—Mrs. Bland; Foible—Mrs. Dunstall; Peg—Miss Ferguson).

1753–54. DL: Oct. 18 (as Nov. 15, 1750, except Petulant—Blakes; Waitwell—Phillips; Mrs. Fainall—Mrs. Mills; Foible—Miss Minors; Mincing omitted). Jan. 3. May 16. CG: Oct. 8 (as May 9, 1751, except Sir Wilful—Shuter; Lady Wishfort—Mrs. Pitt; Millamant—Mrs. Bland; Foible—Mrs. Dunstall; Mincing—Miss Helm; Peg—Miss Ferguson). Nov. 19.

1754–55. DL: Oct. 23 (Fainall—Havard; Mirabell—Palmer; Witwoud—Woodward; Sir Wilful—Yates; Lady Wishfort—Mrs. James; Millamant—Mrs. Pritchard; Mrs. Marwood—Mrs. Clive; Mrs. Fainall—Mrs. Mills; Foible—Miss Minors). Jan. 23 (Lady Wishfort—Mrs. Macklin). May 8 (Fainall—Davies). CG: Sept. 18 (Fainall—Ridout; Mirabell—Ryan; Witwoud—Dyer; Petulant—Cushing; Sir Wilful—Shuter; Waitwell—Arthur; Lady Wishfort—Mrs. Pitt; Millamant—Mrs. Vincent; Mrs. Marwood—Mrs. Elmy; Mrs. Fainall—Mrs. Barrington; Foible—Mrs. Dunstall; Mincing—Miss Helm; Peg—Miss Ferguson). Nov. 25 (Millamant—Mrs. Hamilton). Jan. 9 (Foible—Mrs. Green). Feb. 13. March 4. May 1 (Waitwell—Collins; Millamant—Mrs. Woffington).

1755–56. CG: Oct. 1 (as Sept. 18, 1754, except Millamant—Mrs. Woffington; Foible—Miss Ferguson; Mincing and Peg omitted). Nov. 8. Dec. 23.

1756–57. CG: Oct. 1 (as Sept. 18, 1754, except Millamant—Mrs. Woffington; Foible—Mrs. Green; Mincing and Peg omitted). Nov. 12. Jan. 12. May 11 (Millamant—Mrs. Hamilton).

1757–58. DL: March 16 (as Oct. 23, 1754, except Petulant—Blakes; Waitwell—Walker; Lady Wishfort—Mrs. Clive; Mrs. Marwood—Mrs. Yates; Mrs. Fainall—Mrs. Davies). April 6. CG: Sept. 14 (as Sept. 18, 1754, except Millamant—Mrs. Hamilton; Foible—Mrs. Green; Mincing and Peg omitted). Nov. 15 (Mincing—Miss Helme).

1758–59. DL: Nov. 13 (Fainall—Havard; Mirabell—Palmer; Witwoud —O'Brien; Petulant—Blakes; Sir Wilful—Yates; Waitwell—Mozeen; Lady Wishfort—Mrs. Clive; Millamant—Mrs. Pritchard; Mrs. Marwood—Mrs. Yates; Mrs. Fainall—Mrs. Davies; Foible—Miss Barton; Mincing—Mrs. Simson). Dec. 14. Jan. 11 (Mincing omitted). Feb. 14 (Mincing—Mrs. Simson). April 24 (Mrs. Fainall—Mrs. Bennet; Mincing omitted). CG: Sept. 18 (as Sept. 18, 1754, except Waitwell—Dunstall; Millamant—Mrs. Hamilton; Foible—Mrs. Green; Peg omitted). Feb. 8.

1759–60. DL: Oct. 16 (as Nov. 13, 1758, except Foible—Mrs. Abington; Mincing omitted). Dec. 7 (Waitwell—Bransby; Foible—Mrs. Bennet) . Jan. 8. Feb. 19. CG: May 8 (as Sept. 18, 1754, except Mirabell—Gibson; Petulant—Cresswick; Waitwell—Dunstall; Millamant—Mrs. Hamilton; Mrs. Fainall—Miss Sledge; Foible—Mrs. Ferguson; Peg omitted).

1760–61. DL: Oct. 10 (as Nov. 13, 1758, except Mrs. Marwood—Mrs. Kennedy; Foible—Mrs. Bennet; Mincing omitted). Dec. 15, May 27 (Mincing—Mrs. Simson).

1761–62. DL: Sept. 25 (as Nov. 13, 1758, except Mrs. Marwood—Mrs. Kennedy; Foible—Mrs. Bennet; Mincing omitted). April 14 (Millamant—Mrs. Palmer; Mrs. Marwood—Mrs. Pritchard; Mincing—Mrs. Simson).

1762–63. DL: Nov. 26 (as Nov. 13, 1758, except Waitwell—Bransby; Mrs. Marwood—Mrs. Hopkins; Foible—Mrs. Bennet; Mincing omitted).

1763–64. DL: Jan. 9 (as Nov. 13, 1758, except Petulant—Baddeley; Waitwell—Bransby; Mrs. Marwood—Mrs. Hopkins; Foible—Mrs. Bennet; Mincing omitted).

1764–65. DL: Dec. 18 (Fainall—Havard; Mirabell—Palmer; Witwoud —King; Petulant—Baddeley; Sir Wilful—Yates; Waitwell—Bransby; Lady Wishfort—Mrs. Clive; Millamant—Mrs. Pritchard; Mrs. Marwood—Mrs. Hopkins; Mrs. Fainall—Miss Plym; Foible—Mrs. Bennet). May 20 (Millamant—Mrs. Palmer). CG: Nov. 24 (Fainall—Ross; Mirabell—Smith; Witwoud—Dyer; Petulant—Woodward; Sir Wilful—Shuter; Waitwell—Dunstall; Lady Wishfort—Mrs. Pitt; Millamant—Miss Elliot; Mrs. Marwood—Mrs. Ward; Mrs. Fainall—Mrs. Vincent; Foible—Mrs. Green; Mincing—Miss Vincent; Peg—Mrs. Evans; Betty—Miss Allen). Dec. 1. 6. Jan. 19 (Millamant—Mrs. Bellamy). March 18 (Foible—Mrs. Walker). April 17.

1765–66. DL: May 10 (as Dec. 18, 1764, except Millamant—Mrs. Abington; Mincing—Mrs. Simson). CG: Sept. 25 (as Nov. 24, 1764, except Millamant—Mrs. Bellamy; Peg and Betty omitted). Dec. 7.

1766–67. CG: Dec. 30 (as Nov. 24, 1764, except Waitwell—Anderson; Mrs. Marwood—Mrs. Burden; Peg and Betty omitted). Feb. 27 (Fainall—Hull; Waitwell—Dunstall). May 18 (Fainall—Ross; Witwoud—Cushing; Millamant—Miss Wilford).

1767–68. DL: March 17 (Fainall—Reddish; Mirabell—Palmer; Witwoud—King; Petulant—Baddeley; Sir Wilful—Love; Waitwell—Bransby; Lady Wishfort—Mrs. Clive; Millamant—Mrs. Pritchard; Mrs. Marwood—Mrs. Hopkins; Mrs. Fainall—Mrs. Reddish; Foible—Miss Pope; Mincing—Mrs. Simson).

1770–71. DL: March 18 (Fainall—Reddish; Mirabell—Jefferson; Witwoud—King; Petulant—Baddeley; Sir Wilful—Love; Waitwell—Parsons; Lady Wishfort—Mrs. Hopkins; Millamant—Mrs. Abington; Mrs. Marwood—Mrs. Egerton; Mrs. Fainall—Mrs. Reddish; Foible—Miss Pope). April 12 (Foible—Mrs. Jefferies).

1771–72. CG: April 4 (Fainall—Wroughton; Mirabell—Smith; Witwoud—Dyer; Petulant—Woodward; Sir Wilful—Shuter; Waitwell—Dunstall; Lady Wishfort—Mrs. Pitt; Millamant—Mrs. Bulkley; Mrs. Marwood—Mrs. Mattocks; Mrs. Fainall—Mrs. Baker; Foible—Mrs. Green).

1773–74. DL: March 15 (as March 18, 1771, except Sir Wilful—Yates; Mrs. Marwood—Miss Younge; Mrs. Fainall—Mrs. Jefferson; Foible—Mrs. Davies).

1775–76. DL: Oct. 7 (as March 18, 1771, except Sir Wilful—Yates; Mrs. Marwood—Miss Sherry; Mrs. Fainall—Mrs. Greville; Foible—Mrs. Davies; Mincing—Miss Platt). 27.

1776–77. DL: Dec. 31 (Fainall—Reddish; Mirabell—Smith; Witwoud—King; Petulant—Baddeley; Sir Wilful—Yates; Waitwell—Parsons; Coachman—Griffiths; Messenger—Nash; Servants—Carpenter and Everard; Lady Wishfort—Mrs. Hopkins; Millamant—Mrs. Abington; Mrs. Marwood—Miss Sherry; Mrs. Fainall—Mrs. Greville; Foible—Miss Pope; Mincing—Miss Platt; Betty—Miss Smith; Peg—Mrs. Palmer). Jan. 2. 9 (Mrs. Fainall—Miss Hopkins). 24. April 7 (Mrs.

Marwood—Miss Hopkins; Mrs. Fainall—Miss P. Hopkins). 19 (Mrs. Marwood—Miss Sherry). CG: Nov. 2 (Fainall—Wroughton; Mirabell —Lewis; Witwoud—Lewes; Petulant—Woodward; Sir Wilful—Dunstall; Waitwell—Wilson; Coachman—Fox; Lady Wishfort—Mrs. Pitt; Millamant—Mrs. Barry; Mrs. Marwood—Mrs. Mattocks; Mrs. Fainall—Mrs. Whitfield; Foible—Mrs. Green; Mincing—Mrs. Poussin; Betty—Mrs. White).

1777–78. DL: Jan. 23 (as Dec. 31, 1776, except Mrs. Fainall—Miss P. Hopkins). May 27 (Fainall—Davies).

1778–79. DL: Oct. 19 (as Dec. 31, 1776, except Fainall—Bensley; Coachman, Messenger and Servants omitted; Mrs. Fainall—Mrs. Sharp; Mincing—Miss Collet; Betty and Peg omitted). Nov. 3. March 27 (Witwoud—Dodd). May 1 (Fainall—Farren; Witwoud—King; Millamant—Miss Farren; Mrs. Fainall—Mrs. Davies).

1779–80. DL: Oct. 19 (as Dec. 31, 1776, except Fainall—Bensley; Coachman, Messenger and Servants omitted; Mrs. Fainall—Mrs. Sharp; Mincing—Miss Collet; Betty and Peg omitted). Nov. 4. Dec. 17 (Witwoud—Dodd). March 6. 16 (Fainall—Palmer). April 13.

1780–81. DL: Oct. 31 (as Dec. 31, 1776, except Fainall—Bensley; Coachman, Messenger and Servants omitted; Millamant—Miss Farren; Mrs. Fainall—Mrs. Sharp; Foible—Miss Pope; Mincing—Miss Collet; Betty and Peg omitted). Dec. 20 (Millamant—Mrs. Abington). Jan. 22. Feb. 8 (Mincing—Miss Kirby). May 7.

1781–82. DL: Oct. 13 (as Oct. 31, 1780). Jan. 9 (Millamant—Mrs. Abington). Feb. 6. April 1. 24 (Waitwell—Suett). May 13.

1782–83. CG: Dec. 6 (Fainall—Wroughton; Mirabell—Lewis; Witwoud —Lee Lewes; Petulant—Booth; Sir Wilful—Yates; Waitwell—Quick; Lady Wishfort—Mrs. Pitt; Millamant—Mrs. Abington; Mrs. Marwood—Mrs. Mattocks; Mrs. Fainall—Mrs. Marten; Foible—Mrs. Wilson). 10 (Sir Wilful—Wilson; Mincing—Mrs. Poussin; Maid—Mrs. White). 20.

1783–84. DL: Jan. 28 (Fainall—Bensley; Mirabell—Smith; Witwoud—Lewes; Petulant—Baddeley; Sir Wilful—Moody; Waitwell—Parsons; Lady Wishfort—Mrs. Hopkins; Millamant—Miss Farren; Mrs. Marwood—Mrs. Bulkley; Mrs. Fainall—Mrs. Wilson; Foible—Miss Pope). Feb. 12 (Waitwell—Waldron). April 12 (Fainall—Farren; Witwoud—Dodd; Foible—Mrs. Wrighten). May 18 (Fainall—Bensley; Foible—Miss Pope).

1784–85. DL: April 20 (as Jan. 28, 1784, except Witwoud—King; Sir Wilful—Suett; Mrs. Marwood—Miss E. Kemble). CG: Nov. 11 (Fainall—Farren; Mirabell—Wroughton; Witwoud—Lewis; Petulant—Bonnar; Sir Wilful—Wilson; Waitwell—Quick; Lady Wishfort—Mrs.

Webb; Millamant—Mrs. Abington; Mrs. Marwood—Mrs. Bates; Mrs. Fainall—Mrs. Inchbald; Foible—Mrs. Marten; Mincing—Mrs. Poussin; Maid—Miss Branigan).

1785–86. DL: May 25 (as Jan. 28, 1784, except Mirabell—Barrymore; Witwoud—King; Mrs. Marwood—Mrs. Ward).

1786–87. DL: May 23 (as Jan. 28, 1784, except Witwoud—King; Mrs. Marwood—Mrs. Ward) .

1787–88. DL: May 14 (as Jan. 28, 1784, except Witwoud—King; Petulant—Lamash; Waitwell—Suett; Mrs. Marwood—Mrs. Ward).

1788–89. DL: Nov. 12 (as Jan. 28, 1784, except Mirabell—Kemble; Witwoud—Dodd; Waitwell—R. Palmer; Mrs. Marwood—Mrs. Ward). May 7 (Millamant—Mrs. Goodall).

1789–90. DL: Sept. 15 (as Jan. 28, 1784, except Mirabell—Kemble; Witwoud—Dodd; Waitwell—Suett; Millamant—Mrs. Goodall; Mrs. Marwood—Mrs. Ward; Mincing—Miss Collins). CG: Jan. 13 (as Nov. 11, 1784, except Mirabell—Holman; Petulant—Ryder; Sir Wilful—King; Mrs. Marwood—Mrs. Mattocks; Mrs. Fainall—Miss Chapman; Foible—Miss Stuart). 20.

1797–98. CG: Oct. 28 (Fainall—Murray; Mirabell—Holman; Witwoud—Lewis; Petulant—Knight; Sir Wilful—Munden; Waitwell—Quick; Lady Wishfort—Mrs. Davenport; Millamant—Mrs. Abington; Mrs. Marwood—Mrs. Mattocks; Mrs. Fainall—Mrs. Coats; Foible—Mrs. Gibbs). Nov. 7. Jan. 31 (Mincing—Miss Leserve).

1800–01. DL: Nov. 22 (Fainall—Wroughton; Mirabell—Kemble; Witwoud—Bannister, Jun.; Petulant—Suett; Sir Wilful—King; Waitwell—R. Palmer; Thomas—Wathen; James—Surmount; Coachman—Maddocks; Porter—Evans; Lady Wishfort—Miss Pope; Millamant—Miss Biggs; Mrs. Marwood—Mrs. Powell; Mrs. Fainall—Mrs. Humphries; Mincing—Miss Mellon; Foible—Miss DeCamp; Peg—Miss B. Menage; Barmaid—Miss Tidswell). Dec. 2.

It was revived also at HAY on Dec. 17, 1842, with eleven additional performances in that season.

INDEX

Unless otherwise designated, the theaters listed are London playhouses. As an aid to identification, dates are given whenever possible for eighteenth-century performers and theatrical personnel. Appendix II is not indexed.